# Government and the Arts in Thirties America

## A Guide to Oral Histories and Other Research Materials

# Government and the Arts in Thirties America

A Guide to Oral Histories and
Other Research Materials

Roy Rosenzweig, Editor

Barbara Jones-Smith,
Janet Schrader,
Carolyn Mitchell,
Joan Haring, Associate Editors

Lorraine Brown, Consulting Editor

The
George Mason
University Press

**Copyright © 1986 by**
**George Mason University Press**

4400 University Drive
Fairfax, VA 22030

All rights reserved

Printed in the United States of America

Distributed by arrangement with
University Publishing Associates, Inc.

4720 Boston Way
Lanham, MD 20706

3 Henrietta Street

London WC2E 8LU England


**Library of Congress Cataloging in Publication Data**

Government and the arts in thirties America.

Bibliography: p.
Includes index.
1. Federal aid to the arts—United States.
2. Arts—United States—Sources.    3. Arts and
society—United States—History—20th century.
I. Rosenzweig, Roy.
NX735.G68    1987      026'.7'002573      86-22871
ISBN 0-8026-0002-6 (alk. paper)
ISBN 0-8026-0003-4 (pbk. : alk. paper)

All George Mason University Press books are produced on acid-free
paper which exceeds the minimum standards set by the National
Historical Publications and Records Commission.

To the memory of Warren I. Susman
(1927-1985)

# Table of Contents

# Preface

In May 1937 *Fortune Magazine* commented on the artistic projects launched in 1935 by the Works Progress Administration (WPA): "What the Government experiment in music, painting, and the theatre actually did even in their first year was to work a sort of cultural revolution in America. They brought the American artist and the American audience face to face for the first time in their respective lives and the result was an astonishment needled with excitement." The "cultural revolution" that *Fortune* celebrated proved relatively short-lived: most of these federally-supported artistic endeavors died along with the WPA in the early 1940s. Yet the effects of the four WPA arts projects and related government efforts in the arts have proved more permanent.

Collectively these cultural projects (which include the Federal Art Project, the Federal Music Project, the Federal Theatre Project, and the Federal Writers' Project the Public Works of Art Project, the Treasury Department's Section on Fine Arts, the Treasury Relief Art Project, the Farm Security Administration's historical section, and the United States Film Service) constitute the most ambitious, innovative, and intensive government effort in American history to foster artistic and cultural activity. Under their aegis, artists painted murals on the walls of small town post offices, interviewers collected the life stories of former slaves, symphony orchestras performed in medium-sized industrial communities, photographers captured the faces and landscapes of rural America, and theatre companies dramatized social problems in "Living Newspaper" form. Because of their diversity, their embrace of the traditional as well as the experimental, their relative openness to minorities, their recruitment and development of new audiences, these projects had a significance that went beyond the mere numbers of men and women who actually found employment on them in the late 1930s.

Both the products of these 1930s projects and the people who worked on them have had a central impact on American theatre, dance, music, art, literature, photography, and film in subsequent decades. Indeed, that impact has grown rather than diminished in recent years. Once-forgotten murals on school building walls are now being cleaned and preserved; the Writers' Project's American Guide series is selling thousands of copies in reprint editions; the Theatre Project's plays are being revived in both university and professional productions; exhibits of the Art Project's paintings are touring the nation's museums. And this revival of interest is not just nostalgia. These paintings, plays, photos, and other cultural products still serve as powerful models for current artists who want to acknowledge their heritage as well to link art and politics.

Like the artists, scholars have shown growing interest in the art and culture of the thirties. Dissertations, monographs, articles in a broad range of fields--literature, history, art history, music, theatre, speech, film, and American studies--have appeared in increasing numbers since the mid-1960s. In the last fifteen years more than fifty-five dissertations have been completed on government and the arts in the 1930s. At least ten other dissertations are in progress. And the bibliography of secondary works included within this volume documents the hundreds of other scholarly works produced on this topic since the 1940s.

For those interested in the art and culture of the 1930s--whether from an artistic, humanistic, or social scientific perspective--oral history has been an important research tool. Almost immediately after the cessation of the arts projects in the 1940s, scholars and artists began to interview the project participants about the successes, failures, and inner workings of these projects. Milton Meltzer, for example, comments in his survey of the arts projects, *Violins and Shovels*: "I owe the best parts of this book to those men and women who worked on the WPA arts projects and were willing to share their experiences."

Some of the many interviews with arts projects veterans took place informally and were never recorded; others have been lost or destroyed through accident or neglect. Yet close to

1000 interviews have been preserved on tape and have found their way into archives and libraries. Unfortunately, however, it has often been difficult for researchers to find out what is available in this vast but scattered storehouse of spoken reminiscences. No guide to these materials exists, and even individual archives sometimes have only imperfect records of their own collections.

The primary purpose of this volume is to make more accessible to researchers the approximately one thousand interviews relating to the Depression era arts projects that have been collected over the past thirty years. Part One of this book, thus, includes an alphabetical listing of every relevant interview that we were able to locate either in public or private archives. It also provides indexes to those interviews by project, location, and job. Thus, for example, scholars of American music and theatre will be able to learn that the Archives of American Art- -primarily known as a repository in the history of American art--holds a number of interviews concerning the Music and Theatre projects. And those interested in New England in the thirties will be able to find out which archives hold interviews that talk about Massachusetts, Rhode Island, and Connecticut.

Any complete study of 1930s culture will, of course, use more than oral history. Thus, we have also provided information on other research materials relating to that subject. Part Two of the book includes a preliminary guide to archival collections, secondary sources, and films. Although these guides are not intended to be complete, they are--we believe--the best available introduction to research on government support for the arts in 1930s America.

The primary focus of this volume is on the four arts projects sponsored by the WPA in the second half of the 1930s- -the Federal Art Project (FAP), the Federal Music Project (FMP), the Federal Theatre Project (FTP), and the Federal Writers' Project (FWP). Along with the Historical Records Survey, these projects were known as "Federal One" or, more precisely, as Federal Project No. 1 of the WPA. But we have cast our net more widely than just the WPA projects, although they were the most important and largest of the government efforts at supporting the arts. Our guide includes many references to several other projects of importance: the Public Works of Art Project (PWAP), the Treasury Relief Art Project (TRAP), the Treasury Department Section of Fine Arts (SECT), the historical section of the Resettlement Administration and the Farm Security Administration (RA/FSA), the United States

Film Service (USFS), and the National Youth Administration (NYA), which sponsored some music programs. A brief guide to these projects (as well as guide to using this volume) can be found at the beginning of Part One of this volume.

Like all research guides, this one has some gaps, although we have, of course, striven for accuracy and completeness. Some interviews, for example, probably escaped our notice despite the hundreds of letters that we sent and dozens of announcements we inserted in publications. Naturally, we welcome additions and corrections to both parts of this guide. These listings have been entered into computer databases, and we will continue to add to them as we receive new information. Please address any corrections, additions, or requests for new information to the editors at the Institute on the Federal Theatre Project and New Deal Culture, George Mason University, Fairfax, VA 22030.

A large scale effort to collect information on research materials scattered across the country requires both outside funding and the cooperation of many people. For funding we are primarily indebted to the National Endowment for the Humanities (NEH), which provided a grant to undertake this project. Additional financial support came from GMU's Graduate School, History Department, and Institute on the Federal Theatre Project and New Deal Culture. For their assistance and support, we would like to thank specifically Patricia Shadle, our program officer at NEH, Averett Tombes, Dean of the Graduate School, Michael Fish, head of the Office of Research, and Marion Deshmukh, Chair of the History Department.

Our largest debt for help in assembling this guide is to the numerous archivists, librarians, and scholars who provided details on oral history interviews in their own collections. Although we cannot thank all of them by name, we would like to single out Cathy Keen, the oral history archivist at the Archives of American Art, who was particularly generous with her time. We would also like to thank our distinguished group of academic consultants--Mary Jo Deering, Robert Kvasnika, Gerald Markowitz, Garnett McCoy, Marlene Park, Martha Ross, Robert Snyder, Warren I. Susman, and Jannelle Warren-Findley--who helped us shape the general directions of the project, offered thoughtful criticisms on drafts of specific sections of this volume, and provided detailed information on archival collections, oral history interviews, and secondary sources. The illustrations reproduced here come from the Library of Congress Federal Theatre Project Collection at George Mason University. Our thanks to Ruth Kerns, head of Special Collections and Archives at GMU.

For assistance in turning our computer databases into a published book, we are indebted to Vernon Gras and Isabelle Gibb of George Mason University Press, to Byron Peters and his staff at GMU's office of Communication Network Services, and especially to Pete Brown, Joyce Kubokawa, and Dan Skripkar of GMU's Office of Design and Publication. For both material and moral support over the long course of this project, we extend our heartfelt thanks to our fellow workers at the Institute on the Federal Theatre Project and New Deal Culture: Janet Bouchard, Melanie Mayo, Arthur Peterson, and especially Suzanne McCreight.

Finally, we have dedicated this volume to the memory of Warren I. Susman, a pathbreaking scholar of American culture in the 1930s as well as a generous friend and advisor to this and other projects of the Institute on the Federal Theatre Project and New Deal Culture. In April 1985, Warren had agreed to join us at George Mason University as a Robinson University Professor. His untimely death in that same month was a great loss for us and for all those interested in American culture in the 1930s.

# Part I
# Directory of Oral History
# Interviews

THE FEDERAL THEATRES
ONE THIRD
OF A NATION

OPENING OCT. 17TH
WALNUT ST THEATRE

# 1. How to Use the Directory of Oral History Interviews

This *Directory* is designed to help researchers locate information about the availability of oral history interviews relating to the government-sponsored arts projects of the 1930s. You can begin your search either with the main "Alphabetical Directory of Interviews" on page 11 (if you are interested in a particular person) or with the project, place, or position indexes, which begin on page 217 (if you are looking for information on a particular project, part of the country, or category of artist). Naturally, we have not been able to examine every interview listed; we have generally relied on the information provided by the repository. Nevertheless, all listings contain basic information, which will tell you whether the interview is relevant to a particular project and where the interview is available.

After you have located the interviews that may be useful for your research, you should check the "Guide to Oral History Repositories" (page 257) for details on the archive in which the interview is housed. It is advisable to check with the repository before you plan a research trip, since policies on hours, copying, and inter-library loan as well as restrictions on use may have changed since the publication of the *Directory*. If you are not already familiar with the arts projects and the abbreviations used to identify them, you might want to look first at the "Guide to Arts Projects and Abbreviations" on page 7.

The alphabetical listings contain information on the following:

1) **Name of interviewee:** If the interview involved more than one narrator, we have listed the interview under each person, unless they did not play an important part in the interview. Please note, however, that the repository may have the interview filed only under one person. If you do not find the interview initially, you should also check the names listed under "interview also includes."

2) **Date of birth and/or death:** Where the repository was unable to provide this information, we have tried to add it from standard biographical sources. Nevertheless, these dates are not listed in a large number of cases.

3) **Discusses:** We have indicated up to three projects that the interviewee discusses in this particular interview. This listing enables us to distinguish between people who comment on the arts projects (e.g. art and theatre critics) and those who actually took part. Please keep in mind that the various art projects (FAP, PWAP, TRAP, SECT) are often confused by former participants, by interviewers, and even by scholars. In addition, many artists participated in more than one of these four projects. As a result, it is sometimes difficult to determine which of the four a person discusses in his or her interview. In those cases, we have used FAP as a general catch-all. In other words, in at least a few instances, a person who is listed as discussing (or having participated in) the FAP may have actually worked on PWAP, TRAP, or SECT.

4) **Participated in:** If we knew that a person worked on a particular project, but we were uncertain whether it was discussed in the interview, we have still noted his or her participation under this listing. The caution noted above about the FAP applies here as well.

5) **Position:** We have indicated positions that the person held on the arts projects during the 1930s and not their subsequent jobs. Where the person was not a project participant, we have listed the job held that was relevant to the projects (e.g. art dealer). In the interests of uniformity, we have lumped together certain job titles into more generic categories (e.g. administrator rather than deputy director of the public relations department or artist rather than easel painter). As a result, the positions listed do not always reflect the official job titles held on the project.

6) **Location:** We have listed (by state) up to three places that a person worked, using the standard two letter state abbreviations.

4

7) **Interview date:** If the interview extended over a series of dates, we have indicated that by giving a more general date (e.g. an interview that took place on several days in October 1966 would be listed as 10/66).

8) **Transcript, Tape, or Abstract length:** The term "abstract" refers to a summary (in some cases a timed summary) of the interview.

9) **Repository:** See "Guide to Oral History Repositories" on page 257 for addresses and details on hours and policies.

10) **Restrictions on use:** Some interviews require prior permission from the interviewer, interviewee, or repository before they may be used. The Archives of American Art is seeking to remove restrictions on as many of their interviews as possible; you should, therefore, check with them to see whether an interview has recently been released for general use.

11) **Series:** We have noted whether an interview was part of a special series.

12) **Interview also includes:** In most cases, there is a separate *Directory* entry for the people listed here. As noted above, however, the repository may have filed the interview only under a single name.

13) **Other:** Information is provided here on such matters as sound quality, the availability of the tape, whether it is located in more than one repository, whether it is recorded on videotape, and whether it is indexed.

13) **Description:** We have not been able to complete this item for all the entries. The information provided varies from a brief summary of the topics and/or themes raised in the interview to further information on the interviewee's connection with the arts projects. Because of the peculiarities of the computer program used to prepare the *Directory*, we have been unable to use semicolons in separating items within the description; commas have been used instead.

# 2. Guide to Arts Projects and Abbreviations

The following is a brief summary of the arts and cultural projects covered in this volume. The abbreviations used are in parentheses after the project names. More detailed information on many of the specific projects can be found in William F. McDonald's *Federal Relief Administration and the Arts* (Columbus: Ohio University Press, 1969) and in the works cited in the bibliography. For good brief descriptions of these projects and other New Deal programs, see James S. Olson, ed., *Historical Dictionary of the New Deal* (Westport, Conn.: Greenwood Press, 1985).

**Federal Art Project (FAP):** The FAP was set up in 1935 by the Works Progress Administration as part of Federal Project No. 1 (also known as Federal One), the artistic and professional work relief programs. By December 1935, the FAP employed more than 3,000 persons (about half already on relief) and double that number in March 1936. About half the FAP's workers directly produced art works; the rest worked in art education and art research (e.g. producing the Index of American Design). In addition to thousands of easel paintings, the FAP artists produced sculptures, silk-screens, posters, and graphic art works. Although the Emergency Relief Appropriation Act of 1939 eliminated much federal support for the FAP, it continued to win local funding and produce art work throughout World War II.

**Federal Emergency Relief Administration (FERA):** The FERA was created in May 1933 to administer the allocation of federal grants to the states for direct assistance and work relief

7

and to regulate the proper use of the funds. It ceased to function by July 1, 1935 although some local programs continued to operate.

**Federal Music Project (FMP):** Formed in 1935 to employ unemployed musicians, the FMP had both educational and performing units. Teachers organized choruses, bands, orchestras, and offered group classes in vocal and instrumental music and amateur community productions and group sings. The performing units included symphonies, orchestra, concert bands, dance bands, and ensembles, which gave public performances in diverse settings. The FMP reached an estimated audience of more than 150 million in its first four years of operation and employed 15,000 musicians at its high point in 1936.

**Federal Theatre Project (FTP):** The FTP was established in 1935 to provide jobs for out-of-work actors. By December 1935, 3,350 people were at work--60 percent actors, the rest stagehands, technicians, playwrights, and clerical and administrative workers. The FTP produced plays all over the United States, but it was most active in New York City, Chicago, and Los Angeles. Although most FTP productions were uncontroversial, a small number of plays focusing on social issues became a target for New Deal opponents. As a result, an act of Congress ended the FTP on June 30, 1939, four years before the other arts projects. In those four years, the FTP attracted an audience of thirty million people.

**Federal Writer's Project (FWP):** The FWP employed between 6,000 and 7,000 workers and produced seven twelve-foot bookcases of printed works including almost 400 commercially published books from its creation in 1935 until its end on June 30, 1943. Many of those employed by the project were not professional writers but unemployed teachers, librarians, lawyers, and editors. The FWP took a particular interest in the recovery and preservation of American folk culture and the stories of ordinary Americans. The slave narratives and life histories that FWP workers collected are still being used by scholars today. The most notable project of the FWP was the American Guide Series, which included works on fifty-one states and territories, thirty cities, and twenty regions.

**National Youth Administration (NYA):** The National Youth Administration provided work for high school, college, and jobless youths. Although the work was mostly construction, in some cases, like that at the University of Oklahoma, students with artistic talent were commissioned to embellish schools or campuses. The NYA also sponsored an orchestral music program for high school students.

**Public Works of Art Project (PWAP):** The PWAP, the first large-scale federal art project, was established in the Treasury Department with funds from the Civil Works Administration in December 1933 to provide artists and sculptors with federal relief in the form of employment decorating non-Federal public buildings and parks. Artists employed on the project had to be qualified to produce work that constituted a genuine embellishment of public property. The project aided 3,749 artists before it was terminated in the spring of 1934.

**Resettlement Administration/Farm Security Administration (RA/FSA):** Under the direction of Roy Stryker, the historical section of the RA, which became the FSA in 1937, employed a team of professional photographers to capture on film the trials of the rural poor and the relief efforts of the farm agency. The result of the project was more than 250,000 photographs that are valuable both as sources for the study of the Great Depression and documentary photography itself. In addition to photographing the plight of rural dwellers, the photographers also documented urban blight and the mobilization for war. Among the photographers that served on this team were Dorthea Lange, Walker Evans, Ben Shahn, Arthur Rothstein, Mary Post Wolcott, Gordon Parks, John Vachon, and John Collier. The RA/FSA also sponsored folk music projects and under its auspices Pare Lorentz produced his classic documentary films, *The Plow That Broke the Plains* (1935) and *The River* (1937).

**Section of Painting and Sculpture (SECT):** Originally established in 1934, the unit was renamed the Treasury Department Section of Fine Arts in 1938. The Section commissioned murals and sculpture for newly constructed federal buildings and for eleven hundred post offices. The Section differed from the FAP in that its artists were not employed on the basis of financial need; instead, they competed for individual commissions. The Section of Fine Arts was terminated in 1943 because of the war effort.

**Treasury Relief Art Project (TRAP):** The TRAP, which operated from 1935-39, was created to employ unemployed artists (most of whom were on relief) to decorate some 2,500 federal buildings. The emphasis was on producing permanent embellishments for federal buildings by architectural and sculptural additions to the exteriors or through the use of individual works of art such as sculpture, paints, prints, and murals in the interiors. TRAP also produced posters, curtains, and easel paintings which were allocated to federal departments for use in embassies, hospitals, and offices. Only artists capable of producing work of high artistic quality were eligible to work under the project. Although it operated independently, it used WPA funds; in June 1938 it was absorbed into the FAP.

**United States Film Service (USFS):** The United States Film Service was created in 1938 to produce films about current social and economic problems. President Franklin D. Roosevelt created the USFS after he had seen Pare Lorentz's *The River*, and he named Lorentz head of the agency. In its two-year existence, the USFS produced *The Fight for Life* (1940) and *Power and the Land* (1940). Film industry and congressional opposition killed the USFS in 1940.

**Works Progress Administration (WPA):** Established May 6, 1935, the WPA was designed to coordinate and execute the New Deal work relief program. Under the WPA, approximately 25 percent of Federal and sponsors' funds were expended on public service projects employing white-collar workers. Prominent among these projects was WPA-sponsored Federal Project No. 1 ("Federal One") which consisted of the Federal Art Project, the Federal Theatre Project, the Federal Music Project, the Federal Writers' Project, and the Historical Records Survey. In 1939, the WPA was incorporated into the newly established Federal Works Agency, and its name was changed to the Works Projects Administration. It was terminated in July 1943, because the war effort had generated new public and private jobs.

# 3. Alphabetical Directory of Interviews

**Abbenseth, William**(1898-1972)
Discusses: FAP Participated in: FAP
Position: Photographer Location: CA
Interviewer: McChesney, Mary Fuller Interview date: 11/23/64
Transcript: 23 pages
Repository: Archives of American Art
Permission of archive needed.
Description: FAP assignments, photomurals of San Francisco architecture, photos for Index of American Design, and other projects.

**Abdul, Raoul**(b.1929)
Discusses: FTP
Interview date: 1975
Transcript: 65 pages
Repository: Columbia University
Permission required to quote.
Description: Musical background, journalistic work in Cleveland, Langston Hughes' private secretary, Hughes' views on black culture and art.

**Abel, Christine Jeannette**(1890-1971)
Discusses: FAP Participated in: FAP
Positions: Artist, Sculptor Location: CA
Interviewer: Hoag, Betty Lochrie Interview date: 06/05/65
Transcript: 8 pages
Repository: Archives of American Art
Description: Her experiences assisting Helen Katherine Thorpe

on FAP mural for the Marobia, Calif. Post Office.

**Abel, Don G.**
Discusses: FAP Participated in: FAP
Position: Administrator Location: WA
Interviewer: Bestor, Dorothy Interview date: 06/10/65
Transcript: 12 pages
Repository: Archives of American Art
Permission of interviewee needed.
Description: His work as Washington state administrator, various FAP projects.

**Abelman, Ida**
Discusses: FAP, SECT Participated in: FAP, SECT
Positions: Muralist, Lithographer
Interviewer: Harrison, Helen A. Interview date: 12/08/76
Tape: 105 minutes
Repository: George Mason University
Description: Public Use of Arts Committee (Subway Art), FAP and SECT murals.

**Adams, Kenneth(1897-1966)**
Discusses: TRAP, SECT, PWAP Participated in: TRAP, SECT, PWAP
Position: Artist Locations: NM, KS
Interviewer: Loomis, Sylvia Interview date: 04/23/64
Transcript: 21 pages
Repository: Archives of American Art
Permission of archive needed.
Description: Contracts and methods of TRAP, influence of WPA on his career, PWAP murals project, other WPA artists.

**Agostitni, Peter(b.1913)**
Discusses: FAP Participated in: FAP
Position: Sculptor Location: NY
Interviewer: Roberts, Colette Interview date: 1968
Transcript: 99 pages
Repository: Archives of American Art
Permission of interviewee needed.
Description: Background, education, FAP, teaching, Da Vinci Art School, abstract expressionists, working methods and ideas.

**Aiken, Charlotte**
Discusses: FSA Participated in: FSA
Position: Accountant Location: DC
Interviewer: Doud, Richard Interview date: 04/17/64
Transcript: 42 pages

Repository: Archives of American Art
Permission of interviewee needed.
Interview also includes: Wool, Helen

**Albinson, Dewey**(b.1898)
Discusses: FAP Participated in: FAP
Positions: Administrator, Artist Location: MN
Interviewer: Nagle, Virginia Interview date: 10/27/65
Transcript: 49 pages
Repository: Archives of American Art
Description: FAP murals in St. Paul, Minn., his relationship
with Will Norman, Forbes Watson, and others.

**Albro, Maxine**(1895-1966)
Discusses: PWAP Participated in: PWAP
Position: Artist Location: CA
Interviewer: McChesney, Mary Fuller Interview date:
07/27/64
Transcript: 44 pages
Repository: Archives of American Art
Interview also includes: Hall, Parker
Description: Her PWAP mural at Coit Tower, WPA influence
on her career.

**Alessandro, Victor**(b.1916)
Discusses: WPA, FMP Participated in: FMP
Position: Conductor Location: OK
Interviewer: Loomis, Sylvia Interview date: 05/12/65
Transcript: 21 pages
Repository: Archives of American Art
Description: His work as conductor of the Oklahoma City
Symphony under FMP and the value of WPA arts projects.

**Alexander, Margaret W.**(b.1915)
Discusses: FWP Participated in: FWP
Position: Writer Location: IL
Interviewer: Shockley, Ann Allen Interview date: 07/18/73
Tape: 112 minutes
Transcript is indexed.
Repository: Fisk University Library
Permission of archive needed.
Description: Chicago writers' groups in the 1930s, FWP in
Chicago, other writers.

**Allison, Elitea**
Discusses: FTP
Location: NJ
Interviewer: Brown, Lorraine Interview date: 11/10/78

Abstract: 1 page(s)
Repository: George Mason University
This is an untaped interview, an abstract is available.
Description: Wife of FTP playwright, Hughes Allison.


**Allison, Elitea**
Discusses: FTP
Location: NJ
Interviewers: Hatch, James V. and Billops, Camille Interview
date: 03/09/75
Tape: 90 minutes
Repository: Hatch-Billops Collection, Inc.
Permission of archive needed.
Wife of FTP playwright, Hughes Allison.
Description: Husband's early work reporting for the *Daily Mirror*, plays on Broadway, radio interviews with Mary Bond.


**Alsberg, Henry G.**(1881-1970)
Discusses: FWP Participated in: FERA, FWP
Position: Administrator Location: DC
Interviewer: Mangione, Jerre Interview date: 05/23/68
Repository: University of Rochester
Series: Mangione Collection
Description: Supervisor of reports for FERA in 1934, in August 1935 he was named national director of the FWP.


**Alston, Charles Henry**(1907-1977)
Discusses: PWAP, FAP Participated in: FAP
Position: Artist Location: NY
Interviewer: Phillips, Harlan Interview date: 09/28/65
Transcript: 39 pages
Repository: Archives of American Art
Description: FAP murals at Harlem Hospital, camaraderie among FAP artists.


**Alston, Charles Henry**(1907-1977)
Discusses: FAP Participated in: FAP
Position: Artist Location: NY
Interviewer: Murray, Al Interview date: 10/19/68
Transcript: 26 pages
Repository: Archives of American Art
Description: Background, education, teaching, FAP, Harlem Renaissance, Harlem social and cultural life.


**Ambrusch, Julius Peter**(b.1899)
Discusses: FAP Participated in: FAP
Position: Artist Location: CO

Interviewer: Christy, Helen  Interview date: 08/17/79
Tape: 50 minutes  Abstract: 1 page(s)
Repository: Denver Public Library
Series: Federal Art in Colorado, 1934-1943


**Ames, Arthur**(1906-1975)
Discusses: FAP Participated in: FAP, PWAP
Position: Artist Location: CA
Interviewer: Hoag, Betty Lochrie  Interview date: 06/09/65
Transcript: 30 pages
Repository: Archives of American Art
Interview also includes: Ames, Jean Goodwin
Description: FAP projects in California, including the San
Diego County Courthouse, impact of federal art programs.


**Ames, Jean Goodwin**(b.1903)
Discusses: FAP Participated in: FAP
Position: Artist Location: CA
Interviewer: Hoag, Betty Lochrie  Interview date: 06/09/65
Transcript: 30 pages
Repository: Archives of American Art
Interview also includes: Ames, Arthur
Description: Mural, mosaic, and tapestry techniques, and work
of Maxine Albro and Helen and Margaret Bruton.


**Anderson, Guy**(b.1906)
Discusses: FAP Participated in: FAP, PWAP
Position: Muralist Location: WA
Interviewers: Hoppe, William and Wehr, Wesley Interview date:
06/06/74
Transcript: 71 pages
Repository: University of Washington
Series: Archives of Northwest Art
Description: His training, techniques, methods, teaching, and
relations with other artists.


**Anderson, Guy**(b.1906)
Discusses: FAP Participated in: FAP, PWAP
Position: Muralist Location: WA
Interviewer: Kingsbury, Martha  Interview date: 02/01/83
Transcript: 86 pages Tape: 270 minutes
Repository: Archives of American Art
Series: Northwest Oral History Project
Description: Teaching experience in Spokane, 1939-40, mural
painting in Mt. Vernon, Washington.


**Anderson, Thomas**

Discusses: FTP Participated in: FTP
Positions: Stage Manager, Director Location: NY
Interviewers: Brown, Lorraine and others Interview date: 01/13/78
Tape: 105 minutes Abstract: 5 page(s)
Repository: George Mason University
This is a videotape.
Description: Black FTP reunion: Archer, O., Bates, Add., De Paur, L., Hill, A., LeNoire, R.

### Anderson, Thomas
Discusses: FTP Participated in: FTP
Positions: Stage Manager, Director Location: NY
Interviewer: Brown, Lorraine Interview date: 05/24/78
Transcript: 34 pages Tape: 100 minutes Abstract: 3 page(s)
Repository: George Mason University
Description: Worked under John Houseman at Lafayette Theatre.

### Anderson, Thomas
Discusses: FTP Participated in: FTP
Positions: Stage Manager, Director Location: NY
Interviewer: De Paur, Leonard Interview date: 11/77
Tape: 20 minutes Abstract: 1 page(s)
Repository: George Mason University
Interview also includes: Browne, Theodore and Silvera, John
This is a videotape.
Description: Panel discussion: "Federal Theatre Revisited".

### Andrus, Zoray
Discusses: FTP Participated in: FTP
Position: Costume Designer Location: CA
Interviewer: Wickre, Karen Interview date: 02/24/78
Transcript: 26 pages Tape: 60 minutes Abstract: 4 page(s)
Repository: George Mason University
Description: Produced inexpensive costumes for such plays as *The Farmer's Wife*, *Sabine Women*, and *Beggar on Horseback*.

### Archer, Osceola(b.1890)
Discusses: FTP Participated in: FTP
Positions: Actress, Director Location: NY
Interviewers: Brown, Lorraine and others Interview date: 01/13/78
Tape: 105 minutes Abstract: 5 page(s)
Repository: George Mason University
This is a group videotape.
Description: Black FTP reunion: Anderson, T., Bates, Add.,

De Paur, L., Hill, A., Le Noire, R.

**Archer, Osceola**(b.1890)
Discusses: FTP Participated in: FTP
Positions: Actress, Director Location: NY
Interviewers: Hatch, James V. and Billops, Camille Interview
date: 02/02/72
Tape: 120 minutes Abstract: 1 page(s)
Repository: Hatch-Billops Collection, Inc.
Permission of archive needed.
Description: Repertory Theatre Playhouse, Genet's *The
Screens*, ethnic minorities in Actor's Equity, women in the
theatre, Paul Robeson.

**Archer, Osceola**(b.1890)
Discusses: FTP Participated in: FTP
Positions: Actress, Director Location: NY
Interviewer: Brown, Lorraine Interview date: 01/03/77
Transcript: 32 pages Tape: 90 minutes Abstract: 3 page(s)
Repository: George Mason University
Description: Education, Bennett College, auditioning for Orson
Welles' *Macbeth*, American Negro Theatre, Paul Robeson.

**Armitage, Merle**(1908-1975)
Discusses: PWAP Participated in: PWAP, SECT
Positions: Administrator, Graphic Artist Location: CA
Interviewer: Loomis, Sylvia Interview date: 02/06/64
Transcript: 28 pages
Repository: Archives of American Art
Description: Role as PWAP Regional Director in Southern
Calif., easel painting on project, censorship, opposition to
government-subsidized art.

**Arnason, H. Harvard**(b.1909)
Discusses: FAP Participated in: FAP
Position: Administrator Locations: IL, MN
Interviewer: Cummings, Paul Interview date: 03/03/70
Transcript: 45 pages
Repository: Archives of American Art
Permission of interviewee needed.
Description: Background, education, FAP, Holger Cahill,
Walker Art Center.

**Arndt, Helen**(b.1913)
Discusses: FAP Participated in: FAP
Location: CO
Interviewer: Christy, Helen Interview date: 07/10/79

Tape: 45 minutes
Repository: Denver Public Library
Series: Federal Art in Colorado, 1934-1943

**Atkinson, Brooks**
Discusses: FTP
Position: Drama Critic Location: NY
Interviewer: Berenberg, Benedict Interview date: 07/21/77
Transcript: 30 pages
Repository: Berenberg MA thesis, Univ. of Wisc.
Transcipt in interviewer's MA thesis. Tapes on permanent loan, Wisc. State Historical Society.
Description: *New York Times* drama critic on press coverage of the FTP.

**Ayer, Richard**(1909-1966)
Discusses: FAP Participated in: FAP
Position: Artist Location: CA
Interviewer: McChesney, Mary Fuller Interview date: 09/26/64
Transcript: 26 pages
Repository: Archives of American Art
Description: FAP easel painting project in San Francisco, other artists.

**Ayers, Atlee B.**(1873-1969)
Discusses: WPA, PWAP
Position: Administrator Location: TX
Interviewer: Loomis, Sylvia Interview date: 05/13/65
Transcript: 25 pages
Repository: Archives of American Art
Description: WPA in San Antonio, selection of artists for PWAP exhibits 1934, FAP painting and architectural projects, the growth of arts in Texas.

**Babcock, Alberta Von O.**
Discusses: FAP Participated in: FAP
Position: Artist Location: CA
Interviewer: Hoag, Betty Lochrie Interview date: 05/01/65
Transcript: 22 pages
Repository: Archives of American Art
Interview also includes: Babcock, Paul G.
Description: Easel and mosaic project.

**Babcock, Paul G.**(b.1905)
Discusses: FAP Participated in: FAP
Position: Artist Location: CA

18

Interviewer: Hoag, Betty Lochrie  Interview date: 05/01/65
Transcript: 22 pages
Repository: Archives of American Art
Interview also includes: Babcock, Alberta Von Ottenfeld
Description: Easel and mosaic project.


**Bach, Cile**(b.1910)
Discusses: FAP
Location: CO
Interviewer: Hardwick, Bonnie  Interview date: 07/25/79
Tape: 68 minutes
Repository: Denver Public Library
Permission of archive needed.
Series: Federal Art in Colorado, 1934-1943
Description: FAP artists and the Denver Art Museum.


**Bacon, Ernst**(b.1898)
Discusses: FMP Participated in: FMP
Positions: Administrator, Composer Location: CA
Interviewer: Knoblauch-Franc, Marion  Interview date: 04/23/82
Transcript: 33 pages  Tape: 90 minutes
Repository: George Mason University
Closed until 6/1/86.
Permission of interviewer required, open 6/1/87.
Description: Director of the San Francisco FMP, composer union trouble, *Take Your Choice*.


**Baird, Bil**(b.1904)
Discusses: FTP Participated in: FTP
Positions: Puppeteer, Actor Location: NY
Interview date: 1974
Repository: New York Public Library
Copying not permitted.
Interview also includes: Henson, Jim
Description: People who influenced his career, creating and manipulating puppets, appeal of puppetry for children.


**Baird, Bil**(b.1904)
Discusses: FTP Participated in: FTP
Positions: Puppeteer, Actor Location: NY
Interviewer: Krulak, Mae Mallory  Interview date: 11/08/76
Transcript: 28 pages  Tape: 65 minutes  Abstract: 3 page(s)
Repository: George Mason University
Description: Participated in *Macbeth*, *Faustus*, and *Horse Eats Hat*, trained FTP members to be puppeteers, Group Theatre.

**Baker, Jacob**(1905-1967)
Discusses: FERA, WPA Participated in: FERA, WPA
Position: Administrator Location: DC
Interviewer: Phillips, Harlan Interview date: 09/25/63
Transcript: 85 pages
Repository: Archives of American Art
Description: In charge of FERA'S development of co-operatives among the unemployed, assistant administrator of the WPA, resigned in 1936.

**Baker, Mildred**(b.1905)
Discusses: FAP Participated in: FAP
Position: Administrator Location: DC
Interviewer: Phillips, Harlan Interview date: 09/21/63
Transcript: 77 pages
Repository: Archives of American Art
Description: Assistant to Holger Cahill, Index of American Design, government control of subsidized arts.

**Bakos, Jozef G.**(1891-1977)
Discusses: FAP Participated in: FAP
Position: Artist Location: NM
Interviewer: Loomis, Sylvia Interview date: 04/15/65
Transcript: 26 pages
Repository: Archives of American Art
Description: Education, background, easel painting project of the FAP, feelings about the FAP.

**Balch, Jack**
Discusses: FWP Participated in: FWP
Position: Writer Location: MO
Interviewer: Mangione, Jerre Interview date: 02/11/68
Repository: University of Rochester
Series: Mangione Collection
Description: Selected by Henry Alsberg as editor-in-chief, produced first novel written about the FWP, *Lamps at High Noon*.

**Baldwin, Calvin Benham**
Discusses: RA, FSA Participated in: RA, FSA
Position: Administrator
Interviewer: Hurley, F. Jack Interview date: 08/18/67
Tape: 120 minutes
Repository: Memphis State University
Description: Biography, development of historical section of the Information Division of FSA, photography projects.

**Baldwin, Calvin Benham**
Discusses: RA, FSA Participated in: RA, FSA
Position: Administrator Location: CT
Interviewer: Doud, Richard Interview date: 02/24/65
Transcript: 34 pages
Repository: Archives of American Art
Description: Usefulness of the photography produced by the
FSA, Roy Stryker.

**Bales, Bill**
Discusses: FTP Participated in: FTP
Position: Dancer Location: NY
Interviewer: Wickre, Karen Interview date: 05/22/78
Transcript: 36 pages Tape: 90 minutes Abstract: 3 page(s)
Repository: George Mason University
Description: Role of FTP in the dancer Charles Weidman's
development, sit-in strikes.

**Bales, Richard Horner(b.1915)**
Discusses: FMP Participated in: FMP
Position: Conductor Locations: VA, NC
Interviewer: Warren-Findley, Jannelle Interview date: 6/73
Tape: 60 minutes
Repository: In possession of interviewer
Permission of interviewer needed.
Contact J. Warren-Findley, 2905 Pine Springs Road, Falls
Church, VA 22042.
Description: North Carolina-Virginia Symphony Orchestra.

**Bales, Richard Horner(b.1915)**
Discusses: FMP Participated in: FMP
Position: Conductor Locations: VA, NC
Interviewer: Knoblauch-Franc, Marion Interview date:
06/02/82
Transcript: 12 pages Tape: 30 minutes
Repository: George Mason University
Closed until 5/31/86.
Permission of interviewer required, open 6/1/87.
Description: Virginia Symphony Orchestra, North Carolina-
Virginia Symphony, FMP a beginning for American composers.

**Banfield, Beryl**
Discusses: FTP Participated in: FTP
Position: Dancer Location: NY
Interviewer: Brown, Lorraine Interview date: 05/22/78
Transcript: 13 pages Tape: 30 minutes Abstract: 1 page(s)

Repository: George Mason University
Closed pending release.
Description: Discrimination on FTP, work with Clarence Yates
on *Macbeth*, Harlem Unit of FTP.


**Banks, Bernice Fisher**(b.1906)
Discusses: FAP
Position: Sculptor Location: CA
Interviewer: McChesney, Mary Fuller Interview date:
02/21/65
Transcript: 19 pages
Repository: Archives of American Art
Permission of interviewee needed.


**Baranceanu, Belle**(b.1905)
Discusses: FAP, PWAP, TRAP Participated in: FAP, PWAP,
TRAP
Position: Artist Location: CA
Interviewer: Vitale, Lydia Modi Interview date: 03/09/75
Tape: 50 minutes
Repository: University of Santa Clara
Series: New Deal Art: California
This interview is on 1" videotape and requires special
equipment.


**Baranceanu, Belle**(b.1905)
Discusses: FAP Participated in: FAP, PWAP, TRAP
Position: Artist Location: CA
Interviewer: Hoag, Betty Lochrie Interview date: 08/01/64
Transcript: 35 pages
Repository: Archives of American Art
Permission of interviewee needed.
Interview also includes: Preibisius, Hilda


**Barber, Philip**
Discusses: FTP Participated in: FTP
Position: Administrator Location: NY
Interviewer: Berenberg, Benedict Interview date: 08/10/77
Transcript: 37 pages
Repository: Berenberg MA thesis, Univ of Wisc
Transcript in interviewer's MA thesis. Tapes on permanent
loan, Wisc. State Historical Society.
Description: Work as Regional Director for New York.


**Barber, Philip**
Discusses: FTP Participated in: FTP
Position: Administrator Location: NY

Interviewers: Brown, Lorraine and O'Connor, John Interview date: 11/11/75
Transcript: 159 pages Tape: 300 minutes Abstract: 17 page(s)

Repository: George Mason University
Description: Living Newspapers, Hallie Flanagan, Group Theatre, Houseman-Welles productions, Negro Theatre, bureaucracy, vaudeville.

### Barber, Philip
Discusses: FTP Participated in: FTP
Position: Administrator Location: NY
Interviewer: Sundell, Michael Interview date: 01/11/78
Tape: 60 minutes Abstract: 3 page(s)
Repository: George Mason University
This is a videotape done at the Parsons School Theatre in NY.
Description: Efforts to heal rift with critics, FTP's efforts to try new directions.

### Barber, Philip
Discusses: FTP Participated in: FTP
Position: Administrator Location: NY
Interviewers: Brown, Lorraine and Bowers, Diane Interview date: 02/20/76
Transcript: 32 pages Tape: 70 minutes Abstract: 2 page(s)
Repository: George Mason University
Interview also includes: Hauser, Ethel Aaron
Description: *One Third of a Nation*, *Life and Death of an American*, FTP sparked many fine careers.

### Barlin, Anne Lief
Discusses: FTP Participated in: FTP
Position: Dancer Location: NY
Interviewer: Wickre, Karen Interview date: 02/20/78
Tape: 120 minutes Abstract: 4 page(s)
Repository: George Mason University
This is a videotape.
Description: FTP dancers--demonstration and panel with Bass, P., Garnet, E., Geltman, F., Gerrard, S., Mann, L., Remos, S., Schaff, T.

### Barlin, Anne Lief
Discusses: FTP Participated in: FTP
Position: Dancer Location: NY
Interviewer: Wickre, Karen Interview date: 10/25/77
Transcript: 21 pages Tape: 50 minutes Abstract: 2 page(s)
Repository: George Mason University

Description: Sylvia Manning and Nadia Chilkovsky, work in *Circus* and *Candide*.

**Barnet, Will(b.1911)**
Discusses: FAP Participated in: FAP
Position: Artist Location: NY
Interviewer: Cummings, Paul Interview date: 1968
Transcript: 78 pages
Repository: Archives of American Art
Description: Background, education, FAP, Art Students League, lithographs, cartoons, illustrations.

**Barnet, Will(b.1911)**
Discusses: FAP Participated in: FAP
Position: Artist Location: NY
Interview date: 1976
Transcript: 523 pages
Repository: Columbia University
Permission required to quote.
Microfiche available, part IV.
Description: Education, Art Students League, fine and commercial art, portrait painting.

**Barnouw, Eric**
Discusses: FTP Participated in: FTP
Interviewer: Bowers, Diane Interview date: 05/12/76
Abstract: 1 page(s)
Repository: George Mason University
This is an untaped interview, a one-page abstract is available.
Description: Worked with the radio division of FTP, Arthur Arent, George Kondolf.

**Baron, Paul**
Discusses: FTP Participated in: FTP
Position: Stage Manager Location: NY
Interviewer: O'Connor, John Interview date: 12/01/79
Tape: 85 minutes Abstract: 2 page(s)
Repository: George Mason University
Description: Experiences on *Cherokee Night* and *Monkey's Paw*, recollections of Orson Welles and Joseph Cotton.

**Barrows, Charles**
Discusses: PWAP, FAP Participated in: PWAP, FAP
Location: NM
Interviewer: Loomis, Sylvia Interview date: 03/11/65
Transcript: 15 pages
Repository: Archives of American Art

Description: Art Students League, PWAP, impact of FAP on art and artists, public perception of the WPA.

**Bartlett, Frederic S.(b.1905)**
Discusses: FAP
Position: Museum Director Location: CO
Interviewer: Christy, Helen Interview date: 10/10/79
Tape: 99 minutes
Repository: Denver Public Library
Series: Federal Art in Colorado, 1934-1943
Held no position with FAP, worked with the Denver Art Museum.
Description: Museum director Colorado Springs, Colorado.

**Bartlett, Frederic S.(b.1905)**
Discusses: FAP
Position: Museum Director Location: CO
Interviewer: Loomis, Sylvia
Transcript: 37 pages
Repository: Archives of American Art
Description: Museum director Colorado Springs, Colorado.

**Baskin, Leonard(b.1922)**
Discusses: FAP Participated in: FAP
Positions: Sculptor, Printmaker Location: NY
Interviewer: Cummings, Paul Interview date: 04/17/69
Transcript: 45 pages
Repository: Archives of American Art
Permission of interviewee needed.
Description: Background, education, FAP school, qualities of sculpture.

**Bass, Paula**
Discusses: FTP Participated in: FTP
Position: Dancer Location: NY
Interviewer: Wickre, Karen Interview date: 02/20/78
Tape: 120 minutes Abstract: 4 page(s)
Repository: George Mason University
This is a videotape.
Description: FTP dancers--demonstration and panel with Barlin, A.L., Garnet, E., Geltman, R., Gerrard, S., Mann, L., Remos, S., Schaff, T.

**Bates, Add**
Discusses: FTP Participated in: FTP
Positions: Dancer, Actor Location: NY
Interviewers: Brown, Lorraine and others Interview date:

01/13/78
Tape: 105 minutes  Abstract: 5 page(s)
Repository: George Mason University
This is a videotape.
Description: Black FTP reunion: Anderson, T., Archer, O., De Paur, L., Hill, A., LeNoire, R.

**Bates, Add**
Discusses: FTP Participated in: FTP
Positions: Dancer, Actor Location: NY
Interviewer: Brown, Lorraine Interview date: 11/30/76
Transcript: 25 pages  Tape: 40 minutes  Abstract: 2 page(s)
Repository: George Mason University
Description: Early work with Humphrey-Weidman dancers, FTP work on *Androcles*, *One Third of a Nation*, *Emperor Jones*, Houseman and Welles.

**Bates, Add**
Discusses: FTP Participated in: FTP
Positions: Dancer, Actor Location: NY
Interviewers: Hatch, James V. and Billops, Camille Interview date: 12/29/74
Tape: 135 minutes
Repository: Hatch-Billops Collection, Inc.
Permission of archive needed.
Description: Dancing for FTP in Harlem, Harlem theater and arts in the 1930s.

**Bay, Howard**
Discusses: FTP Participated in: FTP
Position: Set Designer Location: NY
Interviewer: O'Connor, John Interview date: 02/21/76
Transcript: 35 pages  Tape: 85 minutes  Abstract: 4 page(s)
Repository: George Mason University
Description: *One-Third of a Nation*, *Chalk Dust*, *Battle Hymn*, *The Cradle Will Rock*, recollections of Orson Welles.

**Bay, Howard**
Discusses: FTP Participated in: FTP
Position: Set Designer Location: NY
Interviewer: Brown, Lorraine Interview date: 01/09/78
Tape: 95 minutes  Abstract: 4 page(s)
Repository: George Mason University
Interview also includes: Elson, Charles
This is a videotape. It is also available at the NY Public Library.
Description: Set design, conservatism of FTP, work on *One*

*Third of a Nation* and *Cradle Will Rock.*

**Bearden, Romare**(b.1912)
Discusses: FAP
Position: Artist Location: NY
Interviewers: Hatch, James V. and Billops, Camille Interview
date: 12/06/72
Tape: 60 minutes Abstract: 1 page(s)
Repository: Hatch-Billops Collection, Inc.
Permission of archive needed.
Description: Harlem Artists Guild, NYU Art Students League,
Studio 306, Cinque Gallery.

**Becque, Don Oscar**
Discusses: FTP Participated in: FTP
Positions: Dancer, Teacher Location: NY
Tape: 54 minutes Abstract: 1 page(s)
Repository: New York Public Library
Permission of archive needed.
This is a 7" phonotape.
Description: Triangle Theatre, Federal Dance Theatre, NYC
artistic and intellectual environment between 1925 and 1935,
other dancers.

**Bell, Philip Fletcher**(b.1907)
Discusses: FAP Participated in: FAP
Position: Administrator Location: DC
Interviewer: Phillips, Harlan
Transcript: 18 pages
Repository: Archives of American Art
Description: Director of FAP's Children's Art Center in the
District of Columbia.

**Bentley, Eric**
Discusses: FTP
Interviewer: Krulak, Mae Mallory Interview date: 05/12/76
Transcript: 47 pages Tape: 100 minutes Abstract: 3 page(s)
Repository: George Mason University
Interviewee is the son-in-law of Hallie Flanagan.
Description: Recollections of FTP Director Hallie Flanagan.

**Bentley, Joanne Davis**
Discusses: FTP
Interviewer: Krulak, Mae Mallory Interview date: 05/13/76
Tape: 190 minutes Abstract: 4 page(s)
Transcript is indexed.
Repository: George Mason University

Interviewee is the step-daughter of Hallie Flanagan.
Description: FTP Director Hallie Flanagan's life.

**Benton, Thomas Hart**(1889-1975)
Discusses: FAP, TRAP
Positions: Artist, Muralist Location: MO
Interview date: 1964
Transcript: 31 pages Tape: 120 minutes
Repository: George Mason University
Description: Jackson Pollock, murals at the Whitney Museum.

**Benton, Thomas Hart**(1889-1975)
Discusses: FAP, TRAP
Positions: Artist, Muralist Location: MO
Interviewer: Gallagher, Robert S. Interview date: 09/20/72
Transcript: 185 pages
Repository: Columbia University
Description: Art in the 1930s, murals in Missouri, FAP lecture tour, social function of art, regionalist movement.

**Berenberg, Ben**
Discusses: FTP Participated in: FTP
Position: Actor Location: NY
Interviewer: Wickre, Karen Interview date: 09/16/77
Transcript: 19 pages Tape: 60 minutes Abstract: 3 page(s)
Repository: George Mason University
Description: FTP union, strikes and picketing, work on *Revolt of the Beavers*, *Sing for Your Supper*, and *Power*.

**Berger, Josef**(1904-1971)
Discusses: FWP Participated in: FWP
Position: Writer Location: MA
Interviewer: Mangione, Jerre Interview date: 7/24/68
Repository: University of Rochester
Series: Mangione Collection
Description: Berger was on the Massachusetts FWP, wrote *Cape Cod Pilot* and *In Great Waters*, used the pseudonym Jeremiah Digges.

**Berman, Harold**(b.1904)
Discusses: FTP Participated in: FTP
Positions: Playreader, Play Doctor Location: NY
Interviewer: Wickre, Karen Interview date: 11/16/77
Transcript: 51 pages Tape: 90 minutes Abstract: 2 page(s)
Repository: George Mason University
Description: Hostility of theatre owners to FTP.

**Biberman, Edward**(b.1904)
Discusses: FAP, SECT Participated in: FAP, SECT
Positions: Muralist, Printmaker Location: CA
Interviewers: Vitale, Lydia Modi and Gelber, Steven Interview
date: 03/15/75
Tape: 60 minutes
Repository: University of Santa Clara
Series: New Deal Art: California
This interview is on 1" videotape, requires special equipment.

**Biberman, Edward**(b.1904)
Discusses: FAP, SECT Participated in: FAP, SECT
Positions: Muralist, Printmaker Location: CA
Interviewer: Hoag, Betty Lochrie Interview date: 04/15/64
Transcript: 48 pages
Repository: Archives of American Art
Description: Background, education, murals he painted for the
Los Angeles Post Office, FAP contributions to art in
California.

**Biddle, George**(1885-1973)
Discusses: FAP, PWAP Participated in: FAP, PWAP, SECT
Position: Artist Locations: NY, DC, NJ
Interviewer: Phillips, Harlan Interview date: 1963
Transcript: 261 pages
Repository: Archives of American Art
Biddle's papers are available at Library of Congress and
Archives of Am Art.
Description: A schoolmate and friend of FDR, insturmental in
the establishment of the PWAP, believed artists should work
with goverment not for it.

**Billings, Henry**(b.1901)
Discusses: FAP Participated in: FAP, SECT
Positions: Artist, Illustrator Locations: NY, MA, TN
Interviewer: Phillips, Harlan Interview date: 11/25/64
Transcript: 47 pages
Repository: Archives of American Art

**Birchenall, Jack**
Discusses: FTP Participated in: FTP
Position: Costume Designer Location: CA
Interviewer: O'Connor, John Interview date: 11/78
Tape: 70 minutes
Repository: George Mason University
Description: Work with Zoray Andrus in the FTP costume
department, radicals in FTP.

**Bischoff, Elmer Nelson**(b.1916)
Discusses: FAP Participated in: FAP
Positions: Artist, Teacher Location: CA
Interviewer: McChesney, Mary Fuller Interview date: 01/20/65
Transcript: 12 pages
Repository: Archives of American Art
Description: FAP's impact on the community and on American Art, public perception of the project, influence of government support on the arts.

**Bistram, Emil J.**(1895-1976)
Discusses: FAP Participated in: FAP, SECT, PWAP
Positions: Artist, Muralist Locations: NM, TX, DC
Interviewer: Loomis, Sylvia Interview date: 10/17/63
Transcript: 19 pages
Repository: Archives of American Art
Description: Education and background, his FAP murals, the FAP and public interest in art, Taos.

**Black, Ivan**
Discusses: FTP Participated in: FTP
Positions: Publicist, Administrator Location: NY
Interviewer: Brown, Lorraine Interview date: 05/08/77
Abstract: 1 page(s)
Repository: George Mason University
This is an untaped interview, a one-page abstract is available.
Description: Work as publicist for FTP and as Director of Radio Project.

**Blake, Eubie**(1883-1983)
Discusses: FTP Participated in: FTP
Position: Composer
Interviewer: Perlis, Vivian Interview date: 1972
Transcript: 137 pages Tape: 240 minutes
Transcript is indexed.
Repository: Yale University
Permission of archive needed.
Series: "Major Figures in American Music"
Part of a series of interviews by Perlis. A videotaped interview, 07/08/77 is also in Hatch-Billops Collection, Inc.
Description: An in-depth interview on the life and career of Blake, who also wrote music for FTP.

**Blake, Eubie**(1883-1983)
Discusses: FTP Participated in: FTP

Position: Composer Location: NY
Interviewer: Brown, Lorraine Interview date: 01/09/77
Transcript: 22 pages Tape: 40 minutes Abstract: 3 page(s)
Transcript is indexed.
Repository: George Mason University
Also available at Hatch-Billops Collection, Inc.
Description: Wrote *Swing It* for Houseman, Welles, and Virgil
Thomson.

**Blanch, Arnold**(1896-1968)
Discusses: FAP Participated in: FAP, SECT
Position: Artist Locations: MN, NY, CT
Interviewer: Seckler, Dorothy G. Interview date: 1963
Transcript: 31 pages
Repository: Archives of American Art
Description: Background, education, significance of FAP,
Minneapolis School of Fine Art, Art Students League.

**Blankfort, Michael**
Discusses: FTP Participated in: FTP
Position: Playwright Location: NY
Interviewer: Brown, Lorraine Interview date: 07/22/77
Transcript: 17 pages Tape: 40 minutes Abstract: 2 page(s)
Repository: George Mason University
Description: *Battle Hymn*, the variety of FTP.

**Blazek, Anton**(b.1902)
Discusses: FAP
Positions: Artist, Sculptor Location: CA
Interviewer: Hoag, Betty Lochrie Interview date: 04/13/65
Transcript: 34 pages
Repository: Archives of American Art
Permission of interviewee needed.
Description: FAP paintings, lack of government censorship,
value of federal projects.

**Bloch, Lucienne**(b.1909)
Discusses: FAP Participated in: FAP, SECT
Position: Muralist Locations: NY, KY
Interviewer: McChesney, Mary Fuller Interview date:
08/11/64
Transcript: 85 pages
Repository: Archives of American Art
Permission of interviewee needed.

**Block, Irving A.**(b.1910)
Discusses: FAP Participated in: FAP, SECT

Positions: Artist, Teacher Locations: CA, NY, CA
Interviewer: Hoag, Betty Lochrie Interview date: 04/16/65
Transcript: 43 pages
Repository: Archives of American Art

**Block, Lou**(b.1895)
Discusses: FAP
Position: Administrator
Interviewer: Phillips, Harlan Interview date: 05/31/65
Transcript: 43 pages
Repository: Archives of American Art

**Bolotowsky, Ilya**(1907-1981)
Discusses: FAP, PWAP Participated in: FAP, PWAP
Positions: Artist, Muralist Location: NY
Interviewer: Gurin, Ruth Interview date: 11/05/63
Transcript: 22 pages Abstract: 1 page(s)
Repository: Archives of American Art
Permission of archive needed.
Description: Mural projects, various artists' groups, Whitney
Museum, Museum of Modern Art.

**Bolotowsky, Ilya**(1907-1981)
Discusses: FAP, PWAP Participated in: FAP, PWAP
Positions: Artist, Muralist Location: NY
Interviewer: Cummings, Paul Interview date: 1968
Transcript: 165 pages
Repository: Archives of American Art
Permission of archive needed.
Description: Childhood, education, PWAP and FAP projects,
professional organizations, other artists.

**Bolotowsky, Ilya**(1907-1981)
Discusses: FAP, PWAP Participated in: FAP, PWAP
Positions: Artist, Muralist Location: NY
Interviewer: Cummings, Paul Interview date: 1968
Transcript: 140 pages
Repository: Archives of American Art
Description: Background, education, Williamsburg Housing
Project, painting in the 1930s, FAP artists, Art Students
League, politics.

**Bolotowsky, Ilya**(1907-1981)
Discusses: FAP, PWAP Participated in: FAP, PWAP
Positions: Artist, Muralist Location: NY
Interviewer: Bowman, Ruth Interview date: 11/05/63
Transcript: 20 pages

Repository: Archives of American Art
Description: FAP murals, Museum of Modern Art in the 1930s, Willem de Kooning, Ad Reinhardt, social position of artists.

**Bolotowsky, Ilya(1907-1981)**
Discusses: FAP Participated in: FAP, PWAP
Positions: Artist, Muralist Location: NY
Interviewer: Harrison, Helen A. Interview date: 01/30/77
Tape: 60 minutes
Repository: George Mason University
Permission of Andrew Bolotowsky.
Description: Hall of Medicine at the New York World's Fair.

**Bolton, Harold(b.1908)**
Discusses: FTP Participated in: FTP
Position: Director Location: NY
Interviewers: O'Connor, John and Brown, Lorraine Interview date: 11/01/77
Tape: 90 minutes Abstract: 5 page(s)
Repository: George Mason University
Interview also includes: Bolton, Rhoda Rammelkamp, Wheeler, Louanne
This is a videotape.
Description: Contribution of the FTP to American culture, camaraderie of FTP participants, *Mamlock, One Third of a Nation.*

**Bolton, Rhoda Rammelkamp**
Discusses: FTP Participated in: FTP
Position: Costume Designer Location: NY
Interviewer: O'Connor, John Interview date: 11/01/77
Tape: 90 minutes
Repository: George Mason University
Interview also includes: Bolton, Harold

**Bonath, Harry(d.1976)**
Discusses: FAP
Position: Artist Location: WA
Interviewer: Bestor, Dorothy Interview date: 04/03/65
Transcript: 14 pages
Repository: Archives of American Art
Description: FAP mural project at the University of Washington Drama Department, government support for the arts.

**Bontemps, Arna(1902-1973)**

Discusses: FWP Participated in: FWP
Position: Administrator Location: IL
Interviewer: Shockley, Ann Allen Interview date: 07/14/72
Tape: 120 minutes
Repository: Fisk University Library
Permission of archive needed.
An indexed transcript is available.
Description: Autobiographical, writing, writers, librarianship,
Harlem Renaissance.

### Bontemps, Arna(1902-1973)
Discusses: FWP Participated in: FWP
Position: Administrator Location: IL
Interviewer: Collins, Leslie M. Interview date: 01/09/72
Tape: 57 minutes
Repository: Fisk University Library
Permission of archive needed.
An indexed transcript is available.
Description: Harlem Renaissance.

### Booth, Cameron(1892-1980)
Discusses: FAP, PWAP Participated in: FAP, PWAP
Position: Selection Committee Location: MN
Interviewer: Reid, George Interview date: 08/02/77
Transcript: 6 pages Tape: 30 minutes
Repository: Minnesota Historical Society
Series: Federal Art Project in Minnesota
Tape filed under Ibling, Miriam.
Description: How artists were selected, the quality of their art.

### Booth, Cameron(1892-1980)
Discusses: FAP, PWAP Participated in: FAP, PWAP
Position: Selection Committee Location: MN
Interviewer: Waldfogel, Melvin Interview date: 1971
Transcript: 42 pages Tape: 90 minutes
Repository: Minnesota Historical Society
Open only for research.
Description: Art in Minnesota in the 1920s and 1930s, how
artists were selected for PWAP.

### Boratko, Andre(b.1912)
Discusses: FAP Participated in: FAP
Positions: Administrator, Muralist Locations: SD, MN
Interviewer: Reid, George Interview date: 08/09/77
Transcript: 7 pages Tape: 30 minutes
Repository: Minnesota Historical Society

Series: Federal Art Project in Minnesota
Tape filed under Thwaites, Charles.
Description: His experiences as South Dakota State
Administrator (1938-42) and as muralist in Milaca and
Faribault, Minn.

**Borowsky, Maxine**
Discusses: FTP Participated in: FTP
Position: Costume Designer Location: NY
Interviewer: Bowers, Diane Interview date: 06/02/76
Transcript: 43 pages Tape: 90 minutes Abstract: 2 page(s)
Repository: George Mason University
Description: FTP as a political football, Hallie Flanagan, FTP
developed actors, designers, directors, and producers but not
playwrights.

**Bosworth, Francis**
Discusses: FTP Participated in: FTP
Position: Administrator Location: NY
Interviewer: Wickre, Karen Interview date: 09/29/78
Transcript: 57 pages Tape: 160 minutes Abstract: 7 page(s)
Repository: George Mason University
Description: Head of a playreading department, early days in
the FTP, cultivation of new audiences, *It Can't Happen Here.*

**Bothwell, Dorr**(b.1902)
Discusses: FAP Participated in: FAP
Positions: Artist, Printmaker Location: CA
Interviewer: McChesney, Mary Fuller Interview date:
02/27/65
Transcript: 23 pages
Repository: Archives of American Art

**Boyd, Elizabeth**(1903-1974)
Discusses: FAP Participated in: FAP
Position: Administrator Location: NM
Interviewer: Loomis, Sylvia Interview date: 10/08/64
Transcript: 24 pages
Repository: Archives of American Art
Description: Art administrator in Santa Fe, New Mexico,
worked on the Index of American Design from 1936-1937.

**Brandeis, Adele**(d.1975)
Discusses: FAP, TRAP Participated in: FAP
Position: Administrator Location: KY
Interviewer: Phillips, Harlan Interview date: 06/01/65
Transcript: 24 pages

Repository: Archives of American Art
Description: Index of American Design, the Shakers and their work in Kentucky, mural projects for Kentucky artists.

**Brandt, Louise W.**
Discusses: FAP
Position: Administrator Location: CO
Interviewer: Campbell, Jo Interview date: 07/05/79
Tape: 45 minutes
Repository: Denver Public Library
Series: Federal Art in Colorado, 1934-1943

**Brant, Carl**
Discusses: FTP Participated in: FTP
Position: Actor Location: CA
Interviewer: Brown, Lorraine Interview date: 03/16/79
Abstract: 1 page(s)
Repository: George Mason University
This is an untaped interview, a one-page abstract is available.

**Bridaham, Lester B.(b.1899)**
Discusses: FAP
Positions: Artist, Administrator Location: MA
Interviewer: Christy, Helen Interview date: 07/12/79
Tape: 60 minutes
Repository: Denver Public Library
Series: Federal Art in Colorado, 1934-1943

**Brigante, Nicholas P.(b.1895)**
Discusses: FAP Participated in: FAP, PWAP
Position: Artist Location: CA
Interviewer: Hoag, Betty Lochrie Interview date: 05/25/64
Transcript: 17 pages
Repository: Archives of American Art
Description: Worked on the watercolor easel project for the FAP, influenced by Chinese painting, Los Angeles Art Students League.

**Britton, Edgar(1901-1982)**
Discusses: FAP Participated in: FAP, SECT
Positions: Artist, Sculptor Locations: IL, CO, DC
Interviewer: Johnson, Charles Interview date: 08/21/79
Tape: 36 minutes
Repository: Denver Public Library
Series: Federal Art in Colorado, 1934-1943
Description: Chicago FAP, Colorado Springs Fine Arts Center.

**Brocco, Peter**
Discusses: FTP Participated in: FTP
Position: Actor Location: CA
Interviewer: Bowers, Diane Interview date: 06/01/76
Transcript: 28 pages Tape: 40 minutes Abstract: 2 page(s)
Repository: George Mason University
Description: First FTP involvement, Americanism of FTP, various productions.

**Bromley, Robert**
Discusses: FTP Participated in: FTP
Positions: Administrator, Puppeteer Location: CA
Interviewer: Sundell, Michael Interview date: 06/30/77
Transcript: 32 pages Tape: 60 minutes Abstract: 2 page(s)
Repository: George Mason University
Description: Various productions, early background in puppetry, work as director of FTP marionette unit.

**Brook, Alexander(1898-1980)**
Discusses: FAP Participated in: FAP, SECT
Position: Artist Locations: NY, DC
Interviewer: Harrison, Helen A. Interview date: 01/02/79
Tape: 60 minutes
Repository: George Mason University
Closed pending release.
Description: Education and background, work on FAP.

**Brooks, James(b.1906)**
Discusses: FAP Participated in: FAP, SECT
Position: Artist Locations: NY, NJ
Interviewer: Seckler, Dorothy G. Interview date: 1965
Transcript: 36 pages
Repository: Archives of American Art
Permission of interviewee needed.
Description: Early art training, FAP mural projects, Army art projects, other artists.

**Brown, Herbert J.**
Discusses: FAP, FMP Participated in: FAP, FMP
Positions: Administrator, Musician Location: MA
Interviewer: Swift, Geoffrey Interview date: 11/29/65
Transcript: 28 pages
Repository: Archives of American Art
Description: Assistant State Director for Administration, Massachusetts FAP 1939-1941, concert work for FMP, played piano and saxaphone.

**Browne, Rosalind B.**(1916-1979)
Discusses: FAP Participated in: FAP
Positions: Artist, Muralist Location: NY
Interviewer: Sandler, Irving Interview date: 1968
Transcript: 101 pages
Repository: Archives of American Art
Description: Member of Mural Project of the FAP, Art
Students League, Guggenheim Foundation, FAP murals, Hans
Hofmann, WNYC mural.

**Browne, Theodore**
Discusses: FTP Participated in: FTP
Positions: Playwright, Actor Location: WA
Interviewer: De Paur, Leonard Interview date: 11/77
Tape: 20 minutes Abstract: 1 page(s)
Repository: George Mason University
Interview also includes: Anderson, Thomas, and Silvera, John
This is a videotape.
Description: Panel discussion: "Federal Theatre Revisited".

**Browne, Theodore**
Discusses: FTP Participated in: FTP
Positions: Playwright, Actor Locations: WA, MA
Interviewer: Brown, Lorraine Interview date: 10/22/75
Transcript: 37 pages Tape: 90 minutes Abstract: 3 page(s)
Repository: George Mason University
Description: *A Black Woman Called Moses*, *Noah*, *Stevedore*,
*Swing, Gates, Swing*, *Lysistrata*, *Minstrel*, *Natural Man*.

**Bruce, Margaret T.**
Discusses: PWAP, SECT
Interviewer: Phillips, Harlan Interview date: 10/11/63
Transcript: 15 pages
Repository: Archives of American Art
Margaret Bruce is the widow of Edward T. Bruce.
Description: Her husband's career as head of PWAP and SECT.

**Bruskin, Perry**
Discusses: FTP Participated in: FTP
Position: Actor Location: NY
Interviewer: O'Connor, John Interview date: 10/22/76
Transcript: 37 pages Tape: 90 minutes Abstract: 3 page(s)
Repository: George Mason University
Description: Various plays, role of FTP in resurgence of
vaudeville.

**Bruton, Helen**
Discusses: FAP, PWAP, SECT Participated in: FAP, PWAP, SECT
Position: Artist Location: CA
Interviewers: Vitale, Lydia Modi and Gelber, Steven Interview date: 02/26/75
Tape: 100 minutes
Repository: University of Santa Clara
Series: New Deal Art: California
Interview also includes: Bruton, Margaret
This interview is on 1" videotape and needs special equipment to be viewed.

**Bruton, Helen**
Discusses: FAP, PWAP, SECT Participated in: FAP, PWAP, SECT
Position: Artist Location: CA
Interviewer: Ferbrache, Lewis Interview date: 12/04/64
Transcript: 37 pages
Repository: Archives of American Art
Permission of archive needed.
Interview also includes: Bruton, Margaret

**Bruton, Margaret**
Discusses: FAP, PWAP Participated in: FAP, PWAP
Position: Artist Location: CA
Interviewers: Vitale, Lydia Modi and Gelber, Steven Interview date: 02/26/75
Tape: 100 minutes
Repository: University of Santa Clara
Series: New Deal Art: California
Interview also includes: Bruton, Helen
This interview is on 1" videotape and needs special equipment to be viewed.

**Bruton, Margaret**
Discusses: FAP, TRAP Participated in: FAP, TRAP
Position: Artist Location: CA
Interviewer: Ferbrache, Lewis Interview date: 12/04/64
Transcript: 37 pages
Repository: Archives of American Art
Permission of interviewee needed.
Interview also includes: Bruton, Helen

**Bufano, Beniamino(1898-1970)**
Discusses: FAP Participated in: FAP
Position: Sculptor Location: CA

Interviewer: McChesney, Mary Fuller Interview date: 10/04/64
Transcript: 41 pages
Repository: Archives of American Art
Description: In the San Francisco unit of the FAP, work on statue of St. Francis of Assisi.

**Bultman, Fritz(b.1919)**
Discusses: FAP Participated in: FAP
Position: Artist Locations: IL, NY
Interviewer: Sandler, Irving Interview date: 01/06/68
Transcript: 75 pages
Repository: Archives of American Art
Description: Chicago Bauhaus, New Orleans in the 1930s, development of distinctive American art, social aspects of art world.

**Bunce, Louis Dermott(1907-1983)**
Discusses: PWAP, FAP Participated in: PWAP, FAP, SECT
Positions: Artist, Muralist Location: OR
Interviewer: Lafo, Rachel Rosenfield Interview date: 12/03/82
Transcript: 78 pages Tape: 210 minutes
Transcript is indexed.
Repository: Archives of American Art
Series: Northwest Oral History Project
Interview continued on 12/09/82 and 12/13/82 by same interviewer.
Description: FAP in Oregon, Salem Art Center, mural in Grants Pass Federal Building.

**Bunce, Louis Dermott(1907-1983)**
Discusses: FAP Participated in: FAP, PWAP, SECT
Positions: Artist, Muralist Location: OR
Interviewer: Bestor, Dorothy Interview date: 10/26/65
Transcript: 32 pages
Repository: Archives of American Art

**Bunnell, Charles(1897-1967)**
Discusses: PWAP, TRAP, FAP Participated in: PWAP, TRAP, FAP
Positions: Artist, Muralist Location: CO
Interviewer: Loomis, Sylvia Interview date: 11/10/64
Transcript: 27 pages
Repository: Archives of American Art

**Burlin, Paul(1886-1969)**

Discusses: FAP Participated in: FAP, PWAP
Position: Artist Location: NY
Interviewer: Seckler, Dorothy G. Interview date: 12/05/62
Transcript: 40 pages
Repository: Archives of American Art
Permission of widow needed.
Description: Early life, National Academy of Design, working methods, American Artists Congress, American Artists Union, FAP and the 1930s.

### Burris-Meyer, Harold
Discusses: FTP Participated in: FTP
Position: Sound Technician Location: NY
Interviewer: Brown, Lorraine Interview date: 03/14/77
Transcript: 17 pages Tape: 60 minutes Abstract: 2 page(s)
Repository: George Mason University
Description: Experimentation with sound and smell in the theater, *Emperor Jones*.

### Busa, Peter(b.1914)
Discusses: FAP Participated in: FAP
Positions: Artist, Muralist Location: NY
Interviewer: Seckler, Dorothy G. Interview date: 09/05/65
Transcript: 25 pages
Repository: Archives of American Art
Permission of interviewee needed.
Description: FAP murals for Riker's Island, Thomas Hart Benton and his Art Students League students, various artists and art styles.

### Bush, Anita(1883-1974)
Discusses: FTP Participated in: FTP
Position: Actress Location: NY
Interviewers: Hatch, James V. and Billops, Camille Interview date: 02/19/72
Tape: 100 minutes Abstract: 1 page(s)
Repository: Hatch-Billops Collection, Inc.
Permission of archive needed.
Description: Performing in *Swing It*, personal hardships in the theatre.

### Buttita, Tony
Discusses: FTP Participated in: FTP
Position: Publicist Location: NY
Interviewer: Brown, Lorraine Interview date: 01/11/77
Transcript: 34 pages Tape: 50 minutes Abstract: 2 page(s)
Repository: George Mason University

Description: Organization of press department, *Federal Theatre Magazine*, various productions, *Cradle Will Rock* and *Processional*.


**Cabral, Flavio Emmanuel**(b.1918)
Discusses: FAP
Positions: Artist, Teacher Location: CA
Interviewer: Hoag, Betty Lochrie Interview date: 1965
Transcript: 15 pages
Repository: Archives of American Art
Permission of interviewee needed.


**Cadmus, Paul**
Discusses: FAP Participated in: FAP
Positions: Artist, Muralist
Interviewer: Sutherland, David Interview date: 1979-80
Tape: 600 minutes
Repository: George Mason University
Contact-Federal Theatre Project-GMU.
12 oral and videotapes of outakes of "Paul Cadmus: Enfant Terrible at 80".
Description: A comprehensive study of the artist and his work, FAP, other artists.


**Cahill, Holger**(1893-1960)
Discusses: FAP, FTP Participated in: FAP
Position: Administrator Location: DC
Interviewer: Pring, Joan Interview date: 1957
Transcript: 622 pages
Repository: Columbia University
Permission required to quote.
Interview also includes: Caning, Claire, Miller, Dorothy Caning
Available on microfiche, part II.
Description: The Depression, New York World's Fair, relief work for artists.


**Callahan, Kenneth L.**(b.1906)
Discusses: SECT Participated in: SECT
Positions: Muralist, Sculptor Locations: WA, ND
Interviewer: Kendall, Sue Ann Interview date: 10/27/82
Transcript: 75 pages Tape: 560 minutes
Repository: Archives of American Art
Interviews also on 11/21/82 and 12/19/82 by same interviewer.

Description: Mural commissions in Centralia, Wash, Rugby, North Dakota, Anacortes, Wash Post Offices.

**Callahan, Kenneth L.**(b.1906)
Discusses: SECT Participated in: SECT
Positions: Muralist, Sculptor Locations: WA, ND
Interviewer: Bestor, Dorothy Interview date: 03/09/65
Transcript: 15 pages
Repository: Archives of American Art
Description: Section Post Office murals in Centralia and
Anacortes, Wash.

**Campbell, Dick**(b.1904)
Discusses: FTP Participated in: FTP
Position: Administrator Location: NY
Interviewer: Brown, Lorraine Interview date: 11/10/78
Abstract: 1 page(s)
Repository: George Mason University
This is an untaped interview, a one-page abstract is available.
Description: Work as Director of Lafayette Theatre Negro unit
immediately preceding its closing.

**Campbell, Dick**(b.1904)
Discusses: FTP Participated in: FTP
Position: Administrator Location: NY
Interviewers: Hatch, James V. and Billops, Camille Interview
date: 03/16/72
Tape: 60 minutes Abstract: 1 page(s)
Repository: Hatch-Billops Collection, Inc.
Permission of archive needed.
Description: Pioneering in theatre, Harlem political leaders,
reminiscences, FTP performers.

**Camryn, Walter**
Discusses: FTP Participated in: FTP
Position: Dancer Location: IL
Interviewer: Wentink, Andrew Mark Interview date:
09/11/74
Tape: 70 minutes Abstract: 1 page(s)
Repository: New York Public Library
Permission of archive needed.
Interview also includes: Stone, Bentley
This is a phonotape. A transcript of this interview is available.
Description: Teaching methods, Stone-Camryn School, Page-
Stone Ballet, FTP, Ruth Page, Adolf Bolm.

**Candell, Victor**(1903-1977)
Discusses: FAP Participated in: FAP
Position: Artist Location: NY

Interviewer: Seckler, Dorothy G. Interview date: 09/01/65
Transcript: 44 pages
Repository: Archives of American Art
Permission of wife needed.
Description: American Artists Congress, Whitney Museum and the FAP.

**Cardwell, Laurence**
Discusses: FTP Participated in: FTP
Position: Administrator Locations: FL, NY
Interviewer: O'Connor, John Interview date: 03/17/77
Transcript: 12 pages Tape: 30 minutes Abstract: 1 page(s)
Repository: George Mason University
Description: Functions of the personnel office, rights of the participants.

**Carmody, John Michael(1881-1963)**
Discusses: PWAP, WPA Participated in: PWAP, WPA
Position: Administrator Location: DC
Interview date: 1954
Transcript: 763 pages
Repository: Columbia University
Permisssion required to quote.
Available on microfiche.
Description: Cabinet rank position as head of Federal Works Agency (FWA was the successor to the WPA).

**Carter, Clarence Holbrook(b.1904)**
Discusses: FAP Participated in: FAP, SECT
Positions: Artist, Administrator Location: OH
Interviewer: Doud, Richard Interview date: 04/13/64
Transcript: 28 pages
Repository: Archives of American Art

**Carter, Clarence Holbrook(b.1904)**
Discusses: FAP Participated in: FAP, SECT
Positions: Artist, Administrator Location: OH
Interviewer: Harrison, Helen A. Interview date: 1974
Tape: 60 minutes
Repository: George Mason University
Closed pending release.
Description: Administrator of the Cleveland FAP (1937-38), Post Office murals.

**Cassidy, Ina Sizer(b.1869)**
Discusses: PWAP, FWP Participated in: FWP
Position: Administrator Location: NM

Interviewer: Loomis, Sylvia  Interview date: 02/13/64
Transcript: 23 pages
Repository: Archives of American Art
Interviewee is the wife of PWAP muralist, Gerald Cassidy.
Description: PWAP murals painted by her husband Gerald
Cassidy, her work as FWP director in New Mexico.

**Cassimir, John(1898-1964)**
Discusses: FMP  Participated in: FMP
Location: LA
Interviewer: Allen, Richard B.  Interview date: 01/17/59
Tape: 60 minutes
Repository: Tulane University
Description: FMP band.

**Catlett, Elizabeth(b.1919)**
Discusses: FAP
Position: Artist  Location: NY
Interviewer: Van Scott, G.  Interview date: 12/08/81
Transcript: 24 pages  Tape: 120 minutes
Repository: Hatch-Billops Collection, Inc.
Permission of archive needed.
Description: Art Students League.

**Chaivoe, Nick**
Discusses: FTP  Participated in: FTP
Positions: Actor, Stage Manager  Location: OR
Interviewer: Tanzer, Shirley  Interview date: 01/18/78
Transcript: 92 pages  Tape: 160 minutes  Abstract: 6 page(s)
Repository: George Mason University
Description: Performances in various productions, work on
Historical Records Survey.

**Chapman, Kenneth L.(b.1875)**
Discusses: FAP
Position: Administrator  Location: NM
Interviewer: Loomis, Sylvia  Interview date: 12/05/63
Transcript: 16 pages
Repository: Archives of American Art
Description: His work on the FAP, FAP's impact on
printmaking, his opinion of FAP.

**Chase, Mary Coyle**
Discusses: FTP  Participated in: FTP
Position: Playwright  Location: CO
Interviewer: Wickre, Karen  Interview date: 08/09/79
Transcript: 32 pages  Tape: 35 minutes  Abstract: 1 page(s)

Repository: George Mason University
Description: Her FTP play, *Me Third*, FTP actors in Denver, Vassar Summer Conference.

**Chase, Richard**(b.1904)
Discusses: FWP Participated in: FWP
Location: VA
Interviewers: Perdue, Charles and Perdue, Nan Interview date: 11/08/84
Transcript: 7 pages Tape: 240 minutes
Repository: In possession of interviewers
Permission of interviewers needed.
Contact: Charles Perdue, Dept. of English, Univ. of Virginia 22904.
Description: Performed as a teller of Jack tales in Richmond, Virginia.

**Chavez, Edward Arcenio**(b.1917)
Discusses: TRAP, FAP Participated in: TRAP, FAP, SECT
Positions: Artist, Muralist Locations: NY, CO, TX
Interviewer: Trovato, Joseph Interview date: 11/05/64
Transcript: 5 pages
Repository: Archives of American Art
Description: Working for TRAP, murals for FAP and section in high schools and post offices, federal support for the arts.

**Cherry, Herman**(b.1909)
Discusses: FAP Participated in: FAP
Position: Artist Location: CA
Interviewer: Phillips, Harlan Interview date: 09/65
Transcript: 52 pages
Repository: Archives of American Art
Description: Easel painting in Los Angeles.

**Chesse, Ralph**(b.1900)
Discusses: FAP, PWAP Participated in: FAP, PWAP, FTP
Positions: Artist, Puppeteer Location: CA
Interviewers: Vitale, Lydia Modi and Gelber, Steven Interview date: 02/18/75
Tape: 60 minutes
Repository: University of Santa Clara
Series: New Deal Art: California
Chesse also worked on FTP. This interview is on 1" videotape and needs special equipment to be viewed.

**Chesse, Ralph**(b.1900)
Discusses: FTP Participated in: FTP, FAP, PWAP

Positions: Administrator, Puppeteer Location: CA
Interviewer: Chesse, Bruce Interview date: 1974
Tape: 160 minutes Abstract: 3 page(s)
Repository: George Mason University
Also costume designer. Chesse also worked on FAP. Interviewer
is the son of the interviewee.
Description: Early career aspirations, experience with Blanding
Sloan, carving marionette faces, State Director of Marionette
Units.


**Chesse, Ralph**(b.1900)
Discusses: FTP Participated in: FTP, FAP, PWAP
Positions: Administrator, Puppeteer Location: CA
Interviewer: Sundell, Michael Interview date: 06/23/77
Transcript: 29 pages Tape: 60 minutes Abstract: 2 page(s)
Repository: George Mason University
Interview also includes: Chesse, Dion
Description: State Director of Marionette Unit, *Crock of Gold*,
*Alice in Wonderland*, *Mikado*, *Emperor Jones*, *Snow White*, *Rip
Van Winkle*.


**Chesse, Ralph**(b.1900)
Discusses: FAP Participated in: FAP, PWAP, FTP
Positions: Artist, Puppeteer Location: CA
Interviewer: McChesney, Mary Fuller Interview date:
10/22/64
Transcript: 28 pages
Repository: Archives of American Art
Permission of interviewee needed.
Ralph Chesse also worked on FTP.
Description: Coit Tower mural.


**Childress, Alice**(b.1920)
Discusses: FTP
Position: Actress
Interviewers: Hatch, James V. and Billops, Camille Interview
date: 02/21/72
Tape: 120 minutes Abstract: 1 page(s)
Repository: Hatch-Billops Collection, Inc.
Permission of archive needed.
Childress was not a FTP participant. Childress was the wife of
FTP actor, Alvin Childress.
Description: Editing *Black Scenes*, the American Negro
Theatre, racism in the theatre, Langston Hughes.


**Chilkovsky, Nadia**
Discusses: FTP Participated in: FTP

Positions: Choreographer, Dancer Location: NY
Interviewer: Wickre, Karen Interview date: 05/25/78
Transcript: 25 pages Tape: 60 minutes Abstract: 2 page(s)
Repository: George Mason University
Description: Taught modern dance, Doris Humphrey, Martha Graham, *Mother Goose on Parade.*

**Chinn, Andrew**
Discusses: FAP Participated in: FAP
Position: Artist Location: WA
Interviewer: Bestor, Dorothy Interview date: 05/24/65
Transcript: 27 pages
Repository: Archives of American Art
Description: FAP in Washington, Fay Chong, William Cummings, Jacob Elshin, and Morris Graves.

**Chodorow, Eugene(b.1910)**
Discusses: FAP
Positions: Sculptor, Artist Location: CA
Interviewer: Hoag, Betty Lochrie Interview date: 08/04/65
Transcript: 25 pages
Repository: Archives of American Art
Permission of interviewee needed.

**Chong, Fay(d.1973)**
Discusses: FAP Participated in: FAP
Positions: Artist, Printmaker Location: WA
Interviewer: Hoppe, William Interview date: 07/17/72
Transcript: 17 pages
Repository: University of Washington
Series: Archives of Northwest Art
Correspondence, catalogs and photographs, also available.
Description: Seattle in the 1930s, FAP, regionalism, artistic philosophy, other artists.

**Chong, Fay(d.1973)**
Discusses: FAP Participated in: FAP
Positions: Artist, Printmaker Location: WA
Interviewer: Bestor, Dorothy Interview date: 02/65
Transcript: 14 pages
Repository: Archives of American Art
Description: Work on FAP easel painting project, FAP's impact on Seattle and its artists.

**Churchman, Edwin(b.1904)**
Discusses: FAP Participated in: FAP
Positions: Model Maker, Sculptor Location: CA

Interviewer: Hoag, Betty Lochrie  Interview date: 08/27/65
Transcript: 14 pages
Repository: Archives of American Art
Permission of interviewee needed.
Interview also includes: Churchman, Isabelle Schultz
Description: Made model furniture for dioramas.

**Churchman, Isabelle S.(b.1896)**
Discusses: FAP Participated in: FAP
Position: Sculptor Location: CA
Interviewer: Hoag, Betty Lochrie  Interview date: 08/27/65
Transcript: 14 pages
Repository: Archives of American Art
Permission of interviewee needed.
Interview also includes: Churchman, Edwin
Description: Sculpted diaramas.

**Cikovsky, Nicolai**
Discusses: FAP, SECT Participated in: FAP, SECT
Position: Artist Locations: IL, DC
Interviewer: Harrison, Helen A.  Interview date: 07/18/80
Tape: 60 minutes
Repository: George Mason University
Description: Youth in Russia, John Reed Club, FAP and SECT jobs.

**Clapp, Thaddeus**
Discusses: FAP Participated in: FAP
Position: Administrator Location: MA
Interviewer: Swift, Gregory  Interview date: 11/19/65
Transcript: 52 pages
Repository: Archives of American Art
Permission of interviewee needed.
Description: First director of the Index of American Design in Massachusetts, from 1938 he was Massachusetts State Director of FAP.

**Clark, Helen Fisher**
Discusses: FTP Participated in: FTP
Position: Researcher Location: NY
Interviewers: O'Connor, John and Brown, Lorraine Interview date: 08/07/76
Transcript: 37 pages Tape: 75 minutes Abstract: 2 page(s)
Repository: George Mason University
Closed until 08/07/86.
Interview also includes: Clark, Maurice
Description: Studied responses of children to children's theatre.

**Clark, Maurice**
Discusses: FTP Participated in: FTP
Position: Director Location: NY
Interviewers:  O'Connor, John and Brown, Lorraine Interview
date:  08/07/76
Transcript: 37 pages  Tape: 75 minutes  Abstract:  2 page(s)
Repository:  George Mason University
Closed until 08/07/86.
Interview also includes:  Clark, Helen Fisher
Description:  President of Local 100 of CIO's United Federal
Workers of America, directed *Haiti*, *Horse Play*, *Emperor's
New Clothes*.

**Clark, Maurice**
Discusses: FTP Participated in: FTP
Position: Director Location: NY
Interviewers:  O'Connor, John and Brown, Lorraine Interview
date:  08/13/79
Tape: 75 minutes  Abstract:  2 page(s)
Repository:  George Mason University
Closed until 08/13/89.

**Clarke, David**
Discusses: FTP Participated in: FTP
Position: Assistant Stage Manager Location: NY
Interviewer:  Brown, Lorraine  Interview date:  07/21/77
Transcript: 22 pages  Tape: 40 minutes  Abstract:  1 page(s)
Repository:  George Mason University
Description:  Welles' imagination, placement of actors in new
theatre.

**Clarke, Helen Bess(b.1904)**
Discusses: FAP Participated in: FAP
Location: CA
Interviewer:  Hoag, Betty Lochrie  Interview date:  06/24/64
Transcript:  48 pages
Repository:  Archives of American Art
Permission of interviewee needed.
Interview also includes:  Clarke, James Mitchell
Description:  Worked on the Curriculum Project of the FAP.

**Clarke, James Mitchell(b.1903)**
Discusses: FAP Participated in: FAP
Positions: Artist, Muralist Location: CA
Interviewer:  Hoag, Betty Lochrie  Interview date:  06/24/64

Transcript: 48 pages
Repository: Archives of American Art
Permission of interviewee needed.
Interview also includes: Clarke, Helen Bess
Description: Community mural painting.

### Clebanoff, Herman
Discusses: FMP Participated in: FMP
Position: Concertmaster Location: IL
Interviewer: Knoblauch-Franc, Marion    Interview date: 04/21/82
Transcript: 11 pages Tape: 30 minutes
Repository: George Mason University
Closed until 5/31/86.
Permission of interviewer until 5/31/87 open from 6/1/87.
Description: Concertmaster of the Illinois Symphony Orchestra, Albert Goldberg, FMP provided opportunities for composers to hear their work.

### Clugston, Katherine T.(b.1890)
Discusses: FTP Participated in: FTP
Position: Administrator Location: NY
Interviewer: Brown, Lorraine Interview date: 12/28/84
Transcript: 36 pages Tape: 180 minutes
Repository: George Mason University
Closed pending release.
Description: Director of Play Bureau, Hallie Flanagan, theatre techniques, Elmer Rice, *Power*, *Ethiopia*, delegations to D.C. about personnel cuts.

### Clugston, Katherine T.(b.1890)
Discusses: FTP Participated in: FTP
Position: Administrator Location: NY
Interviewers: Hahn, Pauline and Brown, Lorraine
Transcript: 63 pages
Repository: George Mason University
Closed until dissertation completed.
Contact: Pauline Hahn, 74A Forest Dr. Springfield, NJ 07081.

Description: Director of the Play Bureau, Hallie Flanagan, delegations to Washington D.C. about personnel cuts.

### Cohen, Elizabeth Elson
Discusses: FTP Participated in: FTP
Position: Administrator Location: CA
Interviewer: Brown, Lorraine Interview date: 01/14/77
Transcript: 21 pages Tape: 60 minutes Abstract: 3 page(s)

Repository: George Mason University
Administrator of San Francisco FTP.
Description: Ralph Chesse, FTP apprenticeships, several productions, San Francisco FTP.

**Cohn, Arthur**
Discusses: FMP Participated in: FMP
Positions: Administrator, Conductor Location: PA
Interviewer: Knoblauch-Franc, Marion Interview date: 05/06/82
Transcript: 12 pages Tape: 30 minutes
Repository: George Mason University
Closed until 5/31/86.
Permission of interviewer until 5/31/87, open from 6/1/87.
Description: Supervisor of the Copyists' Unit of the FMP in Philadelphia, conducting the Philadelphia Orchestra.

**Coleman, Ralf(1898-1976)**
Discusses: FTP Participated in: FTP
Position: Director Location: MA
Interviewer: Brown, Lorraine Interview date: 11/21/75
Tape: 90 minutes
Repository: George Mason University
Also available at Hatch-Billops Inc.
Description: Massachusetts Negro FTP.

**Coleman, Ralf(1898-1976)**
Discusses: FTP Participated in: FTP
Position: Director Location: MA
Interviewer: Singer, Paula Interview date: 11/24/72
Transcript: 25 pages Tape: 80 minutes Abstract: 8 page(s)
Repository: Hatch-Billops Collection, Inc.
Permission of archive needed.
Available at Archives of American Art. An 8-page abstract is available at GMU, filed with other Coleman interview.
Description: Negro FTP, civil rights plays, memoirs, black community theatre in Boston.

**Colin, Ralph Frederick(b.1900)**
Discusses: FAP
Position: Art Collector Location: NY
Interviewer: Phillips, Harlan Interview date: 03/12/65
Transcript: 58 pages
Repository: Archives of American Art
Permission of interviewee needed.
Description: Politics of government support for the arts, trends in painting.

**Collier, John**
Discusses: FSA Participated in: FSA
Position: Photographer Location: CA
Interviewer: Doud, Richard Interview date: 01/18/65
Transcript: 33 pages
Repository: Archives of American Art
Permission of interviewee needed.
Description: Joined the historical section of the FSA in 1941.

**Collier, Nina Perera**(b.1907)
Discusses: PWAP Participated in: PWAP
Position: Administrator Location: NM
Interviewer: Loomis, Sylvia Interview date: 10/29/64
Transcript: 34 pages
Repository: Archives of American Art
Permission of interviewee needed.
Description: Education, background, PWAP work on survey of
Native American arts and crafts.

**Collins, Dorothy**(b.1893)
Discusses: FAP
Position: Artist Location: CA
Interviewer: McChesney, Mary Fuller Interview date:
07/07/64
Transcript: 65 pages
Repository: Archives of American Art
Permission of interviewee needed.

**Connelly, Marc**(b.1890)
Discusses: FTP Participated in: FTP
Position: Playwright Location: NY
Interviewer: O'Connor, John Interview date: 10/23/76
Abstract: 1 page(s)
Repository: George Mason University
This is an untaped interview, a one-page abstract is available.
Description: Connelly's plays were produced in various FTP
units, e.g., *The Farmer Takes a Wife* and *Everywhere I Roam*
with A. Sungaard.

**Conroy, Jack**
Discusses: FWP Participated in: FWP
Position: Writer Locations: MO, IL
Interviewer: Mangione, Jerre Interview date: 06/14/68
Repository: University of Rochester
Series: Mangione Collection
Description: Worked on the American Guide Series.

**Constantine, Mildred(b.1914)**
Discusses: FAP
Position: Art Historian Location: NY
Interviewer: Phillips, Harlan Interview date: 10/15/65
Transcript: 59 pages
Repository: Archives of American Art

**Corey, Jeff**
Discusses: FTP Participated in: FTP
Position: Actor Location: NY
Interviewer: Wickre, Karen Interview date: 10/24/77
Transcript: 19 pages Tape: 40 minutes Abstract: 2 page(s)
Repository: George Mason University
Description: Early life, Group Theatre, effect of blacklisting, several plays.

**Cornish, Mary Elizabeth(b.1916)**
Discusses: FAP
Location: CO
Interviewer: Bardwell, Lisa Interview date: 07/14/79
Tape: 50 minutes
Repository: Denver Public Library
Series: Federal Art in Colorado, 1934-1943
An abstract is available. Interviewee is the daughter of FAP participant, C. Waldo Love.
Description: Dioramas done by C. Waldo Love for the Denver Museum of Natural History and the Colorado State Historical Society.

**Corwin, Norman(b.1910)**
Interview date: 1966
Transcript: 100 pages
Repository: Columbia University
Closed during lifetime.
Series: Radio Pioneers
Description: Early radio, reaction of radio industry, advertising agencies, and the public to "Red Channels".

**Cotten, Joseph**
Discusses: FTP Participated in: FTP
Position: Actor Location: NY
Interviewer: Wickre, Karen Interview date: 02/22/78
Transcript: 19 pages Tape: 45 minutes Abstract: 2 page(s)
Repository: George Mason University
Description: Orson Welles, early life, *Horse Eats Hat*, *Faustus*, and *Shoemaker's Holiday*.

**Cotten, Joseph**
Discusses: FTP Participated in: FTP
Position: Actor Location: NY
Interviewer: Goldman, Harry
Transcript: 17 pages
Repository: Columbia University
Available 5 years after publication.
Series: History of the Mercury Theatre
Description: Mercury Theatre grew out of the Orson
Welles/John Houseman FTP Lafayette Theatre in New York
City, *Horse Eats Hat.*

**Couch, William Terry(b.1901)**
Discusses: FWP Participated in: FWP
Position: Administrator Location: NC
Interview date: 1970
Transcript: 564 pages
Repository: Columbia University
Permission required to quote.
Available on microfiche, part V.
Description: Regional FWP director (1937-1939), helped to
publish *These Are Our Lives.*

**Courlander, Harold**
Discusses: FTP Participated in: FTP
Position: Playwright Location: NY
Interviewer: Brown, Lorraine Interview date: 08/10/77
Transcript: 22 pages Tape: 50 minutes Abstract: 1 page(s)
Repository: George Mason University
Description: Wrote plays with Black folk themes, *Swamp Mud.*

**Cowell, Henry(1897-1965)**
Interview date: 1963
Transcript: 142 pages
Repository: Columbia University
Description: Music, OWI, folk and orential music, publishing,
lecture anecdotes on musicals, Columbia, New School, Charles
Ives.

**Cowell, Sidney Robertson(b.1903)**
Discusses: RA, FMP, NYA Participated in: RA, FMP
Positions: Folk Song Collector, Administrator Locations: CA,
MN, DC
Interviewer: Warren-Findley, Jannelle Interview date: 07/81
Repository: In possession of interviewer

Permission of J. Warren-Findley.
Contact: J. Warren-Findley at 2905 Pine Springs Rd. Falls Church, VA 22042.
Description: Cowell was a folk song collector, a recreation specialist, and Calif. music history project director.

**Cox, Margaret**
Discusses: FTP Participated in: FTP
Positions: Secretary, Administrative Assistant Locations: DC, NY
Interviewer: Bowers, Diane Interview date: 02/05/76
Transcript: 32 pages Tape: 65 minutes Abstract: 2 page(s)
Repository: George Mason University
Description: Cox was secretary to William Farnsworth, who was national deputy director of FTP, McLean Mansion(FTP headquarters), other secretaries.

**Coye, Lee Brown(d.1981)**
Discusses: FAP Participated in: FAP
Position: Artist Location: NY
Interviewer: Trovato, Joseph Interview date: 05/26/64
Transcript: 9 pages
Repository: Archives of American Art
Description: The impact of FAP on his career and on the lives and work of other artists.

**Craft, Paul**
Discusses: FAP
Position: Museum Director Location: SC
Interviewer: Phillips, Harlan Interview date: 06/03/65
Transcript: 58 pages
Repository: Archives of American Art
Permission of interviewee needed.

**Crampton, Rollin McNeil(1886-1970)**
Discusses: FAP Participated in: FAP
Position: Administrator Location: NY
Interviewer: Trovato, Joseph Interview date: 01/29/65
Transcript: 8 pages
Repository: Archives of American Art
Description: Supervisor of the New York City FAP mural project, effects of FAP on his career.

**Cravath, Dorothy(b.1901)**
Discusses: FAP Participated in: FAP, SECT
Position: Artist Location: CA
Interviewer: Martin, Minette Interview date: 05/27/64

Transcript: 11 pages
Repository: Archives of American Art
Permission of interviewee needed.
Interview also includes: Hamlin, Edith

   **Cravath, Dorothy(b.1901)**
Discusses: FAP Participated in: FAP, SECT
Position: Artist Location: CA
Interviewers: Teiser, Ruth and Harroun, Catherine Interview
date: 1974/75
Transcript: 365 pages
Transcript is indexed.
Repository: University of California, Berkeley
Permission of archive needed.
Interview also includes: Cravath, Ruth
Part of published interview: *Two S.F. Artists and Their
Contemporaries.*
Description: FAP artists, mural art, other San Francisco artists,
sculptors, and architects.

   **Cravath, Ruth(b.1902)**
Discusses: FAP
Location: CA
Interviewers: Teiser, Ruth and Harroun, Catherine Interview
date: 1974/75
Transcript: 365 pages
Transcript is indexed.
Repository: University of California-Berkeley
Permission of archive needed.
Interview also includes: Cravath, Dorothy Wagner Puccinelli
Part of published interview: *Two S.F. Artists and Their
Contemporaries.*
Description: FAP artists, mural art, other San Francisco artists,
sculptors, and architects.

   **Crawford, Phyllis**
Discusses: FAP Participated in: FAP
Position: Artist Location: NM
Interviewer: Loomis, Sylvia Interview date: 08/27/64
Transcript: 27 pages
Repository: Archives of American Art
Permission of interviewee needed.
Description: Worked on the Index of American Design.

   **Crichlow, Ernest(b.1914)**
Discusses: FAP Participated in: FAP
Position: Artist Location: NY

Interviewer: Ghent, Henri  Interview date: 08/20/68
Transcript: 25 pages
Repository: Archives of American Art
Permission of interviewee needed.
Description: Early life, role of black artists, prejudice in the arts, painting techniques, politics and FAP.

**Crockwell, S. Douglas**(1904-1968)
Discusses: FAP  Participated in: FAP, PWAP, SECT
Positions: Artist, Illustrator  Locations: NY, MS, VT
Interviewer: Trovato, Joseph  Interview date: 02/21/65
Transcript: 14 pages
Repository: Archives of American Art
Description: Background and education in commerical art, involvement in FAP.

**Cronbach, Robert**
Discusses: FAP  Participated in: FAP, SECT
Position: Sculptor  Location: NY
Interviewer: Harrison, Helen A.  Interview date: 02/26/76
Repository: George Mason University
Closed pending release.
Description: Public Use of Art Committee and subway art.

**Cronin, Ann**
Discusses: WPA  Participated in: WPA
Position: Administrative Assistant  Location: DC
Interviewer: Phillips, Harlan  Interview date: 03/30/65
Transcript: 42 pages
Repository: Archives of American Art
Permission of interviewee needed.
Description: Administrative assistant to Ellen Woodward, WPA's head of Women's and Professional Division.

**Croydon, Joan**
Discusses: FTP  Participated in: FTP
Position: Actress  Location: NY
Interviewer: Wickre, Karen  Interview date: 12/16/77
Transcript: 17 pages  Tape: 30 minutes  Abstract: 2 page(s)
Repository: George Mason University
Description: Theatre background, Ethel Barrymore her mentor, audiences unresponsive to avant-garde plays.

**Cumming, William**
Discusses: FAP  Participated in: FAP
Position: Artist  Location: WA
Interviewer: Hoppe, William  Interview date: 08/02/72

Transcript: 29 pages  Abstract: 29 page(s)
Repository: University of Washington
Duplication not permitted.
Series: Archives of Northwest Art
Description: His career, the Seattle art community of the 1930s.

**Cumming, William**
Discusses: FAP Participated in: FAP
Position: Artist Location: WA
Interviewer: Bestor, Dorothy Interview date: 04/03/65
Transcript: 35 pages
Repository: Archives of American Art
Permission of interviewee needed.
Description: Getting work on FAP, destruction of some of the art work produced by the project, government support for the arts.

**Cunningham, Benjamin F.(1904-1975)**
Discusses: FAP Participated in: FAP, SECT
Positions: Artist, Muralist Locations: NY, CA
Interviewer: Phillips, Harlan Interview date: 10/24/64
Transcript: 58 pages
Repository: Archives of American Art
Description: Murals for the FAP, political problems on the project, strikes, Index of American Design in California.

**Cunningham, Michele E.**
Discusses: FTP Participated in: FTP
Positions: Actress, Dancer Locations: OR, CA
Interviewer: Krulak, Mae Mallory Interview date: 05/28/76
Tape: 240 minutes  Abstract: 6 page(s)
Repository: George Mason University
Description: Her experiences as dancer, actress, FTP prompt girl, radio script writer, Ralph Chesse and William Watts.

**Cunningham, Patricia S.**
Discusses: FAP Participated in: FAP
Positions: Muralist, Sculptor Location: CA
Interviewer: McChesney, Mary Fuller Interview date: 07/28/64
Transcript: 24 pages
Repository: Archives of American Art
Description: Public school murals, easel painting project, the FAP and her career.

**Curtis, Philip Campbell(b.1907)**

Discusses: FAP Participated in: FAP
Positions: Artist, Administrator Location: AZ
Interviewer: Loomis, Sylvia Interview date: 03/31/65
Transcript: 27 pages
Repository: Archives of American Art
Description: Supervisor of the FAP Mural Project, how the FAP affected art in Arizona.

**Da Silva, Howard**(1909-1986)
Discusses: FTP Participated in: FTP
Positions: Actor, Director Location: NY
Interviewer: Schulman, Sol Interview date: 05/24/76
Transcript: 51 pages Tape: 90 minutes Abstract: 3 page(s)
Repository: George Mason University
Description: Federal Radio Theatre series(*Labor on the March*, *Great Drama*), Living Newspapers: *Triple-A*, *Spirochete*, *One Third of A Nation*.

**Da Silva, Howard**(1909-1986)
Participated in: FTP
Positions: Actor, Director Location: NY
Interviewer: Goldman, Harry
Transcript: 21 pages
Repository: Columbia University
Available 5 years after publication.
Series: History of the Mercury Theatre

**Daggett, Helen Cross**
Discusses: FTP Participated in: FTP
Positions: Director, Teacher Location: CA
Interviewer: Kahn, David Interview date: 04/18/83
Transcript: 16 pages
Repository: George Mason University
Description: Worked on: *Battle Hymn*, *It Can't Happen Here*, *Emperor Jones*, and *Power*.

**Dailey, Dan**(1915-1978)
Discusses: FTP Participated in: FTP
Positions: Dancer, Actor Location: NY
Interviewer: Cullum, Sally G. Interview date: 1974
Transcript: 100 pages Tape: 160 minutes Abstract: 1 page(s)
Transcript is indexed.
Repository: Southern Methodist University
Series: Performing Arts in the U.S.
Description: Overview of Dailey's career.

**Daly, Frank**

Discusses: FTP Participated in: FTP
Position: Actor Location: NY
Interviewer: Wickre, Karen Interview date: 06/11/77
Transcript: 25 pages Tape: 55 minutes Abstract: 2 page(s)
Repository: George Mason University
Description: Pre-FTP NY State theatre activity, FTP was padded, FTP created theatre audiences, Welles' accomplishments.

**Dana, Homer**(b.1900)
Discusses: FAP Participated in: FAP
Position: Sculptor Location: CA
Interviewer: Hoag, Betty Lochrie Interview date: 07/30/64
Transcript: 16 pages
Repository: Archives of American Art
Description: FAP's impact on artists.

**Daniels, Jonathan**(d.1981)
Discusses: FSA
Position: Writer Location: NC
Interviewer: Doud, Richard Interview date: 06/14/65
Transcript: 10 pages
Repository: Archives of American Art
Description: Wrote a book, *A Southerner Discovers the South*, preserving Roy Stryker's collection of photographs.

**Danysh, Joseph**
Discusses: FAP Participated in: FAP
Position: Administrator Location: CA
Interviewer: Vitale, Lydia Modi Interview date: 04/24/75
Tape: 110 minutes
Repository: University of Santa Clara
Series: New Deal Art: California
This interview is on 1" videotape and needs special equipment to be viewed.

**Danzig, Frank**
Discusses: FTP Participated in: FTP
Position: Writer Location: NY
Interviewer: Brown, Lorraine Interview date: 07/19/77
Transcript: 9 pages Tape: 20 minutes Abstract: 1 page(s)
Repository: George Mason University
Description: Radio drama in the 1930s, FTP had mostly prime-time shows, primarily educational in nature.

**Darley, Eunice Welch**
Discusses: FAP Participated in: FAP

Position: Artist Location: CO
Interviewer: Whistler, Nancy Interview date: 10/30/79
Tape: 60 minutes
Repository: Denver Public Library
Description: Colorado State Historical Society dioramas.

**Dasburg, Andrew Michael(1887-1979)**
Discusses: FAP Participated in: FAP, PWAP
Position: Artist Location: NM
Interviewer: Loomis, Sylvia Interview date: 07/02/64
Transcript: 20 pages
Repository: Archives of American Art

**Davidson, Julius**
Discusses: WPA Participated in: WPA
Position: Administrator Location: DC
Interviewers: Krulak, Mae Mallory and Brown, Lorraine
Interview date: 12/14/76
Transcript: 64 pages Tape: 180 minutes Abstract: 3 page(s)
Repository: George Mason University
Finance officer on Federal One.
Description: Problems of artists working for government, FTP
hierarchy, FTP as a relief program, budget cuts, FMP
orchestras.

**Davidson, Julius**
Discusses: WPA Participated in: WPA
Position: Administrator Location: DC
Interviewer: Phillips, Harlan Interview date: 1964
Transcript: 66 pages
Repository: Archives of American Art
Description: Finance officer of Federal One.

**De Koven, Roger(b.1907)**
Discusses: FTP Participated in: FTP
Position: Actor Location: NY
Interviewer: Burch, Jeanne S. Interview date: 01/08/80
Tape: 55 minutes Abstract: 2 page(s)
Repository: George Mason University
Closed pending release.
Description: FTP's purpose more for relief than for
innovation, *Murder in the Cathedral*, cultural impact of FTP.

**De Paur, Leonard(b.1919)**
Discusses: FTP Participated in: FTP
Positions: Composer, Musician Location: NY
Interviewer: Brown, Lorraine Interview date: 12/02/76

Tape: 115 minutes  Abstract:  6 page(s)
Repository:  George Mason University
Also available at the Hatch-Billops Collection Inc.
Description:  Work as music director for Lafayette Unit of
FTP, audience reaction, racism, permanent effects of Negro
Federal Theatre.


   **De Paur, Leonard**(b.1919)
Discusses: FTP Participated in: FTP
Positions: Composer, Musician Location: NY
Interviewers:  Hatch, James V. and Billops, Camille Interview
date:  02/15/75
Tape: 80 minutes  Abstract:  1 page(s)
Repository:  Hatch-Billops Collection, Inc.
Permission of archive needed.
Description:  Music director of Layfayette Theatre in Harlem,
Welles' *Macbeth*.


   **De Rivera, Jose**(1904-1985)
Discusses: FAP Participated in: FAP
Position: Sculptor Locations: IL, NY
Interviewer:  Cummings, Paul  Interview date:  02/24/68
Transcript:  60 pages
Repository:  Archives of American Art
Permission of archive needed.
Description:  Transition from figurative to abstract sculpture,
working methods, the FAP.


   **Dean, Mallette**(1907-1975)
Discusses: TRAP, PWAP Participated in: PWAP, TRAP
Position: Artist Location: CA
Interviewer:  Teiser, Ruth  Interview date:  1969
Transcript:  105 pages
Transcript is indexed.
Repository:  University of California, Berkeley
Description:  Coit Tower murals.


   **Deane, Martha Blanchard**(b.1896)
Discusses: FTP
Position: Administrator Location: CA
Interviewer:  Schippers, Donald J.  Interview date:  1966
Transcript:  212 pages  Tape: 480 minutes
Transcript is indexed.
Repository:  Univ. of California, Los Angeles
Description:  FTP organizer in San Francisco and Los Angeles,
Ralph Freud.

**Deeter, Jasper**
Discusses: FAP
Position: Administrator
Interviewer: Doud, Richard    Interview date:  1964
Transcript:  36 pages
Repository:  Archives of American Art
Permission of archive needed.

**Defenbacher, Daniel S.(b.1906)**
Discusses: FAP Participated in: FAP
Position: Administrator Location: NC
Interviewer:    McChesney, Mary Fuller    Interview date:
04/16/65
Transcript:  60 pages
Repository:  Archives of American Art
Permission of interviewee needed.
Description:  State director for North Carolina.

**Dehn, Adolph Arthur(1895-1968)**
Discusses: FAP Participated in: FAP, PWAP
Position: Artist Locations: MN, NY
Interviewer: Seckler, Dorothy G.  Interview date:  1964
Transcript:  50 pages
Repository:  Archives of American Art
Permission of widow needed.
Description:  Graphics under the FAP, Art Students League,
experiments with lithography, magazine illustrations, the
Depression.

**Dehn, Mura**
Discusses: FTP Participated in: FTP
Positions: Dancer, Choreographer Location: NY
Interviewer:  Wickre, Karen  Interview date:  04/20/78
Transcript:  21 pages  Tape: 50 minutes  Abstract:  3 page(s)
Repository:  George Mason University
Description:  Struggle of Dance Project and FTP in general,
FTP introduced opportunities for "social-political" life.

**Del Bourgo, Fanya Geltman**
See Geltman, Fanya.

**Delano, Irene**
Discusses: FSA
Position: Artist
Interviewer:  Doud, Richard  Interview date:  06/12/65
Transcript:  63 pages
Repository:  Archives of American Art

Interview also includes: Delano, Jack
Description: Irene Delano is an artist, did not work on the FSA.

**Delano, Jack(b.1914)**
Discusses: FSA Participated in: FSA
Position: Photographer
Interviewer: Doud, Richard  Interview date: 06/12/65
Transcript: 63 pages
Repository: Archives of American Art
Interview also includes: Delano, Irene

**Denby, Edwin(1903-1983)**
Discusses: FTP Participated in: FTP
Positions: Play Adapter, Choreographer Location: NY
Interviewer: Krulak, Mae Mallory  Interview date: 03/02/77
Transcript: 18 pages  Tape: 60 minutes  Abstract: 2 page(s)
Repository: George Mason University
Description: *Horse Eats Hat*, *Faustus*, Rudolph Burckhardt's career, audience response, value of FTP.

**Deutsch, Boris(1892-1978)**
Discusses: FAP, SECT Participated in: SECT
Position: Artist Locations: CA, NM
Interviewer: Hoag, Betty Lochrie  Interview date: 1964
Transcript: 44 pages
Repository: Archives of American Art

**Dickey, Roland**
Discusses: FAP
Position: Administrator Location: NM
Interviewer: Loomis, Sylvia  Interview date: 01/16/64
Transcript: 29 pages
Repository: Archives of American Art
Description: County Superivsor for the FAP, involvement with the Index of American Design, public reaction to FAP.

**Dieterich, Hebert R., Jr.(b.1925)**
Discusses: FAP
Location: WY
Interviewer: Chapman, Anne  Interview date: 05/05/79
Tape: 34 minutes
Repository: Denver Public Library
Series: Federal Art in Colorado, 1934-1943
Description: Various projects in Wyoming.

**Dike, Philip(b.1906)**

Discusses: FAP
Position: Artist Location: CA
Interviewer: Hoag, Betty Lochrie Interview date: 06/09/65
Transcript: 7 pages
Repository: Archives of American Art

**Diller, Burgoyne**(1906-1965)
Discusses: FAP Participated in: FAP, PWAP
Positions: Administrator, Artist Location: NY
Interviewer: Gurin, Ruth Interview date: 03/21/64
Transcript: 14 pages
Repository: Archives of American Art
Description: Mural supervisor, Art Students League, comments on federal art programs in the late 1930s.

**Diller, Burgoyne**(1906-1965)
Discusses: FAP Participated in: FAP, PWAP
Positions: Administrator, Artist Location: NY
Interviewer: Phillips, Harlan Interview date: 10/02/64
Transcript: 81 pages
Repository: Archives of American Art

**Dixon, Harry**(b.1907)
Discusses: FAP
Position: Craftsperson Location: CA
Interviewer: McChesney, Mary Fuller Interview date: 05/01/64
Transcript: 25 pages
Repository: Archives of American Art
Permission of interviewee needed.

**Dorais, Leon (Bill)**
Discusses: FWP Participated in: FWP
Position: Writer Location: CA
Interviewer: Mangione, Jerre Interview date: 05/28/68
Repository: University of Rochester
Series: Mangione Collection
Description: Headed the Los Angeles office of the California FWP.

**Dornbush, Adrian**
Discusses: FAP Participated in: PWAP, FAP, RA
Position: Administrator Location: FL
Interviewer: Doud, Richard Interview date: 06/13/65
Transcript: 17 pages
Repository: Archives of American Art
Description: FAP work included the rehabilitation of Key

West, supervised art activities for the RA.

**Douglas, Helen Gahagan**(b.1900)
Discusses: WPA
Positions: Actress, Congresswoman
Interviewers: Fry, Amelia and Chall, Malca Interview date: 1973-78
Transcript is indexed.
Repository: University of California, Berkeley
Series: Helen Gahagan Douglas Oral History
Description: Member of FDR's national WPA advisory committee.

**Dowell, George**
Discusses: FTP
Interviewer: Krulak, Mae Mallory Interview date: 04/30/76
Tape: 120 minutes Abstract: 3 page(s)
Repository: George Mason University
Closed pending release.
Description: Associate of Hallie Flanagan at Smith and Vassar, Vassar Experimental Theatre, Flanagan's charisma and friends.

**Dowling, Eddie**(1894-1976)
Discusses: FTP Participated in: FTP
Position: Actor
Interview date: 1963
Transcript: 838 pages
Repository: Columbia University
Permission required to quote.
Available on microfilm, Micro III.
Description: Early career in vaudeville, actor's strikes.

**Dows, Olin**(1904-1981)
Discusses: PWAP, TRAP, FAP Participated in: PWAP, TRAP, SECT
Positions: Artist, Administrator Location: NY
Interview date: 07/07/78
Transcript: 51 pages
Repository: Franklin D. Roosevelt Library
Other interview 08/08/78.
Description: Murals for the Hyde Park and Rhinebeck, New York Post Offices, first interview on FAP, other interview on Roosevelt family.

**Dows, Olin**(1904-1981)
Discusses: PWAP, TRAP, FAP Participated in: PWAP, TRAP, SECT

Positions: Artist, Administrator Location: NY
Interviewer: Phillips, Harlan Interview date: 10/31/63
Transcript: 111 pages
Repository: Archives of American Art
Description: His education and background, how the PWAP was administered, mural competitions.

**Dozier, Otis(b.1904)**
Discusses: SECT, PWAP Participated in: SECT, PWAP
Positions: Artist, Printmaker Location: TX
Interviewer: Loomis, Sylvia Interview date: 06/10/65
Transcript: 16 pages
Repository: Archives of American Art
Permission of interviewee needed.

**Du Von, Jay**
Discusses: FWP Participated in: FWP
Positions: Administrator, Writer Location: IA
Interviewer: Phillips, Harlan Interview date: 11/07/63
Transcript: 32 pages
Repository: Archives of American Art
Permission of interviewee needed.
Description: Field representative, coordinated between the state office and the national office in Washington.

**DuBois, Shirley Graham(1907-1977)**
Discusses: FTP Participated in: FTP
Position: Playwright Location: IL
Interviewers: Hatch, James V. and Billops, Camille Interview date: 05/28/75
Tape: 150 minutes Abstract: 1 page(s)
Repository: Hatch-Billops Collection, Inc.
Permission of archive needed.
Description: Early life, Negro FTP in Chicago.

**Dudley, Edward, Jr.**
Discusses: FTP Participated in: FTP
Position: Assistant Stage Manager Location: NY
Interviewer: Brown, Lorraine Interview date: 10/27/77
Transcript: 19 pages Tape: 40 minutes Abstract: 2 page(s)
Repository: George Mason University
Description: Background, FTP was umbrella for established players as well as part-time players, Lafayette Unit, value of FTP, *Macbeth.*

**Dudley, Jane**
Discusses: FTP Participated in: FTP

Position: Dancer Location: NY
Interviewer: Wormser, Richard Interview date: 1981
Tape: 45 minutes
Repository: New York University
Series: Oral History of the American Left
Description: FTP Dance Project, Martha Graham.

**Dunham, Katherine(b.1910)**
Discusses: FTP
Positions: Dancer, Choreographer Locations: IL, MO
Interviewers: Hatch, James V. and Billops, Camille Interview date: 10/26/74
Tape: 90 minutes Abstract: 1 page(s)
Repository: Hatch-Billops Collection, Inc.
Permission of archive needed.
Description: Chicago Negro Dance Group, early influences, dance techniques and theory.

**Durham, C.J.S. (Jack)**
Discusses: WPA, FTP Participated in: WPA
Location: DC
Interviewers: Brown, Lorraine and Hogg, Rosemary Interview date: 06/23/83
Transcript: 20 pages Tape: 60 minutes
Repository: George Mason University
Description: Herbert Hoover's press office, worked in Harry Hopkin's press office, responsible for censorship for the FTP, little censorship done.

**Ebsen, Nancy Wolcott**
Discusses: FTP
Interviewer: Krulak, Mae Mallory Interview date: 06/01/76
Tape: 105 minutes Abstract: 2 page(s)
Repository: George Mason University
Description: Student of Hallie Flanagan at Vassar, Flanagan as teacher, Philip Davis, Flanagan's later years.

**Edson, Eda**
Discusses: FTP Participated in: FTP
Positions: Administrator, Director Location: CA
Interviewer: Bowers, Diane Interview date: 05/30/76
Transcript: 25 pages
Repository: George Mason University
This is an untaped interview.
Description: Director of the Los Angeles vaudeville unit of the FTP, *Follow the Parade*.

**Edwards, Ben**
Discusses: FTP Participated in: FTP
Position: Actor Location: NY
Interviewer: O'Connor, John Interview date: 12/28/76
Transcript: 30 pages Tape: 60 minutes Abstract: 2 page(s)
Repository: George Mason University
Closed pending release.
Description: FTP training invaluable, no rivalry between units.

**Egri, Ted**(b.1913)
Discusses: FAP
Positions: Artist, Sculptor Location: NM
Interviewer: Loomis, Sylvia Interview date: 03/22/65
Transcript: 30 pages
Repository: Archives of American Art

**Eichenberg, Fritz**(b.1902)
Discusses: FAP Participated in: FAP
Positions: Illustrator, Printmaker Location: NY
Interviewer: Cummings, Paul Interview date: 11/03/70
Transcript: 38 pages
Repository: Archives of American Art
Permission of interviewee needed.
Description: Background, lithography, Academy of Graphic
Arts, book illustration, political cartooning, the New School,
Pratt Institute.

**Eichenberg, Fritz**(b.1902)
Discusses: FAP Participated in: FAP
Positions: Illustrator, Printmaker Location: NY
Interviewer: Phillips, Harlan Interview date: 12/03/64
Transcript: 35 pages
Repository: Archives of American Art

**Eichenberg, Fritz**(b.1902)
Discusses: FAP Participated in: FAP
Positions: Illustrator, Printmaker Location: NY
Interviewer: Brown, Robert Interview date: 1980
Transcript: 36 pages
Repository: Archives of American Art

**Eldridge, Elaine**
Discusses: FTP Participated in: FTP
Position: Actress Location: NY
Interviewer: Wickre, Karen Interview date: 11/27/78
Transcript: 22 pages Tape: 150 minutes Abstract: 2 page(s)
Repository: George Mason University

Description: Background, Children's Theatre, types of people who worked for FTP, unemployment.

**Ellison, Ralph**(b.1914)
Discusses: FWP Participated in: FWP
Position: Writer
Interviewer: Neal, Larry Interview date: 1973
Tape: 55 minutes
Repository: Hatch-Billops Collection, Inc.
Permission of archive needed.
Description: Music, black culture, American writing.

**Elshin, Jacob**(b.1892)
Discusses: FAP Participated in: FAP, PWAP, SECT
Position: Artist Location: WA
Interviewer: Bestor, Dorothy Interview date: 04/21/65
Transcript: 41 pages
Repository: Archives of American Art

**Elson, Charles**(b.1909)
Discusses: FTP Participated in: FTP
Position: Set Designer Location: CA
Interviewer: Brown, Lorraine Interview date: 12/11/76
Transcript: 37 pages Tape: 75 minutes Abstract: 2 page(s)
Repository: George Mason University
Interview also includes: Elson, Diana Rivers
Description: FTP as training ground for young actors as well as showcase for accomplished actors.

**Elson, Charles**(b.1909)
Discusses: FTP Participated in: FTP
Position: Set Designer Location: CA
Interviewer: Brown, Lorraine Interview date: 01/09/78
Tape: 95 minutes Abstract: 4 page(s)
Repository: George Mason University
Interview also includes: Bay, Howard
This is a videotape. Also available at New York Public Library.
Description: *House of Connelly*, *Triple-A Plowed Under*, FTP lighting, design philosophy crystalized during FTP experience.

**Elson, Diana Rivers**
Discusses: FTP Participated in: FTP
Position: Actress Location: CA
Interviewer: Brown, Lorraine Interview date: 12/11/76
Transcript: 37 pages Tape: 75 minutes Abstract: 2 page(s)
Repository: George Mason University
Interview also includes: Elson, Charles

Description: Experiences with FTP's Southwest Unit, actress in 1930s, *Tomorrow's a Holiday*, *Class of '29*.


**Emery, Edwin(b.1918)**
Discusses: FAP Participated in: FAP
Positions: Artist, Muralist Location: CA
Interviewer: Hoag, Betty Lochrie Interview date: 05/24/65
Transcript: 38 pages
Repository: Archives of American Art
Permission of interviewee needed.
Description: Community mural painting.


**Engard, Robert Oliver**
Discusses: FAP Participated in: FAP
Positions: Artist, Engraver Location: WA
Interviewer: Bestor, Dorothy Interview date: 11/26/65
Transcript: 21 pages
Repository: Archives of American Art
Permission of interviewee needed.
Description: Taught engraving at Spokane Art Center.


**Engel, Lehman(1910-1982)**
Discusses: FMP, FTP Participated in: FMP, FTP
Position: Composer Location: NY
Interviewer: Brown, Lorraine Interview date: 10/23/76
Transcript: 20 pages Tape: 50 minutes Abstract: 2 page(s)
Transcript is indexed.
Repository: George Mason University
Description: Welles-Houseman's crowded schedule, FTP most vigorous of arts projects, *Cradle Will Rock*, *Shoemaker's Holiday*.


**Engel, Lehman(1910-1982)**
Discusses: FMP, FTP Participated in: FMP, FTP
Position: Composer Location: NY
Interview date: 1975
Repository: New York Public Library
Permission of archive needed.
Interview also includes: Addy, Wesley
Description: Association with Margaret Webster, her talents as actress, director, and lecturer.


**Engel, Lehman(1910-1982)**
Discusses: FMP, FTP Participated in: FMP, FTP
Position: Composer Location: NY
Interviewer: Perlis, Vivian Interview date: 10/69
Transcript: 19 pages Tape: 30 minutes

Repository: Yale University
Permission of archive needed.
Series: Charles Ives Project
Description: Memories of Charles Ives, madrigal singers.

**Engel, Lehman(1910-1982)**
Discusses: FMP, FTP Participated in: FMP, FTP
Position: Composer Location: NY
Interviewer: Knoblauch-Franc, Marion   Interview date: 05/08/82
Transcript: 22 pages
Repository: George Mason University
Closed until 6/1/86.
Permission of interviewer required, open from 6/1/87.
Description: Formed and directed the Madrigal Singers, a NYC unit, wrote music for *Shoemaker's Holiday*, value of FMP and FTP.

**Epstein, Samuel**
Discusses: FWP
Interviewer: Mangione, Jerre Interview date: 07/25/68
Repository: University of Rochester
Series: Mangione Collection

**Etcheverry, Louisa(1911-1966)**
Discusses: FAP Participated in: FAP
Position: Artist Location: CA
Interviewer: Hoag, Betty Lochrie Interview date: 09/23/64
Transcript: 11 pages
Repository: Archives of American Art
Description: Art Students League, worked on the mosaic for Long Beach.

**Everett, Eugenia(b.1908)**
Discusses: PWAP Participated in: PWAP
Positions: Sculptor, Artist Location: CA
Interviewer: Hoag, Betty Lochrie Interview date: 10/14/64
Transcript: 18 pages
Repository: Archives of American Art
Permission of interviewee needed.

**Evergood, Philip(1901-1973)**
Discusses: FAP Participated in: FAP, SECT, PWAP
Positions: Artist, Muralist Locations: NY, GA
Interviewer: Selvig, Forrest Interview date: 12/03/68
Transcript: 51 pages
Repository: Archives of American Art

Permission of his widow needed.
Description: Life in New York City in the 1930s, the Depression, the mural for the Jackson, Georgia Post Office.

**Evergood, Philip(1901-1973)**
Discusses: FAP Participated in: FAP, SECT, PWAP
Positions: Artist, Muralist Locations: NY, GA
Interviewer: Selvig, Forrest Interview date: 12/69
Transcript: 44 pages
Repository: Archives of American Art
Permission of his widow needed.
Description: Education, background, Art Students League, various artists, early exhibitions, the Depression, John Reed Club, social problems, FAP.

**Ewing, Kay**
Discusses: FTP Participated in: FTP
Position: Director Location: IL
Interviewers: Burch, Jeanne S. and Greene, Brenda Z. Interview date: 11/27/79
Tape: 105 minutes Abstract: 3 page(s)
Repository: George Mason University
Closed pending release.
Description: Hallie Flanagan's personality, life, and attitude toward theatre.

**Falkenstein, Claire(b.1908)**
Discusses: FAP
Position: Sculptor Location: CA
Interviewer: Hoag, Betty Lochrie Interview date: 04/13/65
Transcript: 4 pages
Repository: Archives of American Art
Permission of interviewee needed.

**Farmer, Virginia**
Discusses: FTP Participated in: FTP
Position: Director Location: CA
Interviewer: Cohen, Gail Interview date: 08/20/76
Transcript: 21 pages
Repository: George Mason University
Closed pending release.
Description: Group Theatre, Jessie Bonstelle, Hedgerow Theatre Collective.

**Farmer, Virginia**
Discusses: FTP Participated in: FTP
Position: Director Location: CA

Interviewer: Cohen, Gail Interview date: 06/83
Transcript: 39 pages
Repository: George Mason University
Closed pending release.
Description: J. Howard Miller, *The Sun Rises in the West*, Will Geer, Hedgerow Theatre Collective.


### Farmer, Virginia
Discusses: FTP Participated in: FTP
Position: Director Location: CA
Interviewer: Brown, Lorraine Interview date: 08/11/76
Transcript: 34 pages Tape: 75 minutes Abstract: 4 page(s)
Transcript is indexed.
Repository: George Mason University
Description: Work as director of the Southwest Experimental Unit, *House of Connelly*, *Johnny Johnson*, *Class of 29*, other plays.


### Farmer, Virginia
Discusses: FTP Participated in: FTP
Position: Director Location: CA
Interviewer: Relph, Ann Interview date: 10/77
Tape: 20 minutes Abstract: 3 page(s)
Repository: George Mason University
This is a videotape.
Description: The Southwest Experimental Unit and its problems.


### Farnsworth, William
Discusses: FTP Participated in: FTP
Position: Administrator Location: CA
Interviewer: O'Connor, John Interview date: 03/16/77
Transcript: 23 pages Tape: 65 minutes Abstract: 2 page(s)
Repository: George Mason University
Description: National Deputy Director to Hallie Flanagan, working with unions, opinions about Flanagan, various performances, accomplishments of FTP.


### Farr, Charles Griffin(b.1908)
Discusses: FAP
Positions: Artist, Sculptor Location: CA
Interviewer: McChesney, Mary Fuller Interview date: 10/22/64
Transcript: 23 pages
Repository: Archives of American Art
Description: Education and background, work as a sculptor and pottery restorer on FAP, influence of FAP on his career.

**Farran, Don**(b.1902)
Discusses: FMP, FWP, FTP Participated in: FMP, FWP, FTP
Position: Administrator Locations: IL, DC
Interviewer: O'Connor, John Interview date: 01/03/76
Transcript: 48 pages Tape: 120 minutes Abstract: 3 page(s)
Repository: George Mason University
Description: Participated in FMP, FWP, FTP, American
Imprints Inventory: Manual of Procedure for HRS, trouble
with Musicians' Union in Chicago.

**Fax, Elton C.**(b.1909)
Discusses: FAP Participated in: FAP
Positions: Teacher, Illustrator Locations: NY, MD
Interview date: 1976
Transcript: 161 pages
Repository: Columbia University
Permission required to quote.
Description: Family background, education, teaching at the
Harlem Cultural Center.

**Feder, Abe**(b.1909)
Discusses: FTP Participated in: FTP
Position: Lighting Designer Locations: NY, TX
Interviewer: Wenslovas, LaVerne Interview date: 04/26/83
Tape: 108 minutes
Repository: New York Public Library
Permission of archive needed.
This is a videotape.
Description: His career, working with Orson Welles in 1937
and Hallie Flanagan in Dallas.

**Feder, Abe**(b.1909)
Discusses: FTP Participated in: FTP
Position: Lighting Designer Location: NY
Interviewers: O'Connor, John and Krulak, Mae Mallory
Interview date: 05/13/76
Transcript: 37 pages Tape: 90 minutes Abstract: 3 page(s)
Repository: George Mason University
Closed pending release.
Description: His work on various productions.

**Feitelson, Lorser**(1898-1980)
Discusses: FAP Participated in: FAP, PWAP
Positions: Administrator, Muralist Location: CA
Interviewers: Vitale, Lydia Modi and Gelber, Steven Interview
date: 03/14/75

Tape: 120 minutes
Repository: University of Santa Clara
Series: New Deal Art: California
Interview also includes: Lundberg, Helen
This interview is on 1" videotape and needs special equipment
to be viewed.

**Feitelson, Lorser(1898-1980)**
Discusses: FAP Participated in: FAP, PWAP
Positions: Administrator, Muralist Location: CA
Interviewer: Hoag, Betty Lochrie Interview date: 1964
Transcript: 52 pages
Repository: Archives of American Art
Description: Administrator of Southern California, produced
five murals, Holger Cahill, FAP political problems, Index of
American Design.

**Ferguson, Kenneth(d.1984)**
Discusses: FTP
Interviewer: Brown, Lorraine Interview date: 09/19/75
Repository: George Mason University
Description: Interviewee was brother of Hallie Flanagan.

**Fields, Earl T.**
Discusses: PWAP Participated in: PWAP
Positions: Artist, Photographer Location: WA
Interviewer: Bestor, Dorothy Interview date: 06/09/65
Transcript: 9 pages
Repository: Archives of American Art

**Fincke, Joy Yeck**
Discusses: FERA, FAP Participated in: FERA, FAP
Position: Secretary Location: NM
Interviewer: Loomis, Sylvia Interview date: 01/09/64
Transcript: 22 pages
Repository: Archives of American Art
Description: Secretary to state director Vernon Hunter, Index
of American Design, how the FAP was run, public perception
of the project and its work.

**Fine, Perle(b.1908)**
Discusses: FAP Participated in: FAP
Position: Artist Location: NY
Interviewer: Seckler, Dorothy G. Interview date: 1/19/68
Transcript: 30 pages
Repository: Archives of American Art
Description: Art Students League, Hans Hofmann, FAP

Exhibitions.

**Fishel, H. L. (Bud)**
Discusses: FTP Participated in: FTP
Position: Administrator Location: NY
Interviewer: Brown, Lorraine Interview date: 10/26/76
Transcript: 31 pages Tape: 90 minutes Abstract: 2 page(s)
Repository: George Mason University
Description: FTP influenced him to try new things, *Horse Eats Hat*, *It Can't Happen Here*, *Jericho*.

**Fisher, Granville**
Discusses: FTP Participated in: FTP
Position: Director Location: FL
Interviewer: O'Connor, John Interview date: 03/19/77
Transcript: 29 pages Tape: 65 minutes Abstract: 1 page(s)
Repository: George Mason University
Description: FTP as training ground, *Green Grow the Lilacs*, *Ninth Guest*, Miami Unit of FTP.

**Fisher, Helen**
SEE Clark, Helen Fisher.

**Fisher, Vardis**
Discusses: FWP Participated in: FWP
Positions: Administrator, Writer Location: ID
Interviewer: Mangione, Jerre Interview date: 06/04/68
Repository: University of Rochester
Series: Mangione Collection
Description: Director of Idaho FWP, published first state guidebook in American Guide Series.

**Fitzgerald, James H.(1899-1973)**
Discusses: FAP, TRAP Participated in: FAP, TRAP
Positions: Administrator, Artist Locations: ID, NY, CO
Interviewer: Bestor, Dorothy Interview date: 10/27/65
Transcript: 14 pages
Repository: Archives of American Art
Permission of interviewees needed.
Interview also includes: Fitzgerald, Margaret Tomkins
Description: Worked in Idaho for TRAP, Boardman Robinson's assistant in 1938 in Colorado Springs, did murals, worked on New York FAP.

**Fitzgerald, Margaret T.**
Discusses: FAP Participated in: FAP
Position: Artist Location: WA

Interviewer: Bestor, Dorothy  Interview date:  10/27/65
Transcript:  14 pages
Repository:  Archives of American Art
Permission of interviewees needed.
Interview also includes:  Fitzgerald, James H.
Description:  Along with her husband(James H. Fitzgerald), she taught classes and ran the Spokane Art Center.

**Fleckenstein, Opal R.(b.1911)**
Discusses: FAP
Positions: Artist, Ceramist Location: WA
Interviewer:  Bestor, Dorothy  Interview date:  11/20/65
Transcript:  36 pages
Repository:  Archives of American Art

**Flint, Leroy W.(b.1909)**
Discusses: FAP Participated in: FAP
Positions: Printmaker, Engraver Location: OH
Interviewer:  Phillips, Harlan  Interview date:  06/04/65
Transcript:  36 pages
Repository:  Archives of American Art
Description:  Joined the FAP in Cleveland, worked in the print section.

**Fogg, Adelaide**
Discusses: FAP
Positions: Artist, Teacher
Interviewer:  Phillips, Harlan  Interview date:  1965
Transcript:  29 pages
Repository:  Archives of American Art
Permission of interviewee needed.

**Forbes, Leon**
Discusses: FTP Participated in: FTP
Position: Actor Location: CA
Interviewer:  Wickre, Karen  Interview date:  07/19/77
Transcript:  29 pages Tape: 60 minutes  Abstract:  2 page(s)
Repository:  George Mason University
Interview also includes:  Wilson, Jack
Description:  Personal background, *Pursuit of Happiness*, *It Can't Happen Here*, *Battle Hymn*.

**Fossum, Syd(1909-1978)**
Discusses: FAP, PWAP Participated in: FAP, PWAP
Position: Artist Location: MN
Interviewer:  Reid, George  Interview date:  08/04/77
Transcript:  9 pages Tape: 30 minutes

Repository: Minnesota Historical Society
Series: Federal Art Project in Minnesota
Description: Minnesota PWAP (1933-34), FAP, Minnesota
Artists Union, the 1938 protests against layoffs.

**Fox, Milton S.**(1904-1971)
Discusses: FAP
Position: Artist
Interviewer: Phillips, Harlan  Interview date: 1964
Transcript: 34 pages
Repository: Archives of American Art

**Francis, Arlene**
Discusses: FTP Participated in: FTP
Position: Actress Location: NY
Interviewers: Wickre, Karen and Maddox, Jean Interview date:
04/17/78
Tape: 35 minutes Abstract: 2 page(s)
Transcript is indexed.
Repository: George Mason University
Description: Association with Orson Welles and Joseph Cotten,
various FTP productions.

**Frank, Allan**
Discusses: FTP Participated in: FTP
Position: Actor Location: NY
Interviewer: O'Connor, John  Interview date: 10/25/76
Transcript: 22 pages Tape: 60 minutes Abstract: 2 page(s)
Repository: George Mason University
Description: *Pinocchio, Murder in the Cathedral, Prologue to
Glory, Hansel and Gretel, Revolt of the Beavers, Jack and the
Beanstalk.*

**Frankel, Lillian Berson**
Discusses: FWP Participated in: FWP
Position: Playwright Location: IL
Interviewer: Wickre, Karen  Interview date: 10/10/77
Transcript: 29 pages Tape: 60 minutes Abstract: 2 page(s)
Repository: George Mason University
Description: Dissolution of projects, investigations, in-fighting,
radical elements, union, merits of FWP, stigma attached to FWP
workers.

**Frankenstein, Alfred V.**(1906-1981)
Discusses: FAP
Positions: Art Critic, Art Historian Location: CA
Interviewer: McChesney, Mary Fuller  Interview date:

11/09/65
Transcript: 31 pages
Repository: Archives of American Art

**Freeman, Charles K.**
Discusses: FTP Participated in: FTP
Positions: Producer, Director Location: NY
Interviewer: O'Connor, John Interview date: 02/20/76
Transcript: 28 pages Tape: 75 minutes Abstract: 3 page(s)
Repository: George Mason University
Description: FTP as a vital part of U.S. theatrical history,
*Adding Machine, Ghost Song, Man and the Masses, Prologue to
Glory, Adelante.*

**Freeman, Don**(1909-1978)
Discusses: FAP Participated in: FAP
Positions: Writer, Illustrator Locations: CA, NY
Interviewer: Hoag, Betty Lochrie Interview date: 06/04/65
Transcript: 19 pages
Repository: Archives of American Art

**Freud, Mayfair**
Discusses: FTP
Location: CA
Interviewer: Krulak, Mae Mallory Interview date: 01/05/76
Transcript: 14 pages Tape: 30 minutes Abstract: 1 page(s)
Repository: George Mason University
Wife of Ralph Freud, theatrical director and actor in Los
Angeles FTP.
Description: Her husband's life, his invitation to be Director
of FTP in San Francisco.

**Freud, Ralph**(1901-1974)
Discusses: FTP Participated in: FTP
Position: Director Location: CA
Interviewer: Duttera, Bonnie Interview date: 1961
Transcript: 139 pages Tape: 240 minutes
Repository: Univ. of California, Los Angeles
Description: Director of FTP San Francisco, Co-director of
Los Angeles FTP.

**Freund, Burton**(b.1915)
Discusses: FAP Participated in: FAP
Positions: Sculptor, Artist Location: IL
Interviewer: Hoag, Betty Lochrie Interview date: 04/20/65
Transcript: 42 pages
Repository: Archives of American Art

Permission of interviewee needed.
Description: On the Illinois FAP and the City of Chicago Project.

**Friar, Kimon**
Discusses: FTP, FWP Participated in: FTP, FWP
Positions: Playreader, Writer Location: MI
Interviewer: Horton, Andrew Interview date: 05/76
Tape: 60 minutes Abstract: 4 page(s)
Repository: George Mason University
Description: Play adaptations.

**Friedman, William M.(b.1909)**
Discusses: FAP
Position: Writer
Interviewer: McChesney, Mary Fuller Interview date: 04/16/65
Transcript: 28 pages
Repository: Archives of American Art
Permission of interviewee needed.
Description: Worked on the Curriculum Project, provided reading materials for schools using artists and writers.

**Fuller, Richard E.(1897-1976)**
Discusses: FAP
Position: Museum Director Location: WA
Interviewer: Bestor, Dorothy Interview date: 06/09/65
Transcript: 7 pages
Repository: Archives of American Art

**Gaethke, George(b.1898)**
Discusses: PWAP Participated in: PWAP
Positions: Artist, Printmaker Location: CA
Interviewer: McChesney, Mary Fuller Interview date: 09/29/69
Transcript: 26 pages
Repository: Archives of American Art
Permission of interviewee needed.

**Gage, Merrell(b.1892)**
Discusses: PWAP Participated in: PWAP
Position: Sculptor Location: CA
Interviewer: Hoag, Betty Lochrie Interview date: 05/27/64
Transcript: 9 pages
Repository: Archives of American Art
Description: His education and background, formation of the PWAP.

**Galea, Manuel**
Discusses: FTP Participated in: FTP
Position: Musician Location: CA
Interviewer: Bowers, Diane Interview date: 02/21/76
Transcript: 7 pages Tape: 85 minutes Abstract: 2 page(s)
Repository: George Mason University
Interview also includes: Myra Kinch (his wife)

**Garnet, Eva Desca**
Discusses: FTP Participated in: FTP
Positions: Administrator, Choreographer Location: NY
Interviewer: Wickre, Karen Interview date: 10/26/77
Transcript: 33 pages Tape: 80 minutes Abstract: 3 page(s)
Repository: George Mason University
Description: *Red Fires*, assistant to Doris Humphrey on the Federal Dance Project.

**Garnet, Eva Desca**
Discusses: FTP Participated in: FTP
Positions: Administrator, Choreographer Location: NY
Interviewer: Wickre, Karen Interview date: 02/20/78
Tape: 120 minutes Abstract: 4 page(s)
Repository: George Mason University
This is a videotape.
Description: FTP dancers--demonstration and panel with Bass, P., Barlin, A.L., Geltman, F., Gerrard, S., Mann, L., Remos, S., Schaff, T.

**Gaskin, William(d.1968)**
Discusses: FAP Participated in: FAP, PWAP
Position: Artist Location: CA
Interviewer: Ferbrache, Lewis Interview date: 02/28/64
Transcript: 71 pages
Repository: Archives of American Art
Description: Education at the San Francisco Institute of Art, involvement with the FAP in SF, FAP mosaic project, impact of FAP on artists' lives.

**Gates, Frank W. (Pancho)(b.1904)**
Discusses: FAP Participated in: FAP, PWAP
Position: Artist Location: CO
Interviewers: Hardwick, Bonnie and Johnson, Charles
Interview date: 08/15/79
Tape: 40 minutes
Repository: Denver Public Library
Permission of archive needed.

Series: Federal Art in Colorado, 1934-1943
Description: Federal Theatre Project.

**Gaw, William A.**(1891-1973)
Discusses: FAP Participated in: FAP
Position: Artist Location: CA
Interviewer: Ferbrache, Lewis Interview date: 03/06/64
Transcript: 48 pages
Repository: Archives of American Art
Description: Education and background, work on the FAP, teaching at Mills College.

**Geer, Will**(1902-1978)
Discusses: FTP Participated in: FTP
Position: Actor Location: NY
Interviewer: Davis, Ronald L. Interview date: 07/29/75
Transcript: 38 pages Tape: 45 minutes Abstract: 1 page(s)
Transcript is indexed.
Repository: Southern Methodist University
Series: Performing Arts in the U.S.
SMU also holds correspondence related to interview.
Description: A biographical interview focusing on the early years of Geer's career.

**Geer, Will**(1902-1978)
Discusses: FTP Participated in: FTP
Position: Actor Location: NY
Interviewer: Bowers, Diane Interview date: 06/01/76
Transcript: 29 pages Tape: 50 minutes Abstract: 2 page(s)
Repository: George Mason University
Description: *Unto Such Glory*, *Cradle Will Rock*, rehearsals with Orson Welles.

**Gellert, Lawrence**
Discusses: FWP, FTP Participated in: FWP, FTP
Position: Folk Song Collector Locations: NY, GA, AL
Interviewer: Brown, Lorraine Interview date: 10/22/76
Transcript: 45 pages Tape: 80 minutes Abstract: 3 page(s)
Repository: George Mason University
Description: Orson Welles, Lafayette Theatre, producers, performers, black actors, prejudices, internal tensions, the Federal Dance Project.

**Geltman, Fanya Del Bourgo**
Discusses: FTP Participated in: FTP
Position: Dancer Location: NY
Interviewer: Wickre, Karen Interview date: 12/16/77

Transcript: 42 pages  Tape: 80 minutes  Abstract: 3 page(s)
Repository: George Mason University
Description: FTP's troubles began with *Cradle Will Rock*, worked for Doris Humphrey, who named her director of her group.


**Geltman, Fanya Del Bourgo**
Discusses: FTP  Participated in: FTP
Position: Dancer  Location: NY
Interviewer: Wickre, Karen  Interview date: 02/20/78
Tape: 90 minutes  Abstract: 3 page(s)
Repository: George Mason University
This is a videotape.
Description: FTP dancers--demonstration and panel with Bass, P., Barlin, A.L., Garnet, E., Gerrard, S., Mann, L., Remos, S., Schaff, T.


**Gerrard, Saida**
Discusses: FTP  Participated in: FTP
Position: Dancer  Location: NY
Interviewer: Wickre, Karen  Interview date: 02/21/78
Transcript: 27 pages  Tape: 50 minutes  Abstract: 3 page(s)
Repository: George Mason University
Description: *Candide*, *A House Divided*, early training.


**Gerrard, Saida**
Discusses: FTP  Participated in: FTP
Position: Dancer  Location: NY
Interviewer: Wickre, Karen  Interview date: 02/20/78
Tape: 90 minutes  Abstract: 3 page(s)
Repository: George Mason University
This is a videotape.
Description: FTP dancers--demonstration and panel with Bass, P., Barlin, A.L., Garnet, E., Geltman, F., Mann, L., Remos, S., Schaff, T.


**Gerrity, John Emmett(1895-1980)**
Discusses: FAP  Participated in: FAP, PWAP
Position: Artist  Location: CA
Interviewer: McChesney, Mary Fuller  Interview date: 01/20/65
Transcript: 24 pages
Repository: Archives of American Art
Description: His work as a water colorist and a muralist for the FAP, effects of the FAP on artists in the San Francisco Bay area.

**Gershoy, Eugenie(b.1905)**
Discusses: FAP Participated in: FAP
Position: Sculptor Location: NY
Interviewer: McChesney, Mary Fuller Interview date: 10/15/64
Transcript: 31 pages
Repository: Archives of American Art
Description: Education and background, Art Students League, FAP in NYC, other sculptors on the project, government support for the arts.

**Gibbs, Howard M., Jr.(1904-1970)**
Discusses: FAP
Position: Artist Location: MA
Interviewer: Swift, Geoffrey Interview date: 11/28/65
Transcript: 26 pages
Repository: Archives of American Art

**Gikow, Ruth(b.1914)**
Discusses: FAP Participated in: FAP
Positions: Artist, Printmaker Location: NY
Interviewer: Selvig, Forrest Interview date: 10/68
Transcript: 53 pages
Repository: Archives of American Art
Permission of interviewee needed.
Description: Early art training, Cooper Union, problems of women artists, mural projects, FAP, working methods.

**Gikow, Ruth(b.1914)**
Discusses: FAP Participated in: FAP
Positions: Artist, Printmaker Location: NY
Interviewer: Phillips, Harlan Interview date: 1964
Transcript: 40 pages
Repository: Archives of American Art

**Gilbert, Lou(1909-1978)**
Discusses: FTP
Position: Actor Location: NY
Interviewer: O'Connor, John Interview date: 04/16/77
Transcript: 30 pages Tape: 120 minutes
Transcript is indexed.
Repository: George Mason University
Description: Founding of Chicago Repertory Group, not eligible for WPA unitl 1939, tried to interest youth in the theatre, the Chicago FTP.

**Gilbertson, Boris(1907-1982)**

Discusses: FAP Participated in: FAP
Position: Sculptor Location: NM
Interviewer: Loomis, Sylvia Interview date: 06/25/65
Transcript: 33 pages
Repository: Archives of American Art
Description: Background and education at the Art Institute of
Chicago, work on the FAP, the project's effect on the politics
of the time.

### Gilder, Rosamond(b.1891)
Discusses: FTP Participated in: FTP
Position: Administrator Location: NY
Interviewer: Bowers, Diane Interview date: 02/19/76
Transcript: 28 pages Tape: 60 minutes Abstract: 3 page(s)
Repository: George Mason University
Description: Director of Research Bureau, compares the
closing of *Ethiopia* and *Cradle Will Rock*, discusses *Murder in
the Cathedral*.

### Gilder, Rosamond(b.1891)
Discusses: FTP Participated in: FTP
Position: Administrator Location: NY
Interviewer: O'Connor, John Interview date: 11/16/75
Transcript: 23 pages Tape: 60 minutes Abstract: 3 page(s)
Repository: George Mason University
Description: Legal problems, loss of control of personal
property if written on FTP time, conflict with Communists.

### Gilien, Ted(1914-1967)
Discusses: FAP Participated in: FAP, SECT
Positions: Artist, Teacher Locations: CA, MO
Interviewer: Hoag, Betty Lochrie Interview date: 03/03/65
Transcript: 35 pages
Repository: Archives of American Art
Permission of archive needed.

### Gilman, Harold
Discusses: FTP Participated in: FTP
Position: Actor Locations: IL, NY
Interviewer: Wickre, Karen Interview date: 11/30/78
Transcript: 59 pages Tape: 100 minutes Abstract: 4 page(s)
Repository: George Mason University
Interview also includes: Ida Galler Gilman
Description: The Oxford Players, Group theatre, Goodman
Theatre, productions and participants, Congressional
investigations, blacklisting, salaries.

### Gilman, Ida Galler
Discusses: FTP Participated in: FTP
Position: Dancer Locations: IL, NY
Interviewer: Wickre, Karen Interview date: 11/30/78
Transcript: 59 pages Tape: 100 minutes Abstract: 4 page(s)
Repository: George Mason University
Interview also includes: Harold Gilman
Description: The Oxford Players, Kay Ewing, Group Theatre, Goodman Theatre, prices, need for national theatre.

### Glassgold, Adolph
Discusses: FAP Participated in: FAP
Positions: Teacher, Administrator Location: NY
Interviewer: Phillips, Harlan Interview date: 12/09/64
Transcript: 41 pages
Repository: Archives of American Art
Permission of interviewee needed.
Description: Attended Art Students League, worked on FAP staff and on the Index of American Design.

### Glidden, Patty Neederman
Discusses: FTP Participated in: FTP
Positions: Actress, Dancer Location: CA
Interviewer: Brown, Lorraine Interview date: 07/23/77
Tape: 30 minutes Abstract: 1 page(s)
Transcript is indexed.
Repository: George Mason University
Description: Value of FTP, Los Angeles vaudeville unit.

### Glyer, Richard
Discusses: FTP Participated in: FTP
Positions: Actor, Director Locations: CA, WA
Interviewer: Wickre, Karen Interview date: 07/19/77
Transcript: 34 pages Tape: 70 minutes Abstract: 2 page(s)
Repository: George Mason University
Description: *Redemption*, *Six Characters*, *Twilight and the Theatre*.

### Goldberg, Albert
Discusses: FMP Participated in: FMP
Position: Administrator Location: IL
Interviewer: Knoblauch-Franc, Marion Interview date: 04/19/82
Transcript: 20 pages Tape: 60 minutes
Repository: George Mason University
Closed until 6/1/86.
Permission of interviewer required until 5/31/87, open 6/1/87.

Description: State director of the Illinois FMP, music critic for *Chicago Tribune*, union problems.

### Goodall, Donald B.(b.1912)
Discusses: FAP Participated in: FAP
Positions: Teacher, Administrator Location: UT
Interviewer: Loomis, Sylvia Interview date: 07/08/65
Transcript: 29 pages
Repository: Archives of American Art
Permission of interviewee needed.
Description: Director of the FAP Community Art Center in Salt Lake City, Utah.

### Goodman, Frank
Discusses: FTP Participated in: FTP
Position: Administrator Location: NY
Interviewer: Wickre, Karen Interview date: 06/09/77
Tape: 45 minutes
Repository: George Mason University
Description: Publicist for the NYC FTP, director of the Scholastic Department within the Department of Information.

### Goodman, Saul(b.1906)
Position: Musician
Interview date: 1976
Transcript: 212 pages
Repository: Columbia University
Permission required to quote.
Description: Career as timpanist, orchestra unionization, performing.

### Goodrich, Lloyd(b.1897)
Discusses: PWAP Participated in: PWAP
Position: Administrator Location: NY
Interviewer: Phillips, Harlan Interview date: 1962-63
Transcript: 511 pages
Repository: Archives of American Art
Permission of interviewee needed.
Description: Pressure from PWAP artists, administrative work for PWAP, congressional attacks on artists, Committee on Government in Art.

### Gordon, Michael
Participated in: FTP
Position: Actor Location: NY
Interviewer: Goldman, Harry
Transcript: 52 pages

Repository: Columbia University
Available 5 years after publication.
Series: History of the Mercury Theatre

**Gordon, Michael**
Discusses: FTP Participated in: FTP
Position: Actor Location: NY
Interviewer: Campbell, Russell Interview date: 03/25/77
Tape: 60 minutes
Repository: New York University
Description: *One Third of A Nation, Faustus*, Frontier Films, Group Theatre.

**Gorelick, Boris(b.1912)**
Discusses: TRAP, FAP Participated in: TRAP, FAP
Positions: Artist, Muralist Locations: NY, DC
Interviewer: Hoag, Betty Lochrie Interview date: 05/20/64
Transcript: 22 pages
Repository: Archives of American Art
Permission of interviewee needed.
Description: National Academy of Design, Art Students League, Columbia Univ., American Artists Union, set up the Phoenix School of Art and Design.

**Gorelik, Mordecai**
Discusses: FTP Participated in: FTP
Positions: Theatre Historian, Director
Interviewer: Brown, Lorraine Interview date: 01/03/76
Abstract: 1 page(s)
Repository: George Mason University
This in an untaped interview, a one-page transcript is available.
Description: Beginning of FTP, unions.

**Goss, Dale**
Discusses: FAP
Positions: Artist, Administrator Location: WA
Interviewer: Bestor, Dorothy Interview date: 06/02/65
Transcript: 20 pages
Repository: Archives of American Art
Permission of interviewee needed.

**Gottlieb, Adolph(1903-1974)**
Discusses: FAP, SECT Participated in: FAP, SECT
Position: Artist Locations: AZ, NV, NY
Interviewer: Seckler, Dorothy G. Interview date: 10/25/67
Transcript: 27 pages
Repository: Archives of American Art

Permission of interviewee needed.
Description: Treasury Dept. murals in Yerington, Nevada Post
Office, jobs, education, family life, exhibits.


**Gottlieb, Harry**
Discusses: FAP Participated in: FAP, PWAP
Position: Artist Location: NY
Interviewer: Gordon, Peter Interview date: 1979-80
Tape: 40 minutes
Repository: LaGuardia College Archives
Sound quality is poor.
Description: FAP in New York, work on the graphic art
project.


**Graham, F. Wynne**
Discusses: FAP
Positions: Artist, Printmaker Location: NM
Interviewer: Loomis, Sylvia Interview date: 07/22/65
Transcript: 25 pages
Repository: Archives of American Art
Permission of interviewee needed.


**Graham, H. Gordon**
Discusses: FTP Participated in: FTP
Position: Director Locations: GA, FL, IL
Interviewer: Brown, Lorraine Interview date: 02/27/77
Transcript: 23 pages Tape: 45 minutes Abstract: 1 page(s)
Repository: George Mason University
Description: *Altars of Steel, 1935, Triple-A Plowed Under,*
Living Newspapers.


**Grant, Campbell(b.1909)**
Discusses: FAP Participated in: FAP, PWAP
Position: Artist Location: CA
Interviewer: Hoag, Betty Lochrie Interview date: 06/04/65
Transcript: 20 pages
Repository: Archives of American Art
Description: Did research and painted in Santa Barbara.


**Green, Paul(b.1894)**
Discusses: FTP Participated in: FTP
Position: Playwright Location: NC
Interview date: 1975
Transcript: 258 pages
Repository: Columbia University
Permission required to quote.
Description: Group Theater, Hollywood 1930s, his work as

playwright, teaching.

**Green, Paul**(b.1894)
Discusses: FTP Participated in: FTP
Position: Playwright Location: NC
Interviewer: Cohen, Gail Interview date: 08/07/77
Transcript: 52 pages
Repository: George Mason University
Closed pending release.
Also available at Hatch-Billops Collection, Inc.
Description: Jasper Deeter, *Johnny Johnson*, Brooks Atkinson, *The Lost Colony*.

**Green, Paul**(b.1894)
Discusses: FTP Participated in: FTP
Position: Playwright Location: NC
Interviewers: O'Connor, John and Krulak, Mae Mallory
Interview date: 12/01/75
Transcript: 60 pages Tape: 160 minutes Abstract: 4 page(s)
Repository: George Mason University
Description: *Common Glory, Hymn to the Rising Sun.*

**Green, Paul**(b.1894)
Discusses: FTP Participated in: FTP
Position: Playwright Location: NC
Interviewer: Doud, Richard Interview date: 07/13/65
Transcript: 39 pages
Repository: Archives of American Art

**Greenwood, Grace**
Discusses: FAP, PWAP Participated in: FAP, PWAP, TRAP
Position: Artist Locations: NY, NJ, TN
Interviewer: Trovato, Joseph Interview date: 01/29/65
Transcript: 7 pages
Repository: Archives of American Art
Permission of interviewee needed.

**Greenwood, Marion**(1909-1970)
Discusses: FAP, PWAP Participated in: FAP, PWAP, TRAP
Positions: Artist, Muralist Locations: NY, NJ, TN
Interviewer: Seckler, Dorothy G. Interview date: 01/31/64
Transcript: 26 pages
Repository: Archives of American Art
Permission of archive needed.
Description: The FAP and reactions against government art projects, social content in mural painting, her mural painting in Mexico.

**Greywacz, Kathryn**
Discusses: PWAP Participated in: PWAP
Position: Administrator Location: NJ
Interviewer: Doud, Richard Interview date: 03/24/64
Transcript: 22 pages
Repository: Archives of American Art
Description: Regional Committee member, selecting artists for
the FAP in New Jersey.

**Gropper, William(1897-1977)**
Discusses: FAP Participated in: FAP, TRAP, SECT
Position: Artist Locations: NY, DC, MI
Interviewer: Hooten, Bruce Interview date: 6/65
Transcript: 20 pages
Repository: Archives of American Art
Permission of archive needed.
Description: FAP, Dept. of Interior Murals in D.C.,
background, newspaper cartoonist, social attitudes of artists.

**Groschwitz, Gustave von**
Discusses: FAP Participated in: FAP
Position: Administrator Location: NY
Interviewer: Doud, Richard Interview date: 12/09/64
Transcript: 21 pages
Repository: Archives of American Art
Permission of interviewee needed.
Description: Supervisor of the Graphic Arts Division of the
FAP (1935-38).

**Gross, Chaim(b.1904)**
Discusses: FAP Participated in: FAP, PWAP, SECT
Position: Sculptor Locations: NY, PA
Interviewer: Seckler, Dorothy G. Interview date: 09/01/64
Transcript: 15 pages
Repository: Archives of American Art
Permission of interviewee needed.
Description: Art training, exhibits, FAP.

**Groves, Wellington**
Discusses: FAP Participated in: FAP
Positions: Artist, Administrator Location: NY
Interviewer: Bestor, Dorothy Interview date: 04/23/65
Transcript: 15 pages
Repository: Archives of American Art
Permission of interviewee needed.
Description: Supervised young staff for Robert Inverarity, did

little painting.

**Gutierrez, Sal**(1905-1974)
Discusses: FMP Participated in: FMP
Location: LA
Interviewer: Allen, Richard B.  Interview date: 01/15/70
Tape: 180 minutes
Repository: Tulane University
Permission of archive needed.
Description: WPA band.

**Gwathmey, Robert**(b.1903)
Discusses: PWAP Participated in: PWAP, SECT
Positions: Artist, Muralist Locations: VA, PA, NY
Interviewer: Cummings, Paul Interview date: 03/05/68
Transcript: 72 pages
Repository: Archives of American Art
Permission of interviewee needed.
Description:  Post Office murals, working methods, the
Depression, founding of Artists' Equity, American Artists'
Union, Cooper Union.

**Hagel, Hansel**(b.1909)
Discusses: FAP Participated in: FAP
Position: Photographer Location: CA
Interviewer:  McChesney, Mary Fuller  Interview date:
10/08/64
Transcript: 22 pages
Repository: Archives of American Art
Permission of interviewee needed.
Description: Photography project in San Francisco.

**Haines, Richard**(b.1906)
Discusses: FAP Participated in: FAP, SECT
Positions: Artist, Muralist Locations: CA, MN, WA
Interviewer: Reid, George Interview date: 08/23/77
Transcript: 7 pages Tape: 30 minutes
Repository: Minnesota Historical Society
Series: Federal Art Project in Minnesota
Tape filed under Haupers, Clement.
Description: Murals he painted in several Minnesota towns,
work in Illinois, Kansas, Missouri, California and Washington.

**Haines, Richard**(b.1906)
Discusses: FAP Participated in: FAP, SECT
Positions: Artist, Muralist Locations: CA, MN, WA
Interviewer: Hoag, Betty Lochrie Interview date: 01/29/65

Transcript: 6 pages
Repository: Archives of American Art

**Hairston, Jester**(b.1901)
Discusses: FTP Participated in: FTP
Position: Musician Locations: CA, NY
Interviewer: Bowers, Diane Interview date: 05/29/76
Transcript: 28 pages Tape: 60 minutes Abstract: 1 page(s)
Repository: George Mason University
Permission required until 1997.
Description: Negro Theatre of the FTP, black playwrights, problems of blacks in the 1930s, FTP contributions to black theatre.

**Hairston, Jester**(b.1901)
Discusses: FTP Participated in: FTP
Position: Musician Locations: NY, UT, SC
Interviewers: Hatch, James V. and Billops, Camille Interview date: 12/27/71
Tape: 120 minutes Abstract: 1 page(s)
Repository: Hatch-Billops Collection, Inc.
Permission of archive needed.
Description: Broadway in 1930s, various productions, conducting in Utah and South Carolina, State Department work in Africa.

**Hale, Laura Virginia**(b.1916)
Discusses: FWP Participated in: FWP
Positions: Field Worker, Researcher Location: VA
Interviewers: Perdue, Charles and Perdue, Nan Interview date: 08/02/84
Transcript: 5 pages Tape: 240 minutes
Repository: In possession of interviewers
Permission of interviewers needed.
Contact: Charles Perdue, Dept. of English, University of Virginia.

**Hall, Bob**(b.1895)
Discusses: FAP
Positions: Artist, Illustrator Location: MT
Interviewer: Hoag, Betty Lochrie Interview date: 11/28/65
Transcript: 85 pages
Repository: Archives of American Art
Permission of interviewee needed.

**Hall, Parker**(b.1898)
Discusses: FAP Participated in: FAP, PWAP

Position: Artist Location: CA
Interviewer: McChesney, Mary Fuller Interview date: 07/27/64
Transcript: 44 pages
Repository: Archives of American Art
Interview also includes: Albro, Maxine
Hall was husband of Maxine Albro.
Description: Coit Tower fresco, other projects.

**Halpert, Edith Gregor**(1900-1970)
Discusses: FAP
Position: Art Dealer Location: NY
Interviewer: Phillips, Harlan Interview date: 01/20/65
Transcript: 22 pages
Repository: Archives of American Art
Restricted unitl 1995.

**Hamilton, Emory L.**(b.1913)
Discusses: FWP Participated in: FWP
Position: Field Worker Location: VA
Interviewers: Perdue, Charles and Perdue, Nan Interview date: 06/21/84
Transcript: 10 pages Tape: 240 minutes
Repository: In possession of interviewers
Permission of interviewers needed.
Contact: Charles Perdue, Dept. of English, University of Virginia.

**Hamlin, Edith**(b.1902)
Discusses: FAP Participated in: FAP, SECT
Position: Muralist Location: CA
Interviewer: Martin, Minette Interview date: 05/27/64
Transcript: 10 pages
Repository: Archives of American Art
Interview also includes: Cravath, Dorothy
Description: Worked in the San Francisco area.

**Harris, Julian H.**
Discusses: FTP Participated in: FTP
Position: Art Director Location: GA
Interviewer: Wickre, Karen Interview date: 10/22/78
Transcript: 22 pages Tape: 60 minutes Abstract: 3 page(s)
Repository: George Mason University
Description: FTP gave employment to professionals and training to amateurs, the Atlanta Federal Theatre (1937-38).

**Harris, Reed**

Discusses: FWP Participated in: FWP, FERA
Position: Administrator Location: DC
Interviewer: Mangione, Jerre Interview date: 01/11/68
Repository: University of Rochester
Series: Mangione Collection
Description: Assistant to Henry Alsberg, head of FWP.

Harris, Wilma(b.1910)
Discusses: FAP Participated in: FAP
Position: Weaver Location: CA
Interviewer: McChesney, Mary Fuller Interview date: 04/22/64
Transcript: 31 pages
Repository: Archives of American Art
Description: Educated at the California School of Fine Arts, worked on FAP from 1941, head of the dyeing department of the Weaving Project in S.F.

Hatch, John Davis(b.1907)
Discusses: FAP
Positions: Art Consultant, Art Historian Location: MA
Interviewer: White, Wade H. Interview date: 06/08/64
Transcript: 52 pages
Repository: Archives of American Art
Permission of interviewee needed.

Haufrecht, Herbert(b.1909)
Discusses: FTP Participated in: RA, FTP
Position: Composer
Interviewer: Durkan, Rhoda Interview date: 07/18/81
Tape: 90 minutes
Repository: George Mason University
Description: A staff composer and arranger for the FTP.

Haufrecht, Herbert(b.1909)
Discusses: RA Participated in: RA, FTP
Position: Composer
Interviewer: Dunaway, David Interview date: 04/14/76
Transcript: 95 pages Tape: 150 minutes
Repository: In possession of interviewer
Permission of interviewer needed.
Series: Pete Seeger and American Folk Music
Contact: Dunaway, Dept of English, Univ. of New Mexico, Albuquerque.
Description: Transition from world of NY composers to music work in RA, New Deal Folklore efforts.

**Haughton, Norris**
Discusses: FTP Participated in: FTP
Positions: Writer, Producer
Interviewer: O'Connor, John  Interview date:  05/13/76
Transcript:  20 pages  Tape: 45 minutes  Abstract:  1 page(s)
Repository:  George Mason University
Description:  Impressions of FTP, Hallie Flanagan's impact on FTP.

**Haupers, Clement B.(1900-1982)**
Discusses: FAP Participated in: FAP, PWAP
Position: Administrator Location: MN
Interviewers:  Reid, George and Archabal, Nina Interview date: 1977
Tape: 175 minutes
Repository:  Minnesota Historical Society
Series:  Federal Art Project in Minnesota
Description:  Haupers' FAP work, other artists.

**Haupers, Clement B.(1900-1982)**
Discusses: FAP Participated in: FAP, PWAP
Position: Administrator Location: MN
Interviewers:  Hancock, Jane and Archabal, Nina Interview date:  1979
Tape: 135 minutes
Repository:  Minnesota Historical Society
Interviewer, Westbrook, Nick. For retrospective at the Minn. Historical Society.
Description:  Art education, participation in art world in 1920s and 1930s, work on FAP.

**Haupers, Clement B.(1900-1982)**
Discusses: FAP Participated in: FAP, PWAP
Position: Administrator Location: MN
Interviewers:  O'Sullivan, Thomas and Knight, Elizabeth
Interview date:  04/03/81
Tape: 70 minutes
Repository:  Minnesota Historical Society
Description:  Comments on prints by FAP artists at Minnesota Historical Society, role as FAP state administrator.

**Haupers, Clement B.(1900-1982)**
Discusses: FAP Participated in: FAP, PWAP
Position: Administrator Location: MN
Tape: 12 minutes
Repository:  Minnesota Historical Society
Series:  Minnesota Living History Series

This is a 3/4" videocassette.

**Haupers, Clement B.**(1900-1982)
Discusses: FAP Participated in: FAP, PWAP
Position: Administrator Location: MN
Interviewer: Hackl, Lloyd Interview date: 1975
Tape: 60 minutes
Repository: Minnesota Historical Society
Research only, no copying allowed.
Series: F. Scott Fitzgerald

**Haupers, Clement B.**(1900-1982)
Discusses: FAP Participated in: FAP, PWAP
Position: Administrator Location: MN
Interviewer: Phillips, Harlan Interview date: 06/15/65
Transcript: 71 pages
Repository: Archives of American Art
Permission of archive needed.

**Hauser, Alonzo**(b.1909)
Discusses: SECT Participated in: SECT
Positions: Artist, Sculptor Locations: NM, MN
Interviewer: Nagle, Virginia Interview date: 10/12/65
Transcript: 18 pages
Repository: Archives of American Art
Permission of interviewee needed.

**Hauser, Ethel Aaron**
Discusses: FTP Participated in: FTP
Position: Stage Manager Location: NY
Interviewers: Brown, Lorraine and Bowers, Diane Interview
date: 02/20/76
Transcript: 33 pages Tape: 70 minutes Abstract: 2 page(s)
Repository: George Mason University
Interview also includes: Barber, Philip
Description: *One-Third of a Nation*, *Life and Death of an
American*, FTP sparked many careers, Living Newspapers.

**Hays, Hoffman R.**
Discusses: FTP Participated in: FTP
Position: Playwright Location: NY
Interviewer: Wickre, Karen Interview date: 06/08/77
Tape: 60 minutes Abstract: 2 page(s)
Repository: George Mason University
Interview also includes: Hays, Julliette
Description: Early days as student, FTP experiences and union.

**Henry, Mary Dill(b.1913)**
Discusses: FAP Participated in: FAP
Positions: Artist, Muralist Location: CA
Interviewer: McChesney, Mary Fuller Interview date: 05/12/64
Transcript: 27 pages
Repository: Archives of American Art
Permission of interviewee needed.
Description: Worked on designing mosaics and murals in Oakland, California.

**Herron, Jason**
Discusses: FAP Participated in: FAP, PWAP
Position: Artist Location: CA
Interviewer: Vitale, Lydia Modi Interview date: 03/06/75
Tape: 120 minutes
Repository: University of Santa Clara
Series: New Deal Art: California
Interview also includes: King, Albert
This interview is on 1" videotape and needs special equipment to be viewed.

**Hesthal, William(b.1908)**
Discusses: PWAP Participated in: PWAP
Position: Artist Location: CA
Interviewer: McChesney, Mary Fuller Interview date: 12/22/64
Transcript: 16 pages
Repository: Archives of American Art

**Hewes, Harry**
Discusses: FMP Participated in: FMP
Position: Writer Location: NY
Interviewer: Phillips, Harlan Interview date: 10/64
Transcript: 65 pages
Repository: Archives of American Art
Permission of interviewee needed.
Interview also includes: Du Von, Jay
Description: Rented theaters for the FMP, Nikolai Sokoloff asked him to work on the FMP.

**Hill, Abram(b.1911)**
Discusses: FTP Participated in: FTP
Positions: Playwright, Playreader Location: NY
Interviewers: Brown, Lorraine and others Interview date: 01/13/78

Tape: 105 minutes  Abstract:  1 page(s)
Repository:  George Mason University
This is a videotape.
Description:  Black FTP reunion: Anderson, T., Archer, O.,
Bates, Add, De Paur. L., LeNoire, R.


**Hill, Abram**(b.1911)
Discusses: FTP Participated in: FTP
Positions: Playwright, Playreader Location: NY
Interviewer:  Brown, Lorraine  Interview date:  02/27/77
Transcript:  18 pages  Tape: 45 minutes  Abstract:  2 page(s)
Repository:  George Mason University
Description:  Experiences with directors, playwrights, and
community-oriented theatre, commitment to educate as well as
amuse.


**Hill, Abram**(b.1911)
Discusses: FTP Participated in: FTP
Positions: Playwright, Playreader Location: NY
Interviewers:  Hatch, James V. and Billops, Camille Interview
date:  01/19/74
Tape: 105 minutes  Abstract:  1 page(s)
Repository:  Hatch-Billops Collection, Inc.
Permission of archive needed.
Description:  The American Negro Theatre in 1940, aims and
philosophy, famous actors, various productions.


**Hirsch, Joseph**(b.1910)
Discusses: FAP Participated in: FAP
Positions: Artist, Muralist Location: PA
Interviewer:  Phillips, Harlan  Interview date:  1965
Transcript:  34 pages
Repository:  Archives of American Art
Description:  Murals in Philadelphia, social realism in the
1930s.


**Hocking, Kay Ewing**
SEE Ewing, Kay.


**Holmes, Jean**(b.1910)
Discusses: FAP
Positions: Artist, Lithographer Location: CA
Interviewer:  McChesney, Mary Fuller  Interview date:
04/12/65
Transcript:  12 pages
Repository:  Archives of American Art
Permission of interviewee needed.

**Holty, Carl**(1900-1973)
Discusses: FAP
Positions: Artist, Art Lecturer
Interviewer: Agee, William C. Interview date: 12/08/64
Transcript: 48 pages
Repository: Archives of American Art
Description: Childhood, early art training, National Academy of Design, Ad Reinhardt, government art programs, Federal Forum lectures.

**Hood, Richard**(b.1910)
Discusses: FAP
Positions: Printmaker, Administrator Location: PA
Interviewer: Doud, Richard Interview date: 12/15/64
Transcript: 22 pages
Repository: Archives of American Art
Description: State Director of FAP in Penn., Graphic Arts section, Index of American Design in Penn., study of Pennsylvania-Dutch designs.

**Hord, Donal**(1902-1966)
Discusses: PWAP Participated in: PWAP
Position: Sculptor Location: CA
Interviewer: Hoag, Betty Lochrie Interview date: 06/25/64
Transcript: 23 pages
Repository: Archives of American Art

**Horn, Axel**
Discusses: FAP Participated in: FAP, SECT
Position: Muralist Locations: NY, OH
Interviewer: Harrison, Helen A. Interview date: 01/03/75
Tape: 50 minutes
Repository: George Mason University
Closed pending release.
Description: Siqueiros workshop, class with Thomas Hart Benton at the Art Students League, Public Use of Art Committee.

**Hough, Henry**
Discusses: FWP Participated in: FWP
Positions: Writer, Administrator Location: CO
Interviewer: Doud, Richard Interview date: 06/11/64
Transcript: 14 pages
Repository: Archives of American Art
Permission of interviewee needed.
Description: State Director of the Colorado FWP.

**Houghton, Norris**
Discusses: FTP
Positions: Producer, Director Location: NY
Interviewer: O'Connor, John Interview date: 05/13/76
Tape: 60 minutes Abstract: 1 page(s)
Repository: George Mason University
Description: Houghton was a designer and director for Broadway theaters in the 1930s, later head of Phoenix Theatre Company.

**Houseman, John(b.1902)**
Discusses: FTP Participated in: FTP
Positions: Director, Producer Location: NY
Interviewer: Berenberg, Benedict Interview date: 06/29/77
Transcript: 7 pages
Repository: Berenberg MA thesis, Univ. of Wisc.
Transcript in interviewer's MA thesis. The tapes are on permanent loan at Wisc. State Historical Society.

**Houseman, John(b.1902)**
Discusses: FTP Participated in: FTP
Positions: Director, Producer Location: NY
Interviewer: Davis, Ronald L. Interview date: 07/19/79
Transcript: 33 pages Tape: 45 minutes Abstract: 1 page(s)
Transcript is indexed.
Repository: Southern Methodist University
Series: Performing Arts in the U.S.
SMU also holds correspondence related to interview.
Description: An overview of his career.

**Houseman, John(b.1902)**
Discusses: FTP Participated in: FTP
Positions: Director, Producer Location: NY
Interviewers: O'Connor, John and Krulak, Mae Mallory
Interview date: 05/11/76
Transcript: 21 pages Tape: 40 minutes Abstract: 2 page(s)
Repository: George Mason University
Description: FTP was "political beachhead", his FTP experiences.

**Houseman, John(b.1902)**
Discusses: FTP Participated in: FTP
Positions: Director, Producer Location: NY
Interviewer: Goldman, Harry
Transcript: 16 pages
Repository: Columbia University

Available 5 years after publication.
Series: History of the Mercury Theatre
Description: The NYC FTP Negro Unit at the Lafayette Theatre headed by Houseman and Welles evolved into the Mercury Theatre.

**Houser, Lowell(1902-1971)**
Discusses: PWAP Participated in: PWAP, SECT
Position: Artist Location: IA
Interviewer: Hoag, Betty Lochrie Interview date: 07/13/64
Transcript: 7 pages
Repository: Archives of American Art

**Howard, Robert Boardman(b.1896)**
Discusses: PWAP, SECT Participated in: PWAP, SECT
Position: Sculptor Location: CA
Interviewer: McChesney, Mary Fuller Interview date: 09/16/64
Transcript: 12 pages
Repository: Archives of American Art

**Hrdy, Olinka(b.1902)**
Discusses: PWAP Participated in: PWAP
Positions: Muralist, Designer Location: CA
Interviewer: Hoag, Betty Lochrie Interview date: 1965
Transcript: 59 pages
Repository: Archives of American Art

**Hudgens, Robert Watts(b.1896)**
Discusses: RA, FSA Participated in: RA, FSA
Position: Administrator Locations: DC, NC
Interviewer: Doud, Richard Interview date: 06/01/65
Transcript: 27 pages
Repository: Archives of American Art
Permission of interviewee needed.
Description: Assistant Administrator of RA and FSA under Rexford Tugwell, Will Winton Alexander and Calvin Benham Baldwin.

**Hudgens, Robert Watts(b.1896)**
Discusses: RA, FSA Participated in: RA, FSA
Position: Administrator Locations: DC, NC
Interview date: 1954
Transcript: 290 pages
Repository: Columbia University
Permission required to quote.
Microfiche available, part II.

Description: Religious, economic, and political conditions in the South, important New Deal personalities, policies, and problems.

**Hughes, Langston**(1902-1967)
Discusses: FTP
Positions: Writer, Playwright
Interviewers: Silver, Dorothy and Silver, Reuben Interview date: 05/06/61
Tape: 90 minutes  Abstract: 1 page(s)
Repository: Hatch-Billops Collection, Inc.
Permission of archive needed.
There are three other interviews in this collection with Hughes.
Description: Various plays, aims of American Negro Theatre.

**Hunt, Lee**
Discusses: FAP Participated in: FAP
Positions: Administrator, Artist Location: IA
Interviewer: Phillips, Harlan
Transcript: 42 pages
Repository: Archives of American Art
Permission of interviewee needed.
Description: Director of the Des Moines Art Center under the FAP.

**Hurd, Peter**(b.1904)
Discusses: PWAP, FAP Participated in: PWAP, FAP, SECT
Positions: Artist, Muralist Locations: NM, TX
Interviewer: Loomis, Sylvia  Interview date: 03/28/64
Transcript: 32 pages
Repository: Archives of American Art
Description: Murals for the Procurement Division of the Treasury Department, Fresco painting in Big Spring, Texas.

**Hurwitz, Leo**
Discusses: RA Participated in: RA
Position: Filmmaker
Interviewer: Rollins, Peter  Interview date: 09/27/75
Transcript: 25 pages  Tape: 60 minutes
Repository: George Mason University
Description: Pare Lorentz, the making of *The Plow That Broke the Plains*, *The River*, and, *Native Land*, Frontier Films, *March of Time*.

**Ibling, Miriam**(b.1895)
Discusses: FAP Participated in: PWAP, FAP
Position: Muralist Location: MN

Interviewer: Reid, George  Interview date: 08/04/77
Transcript: 6 pages  Tape: 30 minutes
Repository: Minnesota Historical Society
Series: Federal Art Project in Minnesota
Description: Murals painted in 1930s in Washington County,
Steele County, and St. Paul.


**Inverarity, Robert Bruce**(b.1909)
Discusses: FAP Participated in: FAP, FWP
Positions: Administrator, Museum Director Location: WA
Interviewer: Phillips, Harlan  Interview date: 11/04/64
Transcript: 75 pages
Repository: Archives of American Art
Permission of interviewee needed.
Description: State Director of FAP, finding artists for the
FAP, worked on the Washington State Guide, a FWP project.


**Inverarity, Robert Bruce**(b.1909)
Discusses: FAP Participated in: FAP, FWP
Positions: Administrator, Museum Director Location: WA
Interviewer: Cummings, Paul  Interview date: 03/04/75
Transcript: 109 pages
Repository: Archives of American Art
Permission of interviewee needed.
Description: State Director of the FAP in Washington.


**Ions, Willoughby**
Discusses: FAP Participated in: FAP
Positions: Artist, Teacher Location: VA
Interviewer: Doud, Richard  Interview date: 03/11/64
Transcript: 23 pages
Repository: Archives of American Art
Permission of interviewee needed.
Description: Worked on the FAP in Fairfax, Virginia.


**Isaacs, Lewis**
Discusses: FTP
Interviewer: Brown, Lorraine  Interview date: 11/09/78
Abstract: 1 page(s)
Repository: George Mason University
This is an untaped interview, a one page abstract is available.
Description: Son of Edith Isaacs, who was editor of *Theatre
Arts Magazine*.


**Iselin, Lewis**(b.1913)
Discusses: TRAP Participated in: TRAP
Position: Sculptor Location: NY

Interviewer: Cummings, Paul  Interview date: 04/10/69
Transcript: 45 pages
Repository: Archives of American Art
Description: Background, art education, effects of WPA and depression on arts and artists, TRAP, U.S. War Memorial at Sureness, NY.


**Izenaur, George**
Discusses: FTP Participated in: FTP
Position: Lighting Designer Location: CA
Interviewer: O'Connor, John  Interview date: 02/76
Abstract: 7 page(s)
Repository: George Mason University
This is an untaped interview, a seven-page abstract is available.
Description: Education, FTP, meeting Hallie Flanagan, *Bird of Paradise*.


**Jackson, Everett Gee(b.1900)**
Discusses: FAP Participated in: FAP
Positions: Artist, Illustrator Location: CA
Interviewer: Hoag, Betty Lochrie  Interview date: 07/31/64
Transcript: 16 pages
Repository: Archives of American Art


**Jackson, Sara O.(b.1915)**
Discusses: FTP Participated in: FTP
Position: Actress Location: WA
Interviewer: Pollack, Leona  Interview date: 03/03/81
Transcript: 55 pages Tape: 180 minutes
Repository: University of Washington
Series: Washington Women's Heritage Project
Description: Her life, beginnings of the Seattle Negro Repertory Company, Florence James, who produced *Stevedore* and *Lysistrata* for FTP.


**Javitz, Romana**
Discusses: FSA Participated in: FSA
Position: Photographer
Interviewer: Doud, Richard  Interview date: 02/23/65
Transcript: 36 pages
Repository: Archives of American Art


**Jeakins, Dorothy(b.1914)**
Discusses: FAP Participated in: FAP
Position: Artist Location: CA
Interviewer: Hoag, Betty Lochrie  Interview date: 06/19/64
Transcript: 14 pages

Repository: Archives of American Art
Permission of interviewee needed.
Description: Youngest woman artist on the FAP in Los Angeles, worked on lithographs, oils, and easel painting.

**Jelliffe, Rowena**
Discusses: FTP Participated in: FTP
Interviewers: Silver, Dorothy and Silver, Reuben Interview date: 04/25/61
Tape: 310 minutes Abstract: 1 page(s)
Repository: Hatch-Billops Collection, Inc.
Permission of archive needed.
Interview also includes: Jelliffe, Russell
Description: Karamu House, a Negro theatre group in Ohio, important members, various plays.

**Jerry, Sylvester(b.1904)**
Discusses: FAP
Position: Artist Location: WI
Interviewer: Phillips, Harlan Interview date: 06/11/65
Transcript: 16 pages
Repository: Archives of American Art

**Johnson, Lamont(b.1922)**
Discusses: FTP
Interviewer: Bowers, Diane Interview date: 05/28/76
Tape: 40 minutes Abstract: 1 page(s)
Repository: George Mason University
Not a member of the FTP.
Description: FTP innovations and achievements, Dies Committee and blacklisting, actor Norman Lloyd, Gilmor Brown, head of the Pasadena Playhouse.

**Johnson, Sargent Claude(1888-1967)**
Discusses: PWAP Participated in: PWAP
Position: Sculptor Location: CA
Interviewer: McChesney, Mary Fuller Interview date: 07/31/64
Transcript: 33 pages
Repository: Archives of American Art

**Jonas, Hallie**
Discusses: FTP Participated in: FTP
Position: Publicist Location: NY
Interviewer: Bowers, Diane Interview date: 05/29/76
Transcript: 41 pages Tape: 65 minutes Abstract: 2 page(s)
Repository: George Mason University

Description: *Chalk Dust*, Hallie Flanagan, FTP as education, social philosophy of art for the people.

Jonson, Raymond(1891-1982)
Discusses: PWAP Participated in: PWAP
Positions: Artist, Art Gallery Director Location: NM
Interviewer: Loomis, Sylvia Interview date: 04/23/64
Transcript: 25 pages
Repository: Archives of American Art

Jung, Theodore
Discusses: FERA, RA Participated in: FERA, RA
Position: Photographer
Interviewer: Doud, Richard Interview date: 01/19/65
Transcript: 23 pages
Repository: Archives of American Art
Description: Chart draftsman in FERA.

Junker, Ernest
Discusses: FAP
Interviewers: Bostick, William and McCoy, Garnett Interview date: 12/05/67
Transcript: 21 pages
Repository: Archives of American Art
Permission of interviewee needed.
Description: Manager of the Scarab Club--a social and sketch club in Detroit, American Artist Congress, Artists Union, Artists Equity, FAP.

Kadish, Reuben(b.1913)
Discusses: TRAP Participated in: TRAP, PWAP
Positions: Administrator, Muralist Location: CA
Interviewer: Phillips, Harlan Interview date: 10/22/64
Transcript: 33 pages
Repository: Archives of American Art
Permission of interviewee needed.
Description: Murals in San Francisco, supervisor of San Francisco and Northern California.

Kahn, Emily Mason
Discusses: FMP Participated in: FMP
Position: Administrator Location: DC
Interviewer: Phillips, Harlan Interview date: 01/27/65
Transcript: 36 pages
Repository: Archives of American Art
Permission of interviewee needed.
Emily Mason Kahn is wife of Lloyd Kahn.

Description:  Directed the education section of the FMP.

**Kaminsky, Dora**(b.1909)
Discusses: FAP Participated in: FAP
Position: Artist Location: NY
Interviewer:  Loomis, Sylvia  Interview date:  04/22/65
Transcript:  31 pages
Repository:  Archives of American Art
Description:  Graphic division in New York, Illustration division.

**Kantor, Morris**(1896-1974)
Discusses: FAP Participated in: FAP
Position: Artist Location: NY
Interviewer:  Baker, Richard Brown  Interview date:  01/23/63
Transcript:  68 pages
Repository:  Archives of American Art
Permission of his widow needed.
Description:  Use of color technique, family background, Art Students League, fine and commercial art, FAP.

**Kantor, Morris**(1896-1974)
Discusses: FAP Participated in: FAP
Position: Artist Location: NY
Interviewer:  Trovato, Joseph  Interview date:  01/16/65
Transcript:  7 pages
Repository:  Archives of American Art
Permission of his widow needed.

**Kaplan, Leonard**(b.1922)
Discusses: FAP
Positions: Artist, Art Dealer Location: CA
Interviewer:  Hoag, Betty Lochrie  Interview date:  06/19/65
Transcript:  10 pages
Repository:  Archives of American Art

**Kassler II, Charles**
Discusses: PWAP, SECT, TRAP Participated in: PWAP, SECT, TRAP
Position: Artist Location: CA
Interviewer:  Vitale, Lydia Modi  Interview date:  03/10/75
Tape: 70 minutes
Repository:  University of Santa Clara
Series:  New Deal Art: California
This interview is on 1" videotape and needs special equipment to be viewed.

**Kayes, Alan**
Discusses: FMP Participated in: FMP
Position: Administrator Location: NY
Interviewer: Knoblauch-Franc, Marion Interview date: 05/11/82
Transcript: 12 pages Tape: 30 minutes
Repository: George Mason University
Closed until 6/1/86.
Permission of interviewer until 5/31/87 open from 6/1/87.
Description: Director of Information, FMP in NYC, operatic groups, chamber-music quartets, chamber orchestras, American Federation of Musicians.

**Kendall, Marion(b.1891)**
Discusses: FAP Participated in: FAP
Position: Weaver Location: CA
Interviewer: Hoag, Betty Lochrie Interview date: 08/26/65
Transcript: 40 pages
Repository: Archives of American Art
Permission of interviewee needed.
Description: San Diego Fine Arts Gallery.

**Kennedy, Donald Scott**
Discusses: FTP Participated in: FTP
Position: Actor Locations: CA, NY
Interviewer: O'Connor, John Interview date: 08/76
Tape: 50 minutes Abstract: 2 page(s)
Repository: George Mason University
Description: Orson Welles, various plays, value of FTP.

**Kennedy, Michael Stephen(b.1912)**
Discusses: FERA, FWP Participated in: FERA, FWP
Positions: Writer, Administrator Location: MT
Interviewer: Hoag, Betty Lochrie Interview date: 11/26/65
Transcript: 19 pages
Repository: Archives of American Art
Permission of interviewee needed.
Description: Did press and publicity for FERA, director of the FMP in Montana.

**Kent, Charlotte**
Discusses: FTP Participated in: FTP
Positions: Songwriter, Composer Location: NY
Interviewer: Wickre, Karen Interview date: 12/15/77
Transcript: 15 pages Tape: 35 minutes Abstract: 2 page(s)
Repository: George Mason University
Description: Background, FTP people were a happy group,

pressures of the professional theatre were lifted, *Sing for Your Supper*.

**Kerr, Florence**(1890-1975)
Discusses: WPA Participated in: WPA
Position: Administrator Locations: IL, DC
Interviewer: Phillips, Harlan Interview date: 1963
Transcript: 207 pages
Repository: Archives of American Art
Permission of interviewee needed.
Description: Midwest Regional Director, Women's and Professional Projects, WPA(1935-38), appointed administrator of Federal One in 1939.

**Kerr, Florence**(1890-1975)
Discusses: WPA Participated in: WPA
Position: Administrator Locations: IL, DC
Interview date: 1974
Transcript: 110 pages
Repository: Columbia University
Permission required to quote.
Available on microfiche, part III.
Description: Midwest Regional Director, Women's and Professional Projects, WPA(1935-38), Washington Assistant Commissioner, WPA 1939, Arts Projects.

**Kidd, Edythe**
Discusses: FAP
Interviewer: Loomis, Sylvia Interview date: 08/05/65
Transcript: 8 pages
Repository: Archives of American Art
Permission of interviewee needed.
Not on the FAP herself, talks about husband's career on the FAP.
Description: Hari Kidd was a muralist on the FAP.

**Kinch, Myra**
Discusses: FTP Participated in: FTP
Positions: Dancer, Choreographer Location: CA
Interviewer: Bowers, Diane Interview date: 02/21/76
Transcript: 7 pages Tape: 60 minutes Abstract: 2 page(s)
Transcript is indexed.
Repository: George Mason University
Interview also includes: Galea, Manuel
Tape is of poor quality and incomplete.
Description: Relationship of FTP Dance Project to other dance companies in Los Angeles, political and social problems, success

of the FTP.

**King, Albert Henry(b.1900)**
Discusses: FAP Participated in: FAP, PWAP
Positions: Artist, Administrator Location: CA
Interviewer: Vitale, Lydia Modi Interview date: 03/06/75
Tape: 120 minutes
Repository: University of Santa Clara
Series: New Deal Art: California
Interview also includes: Herron, John
This interview is on 1" videotape and needs special equipment
to be viewed.

**King, Albert Henry(b.1900)**
Discusses: FAP Participated in: FAP, PWAP
Positions: Artist, Administrator Location: CA
Interviewer: Hoag, Betty Lochrie Interview date: 06/10/64
Transcript: 32 pages
Repository: Archives of American Art
Permission of interviewee needed.
Description: Supervisor of mosaics in Southern California.

**Kingman, Dong M.(b.1911)**
Discusses: FAP Participated in: FAP
Positions: Artist, Muralist Location: CA
Interviewer: Phillips, Harlan Interview date: 01/12/65
Transcript: 28 pages
Repository: Archives of American Art
Description: Water color artist, did murals in San Francisco.

**Kingston, Lenore**
Discusses: FTP Participated in: FTP
Position: Actress Location: CA
Interviewer: Wickre, Karen Interview date: 10/24/77
Tape: 30 minutes Abstract: 1 page(s)
Repository: George Mason University
Description: Vaudeville, FTP experiences, San Bernardino
stock company.

**Kinnard, Henry**
Discusses: FTP Participated in: FTP
Position: Stagehand Location: NY
Interviewer: Brown, Lorraine Interview date: 01/03/77
Transcript: 22 pages Tape: 90 minutes Abstract: 3 page(s)
Repository: George Mason University
Closed pending release.
Description: FTP experiences, the Lafayette Theatre.

**Kirkland, Vance H.(b.1904)**
Discusses: FAP, SECT Participated in: FAP, SECT
Positions: Artist, Muralist Locations: OK, KS
Interviewer: Hardwick, Bonnie Interview date: 08/09/79
Tape: 90 minutes
Transcript is indexed.
Repository: Denver Public Library
Series: Federal Art in Colorado, 1934-1943
Description: Treasury Department Post Office murals in
Oklahoma and Kansas.

**Klonis, Stewart(b.1901)**
Discusses: FAP, PWAP Participated in: FAP, PWAP
Positions: Artist, Administrator Location: NY
Interviewer: Hooten, Bruce Interview date: 1965
Transcript: 12 pages
Repository: Archives of American Art
Permission of interviewee needed.
Description: Art Students League, artist's problems in the
1930s, Washington Square art shows, teaching, procedures of
Art Students League Board.

**Klonis, Stewart(b.1901)**
Discusses: FAP, PWAP Participated in: FAP, PWAP
Position: Artist Location: NY
Interviewer: Cummings, Paul Interview date: 02/03/70
Transcript: 51 pages
Repository: Archives of American Art
Permission of interviewee needed.
Description: Background, Art Students League, Washington
Square art shows, the Depression.

**Kloss, Gene(b.1903)**
Discusses: FAP Participated in: FAP, PWAP
Positions: Etcher, Artist Location: NM
Interviewer: Loomis, Sylvia Interview date: 06/11/64
Transcript: 21 pages
Repository: Archives of American Art

**Knaths, Karl(1891-1971)**
Discusses: FAP, PWAP Participated in: FAP, PWAP, SECT
Position: Artist Locations: MA, DE
Interviewer: Seckler, Dorothy G. Interview date: 1962
Transcript: 35 pages
Repository: Archives of American Art
Permission of his widow needed.

Description:   Background, Art Institute of Chicago, FAP in
Falmouth, Mass., artists' procedures and concepts.

### Kneass, Amelie
Discusses: FERA, FAP Participated in: FERA, FAP
Position: Administrator Location: CA
Interviewer:   McChesney, Mary Fuller   Interview date:
03/28/65
Transcript: 15 pages
Repository:  Archives of American Art
Permission of interviewee needed.
Description:   Director of FAP in Monterey, then state director.

### Knight, Harry
Discusses: PWAP, FAP Participated in: PWAP, FAP
Position: Administrator Location: DC
Interviewer:  Phillips, Harlan
Transcript: 58 pages
Repository:  Archives of American Art
Permission of interviewee needed.
Description:   Establishment of the FAP, how it was organized,
working with Audrey McMahon, Index of American Design.

### Knotts, Ben
Discusses: FAP Participated in: FAP
Positions: Administrator, Muralist Location: NY
Interviewer:  Phillips, Harlan Interview date:  07/24/64
Transcript: 14 pages
Repository:  Archives of American Art
Permission of interviewee needed.
Description:   Worked as assistant to Audrey McMahon, murals
for Julia Richmond High School.

### Koch, Howard
Discusses: FTP Participated in: FTP
Position: Playwright Location: NY
Interviewer: O'Connor, John Interview date:  10/26/76
Transcript: 17 pages Tape: 60 minutes Abstract: 2 page(s)
Repository:  George Mason University
Description:   Working conditions, Welles, Houseman, and
Mercury Theatre, *Three Ways to Rob a Lady*, *The Lonely Man*.

### Korff, Alice Graham
Discusses: PWAP
Position: Art Critic Location: DC
Interviewer:  Phillips, Harlan Interview date:  10/07/64
Transcript: 34 pages

Repository: Archives of American Art
Permission of interviewee needed.
Description: Art Critic for the *Washington Post*, establishment of the PWAP by Edward Bruce.

**Krakow, Leo**
Discusses: FMP Participated in: FMP
Position: Concertmaster Location: MI
Interviewer: Knoblauch-Franc, Marion Interview date: 04/30/82
Transcript: 6 pages
Repository: George Mason University
Closed until 6/1/86.
Permission of interviewer until 5/31/87 open from 6/1/87.
Description: FMP and young musicians: "We in the WPA were really a people's orchestra", Concermaster of FMP Grand Rapids orchestra later conductor.

**Krasner, Lee(b.1908)**
Discusses: FAP Participated in: FAP
Position: Artist Location: NY
Interviewer: Rose, Barbara Interview date: 07/31/66
Transcript: 21 pages
Repository: Archives of American Art
Permission of New York AAA Office.
Description: Types of government murals, value of federal projects, galleries, schools, American Artists Union politics.

**Krasner, Lee(b.1908)**
Discusses: FAP Participated in: FAP
Position: Artist Location: NY
Interviewer: Seckler, Dorothy G. Interview date: 11/02/64
Transcript: 28 pages
Repository: Archives of American Art
Permission of New York AAA Office.
Description: National Academy of Design, Burgoyne Diller and his effect on FAP artists, Jackson Pollock, Hans Hofmann.

**Krause, Erik Hans(b.1899)**
Discusses: FAP Participated in: FAP
Positions: Artist, Administrator Location: NY
Interviewer: Trovato, Joseph Interview date: 01/23/65
Transcript: 11 pages
Repository: Archives of American Art
Interview also includes: Moore, Gertrude Herdle
Description: Supervisor of Rochester FAP.

**Kupferman, Lawrence(1909-1982)**
Discusses: FAP
Positions: Artist, Printmaker Location: MA
Interviewer: Swift, Geoffrey Interview date: 11/12/65
Transcript: 32 pages
Repository: Archives of American Art

**Kurtz, Wilbur(b.1882)**
Discusses: FAP
Positions: Artist, Illustrator
Interviewer: Doud, Richard Interview date: 06/05/65
Transcript: 13 pages
Repository: Archives of American Art
Permission of interviewee needed.

**La Branche, Dolores**
Discusses: FAP Participated in: FAP
Position: Printmaker Location: MT
Interviewer: Hoag, Betty Lochrie Interview date: 09/28/65
Transcript: 36 pages
Repository: Archives of American Art
Interview also includes: Richards, Lavina

**La Farge, Henry**
Discusses: FAP Participated in: FAP
Position: Administrator Location: DC
Interviewer: Phillips, Harlan
Transcript: 11 pages
Repository: Archives of American Art
Permission of interviewee needed.

**Labaudt, Marcelle**
Discusses: PWAP
Positions: Artist, Muralist Location: CA
Interviewer: McChesney, Mary Fuller Interview date: 09/16/64
Transcript: 22 pages
Repository: Archives of American Art
Widow of Lucien Labaudt.
Description: Coit Tower mural called "Beach Chalet".

**Lahti, Aarre K.**
Discusses: FAP Participated in: FAP
Positions: Artist, Sculptor
Interviewer: Ehrlich, Heyward Interview date: 1964
Transcript: 52 pages
Repository: Archives of American Art

Description: Chicago Art Institute.

**Lane, Esther Porter**
Discusses: FTP Participated in: FTP
Positions: Stage Manager, Administrator Locations: DC, NY
Interviewer: Krulak, Mae Mallory Interview date: 09/07/76
Transcript: 44 pages Tape: 90 minutes Abstract: 4 page(s)
Repository: George Mason University
Description: Lane's experiences as administrator, director, and stage manager for the FTP.

**Lane, Esther Porter**
Discusses: FTP Participated in: FTP
Positions: Stage Manager, Administrator Locations: DC, NY
Interviewers: O'Connor, John and Wickre, Karen Interview date: 07/11/77
Transcript: 37 pages Tape: 75 minutes Abstract: 3 page(s)
Repository: George Mason University
Description: *Is Zat So?*, *Mother Goose*, *Black Empire*, speeches to WPA regional and local officials.

**Lange, Dorothea**(1895-1965)
Discusses: RA, FSA Participated in: RA, FSA
Position: Photographer
Interviewer: Riess, Suzanne B. Interview date: 1960-61
Transcript: 257 pages
Transcript is indexed.
Repository: University of California, Berkeley
Permission of archive needed.
Description: A life history interview covering Lange's work for the RA and FSA.

**Lange, Dorothea**(1895-1965)
Discusses: RA, FSA Participated in: RA, FSA
Position: Photographer
Interviewer: Doud, Richard Interview date: 05/22/64
Transcript: 23 pages
Repository: Archives of American Art

**Laning, Clair**
Discusses: FWP Participated in: FERA, FWP
Position: Administrator Location: DC
Interviewer: Loomis, Sylvia Interview date: 04/02/64
Transcript: 26 pages
Repository: Archives of American Art
Interview also includes: Perry, Mary
Description: Chief assistant to Henry Alsberg, director of

FWP, a field supervisor for two years then assistant director of FWP.

**Lantz, Louis**
Discusses: FTP Participated in: FTP
Positions: Playwright, Playreader Location: NY
Interviewer: Bowers, Diane Interview date: 05/26/76
Transcript: 44 pages Tape: 75 minutes Abstract: 3 page(s)
Repository: George Mason University
Closed pending release.
Description: Interest in playwrighting and influence of other playwrights on him, innovation and experimentation on FTP and bureaucratic problems.

**Lantz, Louis**
Discusses: FTP Participated in: FTP
Positions: Playwright, Playreader Location: NY
Interviewer: Berenberg, Benedict Interview date: 06/10/77
Transcript: 20 pages
Repository: Berenberg MA thesis, Univ. of Wisc.
Interview also includes: Saul, Oscar
Transcript in interviewer's MA thesis. These tapes are on permanent loan at Wisc. State Historical Society.

**Lassaw, Ibram**(b.1913)
Discusses: PWAP, FAP Participated in: PWAP, FAP
Position: Sculptor Location: NY
Interviewer: Sandler, Irving Interview date: 08/26/68
Transcript: 59 pages
Repository: Archives of American Art
Description: American Artists Union, art scene in New York from the 1930s to the 1950s.

**Lassaw, Ibram**(b.1913)
Discusses: FAP Participated in: PWAP, FAP
Position: Sculptor Location: NY
Interviewer: Bowman, Ruth Interview date: 1964
Transcript: 28 pages
Repository: Archives of American Art
Description: The Clay Club, Beaux Arts Institute, FAP, teaching, kinetic sculpture, ideas, methods, and materials, American Artists Union.

**Lassaw, Ibram**(b.1913)
Discusses: FAP Participated in: PWAP, FAP
Position: Sculptor Location: NY
Interviewer: Seckler, Dorothy G. Interview date: 11/64

Transcript: 33 pages
Repository: Archives of American Art
Description: Government art projects, freedom of expression under FAP, American Artists Union, exhibitions, techniques.

**Laub, Lili Mann**
SEE Mann, Lili.

**Laufman, Sidney(b.1891)**
Discusses: FAP Participated in: FAP, PWAP
Position: Artist Locations: FL, NY
Interviewer: Trovato, Joseph Interview date: 01/29/64
Transcript: 12 pages
Repository: Archives of American Art
Description: Education and background, Art Students League, FAP in Key West, Florida, effects of the FAP on his career.

**Laurence, Paula**
Discusses: FTP Participated in: FTP
Position: Actress Location: NY
Interviewer: Wickre, Karen Interview date: 04/20/78
Transcript: 28 pages Tape: 60 minutes Abstract: 3 page(s)
Repository: George Mason University
Description: *Sing for Your Supper* rehearsals, Houseman and Welles.

**Lavery, Emmet(b.1902)**
Discusses: FTP Participated in: FTP
Position: Administrator Location: NY
Interviewer: O'Connor, John Interview date: 10/17/77
Transcript: 43 pages Tape: 105 minutes Abstract: 2 page(s)
Repository: George Mason University
Description: Evolution of functions of National Service Bureau, friendship and working relationship with Hallie Flanagan.

**Lavery, Emmet(b.1902)**
Discusses: FTP Participated in: FTP
Position: Administrator Location: NY
Interviewer: O'Connor, John Interview date: 08/76
Tape: 110 minutes Abstract: 4 page(s)
Repository: George Mason University
Interview also includes: Randolph, John and Lloyd, Norman
This is a videotape. Also available at the New York Public Library.
Description: Shame of many actors at being in FTP, need for FTP, conditions which gave rise to it, need for relief programs,

National Service Bureau.

**Lavery, Emmet(b.1902)**
Discusses: FTP Participated in: FTP
Position: Administrator Location: NY
Interviewers: O'Connor, John and Krulak, Mae Mallory
Interview date: 01/05/76
Transcript: 68 pages Tape: 150 minutes Abstract: 5 page(s)
Repository: George Mason University
Description: *Murder in the Cathedral, It Can't Happen Here.*

**Lavery, Emmet(b.1902)**
Discusses: FTP Participated in: FTP
Position: Administrator Location: NY
Interviewers: Dixon, Elizabeth I. and Duttera, Bonnie
Interview date: 07/61
Transcript: 196 pages
Repository: Univ. of California, Los Angeles
Description: Director of the National Service Bureau, colleague of Hallie Flanagan, helped Flanagan with her book *Arena.*

**Lawrence, Jacob(b.1917)**
Discusses: FAP Participated in: FAP
Position: Artist Location: NY
Interviewer: Greene, Carroll Interview date: 10/26/68
Transcript: 50 pages
Repository: Archives of American Art
Permission of interviewee needed.
Description: Early influences, FAP, art scene in Harlem, position of black artists in society.

**Lawson, Kathryn Drain(b.1894)**
Discusses: FTP Participated in: FTP
Position: Technical Director Location: NY
Interviewer: Krulak, Mae Mallory Interview date: 01/03/76
Transcript: 64 pages Tape: 55 minutes Abstract: 2 page(s)
Repository: George Mason University
Description: Her early life, opposition to Hallie Flanagan, FTP's impact on American theatre.

**Lazzari, Pietro(1898-1979)**
Discusses: FAP Participated in: FAP, SECT
Positions: Sculptor, Artist Locations: NY, NC, FL
Interviewer: Phillips, Harlan Interview date: 1964
Transcript: 77 pages
Repository: Archives of American Art

**Le Seur, Meridel**
Discusses: WPA Participated in: WPA
Location: MN
Interviewer: Bloom, Jon  Interview date: 05/01/82
Tape: 45 minutes
Repository: New York University
Series: Oral History of the American Left
Description: Minnesota Depression radicalism, 1930s, women
and the arts projects.


**LeNoire, Rosetta(b.1911)**
Discusses: FTP Participated in: FTP
Position: Actress Location: NY
Interviewers: Brown, Lorraine and others Interview date:
01/13/78
Transcript: 23 pages  Tape: 105 minutes  Abstract: 5 page(s)
Repository: George Mason University
This is a videotape.
Description: Black FTP reunion: Anderson, T., Archer, O.,
Bates, Add., Hill, A., De Paur, L.


**LeNoire, Rosetta(b.1911)**
Discusses: FTP Participated in: FTP
Position: Actress Location: NY
Interviewers: Hatch, James V. and Billops, Camille Interview
date: 12/06/71
Tape: 60 minutes  Abstract: 1 page(s)
Repository: Hatch-Billops Collection, Inc.
Permission of archive needed.
Description: Biography, Bill Robinson.


**LeNoire, Rosetta(b.1911)**
Discusses: FTP Participated in: FTP
Position: Actress Location: NY
Interviewer: Brown, Lorraine  Interview date: 01/08/77
Transcript: 23 pages  Tape: 60 minutes  Abstract: 2 page(s)
Repository: George Mason University
Closed during lifetime.
Description: FTP opened doors for blacks, influence of FTP
on American Negro Theatre.


**Leavitt, Max**
Discusses: FTP Participated in: FTP
Position: Puppeteer Location: NY
Interviewer: Wickre, Karen  Interview date: 11/28/78
Tape: 60 minutes  Abstract: 2 page(s)
Repository: George Mason University

Closed during lifetime.
Description: FTP a help for unknown talent, effect of FTP on life.

**Leavitt, Max**
Discusses: FTP Participated in: FTP
Position: Puppeteer Location: NY
Interviewer: Goldman, Harry
Transcript: 10 pages
Repository: Columbia University
Available 5 years after publication.
Series: History of the Mercury Theatre
Description: Mercury Theatre grew out of the FTP's New York City Negro Unit at the Layfayette Theatre.

**Lee, Doris**(b.1905)
Discusses: FAP Participated in: FAP, SECT
Positions: Artist, Illustrator Locations: NY, DC, GA
Interviewer: Trovato, Joseph Interview date: 11/04/64
Transcript: 6 pages
Repository: Archives of American Art
Permission of interviewee needed.

**Lee, J. Edward**
Discusses: FTP Participated in: FTP
Position: Publicist Locations: IL, NY
Interviewer: Brown, Lorraine Interview date: 07/20/77
Transcript: 28 pages Tape: 65 minutes Abstract: 2 page(s)
Repository: George Mason University
Description: *Dr Faustus* with Orson Welles, racism, strength of FTP, no real star system, a chance to act without fear of losing jobs.

**Lee, Jean**
Discusses: FSA, RA
Interviewer: Doud, Richard Interview date: 06/02/64
Transcript: 41 pages
Repository: Archives of American Art
Interview also includes: Lee, Russell
Description: Work with husband Russell Lee.

**Lee, Russell**(b.1903)
Discusses: RA, FSA Participated in: RA, FSA
Position: Photographer Locations: IL, OH
Interviewer: Doud, Richard Interview date: 06/02/64
Repository: Archives of American Art
Interview also includes: Lee, Jean

Description: Replaced Carl Mydans in Stryker's historical section of RA in the summer of 1936, covered agricultural problems in Illinois and Ohio.

### Lee, Will
Discusses: FTP Participated in: FTP
Position: Actor Location: NY
Interviewer: O'Connor, John Interview date: 10/22/76
Transcript: 36 pages Tape: 80 minutes Abstract: 2 page(s)
Repository: George Mason University
Description: Reasons for closing of FTP, FTP was economically helpful for young actors while allowing them to develop their talents.

### Lee-Smith, Hughie(b.1915)
Discusses: FAP
Positions: Artist, Printmaker Location: MI
Interviewer: Greene, Carroll Interview date: 1968
Transcript: 34 pages
Repository: Archives of American Art
Permission of interviewee needed.
Description: Background and education, teaching, paintings for *History of the Negro in U.S. Navy*, FAP, printmaking.

### Lehac, Ned
Discusses: FTP Participated in: FTP
Position: Songwriter Location: NY
Interviewer: Brown, Lorraine Interview date: 1977
Transcript: 19 pages Tape: 50 minutes Abstract: 2 page(s)
Repository: George Mason University
Description: The production of *Sing For Your Supper*.

### Lehman, Carlton(b.1911)
Discusses: FAP Participated in: FAP
Positions: Artist, Administrator Location: CA
Interviewer: McChesney, Mary Fuller Interview date: 12/17/64
Transcript: 27 pages
Repository: Archives of American Art
Permission of interviewee needed.
Description: Director of the Sacramento Art Center (1939-40), Assistant State Supervisor under Joseph Allen.

### Lenshaw, Ernest(b.1892)
Discusses: FAP Participated in: FAP
Positions: Artist, Muralist Location: CA
Interviewer: McChesney, Mary Fuller Interview date:

05/19/64
Transcript: 29 pages
Repository: Archives of American Art
Permission of interviewee needed.
Description: Worked on Acquatic Park murals in San Francisco.

**Lenson, Michael**(1903-1971)
Discusses: SECT Participated in: SECT
Position: Artist Location: WV
Interviewer: Phillips, Harlan Interview date: 10/30/64
Transcript: 69 pages
Repository: Archives of American Art
Permission of widow needed.

**Lentz, Josef**
Discusses: FTP Participated in: FTP
Position: Administrator Location: CA
Interviewer: O'Connor, John Interview date: 04/07/77
Transcript: 22 pages Tape: 60 minutes Abstract: 3 page(s)
Repository: George Mason University
Permission of Lentz during his life.
Description: Accomplishments of FTP, his work as Regional Director.

**Lessin, Harry**
Discusses: FTP Participated in: FTP
Position: Actor Location: NY
Interviewer: Brown, Lorraine Interview date: 01/06/76
Abstract: 2 page(s)
Repository: George Mason University
This is an untaped interview, a two-page abstract is available.
Description: Lessin was an actor in several New York City FTP productions, *One Third of a Nation, Professor Mamlock.*

**Leuning, Otto**
Discusses: FMP Participated in: FMP
Position: Conductor Location: VT
Interviewer: Knoblauch-Franc, Marion Interview date: 05/10/82
Transcript: 11 pages Tape: 30 minutes
Repository: George Mason University
Closed until 6/1/86.
Permission of Leuning needed until 2000. Permission of interviewer until 5/31/87 open from 6/1/87.
Description: Composers' Forum, Bennington County Music Association, value of FMP.

**Leve, Samuel**
Discusses: FTP Participated in: FTP
Position: Set Designer Location: NY
Interviewer: O'Connor, John Interview date: 02/21/76
Transcript: 21 pages Tape: 50 minutes Abstract: 2 page(s)
Repository: George Mason University
Description: *Cherokee Night*, *Big Blow*, Paul Robeson.

**Leve, Samuel**
Discusses: FTP Participated in: FTP
Position: Set Designer Location: NY
Interviewer: O'Connor, John Interview date: 12/13/78
Tape: 60 minutes Abstract: 3 page(s)
Repository: George Mason University
This is a videotape. Also available at the New York Public
Library.
Description: FTP offered a chance for self expression, Orson
Welles, *Cherokee Night*.

**Levi, Julian**(b.1900)
Discusses: FAP Participated in: FAP
Position: Artist Locations: NY, PA
Interviewer: Roberts, Colette Interview date: 10/21/68
Transcript: 60 pages
Repository: Archives of American Art
Description: Background, Art Students League, the New
School, Pennsylvania Academy, lithography, New York
galleries.

**Levine, Jack**(b.1915)
Discusses: FAP Participated in: FAP
Position: Artist Location: MA
Interviewer: Selvig, Forrest Interview date: 09/05/68
Transcript: 44 pages
Repository: Archives of American Art
Description: Politics and art, FAP and other government-
sponsored art projects, early work, prices of paintings.

**Levine, Jack**(b.1915)
Discusses: FAP Participated in: FAP
Position: Artist Location: MA
Interview date: 1956
Transcript: 150 pages
Repository: Columbia University
Permission required to quote.
Available on microfiche, part I.

Description: Art, painting, the creative process.

**Lewandowski, Edmund**
Discusses: FAP Participated in: FAP, SECT
Position: Muralist Locations: MN, WI, IL
Interviewer: Reid, George Interview date: 08/12/77
Transcript: 5 pages Tape: 30 minutes
Repository: Minnesota Historical Society
Series: Federal Art Project in Minnesota
Tape filed under Fossum, Syd.
Description: Murals painted in Minnesota, Wisconsin, and Illinois.

**Lewis, Monty(b.1907)**
Discusses: FAP
Positions: Artist, Designer
Interviewer: Hoag, Betty Lochrie Interview date: 06/25/64
Transcript: 15 pages
Repository: Archives of American Art

**Lewitsky, Bella**
Discusses: FTP Participated in: FTP
Position: Dancer Location: CA
Interviewer: Brown, Lorraine Interview date: 03/12/79
Tape: 90 minutes Abstract: 2 page(s)
Repository: George Mason University
Description: Lewitsky was a dancer with the Dance Project of the Los Angeles FTP.

**Lief, Arthur**
Discusses: FMP Participated in: FMP
Positions: Conductor, Teacher Location: NY
Interviewer: Wickre, Karen Interview date: 06/07/77
Transcript: 18 pages Tape: 60 minutes Abstract: 2 page(s)
Repository: George Mason University
Closed during his lifetime.
Description: Important musicians who got a start in FMP.

**Lindemulder, Nel**
Discusses: FTP
Locations: LA, FL
Interviewer: Orear, Leslie F. Interview date: 10/28/84
Repository: George Mason University
Nel Lindemulder's husband was a director on Louisiana and Florida FTP.
Description: *One Third of a Nation* in New Orleans, *Uncle Tom's Cabin* in Jacksonville, *If Ye Break Faith*, costuming,

audiences in Florida.

**Lindneux, Robert Ottokar**(1871-1970)
Discusses: FAP
Position: Artist
Interviewer: Loomis, Sylvia  Interview date:  11/14/64
Transcript: 21 pages
Repository: Archives of American Art

**Lion, Henry**(1900-1966)
Discusses: SECT Participated in: SECT
Positions: Sculptor, Artist Location: CA
Interviewer: Hoag, Betty Lochrie Interview date: 05/21/64
Transcript: 14 pages
Repository: Archives of American Art

**Lishinsky, Abraham**
Discusses: FAP, SECT Participated in: FAP, SECT
Position: Muralist Locations: NY, SC
Interviewer: Harrison, Helen A. Interview date: 03/05/76
Tape: 30 minutes
Repository: George Mason University
Closed pending release.
Description: FAP and Section murals.

**Liston, Ilo Carey**
Discusses: FAP
Position: Museum Director Location: WA
Interviewer: Bestor, Dorothy  Interview date: 06/01/65
Transcript: 18 pages
Repository: Archives of American Art
Permission of interviewee needed.
Description:  Seattle Art Museum staff, FAP benefitted the
artists, the museum was financially successful during the 1930s.


**Litvinoff, Valentina**
Discusses: FTP Participated in: FTP
Position: Dancer Location: NY
Interviewer: Wickre, Karen  Interview date:  11/29/78
Transcript: 14 pages  Tape: 30 minutes
Transcript is indexed.
Repository: George Mason University
Description: *Emperor's New Clothes*, conflicts with Sylvia
Manning over choreography concepts, independent attitude and
conflicts.

**Lloyd, Joel**
Discusses: FTP Participated in: FTP
Position: Puppeteer Location: NY
Interviewer: Wickre, Karen Interview date: 11/14/78
Transcript: 28 pages Tape: 60 minutes Abstract: 2 page(s)
Repository: George Mason University
Description: FTP regulations, red tape, administrative
problems, *R.U.R.*, *Ferdinand the Bull*, *String Fever*, strings and
marionette movement.

**Lloyd, Norman(b.1914)**
Participated in: FTP
Position: Actor Location: NY
Interview date: 04/06/73
Repository: Yale University
Permission of archive needed.
Series: Major Figures in American Music
Taped lecture given at Yale School of Music by Lloyd.

**Lloyd, Norman(b.1914)**
Discusses: FTP Participated in: FTP
Position: Actor Location: NY
Interviewer: Davis, Ronald L. Interview date: 1979-80
Transcript: 120 pages Tape: 180 minutes Abstract: 1 page(s)
Transcript is indexed.
Repository: Southern Methodist University
Series: Performing Arts in the U.S.
SMU holds correspondence related to interview.
Description: A biographical approach to his career.

**Lloyd, Norman(b.1914)**
Discusses: FTP Participated in: FTP
Position: Actor Location: NY
Interviewer: O'Connor, John Interview date: 08/76
Tape: 110 minutes Abstract: 4 page(s)
Repository: George Mason University
Interview also includes: Lavery, Emmet, and Randolph, John
This is a videotape. Also available at the New York Public
Library.
Description: FTP created whole new audience, audience impact
on actors, content of plays meaningful to audiences, writers
influenced by audiences.

**Lloyd, Norman(b.1914)**
Discusses: FTP Participated in: FTP
Position: Actor Location: NY
Interviewer: O'Connor, John Interview date: 01/05/76

Transcript: 32 pages  Tape: 60 minutes  Abstract: 3 page(s)
Repository: George Mason University
Description: Living Newspapers with Joseph Losey and Morris
Watson: *Triple-A Plowed Under, Power, Injunction Granted.*


**Lloyd, Norman**
Discusses: FTP Participated in: FTP
Position: Actor Location: NY
Interviewer: Goldman, Harry
Transcript: 29 pages
Repository: Columbia University
Available 5 years after publication.
Series: History of the Mercury Theatre


**Lochrie, Elizabeth D.(b.1890)**
Discusses: SECT Participated in: SECT
Positions: Artist, Sculptor Locations: ID, MT
Interviewer: Hoag, Betty Lochrie Interview date: 1964-65
Transcript: 21 pages
Repository: Archives of American Art


**Loper, Edward L.(b.1916)**
Discusses: FAP
Position: Artist
Interviewer: Doud, Richard Interview date: 03/26/64
Transcript: 20 pages
Repository: Archives of American Art


**Lorentz, Pare(b.1905)**
Discusses: RA, USFS Participated in: RA, USFS
Positions: Filmmaker, Administrator Locations: NY, DC
Interviewer: Snyder, Robert L. Interview date: 10/10/83
Tape: 148 minutes
Transcript is indexed.
Repository: Polk Library, UW-Oshkosh, WI.
Used at collection site only.
Series: Pare Lorentz Oral History
Recorded at Lorentz Home. Series includes four more
interviews up to June 1985, all at Univ. of Wisc.
Description: The focus of this series of tapes is World War II.


**Losey, Blanche Morgan**
Discusses: FTP Participated in: FTP
Position: Costume Designer Location: WA
Interviewer: O'Connor, John Interview date: 01/07/76
Tape: 55 minutes Abstract: 1 page(s)
Repository: George Mason University

Written permission.
Interview also includes: Williams, Guy
Description: Seattle FTP, FTP Negro Theatre, various plays and participants, protest plays.

**Lowe, Peter**(b.1913)
Discusses: FAP
Positions: Artist, Graphic Artist
Interviewer: McChesney, Mary Fuller    Interview date: 03/03/65
Transcript: 16 pages
Repository: Archives of American Art

**Lumet, Sidney**(b.1924)
Discusses: FTP Participated in: FTP
Position: Actor Location: NY
Interview date: 1958
Transcript: 54 pages
Repository: Columbia University
Series: Popular Arts
Available on microfiche, part IV.
Description: Child actor on the FTP, was in *It Can't Happen Here.*

**Lundeberg, Helen**(b.1908)
Discusses: FAP Participated in: FAP, PWAP
Positions: Printmaker, Muralist Location: CA
Interviewers: Vitale, Lydia Modi and Gelber, Steven Interview date: 03/14/75
Tape: 120 minutes
Repository: University of Santa Clara
Series: New Deal Art: California
Interview also includes: Feitelson, Lorser
This interview is on 1" videotape and needs special equipment to be viewed.

**Lundeberg, Helen**(b.1908)
Discusses: FAP Participated in: FAP
Positions: Printmaker, Muralist Location: CA
Interviewer: Hoag, Betty Lochrie Interview date: 03/17/65
Transcript: 42 pages
Repository: Archives of American Art
Interview also includes: Fietelson, Lorser
Description: Education and background, murals and printmaking on FAP, other artists on the FAP.

**Lynch, Dorothea**

Discusses: FTP Participated in: FTP
Position: Administrator Location: FL
Interviewer: O'Connor, John Interview date: 03/14/77
Tape: 125 minutes Abstract: 3 page(s)
Repository: George Mason University
Description: How she got into FTP, audience response in Florida.

**Mac-Gurrin, Buckley(d.1971)**
Discusses: FAP Participated in: FAP, PWAP
Positions: Artist, Muralist Location: CA
Interviewer: Hoag, Betty Lochrie Interview date: 06/20/64
Transcript: 36 pages
Repository: Archives of American Art
Description: Murals for the Los Angeles County Museum and Los Angeles Hall of Records.

**Macchiarini, Peter**
Discusses: FTP Participated in: FTP
Positions: Puppeteer, Sculptor Location: CA
Interviewer: Wickre, Karen Interview date: 02/23/78
Tape: 35 minutes Abstract: 2 page(s)
Repository: George Mason University
Description: Ralph Chesse, San Francisco Marionette Unit, *Cricket on the Hearth*, union struggles of San Francisco FTP workers.

**Macchiarini, Peter**
Discusses: FTP Participated in: FTP
Positions: Puppeteer, Sculptor Location: CA
Interviewer: McChesney, Mary Fuller Interview date: 10/18/64
Transcript: 34 pages
Repository: Archives of American Art
Permission of interviewee needed.

**Maccoy, Genoi**
Discusses: FAP Participated in: FAP
Position: Artist Location: NY
Interviewer: Hoag, Betty Lochrie Interview date: 07/24/64
Transcript: 40 pages
Repository: Archives of American Art
Permission of interviewees needed.
Interview also includes: Maccoy, Guy
Description: Art Students League.

**Macdonald-Wright, Stanton(1890-1973)**

Discusses: FAP Participated in: FAP
Position: Administrator Location: CA
Interviewer: Hoag, Betty Lochrie Interview date: 1964
Transcript: 103 pages
Repository: Archives of American Art
Description: Regional Director of the FAP in Southern California 1935-1940, regional advisor for seven western states.


**Magafan, Ethel(b.1916)**
Discusses: SECT, TRAP Participated in: SECT, TRAP
Positions: Artist, Muralist Locations: DC, OK, CO
Interviewer: Trovato, Joseph Interview date: 11/05/64
Transcript: 10 pages
Repository: Archives of American Art


**Magnani, Margery(b.1918)**
Discusses: FAP Participated in: FAP
Positions: Administrator, Weaver Location: CA
Interviewer: McChesney, Mary Fuller Interview date: 07/07/65
Transcript: 23 pages
Repository: Archives of American Art
Permission of interviewee needed.
Description: On the Arts and Craft Project in San Francisco, assistant supervisor of Arts and Craft Project in charge of weaving.


**Malicoat, Philip(b.1908)**
Discusses: FAP Participated in: FAP
Position: Artist Location: RI
Interviewer: Seckler, Dorothy G. Interview date: 08/30/65
Transcript: 16 pages
Repository: Archives of American Art
Description: Background, art training, FAP, financial difficulties in wartime, Provincetown, exhibits, techniques.


**Maltz, Albert**
Discusses: FTP Participated in: FTP
Position: Playwright Location: NY
Interviewer: Bowers, Diane Interview date: 05/27/76
Transcript: 45 pages Tape: 120 minutes Abstract: 3 page(s)
Repository: George Mason University
Description: Education, theatre and language, *Peace on Earth*, *Stevedore*, *Black Pit*.


**Maltz, Albert**

Participated in: FTP
Position: Playwright Location: NY
Interviewer: Goldman, Harry
Transcript: 48 pages
Repository: Columbia University
Available 5 years after publication.
Series: History of the Mercury Theatre

**Mandelman, Beatrice M.(b.1912)**
Discusses: FAP Participated in: FAP
Positions: Artist, Muralist Location: NY
Interviewer: Loomis, Sylvia Interview date: 07/20/64
Transcript: 22 pages
Repository: Archives of American Art
Description: Art Students League, hospital murals in New York.

**Mann, Dulce Fox**
Discusses: FTP Participated in: FTP
Position: Actress Location: NY
Interviewer: O'Connor, John Interview date: 03/11/80
Tape: 90 minutes Abstract: 2 page(s)
Repository: George Mason University
Description: Work on Project #891, a Houseman/Welles group at the Maxine Elliot Theatre, *Mabel Looks Ahead*, *Horse Eats Hat*, *Cradle Will Rock*.

**Mann, Lili Laub**
Discusses: FTP Participated in: FTP
Position: Dancer Location: NY
Interviewer: Wickre, Karen Interview date: 05/24/78
Transcript: 43 pages Tape: 145 minutes Abstract: 3 page(s)
Repository: George Mason University
Description: President of FTP union, *I'd Rather be Right*.

**Mann, Lili Laub**
Discusses: FTP Participated in: FTP
Position: Dancer Location: NY
Interviewer: Wickre, Karen Interview date: 02/20/78
Tape: 90 minutes Abstract: 3 page(s)
Repository: George Mason University
This is a videotape.
Description: FTP dancers--demonstration and panel with Bass, P., Barlin, A.L., Garnet, E., Geltman, F., Gerrard, S., Remos, S., Schaff,T.

**Mann, Lucile Quarry(b.1897)**

Discusses: PWAP
Location: DC
Interviewer: Henson, Pamela  Interview date: 06/09/77
Transcript: 56 pages  Tape: 90 minutes  Abstract: 1 page(s)
Transcript is indexed.
Repository: Smithsonian Institution Archives
Permission of archive needed.
Interviewee was the wife of William Mann, Dir. of the National Zoo.
Description: Her role in placement of PWAP murals in the zoo.


**Manship, Paul**(1885-1966)
Discusses: SECT  Participated in: SECT
Position: Sculptor  Locations: NY, DC
Interviewer: Morse, John D.  Interview date: 02/18/59
Transcript: 33 pages
Repository: Archives of American Art
Permission of his son needed.
Description: Views on FAP, his Prometheus sculpture at Rockefeller Center, his training, and influences on his work.


**Mantilla, Victor**
Discusses: FAP  Participated in: FAP
Position: Artist
Interviewer: McChesney, Mary Fuller  Interview date: 07/28/64
Transcript: 30 pages
Repository: Archives of American Art
Permission of interviewee needed.
Description: Worked on mosaics.


**Marca-Relli, Conrad**(b.1913)
Discusses: FAP  Participated in: FAP
Position: Artist  Location: MA
Interviewer: Seckler, Dorothy G.  Interview date: 06/10/65
Transcript: 28 pages
Repository: Archives of American Art
Description: Views on FAP and other FAP artists, position of artists in society, freedom under FAP, his techniques and aims.


**Marshall, E.G.**(b.1910)
Discusses: FTP  Participated in: FTP
Position: Actor  Location: IL
Interviewers: Krulak, Mae Mallory and Maddox, Jean  Interview date: 03/03/77

Transcript: 42 pages Tape: 70 minutes Abstract: 2 page(s)
Repository: George Mason University
Description: *Faust, AMACO, Model Tenement, Big Blow,*
commercial condescension toward FTP actors.

#### Martin, Fletcher(1904-1979)
Discusses: FAP Participated in: FAP, SECT
Positions: Printmaker, Artist Locations: TX, CA, ID
Interviewer: Trovato, Joseph Interview date: 11/05/65
Transcript: 10 pages
Repository: Archives of American Art

#### Matthew, John Britton
Discusses: FAP
Position: Administrator Location: CA
Interviewer: McChesney, Mary Fuller Interview date:
10/25/64
Transcript: 23 pages
Repository: Archives of American Art
Description: Executive Secretary of the Citizens Committee
that provided the facilities for the Sacramento Art Center.

#### Mattson, Henry(1887-1971)
Discusses: PWAP, TRAP, FAP Participated in: PWAP, TRAP,
FAP
Position: Artist Location: NY
Interviewer: Trovato, Joseph Interview date: 11/04/64
Transcript: 9 pages
Repository: Archives of American Art
Permission of family needed.

#### Maxwell, Gilbert
Discusses: FTP Participated in: FTP
Position: Actor Location: GA
Interviewer: O'Connor, John Interview date: 03/19/77
Transcript: 38 pages Tape: 65 minutes Abstract: 2 page(s)
Repository: George Mason University
Description: *Boy Meets Girl*, profits, salaries, FTP publicity,
reviews usually sympathetic.

#### Mayer, Bena Frank(b.1900)
Discusses: PWAP, FAP Participated in: PWAP, FAP
Positions: Artist, Educator
Interviewer: Phillips, Harlan
Transcript: 63 pages
Repository: Archives of American Art
Permission of interviewee needed.

Interview also includes: Mayer, Ralph
Description: Worked first on the easel painting project and then on the art education project, had difficulty qualifying for the FAP.

**Mayer, Ralph(1895-1979)**
Discusses: PWAP, FAP Participated in: PWAP, FAP
Position: Artist
Interviewer: Phillips, Harlan
Transcript: 63 pages
Repository: Archives of American Art
Permission of Bena Mayer needed.
Interview also includes: Mayer, Bena Frank
Description: Worked on the Index of American Design.

**McCarthy, Max(b.1896)**
Discusses: FAP Participated in: FAP
Position: Artist Location: CA
Interviewer: McChesney, Mary Fuller Interview date: 10/15/64
Transcript: 25 pages
Repository: Archives of American Art
Permission of interviewee needed.
Description: Mosaic Project at Aquatic Park and Treasure Island for the Golden Gate International Exhibition.

**McChesney, Robert P.(b.1913)**
Discusses: FAP Participated in: FAP
Positions: Artist, Muralist
Interviewer: Ferbrache, Lewis Interview date: 04/04/64
Transcript: 24 pages
Repository: Archives of American Art
Description: Federal building art work for the International Exhibition in 1939.

**McCoy, Guy(b.1904)**
Discusses: FAP Participated in: FAP
Positions: Artist, Muralist Location: NY
Interviewer: Hoag, Betty Lochrie Interview date: 07/24/64
Transcript: 40 pages
Repository: Archives of American Art
Permission of interviewees needed.
Interview also includes: Maccoy, Genoi
Description: Art Students League, Index of American Design.

**McDermott, Thomas**
Discusses: FTP Participated in: FTP

Position: Actor Location: IL
Interviewer: Brown, Lorraine Interview date: 10/23/76
Transcript: 26 pages Tape: 60 minutes Abstract: 2 page(s)
Repository: George Mason University
Closed in interviewee's lifetime.
Description: Experimental unit, Children's Theatre, Yiddish Theatre, value of Living Newspapers, Group Theatre.

### McGraw, James
Discusses: FWP Participated in: FWP
Position: Administrator Location: NY
Interviewer: Mangione, Jerre Interview date: 12/15/67
Repository: University of Rochester
Series: Mangione Collection
Description: Assistant to Orick Johns, who was Director of the New York City FWP.

### McHugh, Vincent
Discusses: FWP Participated in: FWP
Positions: Writer, Editor Location: NY
Interviewer: Mangione, Jerre Interview date: 05/29/68
Repository: University of Rochester
Series: Mangione Collection
Description: Responsible for completing the New York City Guide.

### McLean, Scott Roberts
Discusses: FTP Participated in: FTP
Positions: Actor, Stage Manager Location: FL
Interviewer: O'Connor, John Interview date: 03/20/77
Tape: 60 minutes Abstract: 1 page(s)
Repository: George Mason University
Description: Various productions, other participants, audience characteristics and responses.

### McMahon, Audrey
Discusses: FAP Participated in: FAP
Position: Administrator Location: NY
Interviewer: Harrison, Helen A. Interview date: 12/14/76
Transcript: 30 pages Tape: 45 minutes
Repository: George Mason University
Closed pending release.
Description: Director of the NYC FAP, WPA buildings and murals at New York City World's Fair.

### McMahon, Audrey
Discusses: FAP Participated in: FAP

Position: Administrator Location: NY
Interviewer: Phillips, Harlan Interview date: 11/18/64
Transcript: 63 pages
Repository: Archives of American Art
Permission of interviewee needed.

**McNeil, George**(b.1908)
Discusses: FAP Participated in: FAP
Position: Artist Location: NY
Interviewer: Sandler, Irving Interview date: 01/09/68
Transcript: 78 pages
Repository: Archives of American Art
Description: Pratt Institute, Art Students League, FAP, NYC
art scene and artists of early 1930s, form versus free form in
1930s and 1940s, teaching.

**McNeil, George**(b.1908)
Discusses: FAP Participated in: FAP
Position: Artist Location: NY
Interviewer: Seckler, Dorothy G. Interview date: 06/03/65
Transcript: 20 pages
Repository: Archives of American Art
Description: Art Students League, fellow students, Hans
Hofmann, FAP, teaching.

**McNeil, George**(b.1908)
Discusses: FAP Participated in: FAP
Position: Artist Location: NY
Interviewer: Bowman, Ruth Interview date: 02/12/64
Transcript: 16 pages
Repository: Archives of American Art
Description: American abstract artists, politics, Artists Union,
the artist as part of the community, social realism, FAP.

**McWilliams, Joy Yeck**
Discusses: FAP Participated in: FAP
Position: Administrator Location: NM
Interviewer: Stewart, Janet Interview date: 10/18/79
Transcript: 3 pages
Repository: University of Arizona
Description: Assistant to Russell V. Hunter, FAP Director for
New Mexico, taking art projects to remote communities,
encouragement of native crafts.

**Meadow, Herb**(b.1911)
Discusses: FTP Participated in: FTP
Position: Playwright Location: NY

Interviewer: Brown, Lorraine Interview date: 08/07/76
Transcript: 38 pages Tape: 90 minutes Abstract: 3 page(s)
Repository: George Mason University
Closed during lifetime.
Description: Wrote plays for FTP, editor in Play Bureau, Congressional opposition, censorship, experimentation in FTP, value of FTP.

### Meem, John Gaw(1894-1983)
Discusses: PWAP Participated in: PWAP
Position: Administrator
Interviewer: Loomis, Sylvia Interview date: 12/03/64
Transcript: 21 pages
Repository: Archives of American Art
Description: Served as a member of the Administrative Committee of Region 13 of PWAP.

### Meltzer, Allan
Discusses: FTP Participated in: FTP
Positions: Researcher, Publicist Location: NY
Interviewer: O'Connor, John Interview date: 03/18/77
Tape: 50 minutes Abstract: 2 page(s)
Repository: George Mason University
Description: Researcher, moved to #891 Unit, *Horse Eats Hat*, *Dr. Faustus*, *Cradle Will Rock*, *Ethiopia*, union activity.

### Meltzer, Milton(b.1915)
Discusses: FTP Participated in: FTP
Position: Writer Location: NY
Interview date: 1978
Transcript: 75 pages
Repository: Columbia University
Permission required to quote.
Available on microfiche, part IV.
Description: Background and education in Worcester, Mass., writing for the FTP, political movements at New College, Columbia University in 1936.

### Menchaca, Juan(b.1910)
Discusses: FAP Participated in: FAP
Position: Artist
Interviewer: Loomis, Sylvia Interview date: 11/13/64
Transcript: 11 pages
Repository: Archives of American Art
Permission of interviewee needed.
Description: Portrait painting, reproduced old photographs to paint in oils.

**Mendelowitz, Daniel**
Discusses: SECT Participated in: SECT
Position: Artist Location: CA
Interviewers: Vitale, Lydia Modi and Gelber, Steven Interview
date: 02/17/75
Tape: 28 minutes
Repository: University of Santa Clara
Series: New Deal Art: California
This interview is on 1" videotape and needs special equipment
to be viewed.

**Meredith, Betty Arden**
Discusses: FTP Participated in: FTP
Positions: Actress, Researcher Locations: CA, WA
Interviewer: Wickre, Karen Interview date: 07/18/77
Transcript: 35 pages Tape: 90 minutes Abstract: 3 page(s)
Repository: George Mason University
Description: FTP provided security but little pay, a positive
feeling during FTP.

**Merrill, Anthony French**
Discusses: FERA, WPA Participated in: FERA, WPA
Position: Administrator Location: DC
Interviewer: Phillips, Harlan Interview date: 10/24/63
Transcript: 48 pages
Repository: Archives of American Art
Permission of interviewee needed.
Description: Did retail price study for FERA, began on WPA
in 1935, Supervisor of D.C. WPA Entertainment Unit, which
played CCC camps.

**Merrill, Mary**
Discusses: FTP Participated in: FTP
Position: Costume Designer Location: NY
Interviewer: Walsh, Elizabeth Interview date: 03/08/76
Abstract: 1 page(s)
Repository: George Mason University
This is an untaped interview, a one-page abstract is available.

**Mesa, Fernando**
Discusses: FTP Participated in: FTP
Position: Stage Manager Location: FL
Interviewer: O'Connor, John Interview date: 03/15/77
Tape: 85 minutes Abstract: 2 page(s)
Repository: George Mason University
Closed during lifetime.

Interview also includes: Scott, Isabel and Caminiti, Ida
Description: Children's Theatre, Vaudeville Unit.

**Messenger, Ivan**(b.1895)
Discusses: FAP Participated in: FAP
Position: Artist Location: CA
Interviewer: Hoag, Betty Lochrie   Interview date: 07/31/64
Transcript: 14 pages
Repository: Archives of American Art
Permission of interviewee needed.
Description: Worked on easel painting project in San Diego,
California.

**Messick, Ben Newton**(b.1901)
Discusses: FAP
Positions: Artist, Teacher
Interviewer: Hoag, Betty Lochrie   Interview date: 06/04/65
Transcript: 27 pages
Repository: Archives of American Art
Permission of interviewee needed.

**Meyer, Harriet B.**
Discusses: FTP Participated in: FTP
Position: Administrator
Interviewer: Krulak, Mae Mallory   Interview date: 08/20/75
Abstract: 9 page(s)
Repository: George Mason University
Description: Director of Research Bureau, Hallie Flanagan,
demise of FTP.

**Miller, Arthur**(b.1915)
Discusses: FTP Participated in: FTP
Position: Playreader
Interview date: 1958-60
Transcript: 44 pages
Repository: Columbia University
Series: Popular Arts

**Miller, Arthur**(b.1893)
Discusses: FAP Participated in: FAP
Position: Etcher
Interviewer: Hoag, Betty Lochrie   Interview date: 04/04/65
Transcript: 57 pages
Repository: Archives of American Art

**Miller, Carl**
Discusses: FMP Participated in: FMP

Positions: Administrator, Educator Location: NY
Interviewer: Knoblauch-Franc, Marion Interview date: 05/13/82
Transcript: 14 pages Tape: 30 minutes
Repository: George Mason University
Closed until 6/1/86.
Permission of interviewer until 5/31/87, open 6/1/87.
Description: Miller was on the staff of the FMP Educational Division in NYC and was active in promoting the programming of American works.

### Miller, Dorothy
Discusses: FAP Participated in: FAP
Position: Museum Curator Location: NY
Interviewer: Cummings, Paul Interview date: 1970
Transcript: 170 pages
Repository: Archives of American Art
Description: Assistant to Alfred Barr in the Museum of Modern Art, exhibits, staff acquisitions, other museums, galleries, artists, FAP.

### Miller, J. Howard
Discusses: FTP Participated in: FTP
Position: Administrator Locations: NY, CA
Interviewer: O'Connor, John Interview date: 10/18/77
Transcript: 26 pages Tape: 60 minutes Abstract: 2 page(s)
Repository: George Mason University
Description: LA project more balanced than NY, NY had most research talent, *Johnny Johnson*, *It Can't Happen Here*.

### Miller, J. Howard
Discusses: FTP Participated in: FTP
Position: Administrator Locations: NY, CA
Interviewer: Brown, Lorraine Interview date: 01/05/76
Transcript: 21 pages Tape: 65 minutes Abstract: 2 page(s)
Repository: George Mason University
Description: Experience prior to FTP, FTP in Calif, administrative duties, comparison of LA and NYC units, Living Newspapers.

### Moffett, Ross E.(1888-1971)
Discusses: FAP Participated in: FAP, SECT
Position: Artist Locations: RI, IL, MA
Interviewer: Seckler, Dorothy G. Interview date: 08/27/62
Transcript: 12 pages
Repository: Archives of American Art
Description: Murals, teaching, art schools in Chicago,

Provincetown Art Association.

**Monroe, Charles**
Discusses: FTP Participated in: FTP
Positions: Actor, Technician Location: WA
Interviewer: Brown, Lorraine Interview date: 11/09/78
Transcript: 51 pages Tape: 85 minutes Abstract: 2 page(s)
Repository: George Mason University
Closed to any government agency.
Description: Political views of actors in FTP.

**Moore, Gertrude Herdle**
Discusses: FAP
Position: Administrator Location: NY
Interviewer: Trovato, Joseph Interview date: 01/23/65
Transcript: 11 pages
Repository: Archives of American Art
Interview also includes: Krause, Erik Hans
Description: Director of the Rochester Memorial Art Gallery.

**Morang, Dorothy Alden C.(b.1906)**
Discusses: FAP Participated in: FAP
Position: Artist
Interviewer: Loomis, Sylvia Interview date: 12/03/64
Transcript: 13 pages
Repository: Archives of American Art
Permission of interviewee needed.

**Morcom, James S.**
Discusses: FTP Participated in: FTP
Position: Set Designer Location: NY
Interviewer: Brown, Lorraine Interview date: 05/10/77
Transcript: 32 pages Tape: 50 minutes Abstract: 2 page(s)
Repository: George Mason University
Description: His start with FTP, Orson Welles, Joseph Cotten, importance of FTP to workers, uniqueness of FTP, *Dr Faustus*, *Five Kings*.

**Moreau, Andres Francisco(b.1902)**
Discusses: FAP Participated in: FAP
Position: Artist
Interviewer: McChesney, Mary Fuller Interview date: 06/16/64
Transcript: 30 pages
Repository: Archives of American Art
Permission of interviewee needed.

**Morgenthau, Henry, Jr.(b.1891)**
Discusses: FAP Participated in: FAP, SECT, TRAP
Location: DC
Interviewers:   Rubenstein,  Lewis  and  Rubenstein,  Erica
Interview date:  11/09/64
Transcript:  7 pages
Repository:  Archives of American Art
Permission of interviewee needed.
No taping or note taking allowed during this interview.
Description:  Secretary of the Treasury under FDR, worked with Edward Bruce to support the federally-sponsored art projects.

**Morley, Grace L. McCann(b.1900)**
Discusses: FAP
Position: Museum Director Location: CA
Interviewer:  Riess, Suzanne B.  Interview date:  1960
Transcript:  246 pages
Repository:  University of California, Berkeley
Permission of archive needed.
Description:   Anton  Refregier,  murals  controversy,  San Francisco Museum of Art.

**Morris, Carl(b.1911)**
Discusses: FAP Participated in: FAP, SECT
Position: Administrator Locations: WA, OR
Interviewer:  Kendall, Sue Ann  Interview date:  03/24/83
Transcript:  44 pages
Repository:  Archives of American Art
Permission of interviewee needed.
Series:  Northwest Oral History Project
Description:  Director of Spokane Art Center through 1939, artists at Center, anecdotes about Clyfford Still, obtaining mural commission in Eugene.

**Morris, David(b.1911)**
Discusses: PWAP, WPA, FAP Participated in: PWAP, WPA, FAP
Positions: Clerical Worker, Administrator Location: DC
Interviewer:   McChesney,  Mary  Fuller   Interview  date: 05/04/64
Transcript:  63 pages
Repository:  Archives of American Art
Permission of interviewee needed.
Description:  Worked as a model on PWAP, clerical worker for WPA, District of Columbia supervisor for the FAP.

**Morris, James Stovall(b.1898)**
Discusses: FAP Participated in: FAP
Position: Artist
Interviewer: Loomis, Sylvia Interview date: 05/14/64
Transcript: 10 pages
Repository: Archives of American Art
Permission of interviewee needed.

**Morris, Lawrence S.(1904-1972)**
Discusses: WPA, FTP Participated in: WPA
Position: Administrator Location: NY
Interviewer: Brown, Lorraine Interview date: 01/77
Abstract: 3 page(s)
Repository: George Mason University
This is an untaped interview, a three-page abstract is available.
Description: Role of FTP in promoting an American theatre rather than an extension of the London theatre, FTP a turning point for theatre.

**Morris, Lawrence S.(1904-1972)**
Discusses: WPA Participated in: WPA
Position: Administrator Location: DC
Interviewer: Mangione, Jerre Interview date: 05/17/68
Repository: University of Rochester
Series: Mangione Collection
Description: WPA's administrative supervisor for the four arts programs.

**Morris, Lawrence S.(1904-1972)**
Discusses: WPA Participated in: WPA
Positions: Writer, Editor Location: DC
Interviewer: Phillips, Harlan Interview date: 1964
Transcript: 113 pages
Repository: Archives of American Art

**Morris, Robert Max(b.1909)**
Discusses: FAP
Position: Architect Location: CO
Interviewer: Johnson, Charles Interview date: 07/19/79
Tape: 30 minutes
Repository: Denver Public Library
Series: Federal Art in Colorado, 1934-1943
Description: Architectural models.

**Morrison, Richard C.**
Discusses: PWAP, FAP Participated in: PWAP, FAP
Position: Administrator Location: MA

Interviewer: Phillips, Harlan  Interview date:  07/07/65
Transcript:  40 pages
Repository:  Archives of American Art
Permission of interviewee needed.
Description:  New England Regional Director for the FAP.


**Moss, Carlton**
Discusses: FTP  Participated in: FTP
Position: Director  Location: NY
Interviewer:  Brown, Lorraine  Interview date:  08/06/76
Transcript:  51 pages  Tape: 75 minutes  Abstract:  2 page(s)
Repository:  George Mason University
Description:  Background, hired by FTP, John Houseman, *Walk Together Chillun.*


**Moxom, Jack(b.1913)**
Discusses: PWAP, FAP  Participated in: PWAP, FAP
Positions: Artist, Muralist  Location: CA
Interviewer:  McChesney, Mary Fuller  Interview date: 01/09/65
Transcript:  35 pages
Repository:  Archives of American Art
Interview also includes:  Stackpole, Hebe Daum


**Moxom, Marshall(b.1916)**
Discusses: NYA, FAP  Participated in: NYA
Position: Photographer  Location: CA
Interviewer:  McChesney, Mary Fuller  Interview date: 06/17/65
Transcript:  14 pages
Repository:  Archives of American Art
Description:  Head of Northern Calif. NYA photography project, photographed FAP works of art.


**Moy, Seong(b.1921)**
Discusses: FAP  Participated in: FAP
Positions: Artist, Printmaker  Locations: MI, NY
Interviewer:  Cummings, Paul  Interview date:  01/18/71
Transcript:  34 pages
Repository:  Archives of American Art
Description:  Experiences as a student at FAP School and St. Paul School of Art, printmaking at Walker Art Center, Art Students League, Hans Hofmann.


**Moya Del Pino, Jose(1891-1969)**
Discusses: PWAP, FAP  Participated in: PWAP, FAP, SECT
Positions: Artist, Muralist  Locations: CA, TX

Interviewer: McChesney, Mary Fuller   Interview date: 09/10/64
Transcript: 42 pages
Repository: Archives of American Art
Description: Coit Tower mural, Post Office murals in Stockton, Calif, Alpine, Texas, Redwood City and Lancaster, Calif, Golden Gate Exhibition 1939.

**Mumford, Lewis(b.1895)**
Interviewers: Rubenstein, Lewis and Rubenstein, Erica
Transcript: 8 pages
Repository: Archives of American Art
Permission of interviewee needed.
This is an untaped interview.
Description: Index of American Design.

**Murray, Donald**
Discusses: FTP Participated in: FTP
Position: Playwright Location: CA
Interviewer: Wickre, Karen Interview date: 07/20/77
Transcript: 37 pages Tape: 110 minutes Abstract: 3 page(s)
Repository: George Mason University
Interview also includes: Meredith, Betty Arden
Description: FTP accused of spending too much time on rehearsals, *Sun Rises*, *Class of '29*, *Six Characters*, *Like Falling Leaves*.

**Murray, Justin(b.1912)**
Discusses: FAP Participated in: FAP
Position: Artist Location: CA
Interviewer: McChesney, Mary Fuller
Transcript: 23 pages
Repository: Archives of American Art
Permission of interviewee needed.
Description: On San Francisco FAP easel painting project in 1938.

**Muse, Clarence(b.1889)**
Discusses: FTP Participated in: FTP
Positions: Actor, Director Location: CA
Interviewer: Brown, Lorraine Interview date: 01/04/76
Transcript: 26 pages Tape: 65 minutes Abstract: 2 page(s)
Repository: George Mason University
Also available at Hatch-Billops Collection Inc.
Description: Strong political influences in FTP, long rehearsals, *Run Little Chillun*, *Something About Joe*, various performers.

**Muse, Clarence(b.1889)**
Discusses: FTP Participated in: FTP
Positions: Actor, Director Location: CA
Interviewers: Hatch, James V. and Billops, Camille Interview date: 12/30/71
Tape: 120 minutes Abstract: 1 page(s)
Repository: Hatch-Billops Collection, Inc.
Permission of archive needed.
Description: Plays, theatre groups, Hollywood, Frank Capra, other actors.

**Nadel, Sue Remos**
Discusses: FTP Participated in: FTP
Position: Dancer Location: NY
Interviewer: Wickre, Karen Interview date: 10/23/77
Transcript: 69 pages Tape: 125 minutes Abstract: 4 page(s)
Repository: George Mason University
Interview also includes: Paula Bass Perlowin
Description: Mood of the 1930s, beginnings of Federal Dance Project in 1936, dance background.

**Neff, Earl**
Discusses: FAP Participated in: FAP, TRAP
Position: Administrator Location: OH
Interviewer: Harrison, Helen A. Interview date: 11/29/74
Tape: 90 minutes
Repository: George Mason University
Closed pending release.
Description: Administrator of the Cleveland FAP (1938-39), Communist influence, airport murals.

**Newhall, Beaumont(b.1908)**
Discusses: FAP Participated in: FAP
Position: Administrator Location: MA
Interviewer: Lynes, Russell Interview date: 1970-72
Repository: Archives of American Art
Permission of Newhall and Lynes.
Description: Thirty-two taped interviews done by interviewer for his book, *The Good Old Modern.*

**Newhall, Beaumont(b.1908)**
Discusses: FAP, FSA Participated in: FAP
Position: Administrator Location: MA
Interviewer: Trovato, Joseph Interview date: 01/23/65
Transcript: 29 pages
Repository: Archives of American Art
Description: Administration of FAP in Mass., photography as

art, FSA photography project, 1937 photo exhibit at Museum of Modern Art, photographers.

**Norford, George T.**
Discusses: FTP
Position: Playwright Location: NY
Interviewer: Brown, Lorraine Interview date: 10/25/76
Abstract: 1 page(s)
Repository: George Mason University
This is an untaped interview, a one-page abstract is available.
Description: FTP as genesis of Negro participation in American theatre and as incubator of talent.

**North, Alex(b.1910)**
Discusses: FTP Participated in: FTP
Position: Composer Location: NY
Interviewer: Crowther, Bosley Interview date: 04/07/63
Tape: 60 minutes
Repository: Yale University
Permission of archive needed.
Tape acquired from radio station WQXR, New York, N.Y.
Description: Composed and arranged music for *Life and Death of An American* and *Sing For Your Supper*.

**Norvelle, Lee R.(b.1892)**
Discusses: FTP Participated in: FTP
Position: Administrator Location: IN
Interviewer: Wickre, Karen Interview date: 07/11/79
Transcript: 29 pages Tape: 60 minutes Abstract: 2 page(s)
Repository: George Mason University
Description: Experiences as state director of the Indiana FTP.

**Norvelle, Lee R.(b.1892)**
Discusses: FTP Participated in: FTP
Position: Administrator Location: IN
Interviewer: Doud, Richard Interview date: 06/23/64
Transcript: 26 pages
Repository: Archives of American Art
Description: State director of the Indiana FTP, his education and interest in theater, working with Hallie Flanagan, public reaction to the FTP.

**O'Hanlon, Anne Rice**
Discusses: FAP Participated in: FAP
Position: Artist Location: CA
Interviewer: Gelber, Steven Interview date: 02/19/75
Tape: 110 minutes

Repository: University of Santa Clara
Series: New Deal Art: California
Interview also includes: O'Hanlon, Richard
This interview is on 1" videotape and needs special equipment
to be viewed.

**O'Hanlon, Richard E.**(b.1906)
Discusses: FAP, PWAP, TRAP Participated in: FAP, PWAP,
TRAP
Positions: Artist, Sculptor Location: CA
Interviewer: Gelber, Steven Interview date: 02/19/75
Tape: 110 minutes
Repository: University of Santa Clara
Series: New Deal Art: California
Interview also includes: O'Hanlon, Anne
This interview is on 1" videotape and needs special equipment
to be viewed.

**O'Hanlon, Richard E.**(b.1906)
Discusses: FAP, PWAP, TRAP Participated in: FAP, PWAP,
TRAP
Positions: Artist, Sculptor Location: CA
Interviewer: Ferbrache, Lewis Interview date: 03/04/64
Transcript: 31 pages
Repository: Archives of American Art

**Ocko, Edna**
Discusses: FTP Participated in: FTP
Position: Dancer
Interview date: 1981
Tape: 60 minutes
Repository: New York University
Series: Oral History of the American Left
Description: Member of the FTP Dance Project in the 1930s,
form and content in radicalism and modern dance.

**Oehser, Paul**(b.1904)
Position: Editor Location: DC
Interviewer: Henson, Pamela Interview date: 1974-75
Transcript: 173 pages Tape: 360 minutes Abstract: 1 page(s)
Transcript is indexed.
Repository: Smithsonian Institution Archives
Permission of archive needed.
Description: Smithsonian radio program, "The World is Yours,"
which used unemployed actors and writers.

**Olmsted, Anna Wetherill**

Discusses: PWAP
Position: Museum Director Location: NY
Interviewer: Freundlich, Dean Interview date: 10/22/64
Transcript: 7 pages
Repository: Archives of American Art
Permission of interviewee needed.
Description: Chairman of Central New York Committee PWAP, Syracuse Museum of Fine Art.

**Opper, John**(b.1908)
Discusses: FAP Participated in: FAP
Position: Artist Locations: NY, IL, OH
Interviewer: Sandler, Irving Interview date: 09/01/68
Transcript: 64 pages
Repository: Archives of American Art
Description: Cleveland and Chicago art schools, FAP, artists who influenced his work, American Artists Union, American Artists Congress.

**Ortmayer, Constance**(b.1902)
Discusses: SECT Participated in: SECT
Positions: Sculptor, Teacher Locations: FL, AL
Interviewer: Doud, Richard Interview date: 06/09/65
Transcript: 20 pages
Repository: Archives of American Art
Permission of interviewee needed.

**Ott, Peterpaul**(b.1895)
Discusses: FAP, SECT Participated in: FAP, SECT
Position: Sculptor Location: IL
Interviewer: Hoag, Betty Lochrie Interview date: 06/24/65
Transcript: 48 pages
Repository: Archives of American Art

**Ottenheimer, Albert M.**
Discusses: FTP
Positions: Publicist, Actor Location: WA
Interviewer: O'Connor, John Interview date: 01/10/78
Transcript: 17 pages Tape: 60 minutes
Repository: George Mason University
Closed during lifetime.
Description: *In Abraham's Bosom*, hired as a non-relief worker on publicity.

**Packard, Emmy Lou**(b.1914)
Discusses: FAP Participated in: FAP
Positions: Artist, Muralist Location: CA

Interviewer: McChesney, Mary Fuller  Interview date: 05/11/64
Transcript: 39 pages
Repository: Archives of American Art
Description: Work on the Treasure Island mural.


**Page, Ruth**(b.1900)
Discusses: FTP Participated in: FTP
Positions: Dancer, Choreographer Location: IL
Interviewer: Wickre, Karen Interview date: 04/24/79
Transcript: 21 pages Tape: 40 minutes Abstract: 2 page(s)
Repository: George Mason University
Closed pending release.
Description: Hallie Flanagan, prejudice, *Frankie and Johnny*, *American Pattern*, political overtones, messages in FTP productions.


**Page, Ruth**(b.1900)
Discusses: FTP Participated in: FTP
Positions: Dancer, Choreographer Location: IL
Interviewer: Gruen, John Interview date: 02/17/76
Tape: 55 minutes Abstract: 1 page(s)
Repository: New York Public Library
Permission of archive needed.
Series: "The Sound of Dance"
This is a phonotape recorded by WNCN-FM, New York.
Description: Memories of Anna Pavlova, Adolf Bolm and his "Ballet Intime," economics of ballet during 1930s, FTP, various shows, operas.


**Page, Ruth**(b.1900)
Discusses: FTP Participated in: FTP
Positions: Dancer, Choreographer Location: IL
Interviewer: Wentink, Andrew Mark  Interview date: 09/09/74
Abstract: 1 page(s)
Repository: New York Public Library
Permission of archive needed.
There are three 5" phonotape reels.
Description: Childhood, FTP in Chicago, Adolf Bolm, Pavlova, other famous dancers.


**Painter, Arthur C.**(b.1911)
Discusses: FMP, FAP Participated in: FMP, FAP
Position: Administrator Location: CA
Interviewer: McChesney, Mary Fuller  Interview date: 12/02/64

Transcript: 38 pages
Repository: Archives of American Art
Permission of interviewee needed.
Description: Publicity and public relations for the FMP in San Francisco, transferred to FAP as director of information.

**Palmer, William C.(b.1906)**
Discusses: SECT, PWAP Participated in: SECT, PWAP
Positions: Muralist, Artist Locations: NY, DC, IA
Interviewer: Trovato, Joseph Interview date: 06/12/65
Transcript: 9 pages
Repository: Archives of American Art
Description: Murals in New York City and Washington D.C.

**Palmer, William C.(b.1906)**
Discusses: SECT, PWAP Participated in: SECT, PWAP
Positions: Muralist, Artist Locations: NY, DC, IA
Interviewer: Brown, Robert Interview date: 08/05/80
Repository: Archives of American Art
Untranscribed, two 5" tapes.
Description: Education and background, his murals in New York City and Washington D.C.

**Parker, Thomas C.**
Discusses: FAP Participated in: FAP
Position: Administrator
Interviewer: Phillips, Harlan Interview date: 10/14/63
Transcript: 33 pages
Repository: Archives of American Art
Permission of interviewee needed.
Description: Regional director of the twelve southern states for the FAP.

**Parks, Gordon(b.1912)**
Discusses: FSA Participated in: FSA
Position: Photographer
Interviewer: Doud, Richard Interview date: 12/30/64
Transcript: 16 pages
Repository: Archives of American Art
Description: Joined FSA in 1942 as a Rosenwald Fellow.

**Parshall, Douglass Ewell(b.1899)**
Discusses: FAP
Position: Artist
Interviewer: Hoag, Betty Lochrie Interview date: 06/04/65
Transcript: 16 pages
Repository: Archives of American Art

Permission of interviewee needed.

**Partridge, Charlotte R.**
Discusses: FAP
Position: Artist
Interviewer: Phillips, Harlan
Transcript: 50 pages
Repository: Archives of American Art
Permission of interviewee needed.

**Peat, Wilbur D.**
Discusses: PWAP Participated in: PWAP
Position: Administrator Location: IN
Interviewer: Doud, Richard Interview date: 06/25/64
Transcript: 17 pages
Repository: Archives of American Art
Permission of interviewee needed.
Description: State director of the PWAP in Indiana.

**Pendergast, Malina D.(b.1905)**
Discusses: FAP Participated in: FAP
Positions: Artist, Administrator Location: CA
Interviewer: McChesney, Mary Fuller Interview date: 10/25/64
Transcript: 29 pages
Repository: Archives of American Art
Description: Director of the Sacramento Art Center 1938.

**Penney, James(1910-1982)**
Discusses: FAP Participated in: FAP, SECT
Positions: Muralist, Artist Locations: NY, MO
Interviewer: Trovato, Joseph Interview date: 05/19/64
Transcript: 19 pages
Repository: Archives of American Art
Description: Murals for schools and hospitals, administration of the FAP, coming to NYC in the Depression.

**Penney, James(1910-1982)**
Discusses: FAP Participated in: FAP, SECT
Positions: Muralist, Artist Locations: NY, MO
Interviewer: Brown, Robert Interview date: 1981
Repository: Archives of American Art
Untranscribed, two 5" tapes.
Description: Education at Univ. of Kansas and Art Students League, work with Moses Soyer on FAP murals in New York City.

**Pereira, Irene Rice**(1907-1971)
Discusses: FAP Participated in: FAP
Position: Artist Locations: MA, NY
Interviewer: Selvig, Forrest Interview date: 08/26/68
Transcript: 61 pages
Repository: Archives of American Art
Permission of Djelloul Marbrook.
Description: Background, FAP and Laboratory of Design, Art Students League, her poetry and written work, difficulties with Museum of Modern Art.

**Perkins, Frances**(1880-1965)
Discusses: WPA
Position: Administrator Location: DC
Interview date: 1955
Transcript: 5566 pages
Repository: Columbia University
Permission required to quote.
Available on microfiche, part III.
Description: Lengthy career as Federal administrator, includes years before and after serving as Secretary of Labor, (1933-45).

**Perry, Mary**
Discusses: FWP Participated in: FWP
Position: Administrator Location: NM
Interviewer: Loomis, Sylvia Interview date: 04/02/64
Transcript: 26 pages
Repository: Archives of American Art
Interview also includes: Laning, Clair
Description: Director of FWP in New Mexico.

**Peterson, Arthur**(b.1912)
Discusses: FTP Participated in: FTP
Position: Actor Location: IL
Interviewer: Brown, Lorraine Interview date: 07/22/77
Transcript: 15 pages Tape: 45 minutes Abstract: 2 page(s)
Repository: George Mason University
Description: Difficulties of early days, production of *Faust*, *Chalk Dust*, and *Amaco*.

**Pezman, Theodore**
Discusses: FTP Participated in: FTP
Position: Playwright Location: CA
Interviewer: Wickre, Karen Interview date: 10/26/77
Transcript: 15 pages Tape: 30 minutes Abstract: 1 page(s)
Repository: George Mason University

Description: Playwright's politics, long rehearsals, *Sun Rises in the West.*

**Phelps, Eleanor**
Discusses: FTP
Interviewer: Krulak, Mae Mallory Interview date: 12/13/75
Abstract: 2 page(s)
Repository: George Mason University
This is an untaped interview, a two-page abstract is available.
Description: Actress and student of Hallie Flanagan, her relationship with Flanagan.

**Philips, David M.(b.1913)**
Discusses: FAP Participated in: FAP
Position: Artist Location: CO
Interviewer: Christy, Helen Interview date: 08/24/79
Tape: 45 minutes
Repository: Denver Public Library
Series: Federal Art in Colorado, 1934-1943

**Phillips, Wendell**
Discusses: FTP Participated in: FTP
Position: Director Location: NY
Interviewer: Krulak, Mae Mallory Interview date: 05/27/76
Transcript: 34 pages Tape: 75 minutes Abstract: 2 page(s)
Repository: George Mason University
Description: Background, Welles' method and psyche, *Tommy, Cradle, Dr Faustus.*

**Pierce, Evelyn**
Discusses: FTP Participated in: FTP
Position: Administrator Location: NY
Interviewer: Brown, Lorraine Interview date: 11/10/78
Tape: 60 minutes
Repository: George Mason University
Description: Director of Casting, Talent Bureau, New York City FTP.

**Pinska, Klarna**
Discusses: FTP Participated in: FTP
Position: Dancer
Interviewer: Wickre, Karen Interview date: 02/28/78
Tape: 90 minutes Abstract: 2 page(s)
Repository: George Mason University
Description: FTP provided government recognition for dance.

**Poland, Reginald**

Discusses: PWAP, FAP Participated in: PWAP, FAP
Position: Museum Director Location: CA
Interviewer: Doud, Richard Interview date: 06/08/65
Transcript: 23 pages
Repository: Archives of American Art
Permission of interviewee needed.
Description: Director of Fine Arts Gallery in San Diego, government support for the arts.

   **Pollock, Jackson(1912-1956)**
Discusses: FAP Participated in: FAP
Position: Artist Location: NY
Interviewer: Wright, William Interview date: 1954
Transcript: 3 pages
Repository: Archives of American Art
Permission of New York AAA office.
Description: Did 50 FAP paintings, most of which have been lost, meaning of modern art, painting methods, abstract painting compared to music.

   **Pollock, Max**
Discusses: FTP Participated in: FTP
Position: Director Location: CA
Interviewer: Brown, Lorraine Interview date: 01/08/76
Transcript: 33 pages Tape: 65 minutes Abstract: 2 page(s)
Repository: George Mason University
Interview also includes: Warde, Francis and Freud, Mayfair
Description: Hallie Flanagan, honesty of FTP productions, temporary influence of American theatre, *Uncle Vanya*, *Alien Corn*, vaudeville unit.

   **Pollock, Merlin F.(b.1905)**
Discusses: FAP Participated in: FAP, PWAP, SECT
Positions: Artist, Administrator Locations: WI, IL, AK
Interviewer: Trovato, Joseph Interview date: 12/05/64
Transcript: 13 pages
Repository: Archives of American Art

   **Pollock, Merlin F.(b.1905)**
Discusses: FAP Participated in: FAP, PWAP, SECT
Positions: Artist, Administrator Locations: IL, WI, AK
Interviewer: Brown, Robert Interview date: 1979
Repository: Archives of American Art
Untranscribed, three 5" tapes.
Description: Training at the Art Institute of Chicago, supervisor of mural painting for the Illinois FAP 1940-43.

**Polos, Theodore C.(1902-1976)**
Discusses: FAP
Position: Artist
Interviewer:    McChesney, Mary Fuller    Interview date:
01/31/65
Transcript: 29 pages
Repository:  Archives of American Art

**Pomeroy, Florette White(b.1913)**
Discusses: FAP, FTP, FWP Participated in: FAP, FTP, FWP
Position: Administrator Location: CA
Interviewer:  Morris, Gabrielle  Interview date:  1982
Transcript: 383 pages  Abstract:  1 page(s)
Transcript is indexed.
Repository:  University of California, Berkeley
Description:  Worked closely with statewide administration,
observed FTP and FWP, extensive discussion of California
relief activities.

**Pomeroy, Florette White(b.1913)**
Discusses: FAP, RA Participated in: FAP, RA
Position: Administrator Location: CA
Interviewer:  Riess, Suzanne B.  Interview date:  1983
Abstract:  4 page(s)
Repository:  University of California, Berkeley
Description:  Federal art projects and contact between the FAP
offices.

**Ponch, Martin**
Discusses: FTP
Positions: Actor, Director Location: NY
Interviewer:  Krulak, Mae Mallory  Interview date:  05/26/76
Transcript: 11 pages  Tape: 60 minutes  Abstract:  2 page(s)
Transcript is indexed.
Repository:  George Mason University
Interview also includes:  Ponch, Nancy
Only partial transcript available.
Description:  Ponch did not work on FTP, but he discusses its
radicalism and critics as well as NYC Yiddish Theatre and
NYU Repertory Theatre.

**Pond, Donald**
Discusses: FTP
Position: Composer
Interviewer:  Wilson, Bruce D.  Interview date:  06/10/75
Repository:  University of Maryland
Description:  Music for *Young Tramps* for the FTP dance

project.

**Pond, Donald**
Discusses: FTP
Position: Composer
Interviewer: Wilson, Bruce D.    Interview date:  06/16/76
Repository:  University of Maryland
Description:  Music for the dance project of the FTP.

**Poole, Valter**
Discusses: FMP Participated in: FMP
Position: Conductor Location: MI
Interviewer:  Brown, Rae Linda  Interview date:  04/28/83
Transcript:  33 pages
Repository:  George Mason University
Closed pending release.
Description:   Detroit Symphony Orchestra, Michigan WPA
Symphony Orchestra (1937-38), became the conductor in 1938.

**Poole, Valter**
Discusses: FMP Participated in: FMP
Position: Conductor Location: MI
Interviewer:  Ehrlich, Heyward  Interview date:  1964
Transcript:  23 pages
Repository:  Archives of American Art

**Poor, Henry Varnum(1888-1970)**
Discusses: FAP Participated in: FAP, SECT
Positions: Artist, Muralist Locations: DC, CA
Interviewer:  Phillips, Harlan  Interview date:  1964
Transcript:  25 pages
Repository:  Archives of American Art
Description:  Murals for Departments of Interior and Justice,
early art training, Edward Bruce, painting and sculpture.

**Porter, Don**
Discusses: FTP Participated in: FTP
Position: Actor Locations: CA, OR
Interviewer:  Brown, Lorraine  Interview date:  01/08/76
Abstract:  1 page(s)
Repository:  George Mason University
This is an untaped interview, a one-page abstract is available.
Description:  *Taming of the Shrew, Alien Corn, Judgment Day.*

**Post, George Booth(b.1906)**
Discusses: FAP
Position: Artist

Interviewer: Ferbrache, Lewis  Interview date: 04/09/64
Transcript: 13 pages
Repository: Archives of American Art

**Preibisius, Hilda**
Discusses: FAP Participated in: FAP
Position: Artist Location: CA
Interviewer: Vitale, Lydia Modi  Interview date: 03/09/75
Tape: 30 minutes
Repository: University of Santa Clara
Series: New Deal Art: California
This interview is on 1" videotape and needs special equipment
to be viewed.

**Preibisius, Hilda**
Discusses: FAP Participated in: FAP
Position: Artist
Interviewer: Hoag, Betty Lochrie  Interview date: 08/01/64
Transcript: 35 pages
Repository: Archives of American Art
Permission of archive needed.
Interview also includes: Baranceanu, Belle

**Puccinelli, Raymond(b.1904)**
Discusses: FAP Participated in: FAP, PWAP
Position: Sculptor Location: CA
Interviewers: Teiser, Ruth and Harroun, Catherine Interview
date: 1974
Transcript: 76 pages
Repository: University of California, Berkeley
Permission of archive needed.
Description: A life history interview that includes a discussion
of his work on FAP, 1938-40.

**Pucinelli, Dorothy Wagner**
SEE: Cravath, Dorothy Wagner Pucinelli.

**Randall, Byron(b.1918)**
Discusses: FAP
Position: Artist
Interviewer: McChesney, Mary Fuller  Interview date:
05/12/64
Transcript: 32 pages
Repository: Archives of American Art
Permission of archive needed.

**Randolph, John**

Discusses: FTP Participated in: FTP
Position: Actor Location: NY
Interviewer: Bowers, Diane Interview date: 05/28/76
Transcript: 61 pages Tape: 130 minutes Abstract: 2 page(s)
Repository: George Mason University
Interview also includes: Randolph, Sarah Cunningham
Description: FTP's impact on Actors' Equity, influence on
theatrical world, FTP as a uniquely American experience,
*Turpentine.*

### Randolph, John
Discusses: FTP Participated in: FTP
Position: Actor Location: NY
Interviewer: O'Connor, John Interview date: 08/76
Tape: 110 minutes Abstract: 4 page(s)
Repository: George Mason University
Interview also includes: Lavery, Emmet and Lloyd, Norman
This is a videotape. This tape is also available at the NY Public
Library.
Description: FTP not tradition bound, tapped talent that had
been discarded.

### Rannells, Edward Warder(1892-1972)
Discusses: PWAP, FAP Participated in: PWAP
Position: Administrator Location: KY
Interviewer: Phillips, Harlan Interview date: 06/02/65
Transcript: 31 pages
Repository: Archives of American Art
Description: Director of PWAP for Lexington, Kentucky.

### Raphaelson, Samson(1896-1983)
Positions: Writer, Scriptwriter
Interview date: 1959
Transcript: 123 pages
Repository: Columbia University
Permission required to quote.
Series: Popular Arts
Description: Stage and film career, censorship.

### Rather, Lois Rodecap
Discusses: FTP Participated in: FTP
Positions: Researcher, Administrator Location: CA
Interviewer: Wickre, Karen Interview date: 08/24/79
Transcript: 21 pages Tape: 60 minutes Abstract: 2 page(s)
Repository: George Mason University
Description: WPA and FTP as employment opportunities.

**Rauch, Lillian Shapero**
Discusses: FTP Participated in: FTP
Position: Choreographer Location: NY
Interviewer: Wickre, Karen Interview date: 06/10/77
Tape: 60 minutes Abstract: 2 page(s)
Repository: George Mason University
Closed during lifetime.
Description: Devotion of participants to FTP.

**Reed, Florence**
Discusses: FAP
Position: Museum Director Location: WA
Interviewer: Bestor, Dorothy Interview date: 11/18/65
Transcript: 100 pages
Repository: Archives of American Art
Permission of Spokane Art Center.
Description: Group discussion-Spokane Art Center Board--
Guilbert, G., Irving, Mrs. H., Nelson, E.B., Weaver, E.

**Reef, Margaret S.(b.1903)**
Discusses: WPA Participated in: WPA
Position: Administrator Location: CO
Interviewer: Christy, Helen Interview date: 10/01/79
Tape: 80 minutes
Repository: Denver Public Library
Series: Federal Art in Colorado, 1934-1943

**Reese, Amos**
Discusses: FTP Participated in: FTP
Position: Playwright Location: NY
Interviewer: Brown, Lorraine Interview date: 07/20/77
Abstract: 1 page(s)
Repository: George Mason University
This is an untaped interview.
Description: Wrote radio scripts for FTP.

**Refregier, Anton(1905-1980)**
Discusses: FAP Participated in: FAP, SECT
Positions: Artist, Muralist Locations: NY, NJ, CA
Interviewer: Trovato, Joseph Interview date: 11/05/64
Transcript: 20 pages
Repository: Archives of American Art
Description: His involvement with FAP, government support
for the arts, murals he painted for FAP.

**Refregier, Anton(1905-1980)**
Discusses: FAP Participated in: FAP, SECT

Positions: Artist, Muralist Locations: NY, NJ, CA
Interviewer: Harrison, Helen A. Interview date: 01/02/75
Tape: 60 minutes
Repository: George Mason University
Closed pending release.
Description: John Reed Club, WPA buildings at the New York
World's Fair.

### Reich, Molka
Discusses: FTP Participated in: FTP
Positions: Administrator, Puppeteer Location: FL
Interviewer: O'Connor, John Interview date: 03/19/77
Transcript: 21 pages Tape: 60 minutes Abstract: 2 page(s)
Repository: George Mason University
Description: State director of the Florida marionette unit,
*Engaged, Chimes, Chalk Dust, Twelfth Night.*

### Reinhardt, Ad(1913-1967)
Discusses: FAP Participated in: FAP
Position: Artist Location: NY
Interviewer: Bowman, Ruth Interview date: 05/10/64
Transcript: 28 pages
Repository: Archives of American Art
Permission of widow needed.
Description: FAP easel painting project, the 1930s art scene,
censorship, exhibits, museums, social problems.

### Reinhardt, Ad(1913-1967)
Discusses: FAP Participated in: FAP
Position: Artist Location: NY
Interviewer: Phillips, Harlan
Transcript: 53 pages
Repository: Archives of American Art
Permission of widow needed.

### Rella, Ettore
Discusses: FTP
Position: Playwright Location: NY
Interviewer: O'Connor, John Interview date: 11/13/75
Tape: 35 minutes Abstract: 2 page(s)
Repository: George Mason University
Description: FTP rejected his play *Please Communicate*, never
employed by FTP.

### Remos, Sue
Discusses: FTP Participated in: FTP
Position: Dancer Location: NY

Interviewer: Wickre, Karen  Interview date:  02/20/78
Tape: 90 minutes  Abstract:  3 page(s)
Repository:  George Mason University
This is a videotape.
Description:  FTP dancers--demonstration and panel with Bass,
P., Barlin, A.L., Garnet, E., Geltmean, F., Gerrard, S., Mann,
L., Schaff, T.

**Rexroth, Kenneth**(1905-1982)
Discusses: PWAP, FAP  Participated in: PWAP
Positions: Artist, Muralist  Location: CA
Interviewer:  Martin, Minette  Interview date:  04/13/64
Transcript:  29 pages
Repository:  Archives of American Art
Description:  Chicago Art Institute, Art Students League, Coit
Tower murals, Maxine Albro.

**Rhodes, Irwin**
Discusses: FTP  Participated in: FTP
Positions: Administrator, Lawyer
Interviewer:  Brown, Lorraine  Interview date:  05/10/77
Transcript:  18 pages  Tape: 40 minutes  Abstract:  2 page(s)
Repository:  George Mason University
Description:  Discusses Helen Tamiris, Pierre DiRohan, Virgil
Geddes, Madalyn O'Shea, Flanagan's energy.

**Rhodes, Irwin**
Discusses: FTP  Participated in: FTP
Positions: Administrator, Lawyer
Interviewer:  Brown, Lorraine  Interview date:  02/26/77
Transcript:  51 pages  Tape: 80 minutes  Abstract:  2 page(s)
Repository:  George Mason University
Description:  Various units discussed, why FTP was attacked,
FTP in Congress, FTP influence on American theatre.

**Ribak, Louis**(1902-1980)
Discusses: FAP  Participated in: FAP
Position: Artist  Location: NM
Interviewer:  Loomis, Sylvia  Interview date:  07/20/64
Transcript:  18 pages
Repository:  Archives of American Art

**Rich, Daniel Catton**(1904-1976)
Discusses: FAP
Position: Museum Director  Location: IL
Interviewer:  Cummings, Paul  Interview date:  11/11/70
Transcript:  69 pages

Repository: Archives of American Art
Description: Director of Fine Arts at Chicago Art
Institute(1938-45), Director of Art Institute of Chicago(1945),
Century of Progress Exhibit.


**Rich, Shirley**
Discusses: FTP
Interviewer: Krulak, Mae Mallory Interview date: 11/09/76
Tape: 60 minutes
Repository: George Mason University
Interviewee not on the Federal Theatre Project.
Description: Collated Hallie Flanagan's personal papers to
prepare them for the NYPL Theatre Collection at Lincoln
Center, knew H.F. at Smith.


**Richards, Lavina**
Discusses: FAP Participated in: FAP
Position: Printmaker Location: MT
Interviewer: Hoag, Betty Lochrie Interview date: 09/28/65
Transcript: 36 pages
Repository: Archives of American Art
Interview also includes: La Branche, Dolores


**Richardson, Eudora Ramsey(1891-1973)**
Discusses: FWP Participated in: FWP
Position: Administrator Location: VA
Interviewers: Perdue, Charles and Perdue, Nan Interview date:
08/21/72
Transcript: 10 pages
Repository: In possession of interviewers
Permission of interviewers needed.
Contact: Charles Perdue, Dept. of English, University of
Virginia.
Description: State director of FWP for Virginia.


**Rickey, George W.(b.1907)**
Discusses: SECT Participated in: SECT
Positions: Sculptor, Muralist Locations: NY, PA
Interviewer: Trovato, Joseph Interview date: 07/17/65
Transcript: 20 pages
Repository: Archives of American Art
Permission of interviewee needed.


**Rickey, George W.(b.1907)**
Discusses: SECT Participated in: SECT
Positions: Sculptor, Muralist Locations: NY, PA
Interviewer: Cummings, Paul Interview date: 06/11/68

Transcript: 53 pages
Repository: Archives of American Art
Permission of interviewee needed.


**Robbins, LeRoy**
Discusses: FAP Participated in: FAP
Position: Artist Location: CA
Interviewer: Vitale, Lydia Modi Interview date: 03/13/75
Tape: 85 minutes
Repository: University of Santa Clara
Series: New Deal Art: California
This interview is on 1" videotape and needs special equipment
to be viewed.


**Roberts, Gordon**
Discusses: FTP Participated in: FTP
Position: Actor Location: OH
Interviewer: Brown, Lorraine Interview date: 10/30/77
Transcript: 21 pages Tape: 60 minutes
Transcript is indexed.
Repository: George Mason University
Permission of archive needed.
Description: FTP played to 750,000 school children who were
seeing theatre for the first time, community nature of FTP.


**Roberts, Malcolm**
Discusses: FAP Participated in: FAP
Positions: Artist, Muralist
Interviewer: Bestor, Dorothy Interview date: 05/26/65
Transcript: 28 pages
Repository: Archives of American Art
Permission of interviewee needed.
Description: Watercolors, Maritime Building, lithographs.


**Robinson, Earl(b.1910)**
Discusses: FTP Participated in: FMP, FTP
Position: Composer Location: NY
Interviewer: O'Connor, John Interview date: 08/09/76
Transcript: 46 pages Tape: 80 minutes Abstract: 3 page(s)
Repository: George Mason University
Description: Early life, job in the theatre, red tape caused
lengthy rehearsals, *Processional, Life and Death of an
American.*


**Robinson, Earl(b.1910)**
Discusses: FMP, FTP Participated in: FMP, FTP
Position: Composer Location: NY

Interviewer: Dunaway, David  Interview date:  03/18/76
Transcript:  132 pages  Tape: 180 minutes
Repository:  In possession of interviewer
Permission of interviewer needed.
Contact:     David  Dunaway,  Dept.  of  English,  UNM-
Albuquerque.
Description:  Discussion of shift from avant-garde to traditional
American music, folklore efforts, the FTP's "Ballad for an
American".

**Robson, William N.**
Discusses: FTP Participated in: FTP
Positions: Playwright, Director Location: NY
Interviewer:  Wickre, Karen  Interview date:  09/13/77
Transcript:  28 pages  Tape: 60 minutes  Abstract:  2 page(s)
Repository:  George Mason University
Description:  Experiences with FTP radio programming, *No
Help Wanted, Julius Caesar*, problems of funding overtime
work.

**Rogers, Charles B.(b.1911)**
Discusses: SECT Participated in: SECT
Positions: Artist, Museum Director Location: KS
Interviewer:  Hoag, Betty Lochrie  Interview date:  1964
Transcript:  27 pages
Repository:  Archives of American Art

**Romano, Amelia**
Discusses: FTP Participated in: FTP
Position: Actress Location: NY
Interviewers:   Krulak,  Mae  Mallory  and  Maddox,  Jean
Interview date:  03/04/77
Transcript:  38 pages  Tape: 80 minutes  Abstract:  2 page(s)
Repository:  George Mason University
Description:  *Chalk Dust, Sing for Your Supper*, rehearsals,
discipline, energy, worth of regional theatre.

**Romano, Amelia**
Discusses: FTP Participated in: FTP
Position: Actress Location: NY
Interviewer: Goldman, Harry
Transcript:  13 pages
Repository:  Columbia University
Available 5 years after publication.
Series:  History of the Mercury Theatre
Description:  *Big Blow* and the female leading role.

**Rome, Harold**
Discusses: FTP Participated in: FTP
Position: Lyricist Location: NY
Interviewer: O'Connor, John Interview date: 03/13/80
Repository: George Mason University
Description: Wrote original lyrics for "Papa's Got A Job" under
the pseudonym of Hector Troy, *Sing For Your Supper*, *Pins
and Needles*.

**Rosati, James(b.1912)**
Discusses: FAP, FMP Participated in: FAP
Position: Sculptor Location: PA
Interviewer: Fesci, Sevim Interview date: 1968
Transcript: 52 pages
Repository: Archives of American Art
Permission of interviewee needed.
Description: Studying sculpting, the FAP, study of violin,
playing with Pittsburg String Orchestra.

**Rose, David(b.1910)**
Discusses: FAP
Positions: Artist, Illustrator Location: CA
Interviewer: Hoag, Betty Lochrie Interview date: 03/28/65
Transcript: 14 pages
Repository: Archives of American Art

**Rose, Julia Smead(b.1912)**
Discusses: FAP Participated in: FAP
Position: Secretary Location: CO
Interviewer: Bardwell, Lisa Interview date: 08/30/79
Tape: 30 minutes
Repository: Denver Public Library
Series: Federal Art in Colorado, 1934-1943

**Rosen, David(b.1912)**
Discusses: FAP Participated in: FAP
Positions: Artist, Muralist Location: NY
Interviewer: Hoag, Betty Lochrie Interview date: 1965
Transcript: 30 pages
Repository: Archives of American Art
Description: Assistant to Axel Horn on his mural commissions,
American Artists Union.

**Rosenberg, Harold**
Discusses: FWP Participated in: FWP
Positions: Writer, Editor Location: DC
Interviewer: Mangione, Jerre Interview date: 08/20/68

Repository: University of Rochester
Series: Mangione Collection
Description: Art editor on the national staff of the FWP.

**Rosenstock, Fred A.(b.1895)**
Discusses: FAP
Position: Art Dealer Location: CO
Interviewers: Schaefer, Elly and Christy, Helen Interview date: 09/21/79
Tape: 115 minutes
Repository: Denver Public Library
Series: Federal Art in Colorado, 1934-1943
Description: Art dealer's perspective on 1930s artists.

**Rosenwald, Janet**
Discusses: FAP Participated in: FAP
Position: Researcher
Interviewer: Loomis, Sylvia Interview date: 10/17/64
Transcript: 20 pages
Repository: Archives of American Art
Description: Index of American Design.

**Ross, Charlotte Rothstein(b.1912)**
Discusses: FAP Participated in: FAP
Position: Artist Location: IL
Interviewer: Hoag, Betty Lochrie Interview date: 05/10/65
Transcript: 27 pages
Repository: Archives of American Art
Permission of interviewees needed.
Interview also includes: Ross, Sam
Description: Easel project, American Artist Union officer.

**Ross, Sam(b.1912)**
Discusses: FWP Participated in: FWP
Position: Writer Location: IL
Interviewer: Hoag, Betty Lochrie Interview date: 05/10/65
Transcript: 27 pages
Repository: Archives of American Art
Permission of inteerviewees needed.
Interview also includes: Ross, Charlotte Rothstein
Description: American Guide Series, radio writers project.

**Rosskam, Edwin**
Discusses: FSA Participated in: FSA, RA
Position: Photographer
Interviewer: Doud, Richard Interview date: 08/03/65
Transcript: 70 pages

Repository: Archives of American Art
Interview also includes: Rosskam, Louise
Description: Education and background, joining the FSA and working with Roy Stryker, Dorothea Lange, and Richard Wright, political impact of FSA.

**Rosskam, Louise**
Discusses: FSA
Interviewer: Doud, Richard  Interview date: 08/03/65
Transcript: 70 pages
Repository: Archives of American Art
Interview also includes: Rosskam, Edwin

**Rosten, Norman**
Discusses: FTP  Participated in: FTP
Position: Playwright  Location: NY
Interviewer: O'Connor, John  Interview date: 11/14/75
Transcript: 32 pages  Tape: 60 minutes  Abstract: 3 page(s)
Repository: George Mason University
Description: FTP as nucleus of an acting group and company rather than original playwriting program, *One Third of a Nation*, *Dr. Faustus*.

**Roszak, Theodore**(b.1907)
Discusses: FAP  Participated in: FAP, PWAP
Positions: Sculptor, Artist  Locations: NY, IL
Interviewer: Phillips, Harlan  Interview date: 1963
Transcript: 508 pages
Repository: Archives of American Art
Description: Social upheaval in 1930s, FAP and the Design Laboratory, politics in art, the Depression, Chicago Art Institute, racial problems.

**Rothchild, Lincoln**(1902-1983)
Discusses: FAP  Participated in: FAP
Position: Sculptor  Location: NY
Interviewer: Phillips, Harlan  Interview date: 10/29/64
Transcript: 58 pages
Repository: Archives of American Art
Permission of Elizabeth Rothchild.
Publication restricted.

**Rothchild, Lincoln**(1902-1983)
Discusses: FAP  Participated in: FAP
Position: Sculptor  Location: NY
Interviewer: Trovato, Joseph  Interview date: 06/26/64
Transcript: 26 pages

Repository: Archives of American Art
Publication restriction.

**Rothstein, Arthur(b.1915)**
Discusses: FSA Participated in: FSA
Position: Photographer Location: NY
Interviewer: Doud, Richard Interview date: 05/25/64
Transcript: 31 pages
Repository: Archives of American Art

**Rothstein, Arthur(b.1915)**
Discusses: FSA Participated in: FSA
Position: Photographer Location: NY
Interviewer: Crane, Arthur Interview date: 12/68
Transcript: 17 pages
Repository: Archives of American Art
Description: Education and background, his philosophy of photography, positive impact of the FSA photography.

**Royse, Morton W.**
Discusses: FWP Participated in: FWP
Position: Writer Location: DC
Interviewer: Mangione, Jerre Interview date: 06/08/70
Repository: University of Rochester
Series: Mangione Collection
Description: Royse was national consultant for social-ethnic studies for FWP.

**Rubenstein, Lewis**
Discusses: FAP Participated in: FAP, PWAP, SECT
Position: Muralist Locations: MA, NY
Interviewer: Harrison, Helen A. Interview date: 12/14/78
Tape: 60 minutes
Repository: George Mason University
Closed pending release.
Description: Fresco painting.

**Rublee, Bertha Hellman**
Discusses: PWAP Participated in: PWAP
Position: Muralist Location: TX
Interviewer: Loomis, Sylvia Interview date: 05/13/65
Transcript: 14 pages
Repository: Archives of American Art
Permission of interviewee needed.
Description: Education at Pennsylvania Academy of Fine Arts, murals in Houston, Texas.

**Rufty, Hilton**
Discusses: FMP Participated in: FMP
Position: Administrator Location: VA
Interviewer: Doud, Richard Interview date: 11/16/63
Transcript: 13 pages
Repository: Archives of American Art
Permission of archive needed.
Description: Assistant to the Virginia FMP State Director,
Wilfred Pyle.

**Rush, Olive(1873-1966)**
Discusses: FAP Participated in: FAP, SECT, PWAP
Positions: Artist, Muralist Locations: NM, OK
Interviewer: Loomis, Sylvia Interview date: 11/13/63
Transcript: 14 pages
Repository: Archives of American Art
Description: Background and education, the Corcoran School
of Art, murals for the FAP in public buildings in Santa Fe,
public perception of FAP.

**Russak, Ben(b.1920)**
Discusses: FTP Participated in: FTP
Position: Administrator Location: NY
Interviewer: Brown, Lorraine Interview date: 02/19/76
Transcript: 18 pages Tape: 50 minutes
Repository: George Mason University
Permission of interviewee needed.
Description: FTP and the idea of a national theatre, head of
playwriting department in the National Service Bureau.

**Ryan, Beatrice Judd**
Discusses: FAP Participated in: FAP
Position: Administrator Location: CA
Interviewer: Ferbrache, Lewis Interview date: 02/02/64
Transcript: 27 pages
Repository: Archives of American Art
Description: Owned Gallery Beaux Arts in San Francisco
where many FAP artists exhibited, joined FAP in 1936 as State
Director of exhibition project.

**Saccaro, John(1913-1983)**
Discusses: FAP Participated in: FAP
Position: Artist Location: CA
Interviewer: McChesney, Mary Fuller Interview date:
06/18/64
Transcript: 37 pages
Repository: Archives of American Art

**Saccaro, John(1913-1983)**
Discusses: FAP Participated in: FAP
Position: Artist Location: CA
Interviewer: Karlstrom, Paul Interview date: 04/30/74
Transcript: 57 pages
Repository: Archives of American Art
Description: Background and education, abstract expressionism, California School of Art.

**Saks, Lemon**
Discusses: FAP
Position: Art Dealer Location: CO
Interviewer: Chapman, Anne Interview date: 06/13/79
Tape: 94 minutes
Repository: Denver Public Library
Series: Federal Art in Colorado, 1934-1943
Description: Art Dealer's perspective on FAP artists.

**Sanderson, Phillips(b.1908)**
Discusses: FAP Participated in: FAP
Position: Sculptor Location: AZ
Interviewer: Loomis, Sylvia Interview date: 04/01/65
Transcript: 21 pages
Repository: Archives of American Art
Description: Education at Chicago Art Institute, moved to Arizona for health, joined the FAP in 1936.

**Saul, Oscar**
Discusses: FTP Participated in: FTP
Positions: Playwright, Playreader Location: NY
Interviewer: Berenberg, Benedict Interview date: 06/10/77
Transcript: 20 pages
Repository: Berenberg MA thesis, Univ. of Wisc.
Interview also includes: Lantz, Louis
Transcript in interviewer's MA thesis. Tapes on permanent loan at the Wisconsin Historical Society.

**Saul, Oscar**
Discusses: FTP Participated in: FTP
Positions: Playwright, Playreader Location: NY
Interviewer: Bowers, Diane Interview date: 06/02/76
Abstract: 2 page(s)
Repository: George Mason University
Description: FTP gave people a chance to work creatively, *Medicine Show*, *Revolt of the Beavers*, and *Flight*.

**Saulter, Leon**(b.1908)
Discusses: FAP Participated in: FAP
Position: Sculptor
Interviewer: Hoag, Betty Lochrie Interview date: 11/19/64
Transcript: 71 pages
Repository: Archives of American Art
Permission of interviewee needed.

**Saunders, Wardell**
Discusses: FTP Participated in: FTP
Position: Actor Location: NY
Interviewer: Brown, Lorraine Interview date: 10/27/77
Abstract: 1 page(s)
Repository: George Mason University
Description: *Macbeth* at the Layfayette Theatre.

**Savage, George**
Discusses: FTP Participated in: FTP
Position: Playwright Location: WA
Interviewer: O'Connor, John Interview date: 01/06/76
Tape: 50 minutes Abstract: 3 page(s)
Repository: George Mason University
Closed during Guy Williams'lifetime.
Interview also includes: Gladys Savage, Guy Williams
Description: How plays were chosen.

**Sawyer, Charles Henry**(b.1906)
Discusses: FAP
Position: Museum Director Location: MI
Interviewer: Ehrlich, Heyward Interview date: 1964
Transcript: 23 pages
Repository: Archives of American Art

**Saxe, Al**(d.1979)
Discusses: FTP Participated in: FTP
Position: Director Location: NY
Interviewer: O'Connor, John Interview date: 03/18/77
Transcript: 16 pages Tape: 60 minutes Abstract: 2 page(s)
Repository: George Mason University
Closed pending release.
Description: Director of Workers' Laboratory Theatre, FTP as
cultural spur, development of regional actors, playwrights,
impact on other art forms.

**Sazevich, Zygmund**
Discusses: FAP Participated in: FAP, TRAP, SECT
Position: Sculptor Locations: CA, WA

Interviewer: McChesney, Mary Fuller    Interview date: 01/22/65
Transcript: 19 pages
Repository: Archives of American Art
Permission of interviewee needed.


### Schaff, Janet
Discusses: FTP Participated in: FTP
Position: Dancer Location: NY
Interviewer: Wickre, Karen Interview date: 02/20/78
Tape: 90 minutes Abstract: 3 page(s)
Repository: George Mason University
Permission of archive needed.
This is a videotape.
Description: FTP dancers--demonstration and panel with Bass, P., Barlin, A. L., Garnet, E., Geltman, F., Gerrard, S., Mann, L., Remos, S.


### Schanker, Louis(b.1903)
Discusses: FAP Participated in: FAP
Positions: Printmaker, Artist Locations: CT, NY
Interviewer: Phillips, Harlan
Transcript: 74 pages
Repository: Archives of American Art


### Schenker, Augusta W.
Discusses: FTP Participated in: FTP
Position: Administrative Assistant Location: NY
Interviewer: Krulak, Mae Mallory Interview date: 03/02/77
Transcript: 35 pages Tape: 80 minutes Abstract: 2 page(s)
Repository: George Mason University
Description: Worked for John Houseman, impression of Houseman, Virginia Welles, Arlene Francis.


### Scheuer, Suzanne(d.1984)
Discusses: PWAP Participated in: TRAP, SECT, PWAP
Position: Artist Locations: CA, TX
Interviewer: McChesney, Mary Fuller    Interview date: 07/29/64
Transcript: 30 pages
Repository: Archives of American Art


### Schmidt, Katherine(1898-1978)
Discusses: FAP Participated in: FAP
Position: Artist Locations: NY, OH, ME
Interviewer: Cummings, Paul Interview date: 12/06/69
Transcript: 55 pages

Repository: Archives of American Art
Permission of Irvine J. Schubert.
Description: Art Students League, Whitney Museum, Museum of Modern Art, the National Academy, FAP.

**Schnier, Jacques**
Discusses: FAP, PWAP Participated in: FAP, PWAP
Position: Artist Location: CA
Interviewer: Gelber, Steven Interview date: 02/27/75
Tape: 90 minutes
Repository: University of Santa Clara
Series: New Deal Art: California
This interview is on 1" videotape and needs special equipment to be viewed.

**Schnitzer, Marcella C.**
Discusses: FTP Participated in: FTP
Location: NY
Interviewer: O'Connor, John Interview date: 11/17/76
Transcript: 34 pages Tape: 120 minutes Abstract: 2 page(s)
Repository: George Mason University
Interview also includes: Robert Schnitzer
Description: Worked with the radio division in New York City.

**Schnitzer, Robert(b.1906)**
Discusses: FTP Participated in: FTP
Position: Administrator Locations: DE, CA, DC
Interviewer: O'Connor, John Interview date: 11/17/76
Transcript: 34 pages Tape: 120 minutes Abstract: 2 page(s)
Repository: George Mason University
Interview also includes: Schnitzer, Marcella Cisney
Description: Defense of FTP, Hallie Flanagan, role of radical groups, Eddie Goodman and experimental group, J. Howard Miller.

**Schnitzer, Robert(b.1906)**
Discusses: FTP Participated in: FTP
Position: Administrator Locations: DE, CA, DC
Interviewer: Krulak, Mae Mallory Interview date: 11/07/76
Transcript: 37 pages Tape: 75 minutes Abstract: 2 page(s)
Repository: George Mason University
Description: Early years with FTP, Flanagan's view of FTP functions of the FTP, the FTP at the San Francisco World's Fair.

**Schoolman, Mary Sackler**

Discusses: FTP Participated in: FTP
Position: Executive Secretary Location: NY
Interviewers: Brown, Lorraine and Bowers, Diane Interview
date: 06/22/76
Tape: 80 minutes Abstract: 2 page(s)
Repository: George Mason University
Closed during lifetime.
Description: Was executive secretary to Philip Barber, Director
of the NYC FTP, Living Newspapers, message plays, women's
causes, blacks.

### Schrager, Philip
Discusses: FTP, NYA Participated in: FTP, NYA
Position: Assistant Stage Manager Location: NY
Interviewer: Wickre, Karen Interview date: 02/28/79
Tape: 90 minutes Abstract: 3 page(s)
Repository: George Mason University
Closed until 3/24/89.
Description: NYA Radio Workship, camaraderie on FTP, value
of FTP, Living Newspapers.

### Schulman, Rose
Discusses: FTP Participated in: FTP
Position: Administrative Assistant Locations: PA, NJ
Interviewer: Schulman, Sol Interview date: 04/15/76
Transcript: 27 pages Tape: 60 minutes Abstract: 1 page(s)
Repository: George Mason University
Description: Jasper Deeter and 1930s black theatre, Deeter's
association with John Houseman.

### Schulman, Sol
Discusses: FTP
Location: NY
Interviewer: Bowers, Diane Interview date: 01/22/76
Tape: 100 minutes Abstract: 2 page(s)
Repository: George Mason University
Description: Not a member of FTP, he discusses Federal and
commercial theatre in the 1930s, black productions, actors,
Welles-Houseman productions.

### Schuman, William(b.1910)
Discusses: FMP
Position: Composer Location: NY
Interviewer: Knoblauch-Franc, Marion Interview date:
05/03/82
Transcript: 14 pages Tape: 30 minutes
Repository: George Mason University

Closed until 6/1/86.

Permission of interviewer until 5/31/87, open on 6/1/87.

Description: Composers' Forum Laboratory of NYC, speaking on behalf of the projects to the Chairman of the House Labor Committee.

**Schwankovsky, Frederick(b.1885)**
Discusses: FAP Participated in: FAP
Position: Artist
Interviewer: Hoag, Betty Lochrie Interview date: 03/01/65
Transcript: 29 pages
Repository: Archives of American Art
Permission of interviewee needed.
Description: Philadelphia Academy of Fine Arts.

**Scooler, Zvee**
Discusses: FTP Participated in: FTP
Position: Administrator Location: NY
Interviewer: O'Connor, John Interview date: 04/19/77
Transcript: 12 pages Tape: 30 minutes Abstract: 1 page(s)
Repository: George Mason University
Description: *We Live and Laugh, It Can't Happen Here*, Schooler was Director of the Anglo-Jewish Unit.

**Scott, Isabel**
Discusses: FTP Participated in: FTP
Position: Play Adapter Location: FL
Interviewer: O'Connor, John Interview date: 03/15/77
Tape: 85 minutes Abstract: 2 page(s)
Repository: George Mason University
Interview also includes: Mesa, Fernando, Caminiti, Ida
Description: FTP vaudeville, Children's Theatre Unit, her background.

**Seeger, Charles(1886-1979)**
Discusses: FMP Participated in: RA, FMP
Position: Administrator Location: DC
Interviewer: Perlis, Vivian Interview date: 03/16/70
Transcript: 70 pages Tape: 120 minutes
Transcript is indexed.
Repository: Yale University
Permission of archive needed.
Series: Major Figures in American Music
Description: Seeger was Assistant Director of the FMP.

**Seeger, Charles(1886-1979)**
Discusses: RA, FMP, FTP Participated in: RA, FMP

Position: Administrator Location: DC
Interviewer: Reuss, Dick Interview date: 06/67
Tape: 150 minutes
Repository: Indiana University
Permission of archive needed.
Description: Life history interview with emphasis on folk music.

**Seeger, Charles(1886-1979)**
Discusses: RA, FMP Participated in: RA, FMP
Position: Administrator Location: DC
Interviewer: Warren-Findley, Jannelle Interview date: 1973
Tape: 90 minutes
Repository: In possession of interviewer
Permission of interviewer required.
Contact: J. Warren-Findley, 2905 Pine Springs Rd, Falls Church, VA 22042.
Description: RA, FMP, and wartime projects at Pan American Union.

**Seeger, Charles(1886-1979)**
Discusses: FSA Participated in: RA, FMP
Position: Administrator Location: DC
Interviewer: Kahn, Ed Interview date: 1967
Tape: 120 minutes
Repository: In possession of interviewer
Permission of interviewer.
Description: His life, folk music, the Library of Congress, WPA, FSA, Pan American Union.

**Seeger, Charles(1886-1979)**
Discusses: RA, FMP Participated in: RA, FMP
Position: Administrator Location: DC
Interviewer: Dunaway, David
Transcript: 296 pages Tape: 360 minutes
Repository: In possession of interviewer
Serious researchers by application.
Series: Pete Seeger Project
Contact: David Dunaway, Dept. of English, UNM-Albuquerque.
Description: Seeger active in New Deal Folklore efforts, was Assistant Director of the FMP.

**Sepesky, Zolta(1898-1974)**
Discusses: FAP Participated in: FAP, SECT
Positions: Artist, Muralist Locations: MI, NY, IL
Interviewer: Woolfenden, W.E. Interview date: 01/13/63

Transcript: 65 pages
Repository: Archives of American Art
Permission of widow needed.
Description: FAP murals and other commissions, the Scarab
Club, exhibits, National Institute of Arts and Letters.

**Shahn, Ben**(1898-1969)
Discusses: PWAP, FSA Participated in: PWAP, FSA, SECT
Positions: Muralist, Photographer Locations: NY, OH, DC
Interviewer: Doud, Richard Interview date: 04/14/64
Transcript: 31 pages
Repository: Archives of American Art
Permission of widow needed.

**Shahn, Ben**(1898-1969)
Discusses: PWAP, FSA, SECT Participated in: PWAP, FSA,
SECT
Positions: Muralist, Photographer Locations: NY, OH, DC
Interviewer: Phillips, Harlan Interview date: 10/03/65
Transcript: 45 pages
Repository: Archives of American Art
Permission of widow needed.

**Shahn, Ben**(1898-1969)
Discusses: PWAP, FSA, SECT Participated in: PWAP, FSA,
SECT
Positions: Muralist, Photographer Locations: NY, OH, DC
Interviewer: Benison, Saul
Transcript: 154 pages
Repository: Columbia University
Permission needed to quote.

**Shaw, Zachary**
Discusses: FTP Participated in: FTP
Position: Puppeteer Location: NY
Interviewer: Wickre, Karen Interview date: 08/27/79
Transcript: 28 pages Tape: 60 minutes Abstract: 2 page(s)
Repository: George Mason University
Description: FTP union grievance chairman, marionette
performances in schools and YMCAs.

**Sheets, Nan**(b.1889)
Discusses: FAP Participated in: FAP, PWAP
Positions: Artist, Etcher Location: OK
Interviewer: Doud, Richard Interview date: 06/04/64
Transcript: 37 pages
Repository: Archives of American Art

Permission of interviewee needed.

**Sherman, Hiram**
Discusses: FTP Participated in: FTP
Position: Actor Location: NY
Interviewers:  Wickre, Karen and Maddox, Jean Interview date:
04/18/78
Transcript:  32 pages  Tape: 75 minutes  Abstract:  3 page(s)
Repository:  George Mason University
Description:  *Horse Eats Hat*, *Dr Faustus*, *Cradle Will Rock*,
*One Third of a Nation*, Orson Welles, Mercury Theatre.

**Sherman, James Russell(b.1907)**
Discusses: TRAP Participated in: TRAP, SECT
Position: Artist Location: CO
Interviewer:  Christy, Helen  Interview date:  08/20/79
Tape: 57 minutes
Repository:  Denver Public Library
Series:  Federal Art in Colorado, 1934-1943
Description:  Post Office mural in Loveland, Colorado.

**Sherman, Vincent**
Discusses: FTP Participated in: FTP
Positions: Playwright, Director Location: NY
Interviewer:  Berenberg, Benedict  Interview date:  06/25/77
Transcript:  12 pages
Repository:  Berenberg MA Thesis, Univ. of Wisc.
Transcript in interviewer's MA thesis. Tapes on permanent
loan, Wisc. State Historical Society.

**Sherman, Vincent**
Discusses: FTP Participated in: FTP
Positions: Playwright, Director Location: NY
Interviewer:  Brown, Lorraine  Interview date:  01/07/76
Repository:  George Mason University
This is an untaped interview.
Description:  A writer and playwright in New York during
FTP, he collaborated with Sinclair Lewis on *It Can't Happen
Here*, directed *Battle Hymn*.

**Sherman, Vincent**
Participated in: FTP
Positions: Playwright, Director Location: NY
Interviewer:  Goldman, Harry
Transcript:  23 pages
Repository:  Columbia University
Available 5 years after publication.

### Shibley, Eleanor Scherr
Discusses: FTP Participated in: FTP
Position: Actress Location: NY
Interviewer: Brown, Lorraine Interview date: 08/05/76
Abstract: 2 page(s)
Repository: George Mason University
Description: Began acting in CCC Camps, *Chalk Dust*, *Native Ground*, *Processional*, *Life and Death of An American*, and *Sing For Your Supper*.

### Shohet, Max
Discusses: FTP Participated in: FTP
Position: Publicist Location: NY
Interviewer: Wickre, Karen Interview date: 01/26/78
Transcript: 37 pages Tape: 150 minutes Abstract: 3 page(s)
Repository: George Mason University
Description: *Emperor's New Clothes*, *Prologue to Glory*, *The Big Blow*.

### Shonnard, Eugenie F.(b.1886)
Discusses: FAP Participated in: FAP, SECT
Positions: Sculptor, Designer Locations: NM, TX
Interviewer: Loomis, Sylvia Interview date: 1964
Transcript: 29 pages
Repository: Archives of American Art
Permission of interviewee needed.

### Shope, Irvin(1900-1977)
Discusses: PWAP Participated in: PWAP, SECT
Position: Artist Locations: SD, MT
Interviewer: Hoag, Betty Lochrie Interview date: 11/27/65
Transcript: 38 pages
Repository: Archives of American Art

### Shrewsberry, Robert
Discusses: FTP Participated in: FTP
Positions: Actor, Costume Designer Locations: IL, FL
Interviewer: Wickre, Karen Interview date: 06/11/77
Transcript: 24 pages Tape: 40 minutes Abstract: 2 page(s)
Repository: George Mason University
Description: *Enemy of the People*, *Faustus*, *O Say Can You Sing*, *Triple-A Plowed Under*, *Farmer Takes a Wife*, *If Ye Break Faith*.

### Shuster, Will(1893-1969)

Discusses: PWAP, FAP Participated in: PWAP, FAP
Positions: Artist, Muralist Location: NM
Interviewer: Loomis, Sylvia Interview date: 07/30/64
Transcript: 24 pages
Repository: Archives of American Art
Description: Frescos for PWAP, paintings of Carlsbad Caverns
for FAP.

**Shute, Ben E.**(b.1905)
Discusses: FAP
Position: Artist Location: GA
Interviewer: Doud, Richard Interview date: 06/04/65
Transcript: 15 pages
Repository: Archives of American Art

**Siegal, Fritz**
Discusses: FMP Participated in: FMP
Position: Concertmaster Location: IL
Interviewer: Knoblauch-Franc, Marion Interview date:
04/27/82
Transcript: 18 pages Tape: 60 minutes
Repository: George Mason University
Closed until 6/1/86.
Permission of interviewer until 5/31/87 open on 6/1/87.
Description: Concertmaster for the Illinios Symphony in 1936–
37 through 1938-39 seasons.

**Siegmeister, Elie**(b.1909)
Discusses: FMP Participated in: FMP
Position: Composer
Interviewer: Jory, Margaret Fairbank Interview date: 1967
Tape: 60 minutes
Repository: Yale University
Written permission of interviewee.
Series: Major Figures in American Music
Original interview is housed at New York Public Library.

**Siegmeister, Elie**(b.1909)
Discusses: FMP Participated in: FMP
Position: Composer Location: NY
Interview date: 1975
Transcript: 459 pages
Repository: Columbia University
Permission required to quote.
This interview is also at Yale University.
Description: Music, composing, organization of Soviet-
American Music Society.

**Siegmeister, Elie**(b.1909)
Discusses: FMP Participated in: FMP
Position: Composer Location: NY
Interviewer: Knoblauch-Franc, Marion Interview date: 05/08/82
Tape: 60 minutes
Repository: George Mason University
Closed pending release.
Description: Works performed at the FMP's Composers' Forum Laboratory in New York, wrote score for FTP's *Created Equal*.

**Siegriest, Louis Bassi**(b.1899)
Discusses: FAP Participated in: FAP
Positions: Artist, Muralist Location: CA
Interviewers: Gilb, Corrine L. and Mills, Paul Interview date: 1953
Transcript: 95 pages
Repository: University of California, Berkeley
Interview also includes: Siegriest, Lundy
Description: Mural painting, FAP posters, Golden Gate International Exposition.

**Sievan, Maurice**(1898-1981)
Discusses: FAP Participated in: FAP
Positions: Artist, Muralist
Interviewer: Sandler, Irving Interview date: 01/14/63
Transcript: 6 pages
Repository: Archives of American Art
Description: FAP, how titles relate to paintings.

**Sievan, Maurice**(1898-1981)
Discusses: FAP Participated in: FAP
Positions: Artist, Muralist
Interviewer: Seckler, Dorothy G. Interview date: 1965
Transcript: 55 pages
Repository: Archives of American Art
Description: Early art training, mural painting, FAP.

**Sills, Thomas Albert**(b.1914)
Discusses: FAP Participated in: FAP
Position: Artist Locations: NY, MS
Interviewer: Ghent, Henri Interview date: 07/13/68
Transcript: 28 pages
Repository: Archives of American Art
Permission of interviewee needed.
Description: Childhood, his work and techniques, FAP in

185

Mississippi, racisim, future of black artists in America.

**Silvera, John**
Discusses: FTP Participated in: FTP
Position: Playwright Location: NY
Interviewer: Brown, Lorraine Interview date: 07/11/77
Transcript: 14 pages Tape: 30 minutes Abstract: 1 page(s)
Repository: George Mason University
Description: FTP as door-opener, Workers' Alliance efforts for better conditions for blacks, *Walk Together Chillun*, *Turpentine*, *Haiti*.

**Silvera, John**
Discusses: FTP Participated in: FTP
Position: Playwright Location: NY
Interviewer: De Paur, Leonard Interview date: 11/77
Tape: 20 minutes Abstract: 1 page(s)
Repository: George Mason University
Interview also includes: Anderson, Tommy and Browne, Theodore
This is a videotape.
Description: *Macbeth*, budget problems.

**Silvera, John**
Discusses: FTP Participated in: FTP
Position: Playwright Location: NY
Interviewer: Brown, Lorraine Interview date: 07/11/77
Tape: 15 minutes Abstract: 2 page(s)
Repository: George Mason University
This is a videotape.
Description: FTP was greatest experience of his life, FTP helped break down racial barriers, *Macbeth*.

**Simon, Louis(b.1918)**
Discusses: FTP Participated in: FTP
Position: Administrator Locations: NJ, NY
Interviewer: O'Connor, John Interview date: 10/25/76
Transcript: 22 pages Tape: 150 minutes Abstract: 3 page(s)
Repository: George Mason University
Permission required to quote.
Description: State Director in NJ, Director in Rosslyn, NY, political problems, radicalism of some plays, conflict between state WPA and FTP, unions.

**Simon, Louis(b.1918)**
Discusses: FTP Participated in: FTP
Position: Administrator Locations: NJ, NY

Interviewer: O'Connor, John  Interview date:  12/28/76
Transcript:  32 pages  Tape: 90 minutes
Repository:  George Mason University
Permission required to quote.
Description:  State Director of NJ FTP unit and the Rosslyn, NY unit, Philip Barber, Hallie Flanagan, value and closing of FTP, politics.

### Simpson, Marian(b.1899)
Discusses: FAP
Position: Artist
Interviewer:  Ferbrache, Lewis  Interview date:  04/02/64
Transcript:  43 pages
Repository:  Archives of American Art
Permission of interviewee needed.

### Siporin, Mitchell(1910-1976)
Discusses: FAP Participated in: FAP, SECT, PWAP
Positions: Artist, Teacher Locations: IL, MO
Interviewer:  Swift, Geoffrey  Interview date:  11/11/65
Transcript:  47 pages
Repository:  Archives of American Art
Permission of Miriam Siporin needed.

### Sklar, George
Discusses: FTP Participated in: FTP
Position: Playwright Location: NY
Interviewer:  O'Connor, John  Interview date:  01/02/76
Transcript:  30 pages  Tape: 105 minutes
Repository:  George Mason University

### Slane, Michael Andrew
Discusses: FTP Participated in: FTP
Position: Director Location: CO
Interviewer:  Slane, Michael Andrew  Interview date:  05/79
Transcript:  88 pages  Tape: 227 minutes  Abstract:  6 page(s)
Repository:  George Mason University
A self-conducted interview.
Description:  Background, admiration for Hallie Flanagan, *Waiting for Lefty*, *Cinderella*, *Adding Machine*.

### Sloan, Raymond H.(1912-1981)
Discusses: FWP Participated in: FWP
Position: Field Worker Location: VA
Interviewers:  Perdue, Charles and Perdue, Nan Interview date: 06/17/78
Tape: 60 minutes  Abstract:  8 page(s)

Repository: In possession of the interviewers
Permission of interviewers.
Contact: Charles Perdue, Dept. of English, University of Virginia, 22904.

**Smith, Carlton Sprague**
Discusses: FMP Participated in: FMP
Location: NY
Interviewer: Knoblauch-Franc, Marion Interview date: 04/08/82
Transcript: 4 pages Tape: 30 minutes
Repository: George Mason University
Closed until 6/1/86.
Permission of interviewer until 5/31/87 open on 6/1/87.
Description: Composers' Forum and the music copying project.

**Smith, Charles S.,Jr.(b.1913)**
Discusses: FAP
Location: CO
Interviewer: Bardwell, Lisa Interview date: 01/20/80
Tape: 70 minutes
Repository: Denver Public Library
Series: Federal Art in Colorado, 1934-1943
Description: The work of FAP artist Hugh Weller.

**Smith, David(1906-1965)**
Discusses: FAP, TRAP Participated in: FAP, TRAP
Position: Sculptor Location: NY
Interviewer: Sylvester, David Interview date: 06/16/61
Transcript: 10 pages
Repository: Archives of American Art
Permission of interviewee's family.
Description: TRAP murals program, positive influences of FAP, his generation of artists and the government arts programs.

**Smith, Gordon Mackintosh(1906-1979)**
Discusses: FAP Participated in: FAP
Position: Administrator Location: MA
Interviewer: Phillips, Harlan
Transcript: 31 pages
Repository: Archives of American Art
Description: Assistant Regional Director for New England for Index of American Design.

**Smith, Margery Hoffman**

Discusses: WPA, FTP, FAP Participated in: WPA, FAP
Position: Administrator Location: OR
Interviewer: Phillips, Harlan
Transcript: 31 pages
Repository: Archives of American Art
Description: Development of Timberline Lodge for the FAP.

**Smith, Margery Hoffman**
Discusses: WPA, FTP, FAP Participated in: WPA, FAP
Position: Administrator Location: OR
Interviewer: Ferbrache, Lewis Interview date: 04/10/64
Transcript: 45 pages
Repository: Archives of American Art
Description: State Supervisor, Arts and Skills Projects' for
Oregon WPA, supervised work on Timberline Lodge for FAP,
WPA's World's Fair exhibit.

**Smith, Vernon B.(b.1894)**
Discusses: FAP Participated in: PWAP, FAP
Position: Administrator Location: MA
Interviewer: Swift, Geoffrey Interview date: 11/24/65
Transcript: 11 pages
Repository: Archives of American Art
Correspondence, journals, and personal papers are also in AAA.
Description: Supervisor for FAP for Cape Cod and
Southeastern Mass., 1936, 1938-40.

**Sokolow, Anna**
Discusses: FTP Participated in: FTP
Position: Choreographer Location: NY
Interviewer: Krulak, Mae Mallory Interview date: 11/09/76
Abstract: 2 page(s)
Repository: George Mason University
This is an untaped interview, a two-page abstract is available.
Description: FTP promotion of the Dance Project,
experimentation and creativity, dedication of FTP workers.

**Solman, Joseph**
Discusses: FAP Participated in: FAP
Position: Artist Location: NY
Interviewer: Harrison, Helen A. Interview date: 01/75
Tape: 40 minutes
Repository: George Mason University
Closed pending release.
Description: Realism, easel project, urban themes.

**Solomon, Izler**

Discusses: FMP Participated in: FMP
Positions: Conductor, Administrator Location: IL
Interviewer: Doud, Richard Interview date: 06/24/64
Transcript: 22 pages
Repository: Archives of American Art
Permission of interviewee needed.
Description: Head of FMP in Chicago, conductor of Illinois
Symphony under FMP.

**Sour, Robert**
Discusses: FTP Participated in: FTP
Position: Songwriter Location: NY
Interviewer: Brown, Lorraine Interview date: 10/31/77
Transcript: 16 pages Tape: 40 minutes Abstract: 2 page(s)
Repository: George Mason University
Description: *Sing For Your Supper*, government red tape, long
rehearsals, types of shows best done by FTP, problems of FTP
musicals.

**Spayde, Sydney**
Discusses: FTP
Position: Administrator Location: IA
Interviewer: Nash, Anedith Interview date: 07/19/82
Transcript: 26 pages Tape: 60 minutes
Repository: George Mason University
Assistant to E.C. Mabie.
Description: E.C. Mabie, conferred with H. Flanagan about
organizing regional theatres, Elmer Rice, Virgil Geddes,
decentralization of the theatre.

**Spivak, Max(1906-1981)**
Discusses: PWAP, FAP Participated in: PWAP, FAP
Positions: Artist, Designer Location: NY
Interviewer: Phillips, Harlan
Transcript: 58 pages
Repository: Archives of American Art
Description: Art training, Whitney Museum project, politics
and art, American Artists Union, American Artists Congress.

**Spohn, Clay(1898-1977)**
Discusses: FAP Participated in: FAP, SECT
Positions: Artist, Teacher Locations: NY, CA
Interviewer: Phillips, Harlan Interview date: 09/25/65
Transcript: 120 pages
Repository: Archives of American Art

**Spomer, Peter John(b.1906)**

Discusses: FAP Participated in: FAP
Position: Artist Location: CO
Interviewer: Bardwell, Lisa Interview date: 08/22/79
Tape: 60 minutes
Transcript is indexed.
Repository: Denver Public Library
Series: Federal Art in Colorado, 1934-1943
Description: Woodcuts for Colorado State Historical Society.

**Spurgeon, Sarah**(b.1903)
Discusses: FAP Participated in: FAP
Positions: Artist, Teacher
Interviewer: Bestor, Dorothy Interview date: 10/03/63
Transcript: 23 pages
Repository: Archives of American Art

**Stackpole, Hebe Daum**(b.1912)
Discusses: PWAP, FAP Participated in: PWAP, FAP
Positions: Artist, Muralist Location: CA
Interviewer: McChesney, Mary Fuller Interview date: 01/09/65
Transcript: 35 pages
Repository: Archives of American Art
Interview also includes: Moxom, Jack
Description: Coit Tower murals, San Francisco State University murals.

**Stanley, Edward**
Discusses: FSA
Position: Photographer Location: NY
Interviewer: Doud, Richard Interview date: 07/27/65
Transcript: 22 pages
Repository: Archives of American Art
Permission of interviewee needed.
Not a project participant.
Description: Was executive news photo editor for AP in 1930s, discusses FSA and news photography in 1930s.

**Staton, Joseph**
Discusses: FTP Participated in: FTP
Positions: Actor, Director Location: WA
Interviewer: O'Connor, John Interview date: 01/07/76
Transcript: 25 pages Tape: 60 minutes Abstract: 2 page(s)
Repository: George Mason University
Also available in the Hatch-Billops Collection, Inc.
Description: *Stevedore, Taming of the Shrew, Lysistrata,* racism, audiences.

**Stavis, Barrie**
Discusses: FTP Participated in: FTP
Position: Playwright
Interviewer: Krulak, Mae Mallory Interview date: 11/08/76
Transcript: 35 pages Tape: 75 minutes Abstract: 2 page(s)
Repository: George Mason University
Description: Confrontation with Flanagan over delayed
opening of *Sun and I.*

**Stein, Irene Miller(b.1895)**
Discusses: FAP
Position: Artist Location: CO
Interviewer: Schaefer, Elly Interview date: 10/09/79
Tape: 55 minutes
Repository: Denver Public Library
Series: Federal Art in Colorado, 1934-1943
Description: Did not work on FAP, but discusses many FAP
participants.

**Steinbrueck, Victor**
Discusses: PWAP Participated in: PWAP
Position: Illustrator Location: WA
Interviewer: Bestor, Dorothy Interview date: 11/03/65
Tape: 10 minutes
Repository: Archives of American Art
Description: Assigned to the PWAP in 1934 as an illustrator of
the CCC work camps, water colors, crayon sketches.

**Steinert, Alexander(1900-1982)**
Discusses: NYA Participated in: NYA
Position: Conductor Location: CA
Interviewer: Carrington, Mark Interview date: 01/06/82
Transcript: 25 pages Tape: 60 minutes
Transcript is indexed.
Repository: Yale University
Permission of archive needed.
Series: Major Figures in American Music
Description: Life and career, conductor of the NYA youth
orchestra in Los Angeles.

**Steinman, Mrs. Erwin**
Discusses: FAP Participated in: FAP
Position: Secretary Location: DC
Interviewer: Phillips, Harlan Interview date: 10/04/65
Transcript: 32 pages
Repository: Archives of American Art

Permission of interviewee needed.
Description: Secretary to Holger Cahill, Director of FAP.

**Stevens, Frank**
Discusses: FAP Participated in: FAP
Positions: Artist, Administrator
Interviewer: Hoag, Betty Lochrie Interview date: 06/02/64
Transcript: 52 pages
Repository: Archives of American Art
Permission of interviewee needed.
Description: Regional Director for part of the Northwest
Territory under Stanton McDonald-Wright.

**Stewart, George R.(b.1895)**
Discusses: FWP Participated in: FWP
Position: Writer Location: CA
Interviewer: Riess, Suzanne B. Interview date: 1971-72
Transcript: 319 pages
Transcript is indexed.
Repository: University of California, Berkeley
This interview is part of the book *A Little of Myself* by G.R.
Stewart.
Description: FWP, essays, plays.

**Still, William Grant(1895-1978)**
Discusses: FTP Participated in: FTP
Positions: Composer, Musician Location: NY
Interviewer: Gant, Liz Interview date: 11/22/72
Tape: 100 minutes Abstract: 1 page(s)
Repository: Hatch-Billops Collection, Inc.
Permission of archive needed.
Series: Major Figures in American Music
Also available at Yale University.
Description: Background and education, various compositions
for FTP.

**Stoll, John Theodor E.(b.1898)**
Discusses: PWAP Participated in: PWAP
Positions: Artist, Sculptor Location: CA
Interviewer: McChesney, Mary Fuller Interview date:
02/08/65
Transcript: 15 pages
Repository: Archives of American Art
Permission of interviewee needed.

**Stone, Bentley**
Discusses: FTP Participated in: FTP

Position: Dancer Location: IL
Interviewer: Wentink, Andrew Mark Interview date: 09/11/74
Tape: 70 minutes Abstract: 1 page(s)
Repository: New York Public Library
Permission of archive needed.
Interview also includes: Camryn, Walter
This is a phonotape.
Description: Working with Ruth Page, the Page-Stone Ballet, the Stone-Camryn School, FTP, dance during the Depression, *Guns and Castanets.*

### Stone, Gene
Discusses: FTP Participated in: FTP
Positions: Composer, Arranger Location: CA
Interviewer: Brown, Lorraine Interview date: 07/21/77
Transcript: 30 pages Tape: 60 minutes Abstract: 2 page(s)
Repository: George Mason University
Description: LA unit less political than NYC, *Two-A-Day*, *Revue of Revues*, *Follow the Parade*, *Ready.*

### Stover, Frederick
Discusses: FTP Participated in: FTP
Position: Set Designer Location: CA
Interviewer: Wickre, Karen Interview date: 06/08/77
Transcript: 24 pages Tape: 70 minutes Abstract: 3 page(s)
Repository: George Mason University
Description: FTP in LA started crudely, *Merchant of Venice*, *Run Little Chillun*, *House of Connelly*, *It Can't Happen Here.*

### Stryker, Roy Emerson(1893-1975)
Discusses: FSA, RA Participated in: FSA, RA
Position: Administrator Location: DC
Interviewer: Hurley, F. Jack Interview date: 1967
Tape: 120 minutes
Repository: Memphis State University
Description: Biography, photography projects, internal tensions, uniqueness of FSA, various participants.

### Stryker, Roy Emerson(1893-1975)
Discusses: FSA, RA Participated in: FSA, RA
Position: Administrator Location: DC
Interviewer: Doud, Richard Interview date: 10/17/63
Transcript: 38 pages
Repository: Archives of American Art

### Stryker, Roy Emerson(1893-1975)

194

Discusses: FSA, RA Participated in: FSA, RA
Position: Administrator Location: DC
Interviewer: Doud, Richard Interview date: 06/13/64
Transcript: 94 pages
Repository: Archives of American Art

**Stryker, Roy Emerson(1893-1975)**
Discusses: FSA, RA Participated in: FSA, RA
Position: Administrator Location: DC
Interviewer: Doud, Richard Interview date: 01/23/65
Transcript: 60 pages
Repository: Archives of American Art

**Stuckmann, Eugene**
Discusses: FTP, FWP Participated in: FTP, FWP
Positions: Actor, Researcher Location: NH
Interviewer: Bowers, Diane Interview date: 02/23/76
Transcript: 34 pages Tape: 80 minutes Abstract: 2 page(s)
Repository: George Mason University
Description: Background, value of FTP, the FTP stock
company, hostility of commercial theater managers and certain
Congressional leaders.

**Suib, Leonard**
Discusses: FTP Participated in: FTP
Position: Puppeteer Location: NY
Interviewers: Wickre, Karen and Maddox, Jean Interview date:
04/19/78
Tape: 55 minutes Abstract: 2 page(s)
Repository: George Mason University
Description: Grant Street Playhouse, finances and politics,
Living Newspapers.

**Sundgaard, Arnold(b.1909)**
Discusses: FTP Participated in: FTP
Position: Playwright Location: IL
Interviewer: O'Connor, John Interview date: 09/05/76
Transcript: 40 pages Tape: 75 minutes Abstract: 2 page(s)
Repository: George Mason University
Description: *Everywhere I Roam*, *Spirochete*, FTP provided
opportunities for playwrights.

**Swiggett, Jean**
Discusses: FAP, PWAP, SECT Participated in: FAP, PWAP,
SECT
Position: Artist Locations: CA, IN
Interviewer: Vitale, Lydia Modi Interview date: 03/11/75

Tape: 60 minutes
Repository: University of Santa Clara
Series: New Deal Art: California
This interview is on 1" videotape and needs special equipment
to be viewed.

**Talbot, Clarence**
Discusses: FTP Participated in: FTP
Positions: Playwright, Director Locations: WA, IA
Interviewer: Wickre, Karen Interview date: 07/21/77
Transcript: 31 pages Tape: 75 minutes Abstract: 3 page(s)
Repository: George Mason University
Description: Background, *Ah, Wilderness*, *Arms and the Man*.

**Tamotzu, Chuzo(1891-1975)**
Discusses: PWAP, FAP Participated in: PWAP, FAP
Position: Artist Location: NY
Interviewer: Loomis, Sylvia Interview date: 09/03/64
Transcript: 11 pages
Repository: Archives of American Art
Description: Easel project, graphic project.

**Taylor, Edgar J.**
Discusses: FAP Participated in: FAP
Position: Artist Location: CA
Interviewer: Hoag, Betty Lochrie Interview date: 04/05/65
Transcript: 18 pages
Repository: Archives of American Art
Permission of interviewee needed.
Description: Stained glass work in Oakland.

**Taylor, Farwell(1905-1977)**
Discusses: PWAP, FAP Participated in: PWAP, FAP
Position: Artist Location: CA
Interviewer: McChesney, Mary Fuller Interview date:
08/14/64
Transcript: 25 pages
Repository: Archives of American Art
Description: Ground colors for artists at Coit Tower,
watercolor project.

**Taylor, Frank(b.1903)**
Discusses: WPA Participated in: WPA
Position: Administrator Location: DC
Interviewers: Freilicher, Miriam and Henson, Pamela Interview
date: 02/27/74
Transcript: 60 pages Tape: 120 minutes Abstract: 1 page(s)

Transcript is indexed.
Repository: Smithsonian Institution Archives
Permission of archive needed.
HAMMS is Historical American Merchant Marine Survey.
Description: Smithsonian radio program, "The World is Yours,"
which used unemployed actors and writers, Assistant Director
of HAMMS.

**Teichman, Howard**(b.1916)
Discusses: FTP
Position: Stage Manager Location: NY
Interviewer: O'Connor, John Interview date: 04/18/77
Transcript: 19 pages Tape: 90 minutes Abstract: 2 page(s)
Repository: George Mason University
Closed pending release.
Description: Interviewee was not a part of FTP, FTP's
attempts at attracting audiences, critics response, Group
Theatre, Mercury Theatre.

**Terkel, Studs**
Discusses: FWP Participated in: FWP
Position: Writer Location: IL
Interviewer: Mangione, Jerre Interview date: 01/05/69
Repository: University of Rochester
Series: Mangione Collection

**Thall, Victor**(b.1902)
Discusses: FAP Participated in: FAP
Position: Artist Location: NY
Interviewer: Hoag, Betty Lochrie Interview date: 06/08/65
Transcript: 38 pages
Repository: Archives of American Art
Permission of interviewee needed.
Description: Art Students League, lithograph project, easel
project.

**Thiessen, Leonard**(b.1902)
Discusses: FAP Participated in: FAP
Position: Administrator Location: IA
Interviewer: Phillips, Harlan Interview date: 06/10/65
Transcript: 36 pages
Repository: Archives of American Art
Description: Appointed by Helen Cresswell to be supervisor of
the production project in Des Moines, Index of American
Design.

**Thomas, Grace**(b.1884)

Discusses: FAP Participated in: FAP
Position: Artist Location: NM
Interviewer: Loomis, Sylvia Interview date: 11/05/64
Transcript: 11 pages
Repository: Archives of American Art
Permission of interviewee needed.
Description: Index of American Design, Vernon Hunter, antique furniture.

### Thomas, Howard
Discusses: PWAP Participated in: PWAP
Positions: Artist, Administrator Location: WI
Interviewer: Doud, Richard Interview date: 06/03/65
Transcript: 19 pages
Repository: Archives of American Art
Interview also includes: Wescott, Harold
Description: Worked on the Milwaukee arts and craft project, division director.

### Thomas, Ted
Discusses: FTP Participated in: FTP
Positions: Director, Writer Location: NY
Interviewer: O'Connor, John Interview date: 10/19/77
Transcript: 23 pages Tape: 60 minutes Abstract: 2 page(s)
Repository: George Mason University
Closed pending release.
Description: Theatrical director #891 unit, Living Newspapers, Welles, Houseman, Flanagan, politics of FTP, weaknesses and strengths of FTP.

### Thompson, Donald
Discusses: FWP Participated in: FWP
Positions: Writer, Administrator Location: NY
Interviewer: Mangione, Jerre Interview date: 11/17/68
Repository: University of Rochester
Series: Mangione Collection
Description: Appointed acting head of the New York City FWP in the summer of 1937, union troubles.

### Thomson, Virgil(b.1896)
Discusses: FTP Participated in: FTP
Positions: Composer, Musical Director Location: NY
Interviewer: Perlis, Vivian Interview date: 1977–78
Transcript: 107 pages Tape: 240 minutes
Transcript is indexed.
Repository: Yale University
Permission of archive needed.

Series: Major Figures in American Music
Several other interviews with Thomson are available at Yale.
Description: His life and career in music.

**Thomson, Virgil**(b.1896)
Discusses: FTP Participated in: FTP
Positions: Composer, Musical Director Location: NY
Interviewer: Knoblauch-Franc, Marion Interview date: 05/11/82
Transcript: 10 pages Tape: 30 minutes
Repository: George Mason University
Closed until 6/1/86.
Permission of interviewer needed until 5/31/87 open from 6/1/87.
Description: Composers' Forum, *Horse Eats Hat*, *Injunction Granted*.

**Thomson, Virgil**(b.1896)
Participated in: FTP
Positions: Composer, Musical Director Location: NY
Interview date: 1985
Repository: Columbia University
Closed pending release.
Description: Background, music education, musical theatre in the United States.

**Thomson, Virgil**(b.1896)
Discusses: FTP Participated in: FTP
Positions: Composer, Musical Director Location: NY
Interviewer: Brown, Lorraine Interview date: 11/05/76
Tape: 90 minutes
Repository: George Mason University
Description: Musical director of the #891 unit in New York City.

**Thwaites, Charles**
Discusses: TRAP Participated in: TRAP, PWAP, FAP
Position: Muralist Locations: MN, MI, WI
Interviewer: Reid, George Interview date: 08/10/77
Transcript: 9 pages Tape: 30 minutes
Repository: Minnesota Historical Society
Series: Federal Art in Minnesota
Description: His mural painted for the Post Office in Windom, MN.

**Tolegian, Manuel Jerier**(d.1983)
Discusses: FAP Participated in: FAP

Position: Artist Location: CA
Interviewer: Hoag, Betty Lochrie Interview date: 02/12/65
Transcript: 58 pages
Repository: Archives of American Art

**Tomkins, Margaret(b.1916)**
Discusses: FAP
Positions: Artist, Educator Location: WA
Interviewer: Guenther, Bruce Interview date: 06/06/84
Transcript: 39 pages Tape: 75 minutes
Repository: Archives of American Art
Series: Northwest Oral History Project
Description: Tomkins taught art and art history on voluntary basis, her husband James Fitzgerald was director of Spokane Art Center 1940-41.

**Totten, Donald(b.1903)**
Discusses: FAP Participated in: FAP
Positions: Artist, Muralist Location: CA
Interviewer: Hoag, Betty Lochrie Interview date: 05/28/64
Transcript: 25 pages
Repository: Archives of American Art
Description: Art Students League.

**Traher, William Henry(b.1908)**
Discusses: FAP Participated in: FAP, SECT
Positions: Artist, Muralist Locations: CO, AR
Interviewer: Bardwell, Lisa Interview date: 08/10/79
Tape: 111 minutes
Repository: Denver Public Library
Series: Federal Art in Colorado, 1934-1943
Description: His woodcuts for the Colorado State Historical Society.

**Traher, William Henry(b.1908)**
Discusses: FAP Participated in: FAP, SECT
Positions: Artist, Muralist Locations: CO, AR
Interviewer: Loomis, Sylvia Interview date: 11/13/64
Transcript: 22 pages
Repository: Archives of American Art

**Tribble, Charles(b.1910)**
Discusses: FAP Participated in: FAP
Position: Artist Location: CO
Interviewer: Christy, Helen Interview date: 09/24/79
Tape: 65 minutes
Repository: Denver Public Library

Series: Federal Art in Colorado, 1934-1943
Description: His woodcuts for the Colorado State Historical
Society.

**Triest, Shirley Staschen(b.1914)**
Discusses: FAP Participated in: FAP
Position: Artist Location: CA
Interviewer: McChesney, Mary Fuller Interview date: 1964
Transcript: 47 pages
Repository: Archives of American Art
Description: Graphic Art Division of FAP, colored lithographs
done by Alberte Spratt in San Francisco.

**Trubach, Serge(b.1912)**
Discusses: TRAP, PWAP, FAP Participated in: TRAP, PWAP,
FAP
Position: Artist Location: NY
Interviewer: McChesney, Mary Fuller Interview date:
12/05/64
Transcript: 29 pages
Repository: Archives of American Art
Permission of interviewee needed.
Description: Artist grievence committee, being jailed in New
York City, easel painting project.

**Tugwell, Rexford G.**
Discusses: RA Participated in: RA
Position: Administrator Location: DC
Interviewer: Doud, Richard Interview date: 01/21/65
Transcript: 28 pages
Repository: Archives of American Art
Permission of Grace Tugwell needed.
Description: Under Secretary of Agriculture, conceived the
idea of RA.

**Turner, Ida McAfee(b.1897)**
Discusses: TRAP Participated in: TRAP, SECT
Positions: Artist, Muralist Locations: CO, NM, TX
Interviewer: Hardwick, Bonnie Interview date: 08/02/79
Tape: 30 minutes
Repository: Denver Public Library
Series: Federal Art in Colorado, 1934-1943
Description: TRAP mural for the Post Office in Gunnison,
Colorado.

**Tworkov, Jack(1900-1982)**
Discusses: FAP Participated in: FAP, PWAP

Position: Artist Location: NY
Interviewer: Seckler, Dorothy G. Interview date: 08/17/62
Transcript: 10 pages
Repository: Archives of American Art
Description: FAP, political activities of artists in the 1930s,
relationship with other artists, galleries in New York.

**Tyler, Converse**(b.1903)
Discusses: FTP Participated in: FTP
Position: Administrator Location: NY
Interviewers: O'Connor, John and Schulman, Sol Interview
date: 12/15/76
Transcript: 27 pages Tape: 75 minutes Abstract: 2 page(s)
Repository: George Mason University
Description: Receipt and review of scripts, turnover of
playreaders, black theatre, Living Newspapers, FTP style,
Hallie Flanagan.

**Uhler, Ruth Pershing**(1898-1969)
Discusses: FAP
Position: Artist
Interviewer: Loomis, Sylvia Interview date: 05/11/65
Transcript: 14 pages
Repository: Archives of American Art

**Ulbricht, Elsa Emilie**(b.1885)
Discusses: FAP
Positions: Artist, Craftperson
Interviewer: Ehrlich, Heyward Interview date: 1964
Transcript: 37 pages
Repository: Archives of American Art

**Utley, Tabor**(1891-1978)
Discusses: FAP Participated in: FAP, PWAP
Positions: Artist, Muralist Location: CO
Interviewer: Loomis, Sylvia Interview date: 11/11/64
Transcript: 15 pages
Repository: Archives of American Art
Description: Studied with Boardman Robinson, mural for the
Colorado Springs City Auditorium.

**Vachon, John**
Discusses: RA, FSA Participated in: RA, FSA
Position: Administrator Location: DC
Interviewer: Doud, Richard Interview date: 04/28/64
Transcript: 23 pages
Repository: Archives of American Art

Description: Wrote captions for RA photos, in charge of the classification of the files.

**Vaerlen, Basil**
Discusses: FWP Participated in: FWP
Positions: Writer, Administrator Location: CA
Interviewer: Mangione, Jerre Interview date: 07/05/68
Repository: University of Rochester
Series: Mangione Collection
Description: Supervisor of the San Francisco office of the FWP, demoted after shake up.

**Valiant, Margaret(1901-1982)**
Discusses: RA, NYA, FSA Participated in: RA, FSA, NYA
Position: Administrator
Interviewers: Warren-Findley, Jannelle and Evans, Cheryl
Interview date: 4&6/79
Tape: 360 minutes
Transcript is indexed.
Repository: Mississippi State University
Permission of interviewers needed.
Description: RA Homesteads, FSA migrant camps and Washington.

**Van Veen, Stuyvesant**
Discusses: FAP Participated in: FAP, SECT, PWAP
Position: Muralist Locations: NY, PA
Interviewer: Harrison, Helen A. Interview date: 02/26/75
Tape: 50 minutes
Repository: George Mason University
Closed pending release.
Description: Architects, painters, and sculptors collaborative.

**Vanderbilt, Paul(b.1905)**
Discusses: FSA
Positions: Librarian, Archivist Location: DC
Interviewer: Doud, Richard Interview date: 11/10/64
Transcript: 36 pages
Repository: Archives of American Art
Description: Worked with Roy Stryker on the FSA files.

**Velarde, Pablita(b.1918)**
Discusses: FAP Participated in: FAP, PWAP
Positions: Artist, Illustrator Location: NM
Interviewer: Loomis, Sylvia Interview date: 09/29/65
Transcript: 19 pages
Repository: Archives of American Art

Permission of interviewee needed.

**Velie, Jay**
Discusses: FTP Participated in: FTP
Position: Actor Location: NY
Interviewer: Wickre, Karen Interview date: 05/24/78
Transcript: 27 pages Tape: 55 minutes Abstract: 2 page(s)
Repository: George Mason University
Description: *Little Jesse James*, *Corialanus*, *Open Storage*,
FTP kept actors in their profession.

**Velonis, Anthony(b.1911)**
Discusses: FAP Participated in: FAP
Positions: Artist, Designer Location: NY
Interviewer: Phillips, Harlan Interview date: 10/13/65
Transcript: 38 pages
Repository: Archives of American Art
Permission of interviewee needed.

**Vogel, Joseph(b.1911)**
Discusses: TRAP, FAP Participated in: TRAP, FAP
Positions: Muralist, Lithographer Location: NY
Interviewer: Hoag, Betty Lochrie Interview date: 01/05/65
Transcript: 80 pages
Repository: Archives of American Art
Permission of interviewee needed.

**Volz, Herman(b.1904)**
Discusses: FAP Participated in: FAP
Position: Artist Location: CA
Interviewers: Vitale, Lydia Modi and Gelber, Steven Interview
date: 02/28/75
Tape: 180 minutes
Repository: University of Santa Clara
Series: New Deal Art: California
This interview is on 1" videotape and needs special equipment
to be viewed.

**Volz, Herman(b.1904)**
Discusses: FAP Participated in: FAP
Position: Artist Location: CA
Interviewer: McChesney, Mary Fuller Interview date:
06/27/64
Transcript: 91 pages
Repository: Archives of American Art

**Von Meyer, Michael(b.1894)**

Discusses: FAP Participated in: FAP
Position: Sculptor Location: CA
Interviewer:    McChesney, Mary Fuller    Interview date:
02/12/65
Transcript: 21 pages
Repository:  Archives of American Art
Permission of interviewee needed.

   Voris, Mark(1907-1974)
Discusses: PWAP Participated in: PWAP
Positions: Teacher, Artist Location: AZ
Interviewer: Loomis, Sylvia Interview date:  02/11/65
Transcript: 27 pages
Repository:  Archives of American Art

   Vorse, Mary Heaton(1881-1966)
Discusses: FWP
Location: MA
Interview date:  1957
Transcript:  73 pages
Repository:  Columbia University
Permission required to quote.
Not on the FWP, friend of Henry Alsberg.
Description:  Lawrence strike, Elizabethtown, Tenn. textile
strike, I.W.W., Soviet Russia.

   Wallace, Lea
Discusses: FTP Participated in: FTP
Position: Dancer Location: NY
Interviewer:  Burch, Jeanne S.  Interview date:  06/13/80
Tape: 45 minutes  Abstract: 2 page(s)
Repository:  George Mason University
Description:  *Salut Au Monde*, *How Long Brethren*, *Trojan
Incident*, seventeen when she joined FTP, supported her
parents with FTP salary, Tamiris.

   Ward, Theodore(b.1902)
Discusses: FTP Participated in: FTP
Positions: Playwright, Actor Location: IL
Interviewer:  Brown, Lorraine  Interview date:  08/13/76
Transcript: 26 pages  Tape: 65 minutes  Abstract: 2 page(s)
Repository:  George Mason University
Description:  *Big White Fog*, value of FTP.

   Ward, Theodore(b.1902)
Discusses: FTP Participated in: FTP
Positions: Playwright, Actor Location: IL

Interviewers:  Hatch, James V. and Billops, Camille Interview date:  04/07/74
Tape: 240 minutes
Transcript is indexed.
Repository:  Hatch-Billops Collection, Inc.
Permission of archive needed.
Description:  Early years, founding Negro Playwrights Co., writing *Big White Fog*, *John Brown*, *Our Lan'*, *Whole Hog*, Harlem Renaissance.

**Warde, Frances**
Discusses: FTP Participated in: FTP
Position: Actress Location: CA
Interviewer:  Brown, Lorraine  Interview date:  01/08/76
Transcript:  33 pages  Tape: 65 minutes  Abstract:  1 page(s)
Transcript is indexed.
Repository:  George Mason University
Interview also includes:  Pollock, Max and Mayfair Freud
Description:  Her work in plays directed by Max Pollock.

**Wardell, Thomas**
Discusses: FAP Participated in: FAP
Position: Administrator Location: AZ
Interviewer:  Loomis, Sylvia  Interview date:  03/30/65
Transcript:  22 pages
Repository:  Archives of American Art
Description:  Director of the FAP in Arizona from (1940-43).

**Warren, Marijane**
Discusses: FAP Participated in: FAP
Position: Artist Location: WA
Interviewer:  Bestor, Dorothy  Interview date:  11/12/65
Transcript:  19 pages
Repository:  Archives of American Art
Permission of interviewee needed.
Description:  Worked on FAP in Seattle as a graduate student of the University of Washington.

**Warren, William L.**
Discusses: FAP Participated in: FAP
Position: Administrator Location: CT
Interviewer:  Swift, Geoffrey  Interview date:  10/11/65
Transcript:  15 pages
Repository:  Archives of American Art
Permission of interviewee needed.
Description:  Assistant Director of the FAP in Connecticut, Index of American Design.

**Warsaegar, Hyman J.**(b.1909)
Discusses: FAP
Positions: Printmaker, Artist
Interviewer: Phillips, Harlan  Interview date:  10/14/65
Transcript:  48 pages
Repository:  Archives of American Art
Permission of interviewee needed.

**Washington, James W. Jr.**(b.1909)
Discusses: FAP
Positions: Artist, Sculptor Location: WA
Interviewer: Bestor, Dorothy  Interview date:  10/13/65
Transcript:  15 pages
Repository:  Archives of American Art

**Wasserman, Dale**
Discusses: FTP Participated in: FTP
Positions: Stage Manager, Lighting Technician Location: CA
Interviewer: Medovoy, George  Interview date:  01/23/73
Tape: 65 minutes  Abstract:  2 page(s)
Repository:  George Mason University
Description:  Long rehearsals, no set schedule, no opening
dates, *Awake and Sing*, *String of Pearls*, *When Will He Die*,
*Relatives*.

**Wasserman, Dale**
Discusses: FTP Participated in: FTP
Positions: Stage Manager, Lighting Technician Location: CA
Interviewer: Krulak, Mae Mallory  Interview date:  05/30/76
Transcript:  50 pages  Tape: 100 minutes  Abstract:  3 page(s)
Repository:  George Mason University
Description:  Budget problems at FTP's Yiddish Theatre, FTP
was highly compartmentalized, FTP strangled by politics.

**Watkins, Franklin**(1894-1971)
Discusses: PWAP Participated in: PWAP
Positions: Artist, Administrator Location: PA
Interviewer: Cummings, Paul  Interview date:  08/18/71
Transcript:  57 pages
Repository:  Archives of American Art
Description:  Member of PWAP Selection Committee,
background education, cultural life in Philadelphia, 1930s-
1950s, his techniques.

**Watson, Betty Ferguson**
Discusses: FAP, WPA

Location: MN
Interviewer: Paull, Irene  Interview date: 1968
Tape: 70 minutes
Repository: Minnesota Historical Society
Research only, permission needed.
Series: Finnish Radicals
Interview also includes: Watson, Chester
Husband was the state organizer and Pres. Minn. Workers Alliance.
Description: The FAP, People's Lobby, WPA strike, unemployment movement 1936-1940.

### Wayne, June(b.1918)
Discusses: FAP
Positions: Artist, Lithographer  Locations: IL, NY
Interviewer: Cummings, Paul  Interview date: 08/06/70
Transcript: 66 pages
Repository: Archives of American Art
Permission of interviewee needed.
Description: Background, Chicago in the Depression, her painting methods and techniques, the FAP and her first jobs.

### Wayne, June(b.1918)
Discusses: FAP
Positions: Artist, Lithographer  Location: CA
Interviewer: Hoag, Betty Lochrie  Interview date: 06/14/65
Transcript: 39 pages
Repository: Archives of American Art
Permission of interviewee needed.

### Wedin, Elof(b.1901)
Discusses: PWAP  Participated in: PWAP, SECT
Positions: Muralist, Artist  Locations: SD, MN
Interviewers: Reid, George and Archabal, Nina  Interview date: 06/29/77
Transcript: 11 pages  Tape: 30 minutes
Repository: Minnesota Historical Society
Series: Federal Art in Minnesota
Description: Post Office murals, painting of CCC camp activities, artists' club in Minneapolis in the 1930s.

### Weisberg, Sara Thomas
Discusses: FTP  Participated in: FTP
Position: Administrator  Location: GA
Interviewer: O'Connor, John  Interview date: 04/06/77
Transcript: 21 pages  Tape: 40 minutes  Abstract: 2 page(s)
Repository: George Mason University

Description: Value and accomplishments of FTP, her experiences as an administrator of Atlanta FTP.

**Weissberger, Arnold**
Discusses: FTP Participated in: FTP
Position: Lawyer Location: NY
Interviewer: O'Connor, John Interview date: 04/19/77
Transcript: 14 pages Tape: 30 minutes Abstract: 1 page(s)
Repository: George Mason University
Description: Represented Welles and Houseman, *Macbeth*, *Julius Caesar*, *Horse Eats Hat*, *Danton's Death*.

**Welch, Mrs. William H.**
Discusses: WPA Participated in: WPA
Position: Administrator Location: CT
Interviewer: Phillips, Harlan Interview date: 01/02/65
Transcript: 44 pages
Repository: Archives of American Art
Permission of interviewee needed.
Description: Professional and service project, communicated with the newspapers in Conn. to support the WPA arts projects.


**Welles, Halsted**
Discusses: FTP Participated in: FTP
Position: Director Location: NY
Interviewer: O'Connor, John Interview date: 11/17/75
Transcript: 9 pages Tape: 20 minutes Abstract: 2 page(s)
Repository: George Mason University
Description: *Murder in the Cathedral*, Eddie Goodman, Lehman Engel, Communists and FTP.

**Wessels, Glenn Anthony(1895-1982)**
Discusses: FAP, PWAP Participated in: FAP, PWAP
Positions: Administrator, Muralist Location: CA
Interviewer: Gelber, Steven Interview date: 02/22/75
Tape: 110 minutes
Repository: University of Santa Clara
Series: New Deal Art: California
This interview is on 1" videotape and needs special equipment to be viewed.

**Wessels, Glenn Anthony(1895-1982)**
Discusses: FAP, PWAP Participated in: FAP, PWAP
Positions: Administrator, Muralist Location: CA
Interviewer: Riess, Suzanne B. Interview date: 1966
Transcript: 326 pages

Transcript is indexed.
Repository: University of California, Berkeley
Permission of archive needed.
Description: A life history entitled, "Education of an Artist,"
murals, public buildings, FAP art in Oakland and San
Francisco.

#### Wessels, Glenn Anthony(1895-1982)
Discusses: FAP, PWAP Participated in: FAP, PWAP
Positions: Administrator, Muralist Location: CA
Interviewer: Ferbrache, Lewis Interview date: 02/14/64
Transcript: 54 pages
Repository: Archives of American Art
Permission of interviewee needed.

#### West, Harold Edward(b.1902)
Discusses: FAP Participated in: FAP
Positions: Illustrator, Graphic Artist
Interviewer: Loomis, Sylvia Interview date: 05/14/64
Transcript: 17 pages
Repository: Archives of American Art
Permission of interviewee needed.

#### Westcott, Harold(b.1911)
Discusses: PWAP Participated in: PWAP
Position: Artist Location: WI
Interviewer: Doud, Richard Interview date: 06/03/65
Transcript: 19 pages
Repository: Archives of American Art
Permission of interviewee needed.
Interview also includes: Thomas, Howard

#### Wheeler, Louanne
Discusses: FTP Participated in: FTP
Location: NY
Interviewer: O'Connor, John Interview date: 11/01/77
Tape: 90 minutes Abstract: 5 page(s)
Repository: George Mason University
Interview also includes: Bolton, Harold and Bolton, Rhoda
Rammelkamp

#### White, Charles
Discusses: FAP Participated in: FAP
Positions: Artist, Muralist Location: IL
Interviewers: Hatch, James V. and Billops, Camille Interview
date: 12/29/71
Transcript: 22 pages Tape: 120 minutes

Repository: Hatch-Billop Collection, Inc.
Closed pending release.
Description: Murals for FAP, taught at FAP South Side
Community Art Center, Ted Ward, Katherine Dunham, tight
group of those in the arts projects.

**White, Charles Wilbert(1918-1979)**
Discusses: FAP Participated in: FAP
Positions: Artist, Teacher
Interviewer: Hoag, Betty Lochrie  Interview date: 03/09/65
Transcript: 33 pages
Repository: Archives of American Art

**Whitehouse, Harold C.**
Discusses: FAP
Position: Architect Location: WA
Interviewer: Bestor, Dorothy  Interview date: 10/20/65
Transcript: 6 pages
Repository: Archives of American Art
Permission of interviewee needed.
Description: First president of the board of the Spokane Art
Center, which received federal funds that they had to match.

**Whiteman, Frederick J.**
Discusses: FAP Participated in: FAP
Position: Administrator Location: NC
Interviewer: Seckler, Dorothy G.  Interview date: 04/21/65
Transcript: 18 pages
Repository: Archives of American Art
Description: FAP Art Center director in Greensboro, N.C.,
museum design, exhibit design.

**Whiteside, Duncan(b.1910)**
Discusses: FTP Participated in: FTP
Positions: Lighting Director, Technician Location: IL
Interviewer: Wickre, Karen  Interview date: 08/13/78
Transcript: 64 pages  Tape: 145 minutes  Abstract: 5 page(s)
Repository: George Mason University
Description: Background, value of FTP, Kay Ewing, E.G.
Marshall.

**Wilder, Grace**
Discusses: FTP Participated in: FTP
Position: Administrator Location: NY
Interviewer: Wickre, Karen  Interview date: 07/15/77
Tape: 80 minutes  Abstract: 2 page(s)
Repository: George Mason University

Closed until 10/16/97.
Description:  Formation of the puppet unit.

**Wilkes, Nathan**
Discusses: FTP Participated in: FTP
Positions: Lighting Designer, Puppeteer Location: NY
Interviewer:  Wickre, Karen  Interview date:  11/28/78
Transcript:  22 pages  Tape: 45 minutes  Abstract:  2 page(s)
Repository:  George Mason University
Description:  Value of FTP to his career and as a new way of
approaching the arts, administrative structure of puppet units,
*Mighty Mikko.*

**Williams, Guy**
Discusses: FTP Participated in: FTP
Position: Administrator Locations: WA, CA
Interviewer:  O'Connor, John  Interview date:  01/06/76
Tape: 50 minutes  Abstract:  3 page(s)
Repository:  George Mason University
Closed during lifetime.
Interview also includes:  Savage, George and Gladys
Description:  Responsibilities as administrator and director of
Washington FTP and as regional booking supervisor, black
actors.

**Williams, Guy**
Discusses: FTP Participated in: FTP
Position: Administrator Location: WA
Interviewer:  O'Connor, John  Interview date:  01/07/76
Tape: 55 minutes  Abstract:  1 page(s)
Repository:  George Mason University
Interview also includes:  Blance Morgan Losey
Description:  Director of Washington state FTP, Negro
Repertory Theatre, Hallie Flanagan.

**Williams, Jay**
Discusses: FTP Participated in: FTP
Position: Stage Manager Location: NY
Interviewer:  O'Connor, John  Interview date:  09/08/76
Transcript:  42 pages  Tape: 85 minutes  Abstract:  2 page(s)
Repository:  George Mason University
Description:  *The Ascent of F6*, *Dr Faustus*, *Horse Eats Hat*,
*Murder in the Cathedral*, *Revolt of the Beavers*, audience,
critics, unions.

**Williams, Julian(b.1911)**
Discusses: PWAP, FAP Participated in: PWAP, FAP

Positions: Artist, Muralist Location: CA
Interviewer:    McChesney, Mary Fuller    Interview date:
06/14/64
Transcript: 48 pages
Repository: Archives of American Art
Permission of interviewee needed.
Description: Mural for Union High School in Fullerton, Calif.

**Willison, George F.**
Discusses: FWP Participated in: FWP
Positions: Writer, Administrator Locations: MA, DC
Interviewer: Mangione, Jerre Interview date: 11/24/67
Repository: University of Rochester
Series: Mangione Collection
Description: Joined the Provincetown FWP, American Guide
Series, joined the national staff in 1938, eventually became
editor-in-chief.

**Wilson, Ellis(b.1899)**
Discusses: FAP Participated in: FAP
Position: Artist Locations: IL, NY
Interviewer: Billops, Camille Interview date: 02/25/75
Transcript: 73 pages Tape: 120 minutes
Repository: Hatch-Billops Collection, Inc.
Transcript available at George Mason University.
Description: Chicago Art Institute, Abe Hill, the "Negro"
*Macbeth*, South Side Community Arts Center, The Artists'
Union.

**Wilson, Jack**
Discusses: FTP Participated in: FTP
Position: Researcher Location: CA
Interviewer: Wickre, Karen Interview date: 07/19/77
Transcript: 29 pages Tape: 60 minutes Abstract: 2 page(s)
Repository: George Mason University
Interview also includes: Leon Forbes
Description: Researcher, San Francisco theatre history series,
*Pursuit of Happiness*, *It Can't Happen Here*, *Battle Hymn*.

**Wolcott, Marion Post**
Discusses: FSA Participated in: FSA
Position: Photographer Location: DC
Interviewer: Doud, Richard Interview date: 01/18/65
Transcript: 26 pages
Repository: Archives of American Art
Description: Began working with FSA in late 1938.

**Wong, Tyrus**(b.1910)
Discusses: FAP
Positions: Artist, Designer
Interviewer: Hoag, Betty Lochrie  Interview date: 01/30/65
Transcript: 28 pages
Repository: Archives of American Art

**Wood, Mireille Piazzonni**
Discusses: FAP
Location: CA
Interviewer: McChesney, Mary Fuller  Interview date: 06/23/65
Transcript: 5 pages
Repository: Archives of American Art
Wood not on the project.
Description: Discussion of an FAP mural done by her father Gottardo Piazonni in San Francisco.

**Woodruff, Hale A.**(b.1900)
Discusses: FAP
Position: Artist Location: GA
Interviewer: Murray, Al  Interview date: 11/18/68
Transcript: 24 pages
Repository: Archives of American Art
Description: The FAP in Atlanta, background, education, few critics of black art and artists.

**Wool, Helen**
Discusses: FSA Participated in: FSA
Position: Secretary
Interviewer: Doud, Richard  Interview date: 04/17/64
Transcript: 42 pages
Repository: Archives of American Art
Permission of interviewees needed.
Interview also includes: Aiken, Charlotte
Description: Wool served as secretary to Roy Emerson Stryker.

**Workman, James H.**
Discusses: FAP
Location: MN
Interviewer: O'Sullivan, Thomas  Interview date: 12/14/80
Tape: 45 minutes
Repository: Minnesota Historical Society
Description: Workman discusses his father and his murals for the FAP in Minnesota.

**Wright, James Couper**(b.1906)

Discusses: FAP Participated in: FAP, PWAP
Positions: Artist, Stained Glass Maker Location: CA
Interviewer: Hoag, Betty Lochrie Interview date: 06/11/65
Transcript: 17 pages
Repository: Archives of American Art

**Wyckoff, Florence R.**
Discusses: WPA
Location: CA
Interviewer: Morris, Gabrielle Interview date: 1971/74
Transcript is indexed.
Repository: University of California, Berkeley
Series: Bay Area Foundation History, vol III
Description: Foundation history on State Relief Administration
and arts projects.

**Wyllie, Tom(b.1897)**
Discusses: FAP Participated in: FAP
Position: Administrator
Interviewer: Hoag, Betty Lochrie Interview date: 06/25/65
Transcript: 37 pages
Repository: Archives of American Art
Permission of interviewee needed.
Description: Coordinated FAP art shows and helped raise
funds to supplement what the federal government provided for
FAP.

**Yasko, Karel(d.1984)**
Discusses: FAP
Interviewer: Brown, Lorraine Interview date: 1983
Transcript: 24 pages Tape: 60 minutes
Repository: George Mason University
Closed pending release.
Description: Yasko worked for GSA and was insturmental in
recovering many of the lost works done for the FAP in the
1930s, murals in the U.S.

**Yeon, John(b.1910)**
Discusses: FAP
Position: Administrator Location: OR
Interviewer: Kolisch, Marian Interview date: 12/14/82
Tape: 250 minutes
Transcript is indexed.
Repository: Archives of American Art
Series: Northwest Oral History Project
Description: Director of the Regional Planning Commission,
role in developing Oregon's park system and highways,

Columbia River Gorge.

**Young, Beckford(b.1905)**
Discusses: FAP Participated in: FAP
Position: Artist Location: CA
Interviewer: McChesney, Mary Fuller Interview date: 05/19/65
Transcript: 38 pages
Repository: Archives of American Art
Permission of interviewee needed.
Description: 1937 fresco painting in San Francisco.

**Zakheim, Bernard Baruch(b.1898)**
Discusses: FAP, PWAP, SECT Participated in: FAP, PWAP, SECT
Positions: Artist, Muralist Locations: CA, TX
Interviewer: Gelber, Steven Interview date: 02/15/75
Tape: 80 minutes
Repository: University of Santa Clara
Series: New Deal Art: California
This interview is on 1" videotape and needs special equipment to be viewed.

**Zakheim, Bernard Baruch(b.1898)**
Discusses: FAP, PWAP, SECT Participated in: FAP, PWAP, SECT
Positions: Artist, Muralist Locations: CA, TX
Interviewer: Ferbrache, Lewis Interview date: 1964
Transcript: 42 pages
Repository: Archives of American Art

**Zolott, Esther**
Discusses: FAP Participated in: FAP
Positions: Artist, Sculptor Location: IL
Interviewer: Hoag, Betty Lochrie Interview date: 05/20/65
Transcript: 17 pages
Repository: Archives of American Art
Description: Chicago FAP, office work.

**Zornes, James Milford(b.1908)**
Discusses: PWAP Participated in: PWAP, SECT, TRAP
Positions: Muralist, Artist Locations: TX, CA
Interviewer: Hoag, Betty Lochrie Interview date: 06/30/65
Transcript: 45 pages
Repository: Archives of American Art

# 4. Index by Project

A DRAMA OF THE BLACK NAPOLEON
By William Du Bois
LAFAYETTE THEATRE

Note: The following index lists people who either participated in a particular project or discussed that project in their interview.

**FAP**

Abbenseth, William
Abel, Christine Jeannette
Abel, Don G.
Abelman, Ida
Agostitni, Peter
Albinson, Dewey
Alston, Charles Henry
Ambrusch, Julius Peter
Ames, Arthur
Ames, Jean Goodwin
Anderson, Guy
Arnason, H. Harvard
Arndt, Helen
Ayer, Richard
Babcock, Alberta Von O.
Babcock, Paul G.
Bach, Cile
Baker, Mildred
Bakos, Jozef G.
Banks, Bernice Fisher
Baranceanu, Belle
Barnet, Will
Barrows, Charles
Bartlett, Frederic S.
Baskin, Leonard
Bearden, Romare
Bell, Philip Fletcher
Benton, Thomas Hart
Biberman, Edward
Biddle, George
Billings, Henry
Bischoff, Elmer Nelson
Bistram, Emil J.
Blanch, Arnold
Blazek, Anton
Bloch, Lucienne
Block, Irving A.
Block, Lou
Bolotowsky, Ilya
Bonath, Harry
Booth, Cameron
Boratko, Andre
Bothwell, Dorr
Boyd, Elizabeth
Brandeis, Adele
Brandt, Louise W.
Bridaham, Lester B.
Brigante, Nicholas P.
Britton, Edgar
Brook, Alexander
Brooks, James

217

FAP (*continued*)

Brown, Herbert J.
Browne, Rosalind B.
Bruton, Helen
Bruton, Margaret
Bufano, Beniamino
Bultman, Fritz
Bunce, Louis Dermott
Bunnell, Charles
Burlin, Paul
Busa, Peter
Cabral, Flavio Emmanuel
Cadmus, Paul
Cahill, Holger
Candell, Victor
Carter, Clarence Holbrook
Catlett, Elizabeth
Chapman, Kenneth L.
Chavez, Edward Arcenio
Cherry, Herman
Chesse, Ralph
Chinn, Andrew
Chodorow, Eugene
Chong, Fay
Churchman, Edwin
Churchman, Isabelle S.
Cikovsky, Nicolai
Clapp, Thaddeus
Clarke, Helen Bess
Clarke, James Mitchell
Colin, Ralph Frederick
Collins, Dorothy
Constantine, Mildred
Cornish, Mary Elizabeth
Coye, Lee Brown
Craft, Paul
Crampton, Rollin McNeil
Cravath, Dorothy
Cravath, Ruth
Crawford, Phyllis
Crichlow, Ernest
Crockwell, S. Douglas
Cronbach, Robert
Cumming, William
Cunningham, Benjamin F.
Cunningham, Patricia S.
Curtis, Philip Campbell

Dana, Homer
Danysh, Joseph
Darley, Eunice Welch
Dasburg, Andrew Michael
De Rivera, Jose
Deeter, Jasper
Defenbacher, Daniel S.
Dehn, Adolph Arthur
Deutsch, Boris
Dickey, Roland
Dieterich, Hebert R., Jr.
Dike, Philip
Diller, Burgoyne
Dixon, Harry
Dornbush, Adrian
Dows, Olin
Egri, Ted
Eichenberg, Fritz
Elshin, Jacob
Emery, Edwin
Engard, Robert Oliver
Etcheverry, Louisa
Evergood, Philip
Falkenstein, Claire
Farr, Charles Griffin
Fax, Elton C.
Feitelson, Lorser
Fincke, Joy Yeck
Fine, Perle
Fitzgerald, James H.
Fitzgerald, Margaret T.
Fleckenstein, Opal R.
Flint, Leroy W.
Fogg, Adelaide
Fossum, Syd
Fox, Milton S.
Frankenstein, Alfred V.
Freeman, Don
Freund, Burton
Friedman, William M.
Fuller, Richard E.
Gaskin, William
Gates, Frank W. (Pancho)
Gaw, William A.
Gerrity, John Emmett
Gershoy, Eugenie
Gibbs, Howard M., Jr.

**FAP** (*continued*)

Gikow, Ruth
Gilbertson, Boris
Gilien, Ted
Glassgold, Adolph
Goodall, Donald B.
Gorelick, Boris
Goss, Dale
Gottlieb, Adolph
Gottlieb, Harry
Graham, F. Wynne
Grant, Campbell
Greenwood, Grace
Greenwood, Marion
Gropper, William
Groschwitz, Gustave von
Gross, Chaim
Groves, Wellington
Hagel, Hansel
Haines, Richard
Hall, Bob
Hall, Parker
Halpert, Edith Gregor
Hamlin, Edith
Harris, Wilma
Hatch, John Davis
Haupers, Clement B.
Henry, Mary Dill
Herron, Jason
Hirsch, Joseph
Holmes, Jean
Holty, Carl
Hood, Richard
Horn, Axel
Hunt, Lee
Hurd, Peter
Ibling, Miriam
Inverarity, Robert Bruce
Ions, Willoughby
Jackson, Everett Gee
Jeakins, Dorothy
Jerry, Sylvester
Junker, Ernest
Kaminsky, Dora
Kantor, Morris
Kaplan, Leonard
Kendall, Marion

Kidd, Edythe
King, Albert Henry
Kingman, Dong M.
Kirkland, Vance H.
Klonis, Stewart
Kloss, Gene
Knaths, Karl
Kneass, Amelie
Knight, Harry
Knotts, Ben
Krasner, Lee
Krause, Erik Hans
Kupferman, Lawrence
Kurtz, Wilbur
La Branche, Dolores
La Farge, Henry
Lahti, Aarre K.
Lassaw, Ibram
Laufman, Sidney
Lawrence, Jacob
Lazzari, Pietro
Lee, Doris
Lee-Smith, Hughie
Lehman, Carlton
Lenshaw, Ernest
Levi, Julian
Levine, Jack
Lewandowski, Edmund
Lewis, Monty
Lindneux, Robert Ottokar
Lishinsky, Abraham
Liston, Ilo Carey
Loper, Edward L.
Lowe, Peter
Lundeberg, Helen
Mac-Gurrin, Buckley
Maccoy, Genoi
Macdonald-Wright, Stanton
Magnani, Margery
Malicoat, Philip
Mandelman, Beatrice M.
Mantilla, Victor
Marca-Relli, Conrad
Martin, Fletcher
Matthew, John Britton
Mattson, Henry
Mayer, Bena Frank

FAP (*continued*)

Mayer, Ralph
McCarthy, Max
McChesney, Robert P.
McCoy, Guy
McMahon, Audrey
McNeil, George
McWilliams, Joy Yeck
Menchaca, Juan
Messenger, Ivan
Messick, Ben Newton
Miller, Arthur
Miller, Dorothy
Moffett, Ross E.
Moore, Gertrude Herdle
Morang, Dorothy Alden C.
Moreau, Andres Francisco
Morgenthau, Henry, Jr.
Morley, Grace L. McCann
Morris, Carl
Morris, David
Morris, James Stovall
Morris, Robert Max
Morrison, Richard C.
Moxom, Jack
Moxom, Marshall
Moy, Seong
Moya Del Pino, Jose
Murray, Justin
Neff, Earl
Newhall, Beaumont
O'Hanlon, Anne Rice
O'Hanlon, Richard E.
Opper, John
Ott, Peterpaul
Packard, Emmy Lou
Painter, Arthur C.
Parker, Thomas C.
Parshall, Douglass Ewell
Partridge, Charlotte R.
Pendergast, Malina D.
Penney, James
Pereira, Irene Rice
Philips, David M.
Poland, Reginald
Pollock, Jackson
Pollock, Merlin F.

Polos, Theodore C.
Pomeroy, Florette White
Poor, Henry Varnum
Post, George Booth
Preibisius, Hilda
Puccinelli, Raymond
Randall, Byron
Rannells, Edward Warder
Reed, Florence
Refregier, Anton
Reinhardt, Ad
Rexroth, Kenneth
Ribak, Louis
Rich, Daniel Catton
Richards, Lavina
Robbins, LeRoy
Roberts, Malcolm
Rosati, James
Rose, David
Rose, Julia Smead
Rosen, David
Rosenstock, Fred A.
Rosenwald, Janet
Ross, Charlotte Rothstein
Roszak, Theodore
Rothchild, Lincoln
Rubenstein, Lewis
Rush, Olive
Ryan, Beatrice Judd
Saccaro, John
Saks, Lemon
Sanderson, Phillips
Saulter, Leon
Sawyer, Charles Henry
Sazevich, Zygmund
Schanker, Louis
Schmidt, Katherine
Schnier, Jacques
Schwankovsky, Frederick
Sepesky, Zolta
Sheets, Nan
Shonnard, Eugenie F.
Shuster, Will
Shute, Ben E.
Siegriest, Louis Bassi
Sievan, Maurice
Sills, Thomas Albert

FAP (*continued*)
Simpson, Marian
Siporin, Mitchell
Smith, Charles S.,Jr.
Smith, David
Smith, Gordon Mackintosh
Smith, Margery Hoffman
Smith, Vernon B.
Solman, Joseph
Spivak, Max
Spohn, Clay
Spomer, Peter John
Spurgeon, Sarah
Stackpole, Hebe Daum
Stein, Irene Miller
Steinman, Mrs. Erwin
Stevens, Frank
Swiggett, Jean
Tamotzu, Chuzo
Taylor, Edgar J.
Taylor, Farwell
Thall, Victor
Thiessen, Leonard
Thomas, Grace
Thwaites, Charles
Tolegian, Manuel Jerier
Tomkins, Margaret
Totten, Donald
Traher, William Henry
Tribble, Charles
Triest, Shirley Staschen
Trubach, Serge
Tworkov, Jack
Uhler, Ruth Pershing
Ulbricht, Elsa Emilie
Utley, Tabor
Van Veen, Stuyvesant
Velarde, Pablita
Velonis, Anthony
Vogel, Joseph
Volz, Herman
Von Meyer, Michael
Wardell, Thomas
Warren, Marijane
Warren, William L.
Warsaegar, Hyman J.
Washington, James W. Jr.

Watson, Betty Ferguson
Wayne, June
Wessels, Glenn Anthony
West, Harold Edward
White, Charles
White, Charles Wilbert
Whitehouse, Harold C.
Whiteman, Frederick J.
Williams, Julian
Wilson, Ellis
Wong, Tyrus
Wood, Mireille Piazzonni
Woodruff, Hale A.
Workman, James H.
Wright, James Couper
Wyllie, Tom
Yasko, Karel
Yeon, John
Young, Beckford
Zakheim, Bernard Baruch
Zolott, Esther
**FERA**
Alsberg, Henry G.
Baker, Jacob
Fincke, Joy Yeck
Harris, Reed
Jung, Theodore
Kennedy, Michael Stephen
Kneass, Amelie
Laning, Clair
Merrill, Anthony French
**FMP**
Alessandro, Victor
Bacon, Ernst
Bales, Richard Horner
Brown, Herbert J.
Cassimir, John
Clebanoff, Herman
Cohn, Arthur
Cowell, Sidney Robertson
Engel, Lehman
Farran, Don
Goldberg, Albert
Gutierrez, Sal
Hewes, Harry
Kahn, Emily Mason
Kayes, Alan

221

FMP (*continued*)
  Krakow, Leo
  Leuning, Otto
  Lief, Arthur
  Miller, Carl
  Painter, Arthur C.
  Poole, Valter
  Robinson, Earl
  Rosati, James
  Rufty, Hilton
  Schuman, William
  Seeger, Charles
  Siegal, Fritz
  Siegmeister, Elie
  Smith, Carlton Sprague
  Solomon, Izler
FSA
  Aiken, Charlotte
  Baldwin, Calvin Benham
  Collier, John
  Daniels, Jonathan
  Delano, Irene
  Delano, Jack
  Hudgens, Robert Watts
  Javitz, Romana
  Lange, Dorothea
  Lee, Jean
  Lee, Russell
  Newhall, Beaumont
  Parks, Gordon
  Rosskam, Edwin
  Rosskam, Louise
  Rothstein, Arthur
  Seeger, Charles
  Shahn, Ben
  Stanley, Edward
  Stryker, Roy Emerson
  Vachon, John
  Valiant, Margaret
  Vanderbilt, Paul
  Wolcott, Marion Post
  Wool, Helen
FTP
  Abdul, Raoul
  Allison, Elitea
  Anderson, Thomas
  Andrus, Zoray

Archer, Osceola
Atkinson, Brooks
Baird, Bil
Bales, Bill
Banfield, Beryl
Barber, Philip
Barlin, Anne Lief
Barnouw, Eric
Baron, Paul
Bass, Paula
Bates, Add
Bay, Howard
Becque, Don Oscar
Bentley, Eric
Bentley, Joanne Davis
Berenberg, Ben
Berman, Harold
Birchenall, Jack
Black, Ivan
Blake, Eubie
Blankfort, Michael
Bolton, Harold
Bolton, Rhoda Rammelkamp
Borowsky, Maxine
Bosworth, Francis
Brant, Carl
Brocco, Peter
Bromley, Robert
Browne, Theodore
Bruskin, Perry
Burris-Meyer, Harold
Bush, Anita
Buttita, Tony
Cahill, Holger
Campbell, Dick
Camryn, Walter
Cardwell, Laurence
Chaivoe, Nick
Chase, Mary Coyle
Chesse, Ralph
Childress, Alice
Chilkovsky, Nadia
Clark, Helen Fisher
Clark, Maurice
Clarke, David
Clugston, Katherine T.
Cohen, Elizabeth Elson

FTP (*continued*)
Coleman, Ralf
Connelly, Marc
Corey, Jeff
Cotten, Joseph
Courlander, Harold
Cox, Margaret
Croydon, Joan
Cunningham, Michele E.
Da Silva, Howard
Daggett, Helen Cross
Dailey, Dan
Daly, Frank
Danzig, Frank
De Koven, Roger
De Paur, Leonard
Deane, Martha Blanchard
Dehn, Mura
Denby, Edwin
Dowell, George
Dowling, Eddie
DuBois, Shirley Graham
Dudley, Edward, Jr.
Dudley, Jane
Dunham, Katherine
Durham, C.J.S. (Jack)
Ebsen, Nancy Wolcott
Edson, Eda
Edwards, Ben
Eldridge, Elaine
Elson, Charles
Elson, Diana Rivers
Engel, Lehman
Ewing, Kay
Farmer, Virginia
Farnsworth, William
Farran, Don
Feder, Abe
Ferguson, Kenneth
Fishel, H. L. (Bud)
Fisher, Granville
Forbes, Leon
Francis, Arlene
Frank, Allan
Freeman, Charles K.
Freud, Mayfair
Freud, Ralph

Friar, Kimon
Galea, Manuel
Garnet, Eva Desca
Geer, Will
Gellert, Lawrence
Geltman, Fanya
Geltman, Fanya Del Bourgo
Gerrard, Saida
Gilbert, Lou
Gilder, Rosamond
Gilman, Harold
Gilman, Ida Galler
Glidden, Patty Neederman
Glyer, Richard
Goodman, Frank
Gordon, Michael
Gorelik, Mordecai
Graham, H. Gordon
Green, Paul
Hairston, Jester
Harris, Julian H.
Haufrecht, Herbert
Haughton, Norris
Hauser, Ethel Aaron
Hays, Hoffman R.
Hill, Abram
Houghton, Norris
Houseman, John
Hughes, Langston
Isaacs, Lewis
Izenaur, George
Jackson, Sara O.
Jelliffe, Rowena
Johnson, Lamont
Jonas, Hallie
Kennedy, Donald Scott
Kent, Charlotte
Kinch, Myra
Kingston, Lenore
Kinnard, Henry
Koch, Howard
Lane, Esther Porter
Lantz, Louis
Laurence, Paula
Lavery, Emmet
Lawson, Kathryn Drain
LeNoire, Rosetta

FTP (*continued*)

Leavitt, Max
Lee, J. Edward
Lee, Will
Lehac, Ned
Lentz, Josef
Lessin, Harry
Leve, Samuel
Lewitsky, Bella
Lindemulder, Nel
Litvinoff, Valentina
Lloyd, Joel
Lloyd, Norman
Losey, Blanche Morgan
Lumet, Sidney
Lynch, Dorothea
Macchiarini, Peter
Maltz, Albert
Mann, Dulce Fox
Mann, Lili
Mann, Lili Laub
Marshall, E.G.
Maxwell, Gilbert
McDermott, Thomas
McLean, Scott Roberts
Meadow, Herb
Meltzer, Allan
Meltzer, Milton
Meredith, Betty Arden
Merrill, Mary
Mesa, Fernando
Meyer, Harriet B.
Miller, Arthur
Miller, J. Howard
Monroe, Charles
Morcom, James S.
Morris, Lawrence S.
Moss, Carlton
Murray, Donald
Muse, Clarence
Nadel, Sue Remos
Norford, George T.
North, Alex
Norvelle, Lee R.
Ocko, Edna
Ottenheimer, Albert M.
Page, Ruth

Peterson, Arthur
Pezman, Theodore
Phelps, Eleanor
Phillips, Wendell
Pierce, Evelyn
Pinska, Klarna
Pollock, Max
Pomeroy, Florette White
Ponch, Martin
Pond, Donald
Porter, Don
Randolph, John
Rather, Lois Rodecap
Rauch, Lillian Shapero
Reese, Amos
Reich, Molka
Rella, Ettore
Remos, Sue
Rhodes, Irwin
Rich, Shirley
Roberts, Gordon
Robinson, Earl
Robson, William N.
Romano, Amelia
Rome, Harold
Rosten, Norman
Russak, Ben
Saul, Oscar
Saunders, Wardell
Savage, George
Saxe, Al
Schaff, Janet
Schenker, Augusta W.
Schnitzer, Marcella C.
Schnitzer, Robert
Schoolman, Mary Sackler
Schrager, Philip
Schulman, Rose
Schulman, Sol
Scooler, Zvee
Scott, Isabel
Seeger, Charles
Shaw, Zachary
Sherman, Hiram
Sherman, Vincent
Shibley, Eleanor Scherr
Shohet, Max

**FTP** (*continued*)

Shrewsberry, Robert
Silvera, John
Simon, Louis
Sklar, George
Slane, Michael Andrew
Smith, Margery Hoffman
Sokolow, Anna
Sour, Robert
Spayde, Sydney
Staton, Joseph
Stavis, Barrie
Still, William Grant
Stone, Bentley
Stone, Gene
Stover, Frederick
Stuckmann, Eugene
Suib, Leonard
Sundgaard, Arnold
Talbot, Clarence
Teichman, Howard
Thomas, Ted
Thomson, Virgil
Tyler, Converse
Velie, Jay
Wallace, Lea
Ward, Theodore
Warde, Frances
Wasserman, Dale
Weisberg, Sara Thomas
Weissberger, Arnold
Welles, Halsted
Wheeler, Louanne
Whiteside, Duncan
Wilder, Grace
Wilkes, Nathan
Williams, Guy
Williams, Jay
Wilson, Jack

**FWP**

Alexander, Margaret W.
Alsberg, Henry G.
Balch, Jack
Berger, Josef
Bontemps, Arna
Cassidy, Ina Sizer
Chase, Richard

Conroy, Jack
Couch, William Terry
Dorais, Leon (Bill)
Du Von, Jay
Ellison, Ralph
Epstein, Samuel
Farran, Don
Fisher, Vardis
Frankel, Lillian Berson
Friar, Kimon
Gellert, Lawrence
Hale, Laura Virginia
Hamilton, Emory L.
Harris, Reed
Hough, Henry
Inverarity, Robert Bruce
Kennedy, Michael Stephen
Laning, Clair
McGraw, James
McHugh, Vincent
Perry, Mary
Pomeroy, Florette White
Richardson, Eudora Ramsey
Rosenberg, Harold
Ross, Sam
Royse, Morton W.
Sloan, Raymond H.
Stewart, George R.
Stuckmann, Eugene
Terkel, Studs
Thompson, Donald
Vaerlen, Basil
Vorse, Mary Heaton
Willison, George F.

**NYA**

Cowell, Sidney Robertson
Moxom, Marshall
Schrager, Philip
Steinert, Alexander
Valiant, Margaret

**PWAP**

Adams, Kenneth
Albro, Maxine
Alston, Charles Henry
Ames, Arthur
Anderson, Guy
Armitage, Merle

PWAP (*continued*)
Ayers, Atlee B.
Baranceanu, Belle
Barrows, Charles
Biddle, George
Bistram, Emil J.
Bolotowsky, Ilya
Booth, Cameron
Brigante, Nicholas P.
Bruce, Margaret T.
Bruton, Helen
Bruton, Margaret
Bunce, Louis Dermott
Bunnell, Charles
Burlin, Paul
Carmody, John Michael
Cassidy, Ina Sizer
Chesse, Ralph
Collier, Nina Perera
Crockwell, S. Douglas
Dasburg, Andrew Michael
Dean, Mallette
Dehn, Adolph Arthur
Diller, Burgoyne
Dornbush, Adrian
Dows, Olin
Dozier, Otis
Elshin, Jacob
Everett, Eugenia
Evergood, Philip
Feitelson, Lorser
Fields, Earl T.
Fossum, Syd
Gaethke, George
Gage, Merrell
Gaskin, William
Gates, Frank W. (Pancho)
Gerrity, John Emmett
Goodrich, Lloyd
Gottlieb, Harry
Grant, Campbell
Greenwood, Grace
Greenwood, Marion
Greywacz, Kathryn
Gross, Chaim
Gwathmey, Robert
Hall, Parker

Haupers, Clement B.
Herron, Jason
Hesthal, William
Hord, Donal
Houser, Lowell
Howard, Robert Boardman
Hrdy, Olinka
Hurd, Peter
Ibling, Miriam
Johnson, Sargent Claude
Jonson, Raymond
Kadish, Reuben
Kassler II, Charles
King, Albert Henry
Klonis, Stewart
Kloss, Gene
Knaths, Karl
Knight, Harry
Korff, Alice Graham
Labaudt, Marcelle
Lassaw, Ibram
Laufman, Sidney
Lundeberg, Helen
Mac-Gurrin, Buckley
Mann, Lucile Quarry
Mattson, Henry
Mayer, Bena Frank
Mayer, Ralph
Meem, John Gaw
Morris, David
Morrison, Richard C.
Moxom, Jack
Moya Del Pino, Jose
O'Hanlon, Richard E.
Olmsted, Anna Wetherill
Palmer, William C.
Peat, Wilbur D.
Poland, Reginald
Pollock, Merlin F.
Puccinelli, Raymond
Rannells, Edward Warder
Rexroth, Kenneth
Roszak, Theodore
Rubenstein, Lewis
Rublee, Bertha Hellman
Rush, Olive
Scheuer, Suzanne

PWAP (*continued*)
Schnier, Jacques
Shahn, Ben
Sheets, Nan
Shope, Irvin
Shuster, Will
Siporin, Mitchell
Smith, Vernon B.
Spivak, Max
Stackpole, Hebe Daum
Steinbrueck, Victor
Stoll, John Theodor E.
Swiggett, Jean
Tamotzu, Chuzo
Taylor, Farwell
Thomas, Howard
Thwaites, Charles
Trubach, Serge
Tworkov, Jack
Utley, Tabor
Van Veen, Stuyvesant
Velarde, Pablita
Voris, Mark
Watkins, Franklin
Wedin, Elof
Wessels, Glenn Anthony
Westcott, Harold
Williams, Julian
Wright, James Couper
Zakheim, Bernard Baruch
Zornes, James Milford

RA
Baldwin, Calvin Benham
Cowell, Sidney Robertson
Dornbush, Adrian
Haufrecht, Herbert
Hudgens, Robert Watts
Hurwitz, Leo
Jung, Theodore
Lange, Dorothea
Lee, Jean
Lee, Russell
Lorentz, Pare
Pomeroy, Florette White
Rosskam, Edwin
Seeger, Charles
Stryker, Roy Emerson

Tugwell, Rexford G.
Vachon, John
Valiant, Margaret

SECT
Abelman, Ida
Adams, Kenneth
Armitage, Merle
Biberman, Edward
Biddle, George
Billings, Henry
Bistram, Emil J.
Blanch, Arnold
Bloch, Lucienne
Block, Irving A.
Britton, Edgar
Brook, Alexander
Brooks, James
Bruce, Margaret T.
Bruton, Helen
Bunce, Louis Dermott
Callahan, Kenneth L.
Carter, Clarence Holbrook
Chavez, Edward Arcenio
Cikovsky, Nicolai
Cravath, Dorothy
Crockwell, S. Douglas
Cronbach, Robert
Cunningham, Benjamin F.
Deutsch, Boris
Dows, Olin
Dozier, Otis
Elshin, Jacob
Evergood, Philip
Gilien, Ted
Gottlieb, Adolph
Gropper, William
Gross, Chaim
Gwathmey, Robert
Haines, Richard
Hamlin, Edith
Hauser, Alonzo
Horn, Axel
Houser, Lowell
Howard, Robert Boardman
Hurd, Peter
Kassler II, Charles
Kirkland, Vance H.

SECT (*continued*)
Knaths, Karl
Lazzari, Pietro
Lee, Doris
Lenson, Michael
Lewandowski, Edmund
Lion, Henry
Lishinsky, Abraham
Lochrie, Elizabeth D.
Magafan, Ethel
Manship, Paul
Martin, Fletcher
Mendelowitz, Daniel
Moffett, Ross E.
Morgenthau, Henry, Jr.
Morris, Carl
Moya Del Pino, Jose
Ortmayer, Constance
Ott, Peterpaul
Palmer, William C.
Penney, James
Pollock, Merlin F.
Poor, Henry Varnum
Refregier, Anton
Rickey, George W.
Rogers, Charles B.
Rubenstein, Lewis
Rush, Olive
Sazevich, Zygmund
Scheuer, Suzanne
Sepesky, Zolta
Shahn, Ben
Sherman, James Russell
Shonnard, Eugenie F.
Shope, Irvin
Siporin, Mitchell
Spohn, Clay
Swiggett, Jean
Traher, William Henry
Turner, Ida McAfee
Van Veen, Stuyvesant
Wedin, Elof
Zakheim, Bernard Baruch
Zornes, James Milford
TRAP
Adams, Kenneth
Baranceanu, Belle

Benton, Thomas Hart
Brandeis, Adele
Bruton, Margaret
Bunnell, Charles
Chavez, Edward Arcenio
Dean, Mallette
Dows, Olin
Fitzgerald, James H.
Gorelick, Boris
Greenwood, Grace
Greenwood, Marion
Gropper, William
Iselin, Lewis
Kadish, Reuben
Kassler II, Charles
Magafan, Ethel
Mattson, Henry
Morgenthau, Henry, Jr.
Neff, Earl
O'Hanlon, Richard E.
Sazevich, Zygmund
Scheuer, Suzanne
Sherman, James Russell
Smith, David
Thwaites, Charles
Trubach, Serge
Turner, Ida McAfee
Vogel, Joseph
Zornes, James Milford
USFS
Lorentz, Pare
WPA
Alessandro, Victor
Ayers, Atlee B.
Baker, Jacob
Carmody, John Michael
Cronin, Ann
Davidson, Julius
Douglas, Helen Gahagan
Durham, C.J.S. (Jack)
Kerr, Florence
Le Seur, Meridel
Merrill, Anthony French
Morris, David
Morris, Lawrence S.
Perkins, Frances
Reef, Margaret S.

**WPA** (*continued*)
Smith, Margery Hoffman
Taylor, Frank
Watson, Betty Ferguson
Welch, Mrs. William H.
Wyckoff, Florence R.

# 5. Index by Position

**Accountant**
  Aiken, Charlotte
**Actor**
  Baird, Bil
  Bates, Add
  Berenberg, Ben
  Brant, Carl
  Brocco, Peter
  Browne, Theodore
  Bruskin, Perry
  Chaivoe, Nick
  Corey, Jeff
  Cotten, Joseph
  Da Silva, Howard
  Dailey, Dan
  Daly, Frank
  De Koven, Roger
  Dowling, Eddie
  Edwards, Ben
  Forbes, Leon
  Frank, Allan
  Geer, Will
  Gilbert, Lou
  Gilman, Harold
  Glyer, Richard
  Gordon, Michael
  Kennedy, Donald Scott
  Lee, Will
  Lessin, Harry

  Lloyd, Norman
  Lumet, Sidney
  Marshall, E.G.
  Maxwell, Gilbert
  McDermott, Thomas
  McLean, Scott Roberts
  Monroe, Charles
  Muse, Clarence
  Ottenheimer, Albert M.
  Peterson, Arthur
  Ponch, Martin
  Porter, Don
  Randolph, John
  Roberts, Gordon
  Saunders, Wardell
  Sherman, Hiram
  Shrewsberry, Robert
  Staton, Joseph
  Stuckmann, Eugene
  Velie, Jay
  Ward, Theodore
**Actress**
  Archer, Osceola
  Bush, Anita
  Childress, Alice
  Croydon, Joan
  Cunningham, Michele E.
  Douglas, Helen Gahagan
  Eldridge, Elaine

Actress (*continued*)
  Elson, Diana Rivers
  Francis, Arlene
  Glidden, Patty Neederman
  Jackson, Sara O.
  Kingston, Lenore
  Laurence, Paula
  LeNoire, Rosetta
  Mann, Dulce Fox
  Meredith, Betty Arden
  Romano, Amelia
  Shibley, Eleanor Scherr
  Warde, Frances
**Administrative Assistant**
  Cox, Margaret
  Cronin, Ann
  Schenker, Augusta W.
  Schulman, Rose
**Administrator**
  Abel, Don G.
  Albinson, Dewey
  Alsberg, Henry G.
  Armitage, Merle
  Arnason, H. Harvard
  Ayers, Atlee B.
  Bacon, Ernst
  Baker, Jacob
  Baker, Mildred
  Baldwin, Calvin Benham
  Barber, Philip
  Bell, Philip Fletcher
  Black, Ivan
  Block, Lou
  Bontemps, Arna
  Boratko, Andre
  Bosworth, Francis
  Boyd, Elizabeth
  Brandeis, Adele
  Brandt, Louise W.
  Bridaham, Lester B.
  Bromley, Robert
  Brown, Herbert J.
  Cahill, Holger
  Campbell, Dick
  Cardwell, Laurence
  Carmody, John Michael
  Carter, Clarence Holbrook

Cassidy, Ina Sizer
Chapman, Kenneth L.
Chesse, Ralph
Clapp, Thaddeus
Clugston, Katherine T.
Cohen, Elizabeth Elson
Cohn, Arthur
Collier, Nina Perera
Couch, William Terry
Cowell, Sidney Robertson
Crampton, Rollin McNeil
Curtis, Philip Campbell
Danysh, Joseph
Davidson, Julius
Deane, Martha Blanchard
Deeter, Jasper
Defenbacher, Daniel S.
Dickey, Roland
Diller, Burgoyne
Dornbush, Adrian
Dows, Olin
Du Von, Jay
Edson, Eda
Farnsworth, William
Farran, Don
Feitelson, Lorser
Fishel, H. L. (Bud)
Fisher, Vardis
Fitzgerald, James H.
Garnet, Eva Desca
Gilder, Rosamond
Glassgold, Adolph
Goldberg, Albert
Goodall, Donald B.
Goodman, Frank
Goodrich, Lloyd
Goss, Dale
Greywacz, Kathryn
Groschwitz, Gustave von
Groves, Wellington
Harris, Reed
Haupers, Clement B.
Hood, Richard
Hough, Henry
Hudgens, Robert Watts
Hunt, Lee
Inverarity, Robert Bruce

**Administrator** (*continued*)
Kadish, Reuben
Kahn, Emily Mason
Kayes, Alan
Kennedy, Michael Stephen
Kerr, Florence
King, Albert Henry
Klonis, Stewart
Kneass, Amelie
Knight, Harry
Knotts, Ben
Krause, Erik Hans
La Farge, Henry
Lane, Esther Porter
Laning, Clair
Lavery, Emmet
Lehman, Carlton
Lentz, Josef
Lorentz, Pare
Lynch, Dorothea
Macdonald-Wright, Stanton
Magnani, Margery
Matthew, John Britton
McGraw, James
McMahon, Audrey
McWilliams, Joy Yeck
Meem, John Gaw
Merrill, Anthony French
Meyer, Harriet B.
Miller, Carl
Miller, J. Howard
Moore, Gertrude Herdle
Morris, Carl
Morris, David
Morris, Lawrence S.
Morrison, Richard C.
Neff, Earl
Newhall, Beaumont
Norvelle, Lee R.
Painter, Arthur C.
Parker, Thomas C.
Peat, Wilbur D.
Pendergast, Malina D.
Perkins, Frances
Perry, Mary
Pierce, Evelyn
Pollock, Merlin F.

Pomeroy, Florette White
Rannells, Edward Warder
Rather, Lois Rodecap
Reef, Margaret S.
Reich, Molka
Rhodes, Irwin
Richardson, Eudora Ramsey
Rufty, Hilton
Russak, Ben
Ryan, Beatrice Judd
Schnitzer, Robert
Scooler, Zvee
Seeger, Charles
Simon, Louis
Smith, Gordon Mackintosh
Smith, Margery Hoffman
Smith, Vernon B.
Solomon, Izler
Spayde, Sydney
Stevens, Frank
Stryker, Roy Emerson
Taylor, Frank
Thiessen, Leonard
Thomas, Howard
Thompson, Donald
Tugwell, Rexford G.
Tyler, Converse
Vachon, John
Vaerlen, Basil
Valiant, Margaret
Wardell, Thomas
Warren, William L.
Watkins, Franklin
Weisberg, Sara Thomas
Welch, Mrs. William H.
Wessels, Glenn Anthony
Whiteman, Frederick J.
Wilder, Grace
Williams, Guy
Willison, George F.
Wyllie, Tom
Yeon, John
**Architect**
Morris, Robert Max
Whitehouse, Harold C.
**Archivist**
Vanderbilt, Paul

233

**Arranger**
Stone, Gene
**Art Collector**
Colin, Ralph Frederick
**Art Consultant**
Hatch, John Davis
**Art Critic**
Frankenstein, Alfred V.
Korff, Alice Graham
**Art Dealer**
Halpert, Edith Gregor
Kaplan, Leonard
Rosenstock, Fred A.
Saks, Lemon
**Art Director**
Harris, Julian H.
**Art Gallery Director**
Jonson, Raymond
**Art Historian**
Constantine, Mildred
Frankenstein, Alfred V.
Hatch, John Davis
**Art Lecturer**
Holty, Carl
**Artist**
Abel, Christine Jeannette
Adams, Kenneth
Albinson, Dewey
Albro, Maxine
Alston, Charles Henry
Ambrusch, Julius Peter
Ames, Arthur
Ames, Jean Goodwin
Ayer, Richard
Babcock, Alberta Von O.
Babcock, Paul G.
Bakos, Jozef G.
Baranceanu, Belle
Barnet, Will
Bearden, Romare
Benton, Thomas Hart
Biddle, George
Billings, Henry
Bischoff, Elmer Nelson
Bistram, Emil J.
Blanch, Arnold
Blazek, Anton

Block, Irving A.
Bolotowsky, Ilya
Bonath, Harry
Bothwell, Dorr
Bridaham, Lester B.
Brigante, Nicholas P.
Britton, Edgar
Brook, Alexander
Brooks, James
Browne, Rosalind B.
Bruton, Helen
Bruton, Margaret
Bultman, Fritz
Bunce, Louis Dermott
Bunnell, Charles
Burlin, Paul
Busa, Peter
Cabral, Flavio Emmanuel
Cadmus, Paul
Candell, Victor
Carter, Clarence Holbrook
Catlett, Elizabeth
Chavez, Edward Arcenio
Cherry, Herman
Chesse, Ralph
Chinn, Andrew
Chodorow, Eugene
Chong, Fay
Cikovsky, Nicolai
Clarke, James Mitchell
Collins, Dorothy
Coye, Lee Brown
Cravath, Dorothy
Crawford, Phyllis
Crichlow, Ernest
Crockwell, S. Douglas
Cumming, William
Cunningham, Benjamin F.
Curtis, Philip Campbell
Darley, Eunice Welch
Dasburg, Andrew Michael
Dean, Mallette
Dehn, Adolph Arthur
Delano, Irene
Deutsch, Boris
Dike, Philip
Diller, Burgoyne

Artist (*continued*)
Dows, Olin
Dozier, Otis
Egri, Ted
Elshin, Jacob
Emery, Edwin
Engard, Robert Oliver
Etcheverry, Louisa
Everett, Eugenia
Evergood, Philip
Farr, Charles Griffin
Fields, Earl T.
Fine, Perle
Fitzgerald, James H.
Fitzgerald, Margaret T.
Fleckenstein, Opal R.
Fogg, Adelaide
Fossum, Syd
Fox, Milton S.
Freund, Burton
Gaethke, George
Gaskin, William
Gates, Frank W. (Pancho)
Gaw, William A.
Gerrity, John Emmett
Gibbs, Howard M., Jr.
Gikow, Ruth
Gilien, Ted
Gorelick, Boris
Goss, Dale
Gottlieb, Adolph
Gottlieb, Harry
Graham, F. Wynne
Grant, Campbell
Greenwood, Grace
Greenwood, Marion
Gropper, William
Groves, Wellington
Gwathmey, Robert
Haines, Richard
Hall, Bob
Hall, Parker
Hauser, Alonzo
Henry, Mary Dill
Herron, Jason
Hesthal, William
Hirsch, Joseph

Holmes, Jean
Holty, Carl
Houser, Lowell
Hunt, Lee
Hurd, Peter
Ions, Willoughby
Jackson, Everett Gee
Jeakins, Dorothy
Jerry, Sylvester
Jonson, Raymond
Kaminsky, Dora
Kantor, Morris
Kaplan, Leonard
Kassler II, Charles
King, Albert Henry
Kingman, Dong M.
Kirkland, Vance H.
Klonis, Stewart
Kloss, Gene
Knaths, Karl
Krasner, Lee
Krause, Erik Hans
Kupferman, Lawrence
Kurtz, Wilbur
Labaudt, Marcelle
Lahti, Aarre K.
Laufman, Sidney
Lawrence, Jacob
Lazzari, Pietro
Lee, Doris
Lee-Smith, Hughie
Lehman, Carlton
Lenshaw, Ernest
Lenson, Michael
Levi, Julian
Levine, Jack
Lewis, Monty
Lindneux, Robert Ottokar
Lion, Henry
Lochrie, Elizabeth D.
Loper, Edward L.
Lowe, Peter
Mac-Gurrin, Buckley
Maccoy, Genoi
Magafan, Ethel
Malicoat, Philip
Mandelman, Beatrice M.

**Artist** (*continued*)
Mantilla, Victor
Marca-Relli, Conrad
Martin, Fletcher
Mattson, Henry
Mayer, Bena Frank
Mayer, Ralph
McCarthy, Max
McChesney, Robert P.
McCoy, Guy
McNeil, George
Menchaca, Juan
Mendelowitz, Daniel
Messenger, Ivan
Messick, Ben Newton
Moffett, Ross E.
Morang, Dorothy Alden C.
Moreau, Andres Francisco
Morris, James Stovall
Moxom, Jack
Moy, Seong
Moya Del Pino, Jose
Murray, Justin
O'Hanlon, Anne Rice
O'Hanlon, Richard E.
Opper, John
Packard, Emmy Lou
Palmer, William C.
Parshall, Douglass Ewell
Partridge, Charlotte R.
Pendergast, Malina D.
Penney, James
Pereira, Irene Rice
Philips, David M.
Pollock, Jackson
Pollock, Merlin F.
Polos, Theodore C.
Poor, Henry Varnum
Post, George Booth
Preibisius, Hilda
Randall, Byron
Refregier, Anton
Reinhardt, Ad
Rexroth, Kenneth
Ribak, Louis
Robbins, LeRoy
Roberts, Malcolm

Rogers, Charles B.
Rose, David
Rosen, David
Ross, Charlotte Rothstein
Roszak, Theodore
Rush, Olive
Saccaro, John
Schanker, Louis
Scheuer, Suzanne
Schmidt, Katherine
Schnier, Jacques
Schwankovsky, Frederick
Sepesky, Zolta
Sheets, Nan
Sherman, James Russell
Shope, Irvin
Shuster, Will
Shute, Ben E.
Siegriest, Louis Bassi
Sievan, Maurice
Sills, Thomas Albert
Simpson, Marian
Siporin, Mitchell
Solman, Joseph
Spivak, Max
Spohn, Clay
Spomer, Peter John
Spurgeon, Sarah
Stackpole, Hebe Daum
Stein, Irene Miller
Stevens, Frank
Stoll, John Theodor E.
Swiggett, Jean
Tamotzu, Chuzo
Taylor, Edgar J.
Taylor, Farwell
Thall, Victor
Thomas, Grace
Thomas, Howard
Tolegian, Manuel Jerier
Tomkins, Margaret
Totten, Donald
Traher, William Henry
Tribble, Charles
Triest, Shirley Staschen
Trubach, Serge
Turner, Ida McAfee

Artist (*continued*)
Tworkov, Jack
Uhler, Ruth Pershing
Ulbricht, Elsa Emilie
Utley, Tabor
Velarde, Pablita
Velonis, Anthony
Volz, Herman
Voris, Mark
Warren, Marijane
Warsaegar, Hyman J.
Washington, James W. Jr.
Watkins, Franklin
Wayne, June
Wedin, Elof
Westcott, Harold
White, Charles
White, Charles Wilbert
Williams, Julian
Wilson, Ellis
Wong, Tyrus
Woodruff, Hale A.
Wright, James Couper
Young, Beckford
Zakheim, Bernard Baruch
Zolott, Esther
Zornes, James Milford
**Assistant Stage Manager**
Clarke, David
Dudley, Edward, Jr.
Schrager, Philip
**Ceramist**
Fleckenstein, Opal R.
**Choreographer**
Chilkovsky, Nadia
Dehn, Mura
Denby, Edwin
Dunham, Katherine
Garnet, Eva Desca
Kinch, Myra
Page, Ruth
Rauch, Lillian Shapero
Sokolow, Anna
**Clerical Worker**
Morris, David
**Composer**
Bacon, Ernst

Blake, Eubie
De Paur, Leonard
Engel, Lehman
Haufrecht, Herbert
Kent, Charlotte
North, Alex
Pond, Donald
Robinson, Earl
Schuman, William
Siegmeister, Elie
Still, William Grant
Stone, Gene
Thomson, Virgil
**Concertmaster**
Clebanoff, Herman
Krakow, Leo
Siegal, Fritz
**Conductor**
Alessandro, Victor
Bales, Richard Horner
Cohn, Arthur
Leuning, Otto
Lief, Arthur
Poole, Valter
Solomon, Izler
Steinert, Alexander
**Congresswoman**
Douglas, Helen Gahagan
**Costume Designer**
Andrus, Zoray
Birchenall, Jack
Bolton, Rhoda Rammelkamp
Borowsky, Maxine
Losey, Blanche Morgan
Merrill, Mary
Shrewsberry, Robert
**Craftperson**
Ulbricht, Elsa Emilie
**Craftsperson**
Dixon, Harry
**Dancer**
Bales, Bill
Banfield, Beryl
Barlin, Anne Lief
Bass, Paula
Bates, Add
Becque, Don Oscar

**Dancer** (*continued*)
Camryn, Walter
Chilkovsky, Nadia
Cunningham, Michele E.
Dailey, Dan
Dehn, Mura
Dudley, Jane
Dunham, Katherine
Geltman, Fanya
Geltman, Fanya Del Bourgo
Gerrard, Saida
Gilman, Ida Galler
Glidden, Patty Neederman
Kinch, Myra
Lewitsky, Bella
Litvinoff, Valentina
Mann, Lili
Mann, Lili Laub
Nadel, Sue Remos
Ocko, Edna
Page, Ruth
Pinska, Klarna
Remos, Sue
Schaff, Janet
Stone, Bentley
Wallace, Lea

**Designer**
Hrdy, Olinka
Lewis, Monty
Shonnard, Eugenie F.
Spivak, Max
Velonis, Anthony
Wong, Tyrus

**Director**
Anderson, Thomas
Archer, Osceola
Bolton, Harold
Clark, Maurice
Coleman, Ralf
Da Silva, Howard
Daggett, Helen Cross
Edson, Eda
Ewing, Kay
Farmer, Virginia
Fisher, Granville
Freeman, Charles K.
Freud, Ralph

Glyer, Richard
Gorelik, Mordecai
Graham, H. Gordon
Houghton, Norris
Houseman, John
Moss, Carlton
Muse, Clarence
Phillips, Wendell
Pollock, Max
Ponch, Martin
Robson, William N.
Saxe, Al
Sherman, Vincent
Slane, Michael Andrew
Staton, Joseph
Talbot, Clarence
Thomas, Ted
Welles, Halsted

**Drama Critic**
Atkinson, Brooks

**Editor**
McHugh, Vincent
Morris, Lawrence S.
Oehser, Paul
Rosenberg, Harold

**Educator**
Mayer, Bena Frank
Miller, Carl
Tomkins, Margaret

**Engraver**
Engard, Robert Oliver
Flint, Leroy W.

**Etcher**
Kloss, Gene
Miller, Arthur
Sheets, Nan

**Executive Secretary**
Schoolman, Mary Sackler

**Field Worker**
Hale, Laura Virginia
Hamilton, Emory L.
Sloan, Raymond H.

**Filmmaker**
Hurwitz, Leo
Lorentz, Pare

**Folk Song Collector**
Cowell, Sidney Robertson

**Folk Song Collector** (*continued*)
 Gellert, Lawrence
**Graphic Artist**
 Armitage, Merle
 Lowe, Peter
 West, Harold Edward
**Illustrator**
 Billings, Henry
 Crockwell, S. Douglas
 Eichenberg, Fritz
 Fax, Elton C.
 Freeman, Don
 Hall, Bob
 Jackson, Everett Gee
 Kurtz, Wilbur
 Lee, Doris
 Rose, David
 Steinbrueck, Victor
 Velarde, Pablita
 West, Harold Edward
**Lawyer**
 Rhodes, Irwin
 Weissberger, Arnold
**Librarian**
 Vanderbilt, Paul
**Lighting Designer**
 Feder, Abe
 Izenaur, George
 Wilkes, Nathan
**Lighting Director**
 Whiteside, Duncan
**Lighting Technician**
 Wasserman, Dale
**Lithographer**
 Abelman, Ida
 Holmes, Jean
 Vogel, Joseph
 Wayne, June
**Lyricist**
 Rome, Harold
**Model Maker**
 Churchman, Edwin
**Muralist**
 Abelman, Ida
 Anderson, Guy
 Benton, Thomas Hart
 Biberman, Edward

Bistram, Emil J.
Bloch, Lucienne
Bolotowsky, Ilya
Boratko, Andre
Browne, Rosalind B.
Bunce, Louis Dermott
Bunnell, Charles
Busa, Peter
Cadmus, Paul
Callahan, Kenneth L.
Chavez, Edward Arcenio
Clarke, James Mitchell
Cunningham, Benjamin F.
Cunningham, Patricia S.
Emery, Edwin
Evergood, Philip
Feitelson, Lorser
Gorelick, Boris
Greenwood, Marion
Gwathmey, Robert
Haines, Richard
Hamlin, Edith
Henry, Mary Dill
Hirsch, Joseph
Horn, Axel
Hrdy, Olinka
Hurd, Peter
Ibling, Miriam
Kadish, Reuben
Kingman, Dong M.
Kirkland, Vance H.
Knotts, Ben
Labaudt, Marcelle
Lenshaw, Ernest
Lewandowski, Edmund
Lishinsky, Abraham
Lundeberg, Helen
Mac-Gurrin, Buckley
Magafan, Ethel
Mandelman, Beatrice M.
McChesney, Robert P.
McCoy, Guy
Moxom, Jack
Moya Del Pino, Jose
Packard, Emmy Lou
Palmer, William C.
Penney, James

## Muralist (*continued*)
Poor, Henry Varnum
Refregier, Anton
Rexroth, Kenneth
Rickey, George W.
Roberts, Malcolm
Rosen, David
Rubenstein, Lewis
Rublee, Bertha Hellman
Rush, Olive
Sepesky, Zolta
Shahn, Ben
Shuster, Will
Siegriest, Louis Bassi
Sievan, Maurice
Stackpole, Hebe Daum
Thwaites, Charles
Totten, Donald
Traher, William Henry
Turner, Ida McAfee
Utley, Tabor
Van Veen, Stuyvesant
Vogel, Joseph
Wedin, Elof
Wessels, Glenn Anthony
White, Charles
Williams, Julian
Zakheim, Bernard Baruch
Zornes, James Milford
## Museum Curator
Miller, Dorothy
## Museum Director
Bartlett, Frederic S.
Craft, Paul
Fuller, Richard E.
Inverarity, Robert Bruce
Liston, Ilo Carey
Morley, Grace L. McCann
Olmsted, Anna Wetherill
Poland, Reginald
Reed, Florence
Rich, Daniel Catton
Rogers, Charles B.
Sawyer, Charles Henry
## Musical Director
Thomson, Virgil

## Musician
Brown, Herbert J.
De Paur, Leonard
Galea, Manuel
Goodman, Saul
Hairston, Jester
Still, William Grant
## Photographer
Abbenseth, William
Collier, John
Delano, Jack
Fields, Earl T.
Hagel, Hansel
Javitz, Romana
Jung, Theodore
Lange, Dorothea
Lee, Russell
Moxom, Marshall
Parks, Gordon
Rosskam, Edwin
Rothstein, Arthur
Shahn, Ben
Stanley, Edward
Wolcott, Marion Post
## Play Adapter
Denby, Edwin
Scott, Isabel
## Play Doctor
Berman, Harold
## Playreader
Berman, Harold
Friar, Kimon
Hill, Abram
Lantz, Louis
Miller, Arthur
Saul, Oscar
## Playwright
Blankfort, Michael
Browne, Theodore
Chase, Mary Coyle
Connelly, Marc
Courlander, Harold
DuBois, Shirley Graham
Frankel, Lillian Berson
Green, Paul
Hays, Hoffman R.
Hill, Abram

**Playwright** (*continued*)
Hughes, Langston
Koch, Howard
Lantz, Louis
Maltz, Albert
Meadow, Herb
Murray, Donald
Norford, George T.
Pezman, Theodore
Reese, Amos
Rella, Ettore
Robson, William N.
Rosten, Norman
Saul, Oscar
Savage, George
Sherman, Vincent
Silvera, John
Sklar, George
Stavis, Barrie
Sundgaard, Arnold
Talbot, Clarence
Ward, Theodore
**Printmaker**
Baskin, Leonard
Biberman, Edward
Bothwell, Dorr
Chong, Fay
Dozier, Otis
Eichenberg, Fritz
Flint, Leroy W.
Gaethke, George
Gikow, Ruth
Graham, F. Wynne
Hood, Richard
Kupferman, Lawrence
La Branche, Dolores
Lee-Smith, Hughie
Lundeberg, Helen
Martin, Fletcher
Moy, Seong
Richards, Lavina
Schanker, Louis
Warsaegar, Hyman J.
**Producer**
Freeman, Charles K.
Haughton, Norris
Houghton, Norris

Houseman, John
**Publicist**
Black, Ivan
Buttita, Tony
Jonas, Hallie
Lee, J. Edward
Meltzer, Allan
Ottenheimer, Albert M.
Shohet, Max
**Puppeteer**
Baird, Bil
Bromley, Robert
Chesse, Ralph
Leavitt, Max
Lloyd, Joel
Macchiarini, Peter
Reich, Molka
Shaw, Zachary
Suib, Leonard
Wilkes, Nathan
**Researcher**
Clark, Helen Fisher
Hale, Laura Virginia
Meltzer, Allan
Meredith, Betty Arden
Rather, Lois Rodecap
Rosenwald, Janet
Stuckmann, Eugene
Wilson, Jack
**Scriptwriter**
Raphaelson, Samson
**Sculptor**
Abel, Christine Jeannette
Agostitni, Peter
Banks, Bernice Fisher
Baskin, Leonard
Blazek, Anton
Britton, Edgar
Bufano, Beniamino
Callahan, Kenneth L.
Chodorow, Eugene
Churchman, Edwin
Churchman, Isabelle S.
Cronbach, Robert
Cunningham, Patricia S.
Dana, Homer
De Rivera, Jose

**Sculptor** (*continued*)
Egri, Ted
Everett, Eugenia
Falkenstein, Claire
Farr, Charles Griffin
Freund, Burton
Gage, Merrell
Gershoy, Eugenie
Gilbertson, Boris
Gross, Chaim
Hauser, Alonzo
Hord, Donal
Howard, Robert Boardman
Iselin, Lewis
Johnson, Sargent Claude
Lahti, Aarre K.
Lassaw, Ibram
Lazzari, Pietro
Lion, Henry
Lochrie, Elizabeth D.
Macchiarini, Peter
Manship, Paul
O'Hanlon, Richard E.
Ortmayer, Constance
Ott, Peterpaul
Puccinelli, Raymond
Rickey, George W.
Rosati, James
Roszak, Theodore
Rothchild, Lincoln
Sanderson, Phillips
Saulter, Leon
Sazevich, Zygmund
Shonnard, Eugenie F.
Smith, David
Stoll, John Theodor E.
Von Meyer, Michael
Washington, James W. Jr.
Zolott, Esther
**Secretary**
Cox, Margaret
Fincke, Joy Yeck
Rose, Julia Smead
Steinman, Mrs. Erwin
Wool, Helen
**Selection Committee**
Booth, Cameron

**Set Designer**
Bay, Howard
Elson, Charles
Leve, Samuel
Morcom, James S.
Stover, Frederick
**Songwriter**
Kent, Charlotte
Lehac, Ned
Sour, Robert
**Sound Technician**
Burris-Meyer, Harold
**Stage Manager**
Anderson, Thomas
Baron, Paul
Chaivoe, Nick
Hauser, Ethel Aaron
Lane, Esther Porter
McLean, Scott Roberts
Mesa, Fernando
Teichman, Howard
Wasserman, Dale
Williams, Jay
**Stagehand**
Kinnard, Henry
**Stained Glass Maker**
Wright, James Couper
**Teacher**
Becque, Don Oscar
Bischoff, Elmer Nelson
Block, Irving A.
Cabral, Flavio Emmanuel
Daggett, Helen Cross
Fax, Elton C.
Fogg, Adelaide
Gilien, Ted
Glassgold, Adolph
Goodall, Donald B.
Ions, Willoughby
Lief, Arthur
Messick, Ben Newton
Ortmayer, Constance
Siporin, Mitchell
Spohn, Clay
Spurgeon, Sarah
Voris, Mark
White, Charles Wilbert

**Technical Director**
Lawson, Kathryn Drain
**Technician**
Monroe, Charles
Whiteside, Duncan
**Theatre Historian**
Gorelik, Mordecai
**Weaver**
Harris, Wilma
Kendall, Marion
Magnani, Margery
**Writer**
Alexander, Margaret W.
Balch, Jack
Berger, Josef
Conroy, Jack
Daniels, Jonathan
Danzig, Frank
Dorais, Leon (Bill)
Du Von, Jay
Ellison, Ralph
Fisher, Vardis

Freeman, Don
Friar, Kimon
Friedman, William M.
Haughton, Norris
Hewes, Harry
Hough, Henry
Hughes, Langston
Kennedy, Michael Stephen
McHugh, Vincent
Meltzer, Milton
Morris, Lawrence S.
Raphaelson, Samson
Rosenberg, Harold
Ross, Sam
Royse, Morton W.
Stewart, George R.
Terkel, Studs
Thomas, Ted
Thompson, Donald
Vaerlen, Basil
Willison, George F.

NEW YORKER THEATRE
54ᵗʰ St. W. of Bwy
Columbus 5-8464
NIGHTLY 8:40-MAT. SAT. 2:30 PRICES $1.10-83¢-55¢

Gilbert & Sullivan

The MIKADO

Swingcopated

CHICAGO FEDERAL THEATRE PRODUCTION

# 6. Index by Location

245

CA (*continued*)

Dana, Homer
Danysh, Joseph
Dean, Mallette
Deane, Martha Blanchard
Deutsch, Boris
Dike, Philip
Dixon, Harry
Dorais, Leon (Bill)
Edson, Eda
Elson, Charles
Elson, Diana Rivers
Emery, Edwin
Etcheverry, Louisa
Everett, Eugenia
Falkenstein, Claire
Farmer, Virginia
Farnsworth, William
Farr, Charles Griffin
Feitelson, Lorser
Forbes, Leon
Frankenstein, Alfred V.
Freeman, Don
Freud, Mayfair
Freud, Ralph
Gaethke, George
Gage, Merrell
Galea, Manuel
Gaskin, William
Gaw, William A.
Gerrity, John Emmett
Gilien, Ted
Glidden, Patty Neederman
Glyer, Richard
Grant, Campbell
Hagel, Hansel
Haines, Richard
Hairston, Jester
Hall, Parker
Hamlin, Edith
Harris, Wilma
Henry, Mary Dill
Herron, Jason
Hesthal, William
Holmes, Jean
Hord, Donal
Howard, Robert Boardman

Hrdy, Olinka
Izenaur, George
Jackson, Everett Gee
Jeakins, Dorothy
Johnson, Sargent Claude
Kadish, Reuben
Kaplan, Leonard
Kassler II, Charles
Kendall, Marion
Kennedy, Donald Scott
Kinch, Myra
King, Albert Henry
Kingman, Dong M.
Kingston, Lenore
Kneass, Amelie
Labaudt, Marcelle
Lehman, Carlton
Lenshaw, Ernest
Lentz, Josef
Lewitsky, Bella
Lion, Henry
Lundeberg, Helen
Mac-Gurrin, Buckley
Macchiarini, Peter
Macdonald-Wright, Stanton
Magnani, Margery
Martin, Fletcher
Matthew, John Britton
McCarthy, Max
Mendelowitz, Daniel
Meredith, Betty Arden
Messenger, Ivan
Miller, J. Howard
Morley, Grace L. McCann
Moxom, Jack
Moxom, Marshall
Moya Del Pino, Jose
Murray, Donald
Murray, Justin
Muse, Clarence
O'Hanlon, Anne Rice
O'Hanlon, Richard E.
Packard, Emmy Lou
Painter, Arthur C.
Pendergast, Malina D.
Pezman, Theodore
Poland, Reginald

CA (*continued*)
Pollock, Max
Pomeroy, Florette White
Poor, Henry Varnum
Porter, Don
Preibisius, Hilda
Puccinelli, Raymond
Rather, Lois Rodecap
Refregier, Anton
Rexroth, Kenneth
Robbins, LeRoy
Rose, David
Ryan, Beatrice Judd
Saccaro, John
Sazevich, Zygmund
Scheuer, Suzanne
Schnier, Jacques
Schnitzer, Robert
Siegriest, Louis Bassi
Spohn, Clay
Stackpole, Hebe Daum
Steinert, Alexander
Stewart, George R.
Stoll, John Theodor E.
Stone, Gene
Stover, Frederick
Swiggett, Jean
Taylor, Edgar J.
Taylor, Farwell
Tolegian, Manuel Jerier
Totten, Donald
Triest, Shirley Staschen
Vaerlen, Basil
Volz, Herman
Von Meyer, Michael
Warde, Frances
Wasserman, Dale
Wayne, June
Wessels, Glenn Anthony
Williams, Guy
Williams, Julian
Wilson, Jack
Wood, Mireille Piazzonni
Wright, James Couper
Wyckoff, Florence R.
Young, Beckford
Zakheim, Bernard Baruch

Zornes, James Milford
CO
Ambrusch, Julius Peter
Arndt, Helen
Bach, Cile
Bartlett, Frederic S.
Brandt, Louise W.
Britton, Edgar
Bunnell, Charles
Chase, Mary Coyle
Chavez, Edward Arcenio
Cornish, Mary Elizabeth
Darley, Eunice Welch
Fitzgerald, James H.
Gates, Frank W. (Pancho)
Hough, Henry
Magafan, Ethel
Morris, Robert Max
Philips, David M.
Reef, Margaret S.
Rose, Julia Smead
Rosenstock, Fred A.
Saks, Lemon
Sherman, James Russell
Slane, Michael Andrew
Smith, Charles S.,Jr.
Spomer, Peter John
Stein, Irene Miller
Traher, William Henry
Tribble, Charles
Turner, Ida McAfee
Utley, Tabor
CT
Baldwin, Calvin Benham
Blanch, Arnold
Schanker, Louis
Warren, William L.
Welch, Mrs. William H.
DC
Aiken, Charlotte
Alsberg, Henry G.
Baker, Jacob
Baker, Mildred
Bell, Philip Fletcher
Biddle, George
Bistram, Emil J.
Britton, Edgar

247

DC (*continued*)
Brook, Alexander
Cahill, Holger
Carmody, John Michael
Cikovsky, Nicolai
Cowell, Sidney Robertson
Cox, Margaret
Cronin, Ann
Davidson, Julius
Durham, C.J.S. (Jack)
Farran, Don
Gorelick, Boris
Gropper, William
Harris, Reed
Hudgens, Robert Watts
Kahn, Emily Mason
Kerr, Florence
Knight, Harry
Korff, Alice Graham
La Farge, Henry
Lane, Esther Porter
Laning, Clair
Lee, Doris
Lorentz, Pare
Magafan, Ethel
Mann, Lucile Quarry
Manship, Paul
Merrill, Anthony French
Morgenthau, Henry, Jr.
Morris, David
Morris, Lawrence S.
Oehser, Paul
Palmer, William C.
Perkins, Frances
Poor, Henry Varnum
Rosenberg, Harold
Royse, Morton W.
Schnitzer, Robert
Seeger, Charles
Shahn, Ben
Steinman, Mrs. Erwin
Stryker, Roy Emerson
Taylor, Frank
Tugwell, Rexford G.
Vachon, John
Vanderbilt, Paul
Willison, George F.

Wolcott, Marion Post
DE
Knaths, Karl
Schnitzer, Robert
FL
Cardwell, Laurence
Dornbush, Adrian
Fisher, Granville
Graham, H. Gordon
Laufman, Sidney
Lazzari, Pietro
Lindemulder, Nel
Lynch, Dorothea
McLean, Scott Roberts
Mesa, Fernando
Ortmayer, Constance
Reich, Molka
Scott, Isabel
Shrewsberry, Robert
GA
Evergood, Philip
Gellert, Lawrence
Graham, H. Gordon
Harris, Julian H.
Lee, Doris
Maxwell, Gilbert
Shute, Ben E.
Weisberg, Sara Thomas
Woodruff, Hale A.
IA
Du Von, Jay
Houser, Lowell
Hunt, Lee
Palmer, William C.
Spayde, Sydney
Talbot, Clarence
Thiessen, Leonard
ID
Fisher, Vardis
Fitzgerald, James H.
Lochrie, Elizabeth D.
Martin, Fletcher
IL
Alexander, Margaret W.
Arnason, H. Harvard
Bontemps, Arna
Britton, Edgar

IL (*continued*)
- Bultman, Fritz
- Camryn, Walter
- Cikovsky, Nicolai
- Clebanoff, Herman
- Conroy, Jack
- De Rivera, Jose
- DuBois, Shirley Graham
- Dunham, Katherine
- Ewing, Kay
- Farran, Don
- Frankel, Lillian Berson
- Freund, Burton
- Gilman, Harold
- Gilman, Ida Galler
- Goldberg, Albert
- Graham, H. Gordon
- Kerr, Florence
- Lee, J. Edward
- Lee, Russell
- Lewandowski, Edmund
- Marshall, E.G.
- McDermott, Thomas
- Moffett, Ross E.
- Opper, John
- Ott, Peterpaul
- Page, Ruth
- Peterson, Arthur
- Pollock, Merlin F.
- Rich, Daniel Catton
- Ross, Charlotte Rothstein
- Ross, Sam
- Roszak, Theodore
- Sepesky, Zolta
- Shrewsberry, Robert
- Siegal, Fritz
- Siporin, Mitchell
- Solomon, Izler
- Stone, Bentley
- Sundgaard, Arnold
- Terkel, Studs
- Ward, Theodore
- Wayne, June
- White, Charles
- Whiteside, Duncan
- Wilson, Ellis
- Zolott, Esther

IN
- Norvelle, Lee R.
- Peat, Wilbur D.
- Swiggett, Jean

KS
- Adams, Kenneth
- Kirkland, Vance H.
- Rogers, Charles B.

KY
- Bloch, Lucienne
- Brandeis, Adele
- Rannells, Edward Warder

LA
- Cassimir, John
- Gutierrez, Sal
- Lindemulder, Nel

MA
- Berger, Josef
- Billings, Henry
- Bridaham, Lester B.
- Brown, Herbert J.
- Browne, Theodore
- Clapp, Thaddeus
- Coleman, Ralf
- Gibbs, Howard M., Jr.
- Hatch, John Davis
- Knaths, Karl
- Kupferman, Lawrence
- Levine, Jack
- Marca-Relli, Conrad
- Moffett, Ross E.
- Morrison, Richard C.
- Newhall, Beaumont
- Pereira, Irene Rice
- Rubenstein, Lewis
- Smith, Gordon Mackintosh
- Smith, Vernon B.
- Vorse, Mary Heaton
- Willison, George F.

MD
- Fax, Elton C.

ME
- Schmidt, Katherine

MI
- Friar, Kimon
- Gropper, William
- Krakow, Leo

MI (*continued*)
Lee-Smith, Hughie
Moy, Seong
Poole, Valter
Sawyer, Charles Henry
Sepesky, Zolta
Thwaites, Charles
MN
Albinson, Dewey
Arnason, H. Harvard
Blanch, Arnold
Booth, Cameron
Boratko, Andre
Cowell, Sidney Robertson
Dehn, Adolph Arthur
Fossum, Syd
Haines, Richard
Haupers, Clement B.
Hauser, Alonzo
Ibling, Miriam
Le Seur, Meridel
Lewandowski, Edmund
Thwaites, Charles
Watson, Betty Ferguson
Wedin, Elof
Workman, James H.
MO
Balch, Jack
Benton, Thomas Hart
Conroy, Jack
Dunham, Katherine
Gilien, Ted
Penney, James
Siporin, Mitchell
MS
Crockwell, S. Douglas
Sills, Thomas Albert
MT
Hall, Bob
Kennedy, Michael Stephen
La Branche, Dolores
Lochrie, Elizabeth D.
Richards, Lavina
Shope, Irvin
NC
Bales, Richard Horner
Couch, William Terry

Daniels, Jonathan
Defenbacher, Daniel S.
Green, Paul
Hudgens, Robert Watts
Lazzari, Pietro
Whiteman, Frederick J.
ND
Callahan, Kenneth L.
NH
Stuckmann, Eugene
NJ
Allison, Elitea
Biddle, George
Brooks, James
Greenwood, Grace
Greenwood, Marion
Greywacz, Kathryn
Refregier, Anton
Schulman, Rose
Simon, Louis
NM
Adams, Kenneth
Bakos, Jozef G.
Barrows, Charles
Bistram, Emil J.
Boyd, Elizabeth
Cassidy, Ina Sizer
Chapman, Kenneth L.
Collier, Nina Perera
Crawford, Phyllis
Dasburg, Andrew Michael
Deutsch, Boris
Dickey, Roland
Egri, Ted
Fincke, Joy Yeck
Gilbertson, Boris
Graham, F. Wynne
Hauser, Alonzo
Hurd, Peter
Jonson, Raymond
Kloss, Gene
McWilliams, Joy Yeck
Perry, Mary
Ribak, Louis
Rush, Olive
Shonnard, Eugenie F.
Shuster, Will

NM (*continued*)
Thomas, Grace
Turner, Ida McAfee
Velarde, Pablita
NV
Gottlieb, Adolph
NY
Agostitni, Peter
Alston, Charles Henry
Anderson, Thomas
Archer, Osceola
Atkinson, Brooks
Baird, Bil
Bales, Bill
Banfield, Beryl
Barber, Philip
Barlin, Anne Lief
Barnet, Will
Baron, Paul
Baskin, Leonard
Bass, Paula
Bates, Add
Bay, Howard
Bearden, Romare
Becque, Don Oscar
Berenberg, Ben
Berman, Harold
Biddle, George
Billings, Henry
Black, Ivan
Blake, Eubie
Blanch, Arnold
Blankfort, Michael
Bloch, Lucienne
Block, Irving A.
Bolotowsky, Ilya
Bolton, Harold
Bolton, Rhoda Rammelkamp
Borowsky, Maxine
Bosworth, Francis
Brook, Alexander
Brooks, James
Browne, Rosalind B.
Bruskin, Perry
Bultman, Fritz
Burlin, Paul
Burris-Meyer, Harold

Busa, Peter
Bush, Anita
Buttita, Tony
Campbell, Dick
Candell, Victor
Cardwell, Laurence
Catlett, Elizabeth
Chavez, Edward Arcenio
Chilkovsky, Nadia
Clark, Helen Fisher
Clark, Maurice
Clarke, David
Clugston, Katherine T.
Colin, Ralph Frederick
Connelly, Marc
Constantine, Mildred
Corey, Jeff
Cotten, Joseph
Courlander, Harold
Cox, Margaret
Coye, Lee Brown
Crampton, Rollin McNeil
Crichlow, Ernest
Crockwell, S. Douglas
Cronbach, Robert
Croydon, Joan
Cunningham, Benjamin F.
Da Silva, Howard
Dailey, Dan
Daly, Frank
Danzig, Frank
De Koven, Roger
De Paur, Leonard
De Rivera, Jose
Dehn, Adolph Arthur
Dehn, Mura
Denby, Edwin
Diller, Burgoyne
Dows, Olin
Dudley, Edward, Jr.
Dudley, Jane
Edwards, Ben
Eichenberg, Fritz
Eldridge, Elaine
Engel, Lehman
Evergood, Philip
Fax, Elton C.

251

NY (*continued*)
Feder, Abe
Fine, Perle
Fishel, H. L. (Bud)
Fitzgerald, James H.
Francis, Arlene
Frank, Allan
Freeman, Charles K.
Freeman, Don
Garnet, Eva Desca
Geer, Will
Gellert, Lawrence
Geltman, Fanya
Geltman, Fanya Del Bourgo
Gerrard, Saida
Gershoy, Eugenie
Gikow, Ruth
Gilbert, Lou
Gilder, Rosamond
Gilman, Harold
Gilman, Ida Galler
Glassgold, Adolph
Goodman, Frank
Goodrich, Lloyd
Gordon, Michael
Gorelick, Boris
Gottlieb, Adolph
Gottlieb, Harry
Greenwood, Grace
Greenwood, Marion
Gropper, William
Groschwitz, Gustave von
Gross, Chaim
Groves, Wellington
Gwathmey, Robert
Hairston, Jester
Halpert, Edith Gregor
Hauser, Ethel Aaron
Hays, Hoffman R.
Hewes, Harry
Hill, Abram
Horn, Axel
Houghton, Norris
Houseman, John
Iselin, Lewis
Jonas, Hallie
Kaminsky, Dora

Kantor, Morris
Kayes, Alan
Kennedy, Donald Scott
Kent, Charlotte
Kinnard, Henry
Klonis, Stewart
Knotts, Ben
Koch, Howard
Krasner, Lee
Krause, Erik Hans
Lane, Esther Porter
Lantz, Louis
Lassaw, Ibram
Laufman, Sidney
Laurence, Paula
Lavery, Emmet
Lawrence, Jacob
Lawson, Kathryn Drain
Lazzari, Pietro
LeNoire, Rosetta
Leavitt, Max
Lee, Doris
Lee, J. Edward
Lee, Will
Lehac, Ned
Lessin, Harry
Leve, Samuel
Levi, Julian
Lief, Arthur
Lishinsky, Abraham
Litvinoff, Valentina
Lloyd, Joel
Lloyd, Norman
Lorentz, Pare
Lumet, Sidney
Maccoy, Genoi
Maltz, Albert
Mandelman, Beatrice M.
Mann, Dulce Fox
Mann, Lili
Mann, Lili Laub
Manship, Paul
Mattson, Henry
McCoy, Guy
McGraw, James
McHugh, Vincent
McMahon, Audrey

NY (*continued*)
McNeil, George
Meadow, Herb
Meltzer, Allan
Meltzer, Milton
Merrill, Mary
Miller, Carl
Miller, Dorothy
Miller, J. Howard
Moore, Gertrude Herdle
Morcom, James S.
Morris, Lawrence S.
Moss, Carlton
Moy, Seong
Nadel, Sue Remos
Norford, George T.
North, Alex
Olmsted, Anna Wetherill
Opper, John
Palmer, William C.
Penney, James
Pereira, Irene Rice
Phillips, Wendell
Pierce, Evelyn
Pollock, Jackson
Ponch, Martin
Randolph, John
Rauch, Lillian Shapero
Reese, Amos
Refregier, Anton
Reinhardt, Ad
Rella, Ettore
Remos, Sue
Rickey, George W.
Robinson, Earl
Robson, William N.
Romano, Amelia
Rome, Harold
Rosen, David
Rosten, Norman
Roszak, Theodore
Rothchild, Lincoln
Rothstein, Arthur
Rubenstein, Lewis
Russak, Ben
Saul, Oscar
Saunders, Wardell

Saxe, Al
Schaff, Janet
Schanker, Louis
Schenker, Augusta W.
Schmidt, Katherine
Schnitzer, Marcella C.
Schoolman, Mary Sackler
Schrager, Philip
Schulman, Sol
Schuman, William
Scooler, Zvee
Sepesky, Zolta
Shahn, Ben
Shaw, Zachary
Sherman, Hiram
Sherman, Vincent
Shibley, Eleanor Scherr
Shohet, Max
Siegmeister, Elie
Sills, Thomas Albert
Silvera, John
Simon, Louis
Sklar, George
Smith, Carlton Sprague
Smith, David
Sokolow, Anna
Solman, Joseph
Sour, Robert
Spivak, Max
Spohn, Clay
Stanley, Edward
Still, William Grant
Suib, Leonard
Tamotzu, Chuzo
Teichman, Howard
Thall, Victor
Thomas, Ted
Thompson, Donald
Thomson, Virgil
Trubach, Serge
Tworkov, Jack
Tyler, Converse
Van Veen, Stuyvesant
Velie, Jay
Velonis, Anthony
Vogel, Joseph
Wallace, Lea

NY (*continued*)
Wayne, June
Weissberger, Arnold
Welles, Halsted
Wheeler, Louanne
Wilder, Grace
Wilkes, Nathan
Williams, Jay
Wilson, Ellis
**OH**
Carter, Clarence Holbrook
Flint, Leroy W.
Horn, Axel
Lee, Russell
Neff, Earl
Opper, John
Roberts, Gordon
Schmidt, Katherine
Shahn, Ben
**OK**
Alessandro, Victor
Kirkland, Vance H.
Magafan, Ethel
Rush, Olive
Sheets, Nan
**OR**
Bunce, Louis Dermott
Chaivoe, Nick
Cunningham, Michele E.
Morris, Carl
Porter, Don
Smith, Margery Hoffman
Yeon, John
**PA**
Cohn, Arthur
Gross, Chaim
Gwathmey, Robert
Hirsch, Joseph
Hood, Richard
Levi, Julian
Rickey, George W.
Rosati, James
Schulman, Rose
Van Veen, Stuyvesant
Watkins, Franklin
**RI**
Malicoat, Philip

Moffett, Ross E.
**SC**
Craft, Paul
Hairston, Jester
Lishinsky, Abraham
**SD**
Boratko, Andre
Shope, Irvin
Wedin, Elof
**TN**
Billings, Henry
Greenwood, Grace
Greenwood, Marion
**TX**
Ayers, Atlee B.
Bistram, Emil J.
Chavez, Edward Arcenio
Dozier, Otis
Feder, Abe
Hurd, Peter
Martin, Fletcher
Moya Del Pino, Jose
Rublee, Bertha Hellman
Scheuer, Suzanne
Shonnard, Eugenie F.
Turner, Ida McAfee
Zakheim, Bernard Baruch
Zornes, James Milford
**UT**
Goodall, Donald B.
Hairston, Jester
**VA**
Bales, Richard Horner
Chase, Richard
Gwathmey, Robert
Hale, Laura Virginia
Hamilton, Emory L.
Ions, Willoughby
Richardson, Eudora Ramsey
Rufty, Hilton
Sloan, Raymond H.
**VT**
Crockwell, S. Douglas
Leuning, Otto
**WA**
Abel, Don G.
Anderson, Guy

254

WA (*continued*)
Bonath, Harry
Browne, Theodore
Callahan, Kenneth L.
Chinn, Andrew
Chong, Fay
Cumming, William
Elshin, Jacob
Engard, Robert Oliver
Fields, Earl T.
Fitzgerald, Margaret T.
Fleckenstein, Opal R.
Fuller, Richard E.
Glyer, Richard
Goss, Dale
Haines, Richard
Inverarity, Robert Bruce
Jackson, Sara O.
Liston, Ilo Carey
Losey, Blanche Morgan
Meredith, Betty Arden
Monroe, Charles
Morris, Carl

Ottenheimer, Albert M.
Reed, Florence
Savage, George
Sazevich, Zygmund
Staton, Joseph
Steinbrueck, Victor
Talbot, Clarence
Tomkins, Margaret
Warren, Marijane
Washington, James W. Jr.
Whitehouse, Harold C.
Williams, Guy

WI
Jerry, Sylvester
Lewandowski, Edmund
Pollock, Merlin F.
Thomas, Howard
Thwaites, Charles
Westcott, Harold

WV
Lenson, Michael

WY
Dieterich, Hebert R., Jr.

# 7. Guide to Oral History Repositories

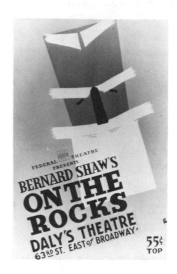

The following lists repositories that contain interviews included in the "Alphabetical Directory of Interviews." Private collections are listed at the end.

**Archives of American Art**
AA-PG Building, Balcony 331
8th & F Streets NW
Washington, D.C. 20560
202-357-4251
Contact: Cathy Keen
Hours: M-F, 10-5
Copying policy: No copying permitted
Inter-library Loan (ILL) policy: Only filmed interviews
Card catalog covers entire oral history collection. No interviews are available for purchase. Many interviews are now being typed and microfilmed and will ultimately be available for inter-library loan. Nothing has as yet been published except a bound card catalog and an oral history catalog, *Catalog of the Oral History Collections of the Archives of American Art*, and those are only partially cross-referenced.

**University of California, Berkeley**
Regional Oral History Office
The Bancroft Library
Berkeley, CA 94720
415-642-7395
Contact: Willa Baum, Department Head
Hours: M-F, 9-5
Copying policy: Copies for sale to libraries and to individuals

with interviewee's permission. Permission required to quote. Catalog of the *Regional Oral History Office* available.

**University of California, Los Angeles**
UCLA Oral History Program
136 Powell Library
405 Hilgard Ave.
Los Angeles, CA 90024
213-825-4932
Oral history collection at Department of Special Collections
University Research Library, UCLA
Contact: David S. Zeiberg, Head, DSC
Hours: M-Sat, 8-5
Copying policy: 25 copies per day; complete transcript copies may be ordered from Director, Oral History Program
ILL policy: Not permitted
    Interviews may be purchased with written request to Dale Treleven, Director, Oral History Program. About one-third of the Oral History Program's interviews involve some aspect of the fine arts at UCLA and in Los Angeles.

**Columbia University**
Oral History Collection
220 M Butler Library
Columbia University
New York, NY
212-280-2273
Contact: Ronald J. Grele, Director
Hours: M-F, 9-5
Copying policy: Copyright law obtains
ILL policy: Not permitted
    All oral history memoirs are indexed for proper names and a catalog abstract is prepared for each memoir. A dictionary catalog, *The Oral History Collection of Columbia University* describes holdings, provides subject cross references, and explains restrictions on access where they exist. Annual reports provide supplementary information.

**Denver Public Library**
Western History Department
1357 Broadway
Denver, CO 80203-2165
303-571-2009
Contact: Bonnie Hardwick, Manuscripts Specialist
Copying policy: Restricted
ILL policy: Available
    In-house catalog available.

**Fisk University**
Special Collections
Nashville, TN 37203
615-329-8580/646
Contact: Ann Allen Shockley, Associate Librarian for Special
Collections and University Archivist
Hours: M-F, 8-5.
Copying policy: Permission required.
ILL policy: Non-circulating collection
   The library has published *An Annotated Bibliography of the
Fisk University Library's Black Oral History Program* by
Veronica Tucker.

**George Mason University**
Special Collections
Fenwick Library
4400 University Drive
Fairfax, VA  22030
703-323-2251
Contact: Ruth Kerns, Director of Special Collections
Hours: M-F, 8:30-5
Copying policy: Inquiries should be directed to the Special
Collections Librarian
ILL policy: Permitted
   Partial   description  of  holdings  in  *Performing  Arts
Resources*, vol. 6 (1980), pp. 63-69. Collection focuses on the
FTP but includes interviews relating to all the government
sponsored art projects of the 1930s. Oral history collection
supplements the "product" material of the Federal Theatre
Project, which the Library of Congress has placed on
permanent deposit at George Mason University.

**Hatch-Billops Collection, Inc.**
491 Broadway, 7th Floor
New York, NY 10012
212-966-3231
Contact: James V. Hatch, Director or Camille J. Billops,
Director
Hours: Open by appointment only
Copying policy: Tapes may not be duplicated without the
artist's permission. Copies of abstracts may be purchased.
ILL policy: Not permitted
   Focus of the collection is on the Afro-American artist in
all disciplines, although artists from other racial groups are
included. Any qualified person may use the collection which is
indexed and cataloged by artist and by art discipline.

**Indiana University**
Archives of Traditional Music
Maxwell Hall 057
Indiana University
Bloomington, IN 47405
812-335-8632
Contact: Anthony Seeger, Director
Hours: M-F, 9-5
Copying policy: Copies of most materials available with permission of collector/depositor
ILL policy: Permitted
　　Card catalog in Archives' library, printed catalog of holdings through 1974: *A Catalog of Phonorecordings of Music and Oral Data Held by the Archives of Traditional Music*. Interviews are available for purchase. Collection holds recordings made by Herbert Halpert and Alton Morris under the auspices of the WPA.

**LaGuardia Community College/CUNY**
LaGuardia Archives
31-10 Thomson Ave.
Long Island City, NY 11101
718-626-5078
Contact: Richard K. Lieberman, Director
Hours: M-F, 10-4
Copying policy: May copy transcripts but not tapes
ILL Loan: Need direct request to archives
　　Collection contains records of the New York City Housing Authority and its involvement with WPA Artists for art in housing projects.

**University of Maryland**
Pillsbury Foundation School Archives
MENC Historical Center, Music Library
College Park, MD 20742
301-454-5611
Contact: Bruce D. Wilson, Curator, Special Collections in Music
Hours: M-F, 8:30-4:30
Copying policy: Duplication available at cost of copying
ILL policy: Permitted with payment for copying

**Memphis State University Library**
Mississippi Valley Collection
Memphis State University
Memphis, TN 38152
901-454-2210

Contact: Eleanor McKay, Curator
Hours: M-F, 8-4:30
Copying policy: Will copy unrestricted tapes; transcripts may not be copied without permission.
ILL policy: Will lend small number of transcripts, to be used in library of borrowing institution.

The library has an extensive shelf list and is developing series descriptions. Potential users must apply in advance in writing and supply research topic as well as credentials.

**Minnesota Historical Society**
Audio Visual Library
690 Cedar Street
St. Paul, MN 55101
612-296-2489
Contact: Bonnie Wilson, Head, Special Libraries
Hours: M-Sat: 8:30-5
Copying policy: Written permission required
ILL policy: Not permitted

Library uses notebooks to describe the tapes. A published catalog, *The Oral History Collections of the Minnesota Historical Society*, is available. Copies of interviews may be purchased for the cost of the blank tape and dubbing time costs. Transcripts are available for 10 cents a page. The majority of the tapes on FAP were made in preparation for an exhibit by the University of Minnesota Gallery.

**New York Public Library at Lincoln Center**
Theater on Film and Tape
111 Amsterdam Ave.
New York, NY 10023
212-870-1661
Oral history collection at Rodgers & Hammerstein Archives of Recorded Sound
Contact: Donald McCormick
Hours: M,Th, 10-7:45; T,W,F, 12-5:45; Sat, 10-5:45
Copying policy: Reserve right to deny. If donor has no objections, it is allowed.
ILL policy: Not permitted

No interviews available for purchase. Collection contains WNYC broadcasts from 1920s to 1960.

**New York University**
Tamiment Institute, Oral History of the American Left
Bobst Library, 70 Washington Square South
New York, NY 10012
212-598-3708

Contact: Jon Bloom
Hours: T,W,F, 10-5:45; M,Th, 10-9; Sat, 10-5
Copying policy: Not permitted
ILL policy: No loan of oral history tapes and transcripts
Indexes available, brief summaries in published guide. No interviews available for purchase. Seven-issue newsletter on Oral History of the American Left project and published guide, *The Guide to the Oral History of the American Left*, are available. Much of the material in the collection was donated from personal collections.

**University of Rochester**
Department of Rare Books and Special Collections, Library
River Campus Station
Rochester, NY 14620
716-275-4477
Contact: Peter Dzwonkoski, Head
Hours: M-F, 9-12 and 1-5
Copying policy: Will not copy tapes
ILL policy: Will not loan tapes
The tapes are part of the Jerre Mangione Papers which are now on deposit in the department but can be used only with the permission of Robert C. Stevens. Tapes will be listed in the Jerre Mangione Papers when they are processed.

**University of Santa Clara**
De Saisset Museum
Santa Clara, CA 95053
408-984-4528
Contact: Brigid Baston, Director
Hours: M-F, 9-5
Copying policy: Not practical (video tape). Tapes are wider than most recorder/players.
ILL policy: Not permitted

**Smithsonian Institution**
Archives Oral History Program
Arts and Industries 2135
Washington, D.C. 20560
202-357-1420
Contact: Pamela M. Henson, Historian
Hours: M-F, 9-5
Copying policy: Very limited, subject to restrictions
ILL policy: Not permitted
Collection holds oral history interviews and archival collections relating to PWAP murals, "The World Is Yours" radio program, and the Historic American Merchant Marine

Survey. Material is scattered throughout an institutional archives and oral history project generated by people who worked on government sponsored arts projects at the Smithsonian. See *Guide to the Smithsonian Archives.*

**Southern Methodist University**
Oral History Program on the Performing Arts
Department of History
Dallas, TX 75275
214-692-2889
Contact: Ronald L. Davis, Director
Copying policy: Will reproduce for a fee
ILL policy: Not permitted
　　　The collection is located in the De Goyler Institute for American Studies, Science Information Center. SMU has published a catalog, *Oral History Collection on the Performing Arts.*

**Tulane University**
William Ransom Hogan Jazz Archives
Howard-Tilton Memorial Library
New Orleans, LA 70118
504-865-6634
Contact: Curtis D. Jerde, Curator
Hours: M-F, 8:30-5
Copying policy: In house duplication of transcripts or summaries available.
ILL policy: Not permitted

**University of Washington**
Libraries, Archives and Manuscript Division
FM-25
Seattle, WA 98195
206-543-1874
Contact: Karyl Winn, Curator of Manuscripts
Hours: M-F, 8-12 and 1-5
Copying policy: Only permitted when copyright held by library
ILL policy: None, prefer to duplicate at cost
　　　Interviews available for purchase if no restrictions by informant. See *Comprehensive Guide to the Manuscript Collection and Personal Papers in the University Archives* and Margot Knight, *Directory of Oral History in Washington State.*

**State Historical Society of Wisconsin**
State Historical Society of Wisconsin Oral History Program
816 State Street
Madison, WI 53706

608-262-3266
Contact: George Talbot, Curator of Visual and Sound Archives
Hours: M-F, 9-5
Copying policy: Tapes, abstracts reproduced for a fee.
Researcher must sign Society's identification form.
ILL policy: Permitted through research centers at various
college and university campuses in Wisconsin.

**Yale School of Music**
Oral History, American Music
96 Wall Street
New Haven, CT 06520
203-432-4169
Contact: Vivian Perlis, Director
Hours: M-F, 9-5
Copying policy: Available for a fee on tapes and transcripts
ILL policy: Not permitted
   Card catalog lists all interviews alphabetically. Interviews
may be purchased if permission is granted. Interviews are
incorporated in general oral history interviews with major
figures in music.


## PRIVATE COLLECTIONS

   The following people hold private collections of interviews,
which can be consulted by special request.

**Dr. Jannelle Warren-Findley**
2905 Pine Springs Road
Falls Church, VA 22042

**Dr. Charles Perdue**
Department of English/Anthropology
University of Virginia
Charlottesville, VA 22904

**Pauline Hahn**
74 A Forest Drive
Springfield, NJ 07081

**David Dunaway**
Dept. of English
University of New Mexico
Albuquerque, NM 87106

**Dr. Robert Snyder**

Dept. of Speech, Radio/TV/Film Division
University of Wisconsin-Oshkosh
Oshkosh, WI 54901

# Part II
# Other Research, Resources:
# Archival Collections,
# Secondary Sources, and Films

# 8. Archival Collections:
## A Preliminary Guide

The following listing of archival collections relevant to the study of the government-sponsored arts projects of the 1930s is not intended to be a definitive guide. Such an exhaustive listing of collections is beyond the scope of this project. Instead, we offer an introductory guide to the best-known national and local collections. The guide is organized into four sections: A. Major Collections (includes collections that are national in scope); B. Local and Regional Collections (organized by state); C. Additional Repositories of FWP Records (A recently published pamphlet provides a comprehensive guide to FWP collections in state repositories; rather than simply repeat the information in this guide we have provided a summary of its contents and have referred readers to it for further information.); D. Major Repositories of New Deal Art (a very brief introduction to the locations of art works produced on the government projects.) Many of the references in the second section are drawn from the *The National Union Catalog of Manuscript Collections*, and additional information on those entries can be found there.

## A. MAJOR COLLECTIONS

**Archives of American Art**
Washington Office, AA-PG Building, Smithsonian Institution, Washington, DC 20560
202-357-2781
Microfilmed holdings are available at the Archives regional centers: 41 E 65th St., New York, NY 10021; 87 Mount Vernon St., Boston, MA 02108; 5200 Woodward Ave.,

Detroit, MI 48202; DeYoung Museum, Golden Gate Park, San Francisco, CA 94118; and Huntington Library and Art Gallery, 1151 Oxford Road, San Marino, CA 91108. They are also available on Inter-library Loan. A guide to the collections is in preparation. But the following published finding aids to the collections are available:

*Archives of American Art, a Directory of Resources.* N.Y., R.R. Bowker, 1972.

*The Card Catalog of the Manuscript Collections of the Archives of American Art.* Wilmington, Delaware, Scholarly Resources, Inc., 1980. 10 vols. and supplement.

*The Card Catalog of the Oral History Collections of the Archives of American Art.* Wilmington, Delaware, Scholarly Resources, Inc., 1984.

Recent acquisitions are described in each issue of the quarterly *Archives of American Art Journal.*

The Archives of American Art is one of the major repositories of records from the art projects of the 1930s as well as the FSA photography project. The following is a partial listing of its holdings.

ADMINISTRATORS' PAPERS: The Archives holds papers of the following arts projects administrators.

\* Edward Bruce: Executive, economist, corporation counsel, semi-professional painter and muralist, and bureaucrat who administered the PWAP and the Section of Fine Arts. Personal papers and official records.

\* Edward Rowan: Deputy administrator of PWAP and the Section of Fine Arts. Personal papers and official records.

\* Olin Dows: Muralist and first director of the TRAP. Personal papers and official records.

\* Charles Christopher Adams: Museum director. Material on FAP

\* Emanuel Mervin Benson: Consultant to FAP. Reports, directives, articles, speeches, clippings. Community Art Centers and Index of American Design covered. Includes mock-up of projected book "Art for the Millions."

\* Holger Cahill: Papers of the head of FAP.

\* Adele Clark: Papers relating to her work as director of FAP in Virginia.

\* Nina Perera Collier: Government official. Material relating to her work in the Federal Emergency Relief Administration, Section for Professional and Non-Manual Projects, and as publicist for the Information Service of the WPA. Includes papers on FAP, FMP, criticism of FWP, alleged Communist propaganda in FTP, and movement for permanent government art program.

270

* Roy Stryker: Head of the FSA historical section. Microfilm copy of correspondence, reports, articles and other publications. Includes material relating to Depression era photographs.

* Paul Vanderbilt: Vanderbilt joined the FSA in 1941 as a classifier and organizer of the photograph file.

ARTISTS' PAPERS: Many, perhaps most, of the major artists born between 1890 and 1910 were employed by or had commissions from the government in the 1930s. That generation is prominently represented in the Archives with papers that almost invariably reflect a connection with the projects, chiefly through correspondence and photographs but occasionally through journals, sketchbooks, and reminiscences. Some specific artists are listed below.

* William Baziotes: Painter. FAP papers and correspondence from major figures in art during the 1930s and 1940s.

* Clarence Holbrook Carter: 200 items of correspondence (1934-56), contracts, memoranda, bulletins, and photos, relating to Carter's painting of post office murals in Portsmouth and Ravenna, Ohio, under the direction of the U.S. Treasury Dept. Section of Painting and Sculpture, and the organization of the Municipal Collection of the Cleveland Art Project under the FAP, journal reproductions and tear sheets of Carter's work.

* George Constant: Correspondence, announcements, reviews and photos. Some letters from Edward Bruce and from administrators of the Graphic Arts Division of the WPA Art Program.

* Helen Stuart Davis: Sculptor. One reel of microfilm of papers dating from 1935-39, relating to her difficulties working with the FAP in Dade County, Fla., and in Berkeley, Calif.

* Eugenie Gershoy: Sculptor. Letters relating FAP experiences.

* F. Wynn Graham: Correspondence relating to artists' organizations and unions in New York City and FAP.

* Julian Levi: Painter. Correspondence pertaining to WPA-New York City art projects, 1930-40.

* Richard Lippold: Material relating to conference on government participation in the arts and humanities.

* Edward Millman: Muralist, art professor. Correspondence, lectures, notes relating to work as WPA artist and State Director of Mural Projects for the WPA Fine Arts Project in Illinois (1934-45).

* Geoffrey Norman: Official correspondence relating to the National Society of Mural Painters and the FAP in New York City (1934-40).

* Irene (Rice) Pereira: Includes lectures delivered to

271

students attending the Design Laboratory sponsored by the FAP.

* Vernon B. Smith: Material on his career as supervisor of FAP Easel Division in Massachusetts, work in Alaska as an FAP painter, and other government art projects.

DEALERS' AND CRITICS' PAPERS: Of particular importance are the extensive files of the Downtown Gallery and the art writer Elizabeth McCausland. The latter contain substantial information on the FAP and the FSA photography project.

* Onya LaTour: Material relating to WPA Federal Art Gallery, New York, N.Y. (1936-37).

* Helen Appleton Read: Art critic and gallery director. Reports from her survey of art in Federal buildings.

OTHER HOLDINGS:

* New York City FAP photographs.

* Microfilm copies of official records at the National Archives: This is not a complete duplication of archives records, but it includes: PWAP correspondence and central office records (17 rolls); TRAP records (25 rolls); Section of Fine Arts Records (18 rolls); FAP records (70 rolls).

* Microfilm copies of official documents from the Franklin D. Roosevelt Library at Hyde Park and several state repositories.

* FAP staff members' records from Virginia, Washington, Delaware, Oregon, and New York.

* Brooklyn Institute of Arts and Sciences: 25 reels of microfilm of records. Includes material on FAP, especially in relation to graphics.

* Fine Arts Federation of New York: Correspondence, minutes, reports, financial records and publications of a council composed of representatives from New York City art organizations. Includes material on Federal art legislation during the Depression.


**Franklin D. Roosevelt Library**
259 Albany Post Road
Hyde Park, NY 12538
914-229-8114

* Harry Hopkins Papers: Correspondence, memoranda, field reports, directives, file of speeches and articles, transcripts of conferences, statistical data, press releases, and newspaper clippings relating to Hopkins' service with the New York Temporary Relief Administration and as Administrator, WPA.

* Howard Hunter Papers: Documents of Deputy Administrator of WPA, 1939-42.
* Eleanor Roosevelt Papers: Series 70 and 100. See especially Woodward, Bruce, Flanagan, Kerr, Dewson, and Lazell files.
* Franklin D. Roosevelt Papers: OF-444C. WPA and WPA miscellaneous files. Also sound recordings.
* Hilda Smith Papers: Director, Workers' Service Program, Federal Emergency Relief Administration and Works Progress Administration, 1933-43. Papers date from 1922-47.
* Charles W. Taussig Papers: Chairman, National Advisory Committee, National Youth Administration, 1935-43. Papers from 1928-48.
* Rexford Guy Tugwell Papers: Correspondence, diary, journal notes, memoranda, newspaper clippings and press releases relating to Tugwell's work as Director of the RA.


**George Mason University**
Special Collections, Fenwick Library
4400 University Drive
Fairfax, VA  22030
703-323-2251
The Federal Theatre Project and the New Deal Culture collections at George Mason University number about 250,000 items. The materials fall into four major groupings:
* Administrative records, including personnel folders, publicity clippings, meeting notes, financial data, reports, policy and procedure memorandums, mailing lists, and correspondence, (the bulk of the administrative records are at the National Archives).
* Research records, including bibliographies and lists, card files, playreader reports, study guides, reports on sources of dramatic literature, factual research for productions, audience surveys, and the Living Newspaper clipping file.
* Production records, including billboard, posters, photographs, music, prompt scripts, film clips, programs, lighting plots, costume and set designs, production notebooks, marionettes, radio scripts, and publicity materials.
* Non-archival Federal Theatre Project materials, including books, magazines, articles, speeches, unpublished research, and oral history memoirs.
In 1974 most of these records were placed on permanent loan by the Library of Congress on the condition that the materials be sorted, inventoried, and made accessible to scholars. FTP records that did not come as part of the major deposit have been donated by former FTP employees. In

addition to the archival records, the University has acquired related books, articles, and unpublished research dealing with the FTP or New Deal culture. Grants from NEH and NHPRC have made possible these acquisitions as well as the processing of the collection.

**Library of Congress**
First St. between East Capitol & Independence Ave. SE
Washington, DC 20540
202-287-5000
The Library of Congress is a major Federal repository of publications, research materials and administrative records produced by the WPA. Among the holdings are the following.

## MANUSCRIPT DIVISION

The Manuscript Division is a repository for transcripts and unpublished manuscripts and the following relevant collections:

* Ex-Slave Narrative Collection: More than two thousand interviews with former slaves done by the FERA and the FWP transcribed, edited, and microfilmed and published in several editions. Auxiliary research materials also in collection.

* Folklore and Social-Ethnic Studies Collection: Research files, correspondence, and publications from the FWP divided into three principal groups: traditional folklore (myths, legends, stories and rhymes), life histories (first and third person narratives about daily living), and urban-ethnic studies, which includes field notes and compilations and a lexicon of trade slang and jargon.

* Unpublished WPA Materials: Numerous containers of unpublished manuscripts, transcripts, and research materials generated by the arts projects, primarily the Historical Records Survey and the FWP. The FWP portion of the collection includes manuscripts that were approved for publication but remained unpublished for various reasons and copies of unedited material thought to be of potential research value.

* Personal Papers: Correspondence and records of people involved in the arts projects.
George Biddle Papers: Includes general and family correspondence, drafts, and printed copies of speeches and articles, sketchbooks (1930-59), scrapbooks of personal clippings, announcements of exhibits, and reviews of Biddle's

books, relating chiefly to his place in American art, his work in behalf of Federal support of art. FAP (1933). Also material about his murals for the Mexican Supreme Court Building and the War Dept. Art Committee.

Katharine Amend Kellock Papers: Includes correspondence, project reports, and other papers relating to Kellock's work with the FWP as a field supervisor and tours editor of the American Guide series.

## MUSIC DIVISION

* Composer File of American Music (twenty thousand typed cards describing compositions).

* Programs from various FMP productions. These holdings are extensive and are kept in storage in a warehouse in Maryland. Researchers interested in this material should specify state and year in their requests.

* Appendices to the FMP final report. [Note: The final report is at the National Archives.]

* Recordings from FMP performances are in the Recorded Sound Division.

## AMERICAN FOLKLIFE CENTER

ARCHIVE OF FOLK SONG: Completed discs from a special recording project conducted in the southern states under the sponsorship of the WPA's Joint Committee on Folk Arts. Also California field studies conducted in ethnic and migrant communities.

## PRINTS AND PHOTOGRAPHS DIVISION

* WPA Posters: Nearly a thousand silk-screened posters produced in the 1930s to publicize FTP productions, exhibits, community activities, and health and educational programs in twenty states.

* WPA Prints: Two Hundred and twenty prints produced by WPA artists. Items listed by artist in the fine prints card index and in the publication *American Prints in the Library of Congress*(Baltimore: Published for the Library of Congress by the Johns Hopkins University Press, 1970).

* FSA Photographs Collection: Photographic record of American life between 1935 and 1942. Collection consists of more than 270,000 photographs that document rural conditions, life in urban communities, and the domestic side of the war effort taken by a team of photographers headed by Roy E. Stryker and including Carl Mydans, Walker Evans, Dorthea

Lange, Ben Shahn, Arthur Rothstein, Russell Lee, and Jack Delano. A portion of the collection (87,000 captioned photographs) is available on microfiche from Chadwyck-Healey, 1021 Prince St., Alexandria, VA 22314.

**National Archives**
Pennsylvania Ave. at 8th St. NW
Washington, D.C. 20408
202-655-4000

The National Archives is the primary repository for administrative records relating to the following government sponsored arts projects.

PUBLIC WORKS OF ART PROJECT: Surviving records of the project are part of Record Group 121, Records of the Public Buildings Service, and include central office correspondence and related records; central office correspondence with artists; newspaper clippings; card lists of allocated paintings and other works of art; and receipt cards for works of art. Holdings also include documents preserved as samples of larger bodies of records that were disposed of. These are selected records of the 16 regional offices (2 linear feet); and correspondence of the Region 2 office with artists (4 linear feet). Additional PWAP materials are in Record Group 69.

TREASURY RELIEF ART PROJECT: TRAP records, in Record Group 121, consist of a general administrative and reference file of the Chief of the Project, 1935-37; central office correspondence with field offices, state supervisors, and others, 1935-39; correspondence of the New York City supervisor with the Washington office, 1935-38; and a card record by artist of art works submitted in competition, 1936-39.

SECTION OF FINE ARTS, PUBLIC BUILDINGS ADMINISTRATION: Records, also in Record Group 121, consist of case files concerning embellishments of Federal Buildings, 1934-43 (55 linear feet), arranged by state and thereunder by building with a separate section for buildings in the District of Columbia; exhibition records, 1939-42; decoration of buildings at the New York World's Fair; the Marian Anderson mural in the Interior Department Building; National Art Week, 1940; national defense and war art projects; and art works produced in Civilian Conservation Corps camps; technical questionnaires, 1936-38; letters received and other records concerning completed murals and works of sculpture and their artists, 1935-42; a biographical data file on artists, 1938; announcements of competitions, 1935-41; and the correspondence 1934-43, of Edward Bruce who served as head of the Section from 1934-43. In addition to the textual records, there are fifteen series of photographic records including photographs of sketches submitted in 1936 for the so-called "48 States Competition" for murals to be placed in public buildings; photographs of sketches of proposed murals and sculpture, 1933-43; and photographs of murals in U.S. Post Offices, 1933-43.

WORKS PROJECTS ADMINISTRATION: Record Group 69 comprises the records of the WPA and its predecessors, the Federal Emergency Relief Administration, the Civil Works Administration, and the Works Progress Administration. The records of each agency include a central correspondence file composed of a "General Subject" series and a "State" series. The "General Subject" series for both the CWA and the FERA include folders for the PWAP; information about other arts projects conducted under these agencies may be found by examining materials filed under general "Projects" headings in the "General Subject" and "State" series. The WPA central files include specific classifications for records relating art, music, theatre, and writers' projects.

WPA'S FEDERAL PROJECT NO. 1: The FAP, the FTP, the FMP, the FWP, and the HRS. Final reports exist for most of the programs. (The appendices that accompany the FMP Final Report are in the Library of Congress.) Originally part of the "State" correspondence series, they have been segregated into one large series arranged by type of project and thereunder by State. The file for the FTP is incomplete, consisting only of reports from Florida, Louisiana, New Hampshire, New Jersey, Oklahoma, Pennsylvania, and Rhode Island. There is a separate set of reports on arts and crafts programs that operated outside the FAP.

Files of the central offices were maintained separately. Some of the documents are:

* Records of the Finance Officer, 1935-39 (6 linear feet), which provide statistical information about the project.

* Records of the FAP, 1935-40 (28 linear feet), consisting of general records, correspondence with state and regional offices; reports of the FAP for New York State, New York City, and New Jersey, 1935-39; small quantities of material from the projects in Illinois, Massachusetts, and Ohio; and copies of speeches, addresses, lectures, and reports, 1937-38, of Holger Cahill, FAP director, and others.

* Records of the FMP, 1935-40 (41 linear feet), includes

correspondence, reports, programs and schedules, material on folk music, music festivals, music research, and American composers; newspaper clippings and magazine articles; material on the Composers Forum; four scrapbooks on FMP activities in New York City, an album of photographs of symphony orchestras, choral groups, jubilee singers, and Mexican tipica orchestras, and press clippings and publicity materials concerning Nikolai Sokoloff, the FMP director, and his concert appearances.

* Records of the FWP, 1935-44 (133 linear feet) consisting of more than 40 series, most of which are arranged by State, including administrative correspondence, 1935-39; editorial correspondence, 1936-39; field reports and reports on FWP activities and plans; publication reports, 1937-42; "Applications for Permission to Publish," 1937-44; administrative memorandums, and office files of the FWP director, Henry G. Alsberg, and other officials; also files on the American Encyclopedia series; the *American Stuff* magazine; architectural, ethnic, Negro, Indian and archaeological studies; proposed studies on the "Lexicon of Trade Jargon" and municipal government; and manuals and instructions; correspondence on folklore and ex-slave studies compiled by the FWP and edited by the Library of Congress Writers' Unit in 1940.

* Records of the FTP, 1935-39, are the most voluminous, consisting of more than 400 linear feet. Correspondence files include general correspondence of the National office, correspondence of the National Director, Hallie Flanagan, and other officials; correspondence with FTP personnel and individuals concerned with FTP; and correspondence with regional offices and state FTP officials. Report files include semi-monthly activity reports, narrative reports, regional reports, reports of various types for Region V, and reports of operations in Southern California. There is a general correspondence file for the Play Policy Board, 1936-37, a large collection of materials for the National Service Bureau, a collection of playscripts (34 linear feet) with separate groups of Yiddish and Civilian Conservation Corps scripts; region and state office records; Living Newspaper files consisting of more than 25 linear feet; bound and unbound production bulletins documenting FTP productions (25 linear feet); publicity materials and related records (61 linear feet); scrapbooks covering FTP activities in ten states Florida, Michigan, New Jersey, New York, North Carolina, Ohio, Oregon, Texas, Washington, and Wisconsin (8 linear feet) and three scrapbooks on the New York Caravan Theatre; FTP Radio Division scripts from units in San Francisco, Los Angeles, New York City,

Syracuse, Buffalo, and Oklahoma.

WPA INFORMATION DIVISION: The Information Division prepared responses to requests from newspapers, public officials and citizens, and compiled data for dissemination in reports, pamphlets, articles, public speeches, and radio broadcasts. The records of the Radio Section include state and general correspondence files, 1936-42, and several series of radio scripts, including some for recorded talks with prominent persons in government, the arts, business, journalism, and the military. Some FTP radio scripts are found in the records of the Radio Section.

A large newspaper clippings file of published news stories, editorials, and columns contains much information about programs under Federal Project No. 1. Filed under the general heading "Arts," are folders for actors, exhibits, models, murals, music, painters, policies, theatre, writers, Writers' Guide, and miscellaneous. The Division also compiled a separate set of materials relating to the National Art Week in 1940.

The principal series of Division records is the Information Service file, 1936-42 (43 linear feet) which is arranged according to a numeric-subject classification system. The 900 section of the file covers "Cultural Projects" under which are separate classification numbers for FAP (910), FTP (920), FMP (930), FWP (940), and American Guide (945).

THE PARE LORENTZ FILMS: Two of the most famous and widely distributed documentary films produced by the Federal Government came from the Information Division of the Resettlement Administration and its successor, the Farm Security Administration: *The Plow That Broke the Plains* (1936) and *The River* (1937). These films and five silent films by the Information Division are part of the audiovisual records of the Farmers Home Administration, Record Group 96.

LOCATION AIDS: The following published inventories should be available at most large libraries. All of the location aids mentioned below are available for use at the National Archives.

* *Preliminary Inventory of the Records of the Public Buildings Service*, PI 110 (1950) compiled by W. Lane Van Neste and Virgil E. Gaugh, describes the records of the Treasury Department programs.

* "Preliminary Checklist of the Central Correspondence Files of the Work Projects Administration and Its Predecessors, 1933-1944," PC 37 (1946) compiled by Frances T. Bourne with the assistance of Betty Herscher. This in-house guide explains

the CWA, FERA, and WPA filing systems and provides a list of file headings for the central files of each agency and an alphabetical listing of subject headings in the WPA classified correspondence files. Also included are listings of FERA and WPA divisional, office, and project records in the National Archives as well as brief administrative histories of the agencies.

   * *Preliminary Inventory of the Records of the Federal Writers' Project, Work Projects Administration, 1935-44*, PI 57 (1953) compiled by Katherine H. Davidson. There records of the FWP are fully described in this volume and draft inventories exist for the FAP, FMP, FTP, the records of the Finance Officer of Federal Project No. 1, and the Division of Information. These drafts contain lists of file headings for individual series of records.

   * Information about the Information Division of the Resettlement Administration and the Farm Security Administration is available in *Preliminary Inventory of the Records of the Farmers Home Administration*, PI 118 (1959) compiled by Stanley W. Brown and Virgil E. Baugh.

**National Gallery of Art**
Constitution at 6th St. NW
Washington, DC 20565
202-842-6604

   The National Gallery is the repository for the Index of American Design, an FAP project to compile a visual survey of the objects of decorative, folk, and popular arts made in America from the time of settlement to 1900. The collection consists of 17,000 watercolors of decorative objects painted by FAP artists, information sheets on the watercolors, documentary photographs, and color microfiche. The complete collection on color microfiche along with a printed catalog, *Consoldiated Catalog to the Index of American Design*, is available from Chadwyck-Healey (1021 Prince St., Alexandria, VA 22314).

### B. LOCAL AND REGIONAL COLLECTIONS
(Organized by state)

### ARIZONA

Arizona State University, The Hayden Library, Tempe, AZ 85281 602-965-3106
   * Philip Curtis Archives: Collection of WPA prints.
   * Thomas Wardell Papers: Correspondence and 55

photographs of furniture and artwork from the FAP.

University of Arizona Museum of Art, Tucson, AZ 85721 602-621-7567
* Typescripts of interviews and other correspondence with various persons connected with the New Deal projects.

## CALIFORNIA

San Francisco Museum of Modern Art, Louise Sloss Ackerman Fine Arts Library, Van Ness & McAllister, San Francisco, CA 94102 415-863-8800
* Files on FAP artists.

University of California, Berkeley Bancroft Library, Berkeley, CA 94720 415-642-3781
* Microfilms of biographical sketches of Utah pioneers prepared by the Historical Records Survey and FWP.

## DISTRICT OF COLUMBIA

Moorland-Spingarn Research Center, Founder's Library, Howard University, Washington, D.C. 20059 202-636-7479
* Isabele Taliaferro Spiller Papers: Photos documenting Mrs. Spiller's work with FMP.

## FLORIDA

Jacksonville University, Swisher Library, Jacksonville, FL 32211 904-744-3950
* Files of Florida FWP.

## IOWA

State University of Iowa Libraries Iowa City, IO 52242 319-353-4450
* Edward Charles Mabie Papers: Correspondence of the Dept. of Speech and Dramatic Art of the University of Iowa, of which Mabie was head; material on the FTP and the Theatre for Victory Council.

## KENTUCKY

Division of Archives and Records Management, Dept. of Library and Archives, 851 East Main St., Frankfort, KY 40601
* Correspondence and material relating to FWP. Project files: America Eats, American Guide Series, American Life Series--Folklore, Kentucky Atlas, Baptists of Kentucky,

Kentucky Factbook, Fairs and Fairmakers, Greeks in America, Hands That Build America, Kentucky Derby, Military Area Guides, Military History of Kentucky, Our Lives, Kentucky Photobook, U.S. Travel Atlas.

University of Louisville, Photographic Archives, Louisville, KY 40208 502-588-6752
* Roy Stryker papers and photographs: Correspondence relating to Stryker's photographic projects for the FSA; newspaper clippings, booklets and article reprints pertaining to Stryker's career in photography; and 2,000 photographs from Stryker's personal collection including FSA and Standard Oil of New Jersey projects. Microfiche edition of papers and photographs available from Chadwyck-Healey.

Western Kentucky University, Kentucky Library Bowling Green, KY 42101 502-745-2592
* Narratives from interviews with former slaves prepared by FWP.

## LOUISIANA

Louisiana Tech University Library Ruston, LA 71270 318-257-3555
* Lavinia Egan Papers: Articles on Louisiana history, some for FWP.

Historic New Orleans Collection, 533 Royal St., New Orleans, LA 70130 504-523-4662
* Extensive artists files that include FAP artists.

## MASSACHUSETTS

Radcliffe College, Arthur and Elizabeth Schlesinger Library on the History of Women in America, 10 Garden St., Cambridge, MA 02138 617-495-8647
* Hilda Worthington Smith Papers: Material on Workers Service Program of the Emergency Relief Administration and the WPA.
* Ellen (Sullivan) Woodward Papers: Includes material relating to her work as the deputy WPA administrator in charge of white collar projects.

## MICHIGAN

Detroit Institute of Arts, Museum Archives and Record Center 5200 Woodward Ave., Detroit, MI 48202 313-833-7900

* Clyde H. Burroughs Papers: Includes material on the controversy over the Diego Rivera murals and the FAP (1933-36). Burroughs was Secretary of the Detroit Arts Commission and director and curator of the Detroit Museum of Art.

University of Michigan Library, Dept. of Rare Books and Special Collections, Ann Arbor, MI 48109  313-764-9377
    * Kenneth Thorpe Rowe Papers: Correspondence between Rowe and FTP officials, undertaken by Rowe on behalf of his playwriting students, including Arthur Miller, Kimon Friar, and Norman Rosten; together with circular letters of Detroit Federal Theatre.
    * Earl Vincent Moore Papers: Letters and other papers of the second director of the FMP.

## MISSISSIPPI

Mississippi State University, Mississippi State, MS 39762  601-325-3060
    * Margaret Valiant papers.

## MISSOURI

Missouri Historical Society, Jefferson Memorial Building, Forest Park, St. Louis, MO 63112  314-361-1424
    * John Green Papers: Physician. Correspondence, journals, records and notes includes material on his daughter Elizabeth's work with artists connected with the WPA, the Professional Workers' Program, the People's Art Center for Negroes in St. Louis, and the development of art in St. Louis.
    * Frank B. Nuderscher Papers: Correspondence, writings, and documents relating to Nuderscher's Civil Works Administration position in charge of artists in the Hospital Division.

## NEW HAMPSHIRE

University of New Hampshire Library, Durham, NH 03824  603-862-1534
    * New Hampshire WPA records: FAP material includes ca. 125 photos of New Hampshire places, artifacts, and activities.

## NEW YORK

George Arents Research Library, Syracuse University, Syracuse, NY 13210  315-423-2093
    * Catalogs, papers, manuscripts, on artists Aaron Bohrod,

Louis Lozowick, Anthony Toney, and Eugenie Gershoy.

Fiorello H. LaGuardia Archives, LaGuardia Community College, The City University of New York, 31-10 Thomson Ave., Long Island City, NY 11101   718-626-5078
   * Papers relating to WPA art in the housing projects.

New York Public Library, Performing Arts Research Center, Dance Collection, 111 Amsterdam Ave., New York, NY 10023   212-870-1641
   * Grant Hyde Code Papers: Poet. Includes letters referring to Code's attempts to collaborate with the FTP in setting up a workshop for young choreographers.
   * Hallie Flanagan Papers: Director of FTP. Correspondence, memoranda, reports relating to FTP.

## NORTH CAROLINA

University of North Carolina at Chapel Hill, Library Chapel Hill, NC 27514   919-962-1345
Southern Historical Collections
   * Travis (Tuck) Jordan Papers: 1500 items from the author and head of Durham, N.C. FWP.

## NORTH DAKOTA

University of North Dakota Library Grand Forks, ND 58206   701-777-2617
   * Collection of Nebraska Farmers' Alliance songs of the 1890's made by Nebraska FWP (1938).

## OHIO

Clark County Historical Society Collections, 818 North Fountain St., Springfield, OH 45501   513-324-0657
   * Zoe Johnson Papers: Author. Includes notes, clippings, personal interviews, copies of records comprising research done for the FWP in Ohio, American Guide Series (1941).

## OKLAHOMA

Oklahoma Art Center, Sheets Collection, 3113 Pershing Blvd., Oklahoma City, OK 73107   405-946-4477
   * Nan Sheets Papers: Artist's unpublished scrapbooks.

Oklahoma Historical Society, Wiley Post Building, Oklahoma City, OK 73105   405-521-2491

* Grant Foreman Papers: Supervisor of FWP Indian interviews. Correspondence and transcripts.
* Local FWP papers and correspondence.

University of Oklahoma Library Norman, OK 73069 405325-4142
* John Willis Stovall Papers: Paleontologist. Material on WPA sponsorship of various museum projects.
* Lida White Papers: Teacher. Correspondence, notes on Oklahoma Indian lore, interviews with survivors of the opening of the Territory in 1889, bibliographical notes, historical pictures and photos, maps, leases and contracts, news clippings, and printed material collected as part of a WPA project.

## OREGON

Oregon Historical Society Library, 1230 Southwest Park Ave., Portland, OR 97205 503-222-1741
* Harry Lane Papers: Transcripts of materials gathered by Oregon FWP for proposed biography of Harry Lane, Mayor of Portland and U.S. Senator.

University of Oregon Library, Eugene, OR 97403 503-686-3053
* Morris Watson Papers: Journalist. Correspondence, dramas, memoranda, and other papers relating to Watson's position as managing producer of Living Newspaper, part of the FTP sponsored by the Newspaper Guild of New York.

## PENNSYLVANIA

Columbia County Historical Society Collection, Bloomsburg, PA 17815
* Records accumulated in 1936 by local unit of the FWP. Includes recorded newspaper interviews relating to canals lumbering.

## SOUTH CAROLINA

South Carolina Historical Society Collections, 100 Meeting St., Charleston, SC 29401 803-723-3225
* Ann King Gregorie Papers: Records of South Carolina Writers' Program directed by Gregorie.

University of South Carolina, South Caroliniana Library, Columbia, SC 29208 803-777-4866
* Louise Jones DuBose Papers: Correspondence, poems,

radio scripts, plays, articles, newspaper clippings documenting DuBose's career as reporter and director of the FWP in S.C.

## SOUTH DAKOTA

South Dakota State Historical Resource Center, 500 East Capital St., Pierre, SD 57501 605-773-3615
* Records of the South Dakota Guide Commission: Correspondence, financial records, advertising, and reviews, pertaining to *South Dakota: A Guide to the State*, produced by the FWP.

## TEXAS

University of Texas at Austin Library, Austin, TX 78712 512-471-3840
* History of the cattle industry done by FWP.

## UTAH

Utah State University Library, Logan, UT 84321 801-750-2663
* WPA history of grazing collection, 1680-1941: Project correspondence with 17 states represented in a history of cattle, sheep, and horse grazing in the West. Also drafts for the national history and complete or partial histories of grazing in Arizona, North Dakota, Oregon, Texas, and Utah.

University of Utah Libraries, Special Collections Dept., Salt Lake City, UT 84112 801-581-8863
* Madeline (Reeder) Thurston McQuown Papers: Correspondence with Dale Lowell Morgan, with whom McQuown worked on the FWP.

## WASHINGTON

Seattle Public Library, 1000 Fourth Ave., Seattle, WA 98104 206-625-2665
* J. Willis Sayre Theatre Collection: 15,000 programs from plays performed in Seattle from 1860s to 1930s, 207-page list of "Complete Index of Plays Given in Seattle" with FTP plays, dates, and theaters inked in, and 197-page list of "Players Who Have Appeared in Seattle."

Tacoma Public Library, 1102 Tacoma Ave. South, Tacoma, WA 98402 206-591-5666
* Correspondence, lists and notes on historical markers

written and compiled by Alfred J. Smith for FWP, Pierce County.

University of Washington Library, Seattle, WA 98105 206-543-9158
  * Oliver King Wilson Papers: Material on the FTP.
  * Photographs of Seattle unit of FTP.


## C. ADDITIONAL REPOSITORIES OF FWP RECORDS

The following list (organized alphabetically by state) is based upon Ann Banks' and Robert Carter's very useful *Survey of Federal Writers' Project Holdings in State Depositories*, which contains much further information and may be obtained from the American Historical Association, 400 A Street SE, Washington, D.C. 20003. The price is $4 for AHA members and ISP subscribers; $5 for non-members and institutions.

State of Alabama, Dept. of Archives and History, Montgomery, AL 36130

State of Arizona, Dept. of Library, Archives and Public Records, 3rd Floor Capitol, 1700 West Washington, Phoenix, AZ 85007

Arkansas History Commission, 300 West Markham St., Little Rock, AR 72201

California State Library, Library-Courts Building, P.O. Box 2037, Sacramento, CA 95809

San Bernardino County, Historical Archives, 104 West Fourth St., San Bernardino, CA 92415

University of California, Los Angeles, The University Library, Dept. of Special Collections, University Research Library, Los Angeles, CA 90024

Colorado Historical Society, The Colorado Heritage Center, 1300 Broadway, Denver, CO 80203

Denver Public Library, 1357 Broadway, Denver, CO 80203

Connecticut State Library, 231 Capitol Ave., Hartford, CT 06115

University of Delaware, Morris Library, Newark, DE 19711

Florida Historical Society Library, The Library, University of South Florida, Tampa, FL 33620

Florida State Archives, Division of Archives, History, and Records Management, State of Florida, The Capitol, Tallahassee, FL 32304

Jacksonville Public Library, Haydon Burns Library, 122 North Ocean St., Jacksonville, FL 32202

The University of Florida, P. K. Yonge Library of Florida

History, The University Libraries, Gainesville, FL 32611

University of Georgia Libraries, Special Collections, Athens, GA 30602

Idaho State University, The Library, Pocatello, ID 83209

Illinois State Historical Library, Old State Capitol, Springfield, IL 62706

Indiana State University, Cunningham Memorial Library, Terre Haute, IN 47809

The University of Iowa, The University Libraries, Iowa City, IA 52242

Salina Public Library, P.O. Box 119, 301 West Elm St., Salina, KS 67401

Wichita State University, University Library, Wichita, KS 67208

Louisiana State Library, Louisiana Section, 760 Riverside North, P.O. Box 131, Baton Rouge, LA 70821

New Orleans Public Library, Louisiana Division, Robert Tallant Papers, 219 Loyola Ave., New Orleans, LA 70140

Northwestern State University Library, Special Collections Division, The Melrose Collection, Natchitoches, LA 71457

Tulane University Library, Howard-Tilton Memorial Library, New Orleans, LA 70118

University of Maryland, McKeldin Library, College Park, MD 20742

Minnesota Historical Society, Division of Archives and Manuscripts, 1500 Mississippi St., St. Paul, MN 55101

State of Mississippi, Dept. of Archives and History, P.O. Box 517, Jackson, MS 39205

University of Missouri, Western Historical Manuscript Collection, 23 Elmer Ellis Library, Columbia, MO 65201

Montana Historical Society, 225 North Roberts St., Helena, MT 59601

Montana State University Library, Bozeman, MT 59715

Nebraska State Historical Society, 1500 R St., Lincoln, NE 68508

Nevada Historical Society, 1650 North Virginia St., Reno, NV 89503

Manchester City Library, New Hampshire Room, Carpenter Memorial Building, 405 Pine St., Manchester, NH 03104

New Hampshire State Library, 20 Park St., Concord, NH 03301

The New Jersey Historical Society, 230 Broadway, Newark, NJ 07104

Museum of New Mexico, History Division Library, P.O. Box 2087, Santa Fe, NM 87503

State of New Mexico, State Records Center and Archives,

404 Montezuma, Santa Fe, NM 87503

The City of New York, Municipal Archives, Dept. of Records & Information Services, 52 Chambers St., New York, NY 10007

The Schomburg Center for Research in Black Culture, The New York Public Library, 515 Lenox Ave., New York, NY 10034

State Archives, The University of the State of New York, The State Education Department, Albany, NY 12234

The Port Jervis Free Library, 138 Pike St., Port Jervis, NY 12771

North Carolina Dept. of Cultural Resources, Division of Archives and History, Raleigh, NC 27611

State Historical Society of North Dakota, Liberty Memorial Building, Bismarck, ND 58505

The Ohio Historical Society, Inc., Archives-Manuscript Division, The Ohio Historical Society Center, I-71 and 17th Ave., Columbus, OH 43211

Oregon Historical Society, 1230 Southwest Park Ave., Portland, OR 97205

Oregon State Library, State Library Building, Salem, OR 97310

Pennsylvania Historical and Museum Commission, Bureau of Archives and History, William Penn Memorial Museum and Archives Building, Box 1026, Harrisburg, PA 17120

The University of South Dakota, The I.D. Weeks Library, Vermillion, SD 57069

Tennessee State Library and Archives, 403 Seventh Ave. North, Nashville, TN 37219

Austin Public Library, Austin-Travis County Collection, Box 2287, Austin, TX 78768

Barker Texas History Center, The General Libraries, The University of Texas, Austin, TX 78712

Fort Worth Public Library, 300 Taylor, Fort Worth, TX 76102

Houston Public Library, 500 McKinney St., Houston, TX 77002

San Antonio Public Library, 203 South St. Mary's St., San Antonio, TX 78205

Texas Library and Historical Commission, Texas State Library, Lorenzo de Zavala State Archives and Library Building, Box 12927 Capitol Station, Austin, TX 78711

State of Utah Dept. of Community and Economic Development, Division of State History, 300 Rio Grande, Salt Lake City, UT 84101

Aldrich Public Library, Barre, VT 05641

Vermont Historical Society, 109 State St., Pavilion

Building, Montpelier, VT 05602

Clinch Valley College of the University of Virginia, John Cook Wyllie Library, Wise, VA 24293

Hampton Institute, Huntington P. Collis Library, East Queen St., Hampton, VA 23668

University of Virginia, Manuscripts Department, Alderman Library, Charlottesville, VA 22901

Virginia State Library, Archives and Records Division, Richmond, VA 23219

The Washington State Historical Society, 315 North Stadium Way, Tacoma, WA 98403

Washington State Library, Washington/Northwest Room, Olympia, WA 98504

Washington State University, Manuscripts, Archives and Special Collections, the Library, Pullman, WA 99164

West Virginia University, Potomac State College Library, Keyser, WV 26726

West Virginia University, West Virginia Collection, Morgantown, WV 26506

Superior Public Library, 1204 Hammond Ave., Superior, WI 54880

The State Historical Society of Wisconsin, 816 State St., Madison, WI 53706

University of Wisconsin-Green Bay, Area Research Center, Library Learning Center, 2420 Nicolet Drive, Green Bay, WI 54302

Wyoming State Archives Museums & Historical Department, Barrett Building, Cheyenne, WY 82002

## D. MAJOR REPOSITORIES OF NEW DEAL ART

The following libraries and museums contain important collections of New Deal art. For further information, see the very helpful guide to Section of Fine Arts and TRAP murals and sculptures in Marlene Park and Gerald E. Markowitz, *Democratic Vistas: Post Offices and Public Art in the New Deal*(Philadelphia: Temple Univ. Press, 1984). The exhibit catalogs listed under "Secondary Sources: A General Bibliography" provide additional information on the location of art works.

University of Arizona Museum of Art, Tucson, AZ 85721

The University Art Collections, Arizona State University, Tempe, AZ 85287

Library of Congress, Prints and Photographs Division, 1st St. between East Capitol and Independence SE, Washington, DC 20540

University of Maryland Art Gallery, College Park, MD 20742

National Museum of American Art, 9 & G Sts. NW, Washington, DC 20004

University of New Mexico, University Art Museum, Albuquerque, NM 87131

New York Public Library, Graphics Collection, 42nd St. & 5th Ave., New York, NY 10017

Newark Museum, 49 Washington St., Newark, NJ 07109

Queensborough Public Library, 89-11 Merrick Blvd., Jamaica, NY 11432

Rochester Museum and Science Center, 657 East Ave., Box 1480, Rochester, NY 14603

Syracuse University Library, Syracuse University, Syracuse, NY 13210

# 9. Secondary Sources: A General Bibliography

The following bibliography covers works on the government-sponsored arts projects of the 1930s that have been published since 1943--the date when most of the projects ended. Although we have attempted to provide a full listing of works specifically relating to the arts projects, no such bibliography could be entirely complete. In deciding what works to include, we have generally followed these guidelines:

1) We have not included direct reprints of works that were originally issued before 1943 (e.g. reprints of the FWP guidebooks). We have, however, included reprints--such as the guidebooks recently reissued by Pantheon--that have new introductions or commentaries. In addition, we have included compilations of documents generated by the arts projects that were not published before the end of the projects (e.g. the various editions of FWP life histories). In one or two cases, we have made exceptions to the 1943 cut-off date for particularly important works.

2) We have tried to be most complete in including references that directly bear on the arts projects sponsored by the WPA and other federal agencies. We faced a more difficult choice on whether to include works that mention the projects or provide a context for understanding them. We have not included basic histories of the 1930s, but we have listed some important general works on the 1930s arts and culture (e.g. books by Susman, Stott, and Pells). We have also listed some basic works on the WPA itself, but the bibliography is far from complete on that subject. We have not been able to list all the

publications that relate to the life and works of the artists, actors, musicians, and writers who participated in the projects. For example, we do not list the many exhibit catalogs of the work of artists who participated in the projects. We do, however, include catalogs from exhibits that focus specifically on the 1930s; we also include a number of books on the life and works of artists who participated in the projects. But this bibliography provides only a general introduction to the vast set of references on art and artists during the Great Depression.

3) We have included some review essays on the arts projects but not book reviews. We have not been able to annotate all items; we have, however, tried to provide annotations where the title of the article does not indicate its content.

1. Aaron, Daniel. *Writers on the Left*. New York: Harcourt, Brace & World, 1961.
2. Abramson, Doris E. *Negro Playwrights in the American Theatre, 1925-1959*. New York: Columbia Univ. Press, 1969.
   Discusses blacks in FTP.
3. Achter, Barbara. "Americanism and American Art Music, 1929-1945." Ph.D. Thesis, Univ. of Michigan, 1978.
4. Adubato, Robert A. "A History of the WPA's Negro Theatre Project in New York City, 1935-1939." Ph.D. Thesis, New York Univ., 1978.
5. Agee, William C. *The 1930's: Painting and Sculpture in America*. New York: Whitney Museum of American Art, 1968.
6. Ajay, Abe. "Working for the WPA." *Art in America*, 60(Sept. 1972), 70-5.
7. Alexander, Charles C. *Here the Country Lies: Nationalism and the Arts in Twentieth Century America*. Bloomington: Indiana Univ. Press, 1980.
8. Alexander, William. *Film on the Left: American Documentary Film from 1931-1942*. Princeton, NJ: Princeton Univ. Press, 1981.
9. Alexander, William. "Frontier Films, 1936-1941: The Aesthetics of Impact." *Cinema Journal*, 15(Fall 1975), 16-28.
10. Alinder, James. *Marion Post Wolcott: FSA Photographs*. California: Friends Photography, 1984.
11. Alsberg, Henry G. "Their Own Baedeker: American Guide." *New Yorker*, 25(Aug. 1949), 17-8.
12. Alsberg, Henry G., ed. *The American Guide*. New York: Hastings House, 1949.
    One-volume condensation of FWP guides with essays. Publisher also reprinted individual guides.
13. Andersen, Wayne. *American Sculpture in Process:*

*1930/1970.* Boston: New York Graphic Society, 1975.

14. Arent, Arthur. "The Techniques of the Living Newspaper." *Theatre Quarterly*, 1(Oct. 1971), 57-9.

15. Arent, Arthur. "Ethiopia: The First *Living Newspaper.*" *Educational Theatre Journal* 20(March 1968), 15-9,+.
Introduction by Dan Isaac.

16. *Art Under the New Deal.* Columbia, SC, 1969.

17. Arthur, Thomas Hahn. "The Political Career of an Actor: Melvyn Douglas and the New Deal." Ph.D. Thesis, Indiana Univ., 1973.

18. Ashton, Dore. *George L.K. Morris: Abstract Art of the Thirties.* New York: Hirschl & Adler Galleries, 1974.

19. Ashton, Dore. *Yes, but. . . A Critical Study of Philip Guston.* New York: The Viking Press, 1976.
On FAP artist.

20. Baigell, Matthew. *The American Scene: American Painting in the 1930's.* New York: Praeger Publishers, 1974.

21. Baigell, Matthew and Julia Williams, eds. *Artists Against War and Fascism: Papers of the First American Artists' Congress.* New Brunswick, NJ: Rutgers Univ. Press, 1986.

22. Baigell, Matthew. "The Beginnings of 'The American Wave' and the Depression." *Art Journal*, 27(Summer 1968), 387-96+.

23. Bain, Reginald Frank. "The Federal Government and Theatre: A History of Federal Involvement in Theatre." Ph.D. Thesis, Univ. of Minnesota, 1972.

24. Balch, Jack. *Lamps at High Noon.* New York: Modern Age, 1941.
Novel about FWP.

25. Baldwin, Sidney. *Poverty and Politics: The Rise and Decline of the Farm Security Administration.* Chapel Hill: Univ. of North Carolina Press, 1968.
See also 1955 Syracuse Univ. Ph.D. thesis.

26. Banks, Ann, ed. *First Person America.* New York: Alfred A. Knopf, 1980.
Selection of 80 FWP life narratives.

27. Banks, Ann. "Tobacco Talk." *Southern Exposure* 8(no.4 1980), 34-45.
On FWP tobacco study.

28. Banks, Ann and Robert Carter. *Survey of Federal Writers' Project Manuscript Holdings in State Depositories.* Washington, DC: American Historical Association, 1985.

29. Barber, James B. and Frederick S. Voss. *Portraits from the New Deal.* Washington, DC: Smithsonian Institution Press, 1983.
Catalog from National Portrait Gallery exhibit, March 4 to September 7, 1983.

30. Barrese, Edward F. "The Historical Records Survey: A Nation Acts to Save Its Memory." Ph.D. Thesis, George Washington Univ., 1980.

31. Barsam, Richard Meran. *Nonfiction Film: A Critical History*. New York: E.P. Dutton, 1973.

32. Baur, John I. H. *Philip Evergood*. New York: Harry N. Abrams, Inc., 1975.

On FAP artist.

33. Beckham, Sue B. "A Gentle Reconstruction: Depression Post Office Murals and Southern Culture." Ph.D. Thesis, Univ. of Minnesota, 1984.

34. Bendiner, Robert. "When Culture Came to Main Street." *Saturday Review*, 50(April 1967), 19-21.

35. Benton, Thomas Hart. "American Regionalism: A Personal History of the Movement." *The University of Kansas City Review*, 18(Fall 1951).

36. Berman, Avis. "WPA Murals in New York." *New York Magazine*, 12(April 1979).

37. Berman, Greta. *The Lost Years: Mural Painting in N.Y. City Under the WPA Federal Art Project, 1935-1943*. New York: Garland Publishing, Inc., 1978.

See also 1975 Columbia Univ. Ph.D. Thesis.

38. Berman, Greta. "Does 'Flight' Have a Future." *Art in America* 64(Sept 1976), 97-9.

On mural at La Guardia Airport.

39. Berman, Greta. "The Walls of Harlem." *Arts Magazine*, 52(Oct. 1977), 122-6.

40. Berman, Greta. "Murals Under Wraps." *Arts Magazine*, 54(Sept. 1979), 168-71.

41. Berman, Greta. "Abstractions for Public Spaces, 1935-1943." *Arts Magazine*, 56(June 1982), 81-6.

42. Bermingham, Peter. *The New Deal in the Southwest: Arizona and New Mexico*. Tucson: Univ. of Arizona Museum of Art, 1980.

Catalog of exhibit at University of Arizona Museum of Art.

43. Bernard, Heinz. "A Theatre for Lefty: U.S.A. in the 1930's." *Theatre Quarterly*, 1(Oct. 1971), 53-6.

44. Bernstein, Joel H. "The Artist and the Government: The P.W.A.P." *Challenges in American Culture*. Ed. Ray Browne, et al. Bowling Green, OH: Bowling Green Univ. Press, 1970.

45. Bevier, Thomas. "A Glass of Sherry with Margaret Valiant." *The Commercial Appeal Mid-South Magazine*, 30(April 1972), 7-8,11.

46. Billings, Alan Gailey. "Design in the Works Progress Administration's Federal Theatre Project, 1935-1939." Ph.D. Thesis, Univ. of Illinois at Urbana-Champaign, 1967.

47. Billington, Monroe. "Black Slavery in Indian Territory: The Ex-Slave Narratives." *Chronicles of Oklahoma*, 60(no.1 1982), 59-65.

48. Billington, Ray A. "Government and the Arts: The WPA Experience." *American Quarterly*, 13(Winter 1961), 466-79.

49. Birdsall, Esther K. "The FWP and the Popular Press." *Challenges in American Culture*. Ed. Ray Browne, et al. Bowling Green, OH: Bowling Green Univ. Popular Press, 1970.

50. Blassingame, John W. "Using the Testimony of Ex-slaves: Approaches and Problems." *Journal of Southern History* 41(Nov. 1975), 473-92.
    Discusses FWP Slave Narratives.

51. Bloch, Lucienne. "On Location with Diego Rivera." *Art in America*, 74(Feb. 1986), 102-23.

52. Bloxom, Marguerite D., ed. *Pickaxe and Pencil: References for the Study of WPA*. Washington, DC: Library of Congress, 1982.

53. Blumberg, Barbara. "The Works Progress Administration in New York City: A Case Study of the New Deal in Action." Ph.D. Thesis, Columbia Univ., 1974.

54. Blumberg, Barbara. *The New Deal and the Unemployed: The View from New York City*. Cranbury, NJ: Bucknell Univ. Press, 1979.

55. Boddy, Julie M. "The Farm Security Administration Photographs of Marion Post Wolcott: A Cultural History." Ph.D. Thesis, State Univ. of New York at Buffalo, 1982.

56. Botkin, Benjamin A. "Living Lore on the New York City Writers' Project." *New York Folklore Quarterly*, 2(Nov. 1946), 252-63.

57. Botkin, Benjamin A. "We Called It 'Living Lore'." *New York Folklore Quarterly*, 14(Fall 1958), 189-201.

58. Botkin, Benjamin A. "The Slave as His Own Interpreter." *Library of Congress Quarterly Journal of Current Acquisitions*, 2(Nov. 1944), 49-50.

59. Botkin, Benjamin A., ed. *Lay My Burden Down: A Folk History of Slavery*. Chicago, IL: Univ. of Chicago Press, 1945.

60. Bowers, Diane. "Ethiopia, the First Living Newspaper." *Phoebe*, 5(Spring 1976), 6-25.

61. Bowman, Ruth. *Murals Without Walls: Arshile Gorky's Aviation Murals Rediscovered*. Newark, NJ: The Newark Museum, 1978.
    Exhibit catalog.

62. Bremer, William W. "Along the 'American Way': The New Deal's Work Relief Program for the Unemployed." *Journal of American History*, 62(Dec. 1975), 636-52.

63. Brewer, Jeutonne Patten. "The Verb 'Be' in Early Black English: A Study Based on the WPA Ex-Slave Narratives." Ph.D. Thesis, Univ. of North Carolina at Chapel Hill, 1974.

64. Browder, Nathaniel Clenroy, ed. *Just Plain Folks: In Their Own Words*. Raleigh, NC: Nathaniel C. Browder, 1983. Abstracts of stories told to those on FWP in the South.

65. Brown, James Seay. *Up Before Daylight: Life Histories from the Alabama Writers' Project, 1938-1939*. University: Univ. of Alabama Press, 1982.

66. Brown, Lorin W. *Hispano Folklife of New Mexico: The Lorin W. Brown Federal Writers' Project Manuscripts*. Albuquerque: Univ. of New Mexico Press, 1978.

67. Brown, Lorraine. "Federal Theatre: Melodrama, Social Protest, and Genius." *Quarterly Journal of the Library of Congress*, 36(Feb. 1979), 18-37.

68. Brown, Lorraine. "A Story Yet to Be Told: The Federal Theatre Research Project." *Black Scholar*, 10(Spring 1979), 70-8.

69. Brown, Lorraine and John O'Connor. *Free, Adult, Uncensored: The Living History of the Federal Theatre Project*. Washington: New Republic Books, 1978.

70. Brown, Lorraine and Michael G. Sundell. "Stylizing the Folk: Hall Johnson's *Run Little Chillun* Photographed by Doris Ulmann." *Prospects*, 7(1982), 335-54.

71. Brown, Milton. *Social Art in America, 1934-1945*. New York: ACA Galleries, 1981.

72. Brown, Milton W. *American Painting from the Armory Show to the Depression*. Princeton, NJ: Princeton Univ., 1955.

73. Brown, Milton W. *Jacob Lawrence*. New York: Whitney Museum of American Art, 1974. On FAP artist.

74. Brown, Milton W. "New Deal Art Projects: Boondoggle or Bargain." *Art News*, 81(April 1982), 82-7.

75. Burroughs, Polly. *Thomas Hart Benton: A Portrait*. Garden City, NY: Doubleday, 1981.

76. Buttitta, Tony and Barry Witham. *Uncle Sam Presents: A Memoir of the Federal Theatre, 1935-1939*. Philadelphia: Univ. of Pennsylvania Press, 1982.

77. Bystryn, Marcia N. "Variation in Artistic Circles." *Sociological Quarterly* 22(no.1 1981), 119-32. Based on data from FAP and the American Artists' Congress.

78. Cahill, Holger. "Artists in War and Peace." *Studio*, 130(July 1945), 1-16.

79. Calcagno, Nicholas A. *New Deal Murals in Oklahoma: A Bicentennial Project*. Miami, OK: Pioneer Print, 1976.

80. Campbell, Russell. "Film and Photo League: Radical

Cinema in the 30s." *Jump Cut*, (no.14  1977), 23-5.
81. Campbell, Russell. "Radical Cinema in the United States, 1930-1942: The Work of the Film and Photo League, Nykino, and Frontier Films." Ph.D. Thesis, Northwestern Univ., 1978.
82. Canon, Cornelius Baird. "The Federal Music Project of the Works Progress Administration:  Music in a Democracy." Ph.D. Thesis, Univ. of Minnesota, 1963.
83. Canon, Neal. "Art for Whose Sake:  The Federal Music Project of the WPA." *Challenges in American Culture*. Ed. Ray Browne, et al.  Bowling Green, OH: Bowling Green University Press, 1970.
84. Carr, Eleanor. "The New Deal and the Sculptor:  A Study of Federal Relief to the Sculptor on the New York City Federal Art Project of the WPA, 1935-1943." Ph.D. Thesis, New York Univ., 1969.
85. Carr, Eleanor. "New York Sculpture During the Federal Project." *Art Journal*, 31(Summer  1972), 397-403.
86. Charles, Searle F. *Minister of Relief: Harry Hopkins and the Depression*.  Syracuse: Syracuse Univ. Press, 1963.
87. Charlot, Jean.  *An Artist on Art:  Collected Essays of Jean Charlot*.  Honolulu: Univ. Press of Hawaii, 1972.
   2 volumes by FAP artist.
88. Charnow, John. *Work Relief Experience in the United States*.  Washington: Social Science Research Council, 1943.
89. Chinoy, Helen Kritch. "Reunion: A Self Portrait of the Group Theatre." *Educational Theatre Journal*, 28(Dec.  1976).
   Subject for December issue.
90. Christensen, Erwin O.  *The Index of American Design*. New York: Macmillan Co., 1967.
91. Christensen, Erwin O. "American Popular Art as Recorded in the Index of American Design." *Art in America*, 35(July  1947), 199-208.
92. Cimbala, Paul A. "Fortunate Bondsmen:  Black 'Musicianers' and Their Role as an Antebellum Southern Plantation Elite." *Southern Studies*  18(no.3  1979), 291-303.
   Based on WPA Slave Narratives.
93. Clayton, Ronnie Wayne. "Federal Writers' Project for Blacks in Louisiana." *Louisiana History*, 19(Summer  1978), 327-35.
94. Clayton, Ronnie Wayne. "A History of the Federal Writers' Project in Louisiana." Ph.D. Thesis, Louisiana State Univ, 1974.
95. Clurman, Harold. *The Fervent Years:  The Story of the Group Theater and the Thirties*.  New York: De Capo Press, 1975.
96. Cole, John Y. "Amassing American 'Stuff': The Library of Congress and the Federal Arts Projects of the 1930s."

*Quarterly Journal of the Library of Congress*, 40(Fall 1983), 356-89.

97. Cole, John Y. "WPA Research Materials at the Library of Congress: A Review and Progress Report." *U.S. Library of Congress Information Bulletin*, 33(Nov. 1974), 243-5.

98. Conkin, Paul K. *Tomorrow a New World: The New Deal Community Program.* Ithaca, NY: Cornell Univ. Press, 1959.

99. Contreras, Belisario R. *Tradition and Innovation in New Deal Art.* Lewisburg: Bucknell Univ. Press, 1983.
See also 1967 American Univ. Ph.D. Thesis.

100. Cook, Charles Orson and James M. Poteet. "'Dem Was Black Times, Sure 'nough": The Slave Narratives of Lydia Jefferson and Stephen Williams." *Louisiana History*, 20(no.3 1979), 281-92.

101. Cooke, H. Lester Jr. *Fletcher Martin.* New York: Harry N. Abrams, 1977.
On FAP artist.

102. Coppock, James. "A Conversation with Arthur Berger." *Partisan Review* 48(no.3 1981), 366-79.
Comments on WPA and the fine arts.

103. Cords, John. "Music in Social Settlement and Community Music Schools, 1893-1939: A Democratic-Esthetic Approach to Musical Culture." Ph.D. Thesis, Univ. of Minnesota, 1970.

104. Corkern, Wilton Claude, Jr. "Architects, Preservationists, and the New Deal: The Historic American Buildings Survey, 1933-1942." Ph.D. Thesis, George Washington Univ., 1984.

105. Corn, Wanda. *Grant Wood: The Regionalist Vision.* New Haven: Yale Univ. Press, 1983.

106. Cosgrove, Stuart. "The Living Newspaper: History, Production and Form." Ph.D. Thesis, Univ. of Hull, 1982.

107. Cosgrove, Stuart. "Cabaret and Counterculture: The Anti-Fascist Theatre in New York." *Theatre Quarterly*, 10(no.40 1981), 49-59.

108. Cowley, Malcolm. "Federal Writers' Project." *New Republic*, 167(Oct. 1972), 23-6.

109. Cowley, Malcolm. "The 1930's Were an Age of Faith." *New York Times Book Review*, 69(Dec. 1964), 16.

110. Cowley, Malcolm. *Think Back on Us. . . A Contemporary Chronicle of the 1930s.* Carbondale: Southern Illinois Univ. Press, 1967.
Reprint of Cowley's *New Republic* essays, many of them on 1930s literature and culture.

111. Craig, Evelyn Q. *Black Drama of the Federal Theater Era: Beyond the Formal Horizons.* Amherst: Univ. of

Massachusetts Press, 1980.

112. Craig, Lois et al. *The Federal Presence: Architecture, Politics, and Symbols in United States Government Building.* Cambridge, MA: The M.I.T. Press, 1978.

113. Crawford, Stephen Cooban. "Quantified Memory: A Study of the WPA and Fisk University Slave Narrative Collections." Ph.D. Thesis, Univ. of Chicago, 1980.

114. Culbert, David H. "The Infinite Variety of Mass Experience: The Great Depression, W.P.A. Interviews, and Student Family History Projects." *Louisiana History*, 19(Winter 1978), 43-63.

115. Culley, John J. and Peter L. Petersen. "Hard Times on the High Plains: FSA Photography During the 1930s." *Panhandle-Plains History Review*, 52(1979), 15-37.

116. Cummings, Paul, ed. *Artists in Their Own Words.* New York: St. Martin's Press, 1979.

Includes artists Kent, Benton, Albright, Schmidt, Walker Evans, Noguchi, Porter.

117. Curtis, James C. and Sheila Curtis Grannen. "Let Us Now Appraise Famous Photographs: Walker Evans and Documentary Photography." *Winterthur Portfolio*, 15(Spring 1980), 1-23.

118. Cutler, Phoebe. *The Public Landscape of the New Deal.* New Haven: Yale Univ. Press, 1986.

119. Czestochowski, Joseph S. *John Steuart Curry and Grant Wood: A Portrait of Rural America.* Columbia: Univ. of Missouri Press, 1981.

120. Davidson, Katherine H., ed. *Preliminary Inventory of the Records of the Federal Writers' Project, Work Projects Administration, 1935-44.* Washington, DC: National Archives, 1953.

121. Davidson, Marshall B. "The WPA's Amazing Artistic Record of American Design." *American Heritage*, 23(Feb. 1972), 65-80.

122. Dawson, Oliver B. "The Ironwork of Timberline." *Oregon History Quarterly*, 76(no.3 1975), 258-68.

123. Day, Greg and Jack Delano. "Folklife and Photography: Bringing the FSA Home." *Southern Exposure*, 5(no.2-3 1977), 122-33.

124. De Saisset Art Gallery, Univ. of Santa Clara. *New Deal Art: California.* Santa Clara, CA: Univ. of Santa Clara, 1976.

Catalog for 1976 exhibit at De Saisset Art Gallery and Museum.

125. DeCordova Museum, Lincoln, Massachusetts. *By the People, for the People: New England.* Lincoln, MA: DeCordova Museum Press, 1977.

Catalog of 1977 exhibit at DeCordova Museum on arts projects in New England.

126. Dent, Tom. "Octave Lilly, Jr.: In Memoriam." *Crisis* 83(no.7 1976), 243-4.

On black insurance executive who worked for FWP.

127. Dieterich, Herbert R. "The New Deal Cultural Projects in Wyoming: A Survey and Appraisal." *Annals of Wyoming*, 52(no.2 1980), 30-44.

128. Dieterich, Herbert R. and Jacqueline Petravage. "New Deal Art in Wyoming: Some Case Studies." *Annals of Wyoming*, 45(Spring 1973), 53-68.

129. Dobak, William A. "Black Regulars Speak." *Panhandle-Plains History Review*, 47(1974), 19-27.

FWP accounts of Black soldiers.

130. Doherty, Robert J. "Farm Security Administration Photographs of the Depression Era." *Camera*, (Oct. 1962), 9-51.

131. Doty, C. Stewart. *The First Franco-Americans: New England Life Histories from the Federal Writers' Project, 1938-1939.* Orono: Univ. of Maine at Orono Press, 1985.

132. Dows, Olin. "The New Deal's Treasury Art Programs, a Memoir." *Arts in Society*, 2(no.4 1964), 50-88.

133. Dunaway, David K. *How Can I Keep from Singing: Pete Seeger.* NY: McGraw-Hill, 1981.

Discusses Charles Seeger and government music projects.

134. Dunaway, David K. "Unsung Songs of Protest - - The Composers Collective of New York." *New York Folklore Quarterly*, 5(no.1 1979), 1-19.

135. Dunfee, Charles Dennis. "Harold H. Burton, Mayor of Cleveland: The WPA Program, 1935-1937." Ph.D. Thesis, Case Western Reserve Univ., 1975.

136. Durniak, John. "Focus on Stryker." *Popular Photography*, (Sept. 1962), 60-5+.

137. Dwyer-Shick, Elizabeth. "The Development of Folklore and Folklife Research in the Federal Writers' Project, 1935-1943." *Keystone Folklore Quarterly*, 20(Fall 1975), 12-4.

138. Dwyer-Shick, Susan. "Review Essay: Folklore and Government Support." *Journal of American Folklore*, 89(Oct. 1976), 476-86.

139. Ebersole, Barbara. *Fletcher Martin.* Gainesville: Univ. of Florida Press, 1954.

On FAP artist.

140. Edwin A. Ulrich Museum of Art, Wichita State Univ. *Art from the Thirties.* Wichita, KS: Edwin A. Ulrich Museum of Art, 1978.

141. "End of WPA Art." *Life*, (April 1944), 85-6.

142. Escott, Paul D. "The Context of Freedom: Georgia's

302

Slaves During the Civil War." *Georgia History Quarterly* 58(no.1 1974), 79-104.
    Uses Slave Narratives.
    143. Ewen, Frederic. "The Thirties, Commitment, and the Theatre." *Science and Society*, 32(Summer 1968), 300-6.
    144. Failing, Patricia. "Timberline Lodge." *Americana*, 8(March 1980), 32-8.
    145. Farran, Don. "The Federals in Iowa: A Hawkeye Guidebook in the Making." *Annals of Iowa*, 41(Winter 1973), 1190-6.
    146. Farrell, James T. "The Literary Left in the Middle Thirties." *New International*, 13(July 1947), 150-4.
    147. Federal Writers' Project. *Slave Narratives: A Folk History of Slavery in the United States, from Interviews with Former Slaves*. St. Clair Shores, MI: Scholarly Press, 1976.
    148. Federal Writers' Project. *The WPA Guide to Minnesota*. St. Paul: Minnesota Historical Society, 1985.
    Reprint, includes new introduction by Frederick Manfred.
    149. Federal Writers' Project. *New York Panorama: A Companion to the WPA Guide to New York City*. New York: Pantheon, 1984.
    Reprint, includes new introduction by Alfred Kazin.
    150. Federal Writers' Project. *The WPA Guide to Washington, D.C.*. New York: Pantheon, 1983.
    Reprint, includes new introduction by Roger G. Kennedy.
    151. Federal Writers' Project. *The WPA Guide to Massachusetts*. New York: Pantheon, 1983.
    Reprint, includes new introduction by Jane Holtz Kay.
    152. Federal Writers' Project. *The WPA Guide to New York City*. New York: Pantheon, 1982.
    Reprint, includes new introduction by William H. Whyte.
    153. Federal Writers' Project. *The WPA Guide to Illinois*. New York: Pantheon, 1983.
    Reprint, edited by Neil Harris and Michael Conzen.
    154. Federal Writers' Project. *The WPA Guide to California*. New York: Pantheon, 1984.
    Reprint.
    155. Federal Writers' Project. *The WPA Guide to Florida*. New York: Pantheon, 1984.
    Reprint.
    156. Federal Writers' Project. *The WPA Guide to Nineteen Thirties Kansas*. Lawrence: Univ. Press of Kansas, 1984.
    Reprint, original title: *Kansas: A Guide to the Sunflower State*.
    157. Feld, Ross. *Philip Guston*. New York: George Braziller, Inc., 1980.
    On FAP artist.

158. Feldman, Frances T. "American Painting During the Great Depression, 1929-1939." Ph.D. Thesis, New York Univ., 1963.

159. Fielding, Dennis L. *Inventory of the Records of the Work Projects Administration in Kentucky.* Frankfort, KY: Division of Archives and Records Management, 1979.

160. Flanagan, Hallie. *Arena.* New York: Duell, Sloane and Pearce, 1940.
Originally published under the name Hallie Flanagan Davis.

161. Flanagan, Hallie. "A Theatre for the People." *American Magazine of Art*, 29(Aug. 1946), 494-503.

162. Flynn, George Q. "The New Deal and Local Archives: The Pacific Northwest." *American Archivist*, 33(Jan. 1970), 41-52.

163. Fox, Daniel M. "The Achievement of the Federal Writers' Project." *American Quarterly*, 13(Spring 1961), 3-19.

164. France, Richard. *The Theatre of Orson Welles.* Lewisburg, PA: Bucknell Univ. Press, 1977.

165. France, Richard. "The 'Voodoo' *Macbeth* of Orson Welles." *Yale/Theatre*, 5(no.3 1974), 66-78.

166. Frankel, Ronni Ann. "Photography and the Farm Security Administration: The Visual Politics of Dorothea Lange and Ben Shahn." Senior Thesis, Cornell Univ., 1969

167. Garver, Thomas H., ed. *Just Before the War: Urban America as Seen by Photographers of the Farm Security Administration.* Boston: October, 1968.

168. Gelber, Steven M. "Working to Prosperity: California's New Deal Murals." *California History*, 58(Summer 1979), 98-127.

169. Getlein, Frank. *Jack Levine.* New York: Harry N. Abrams, Inc., 1966.
On FAP artist.

170. Getlein, Frank. *Chaim Gross.* New York: Abrams, 1974.

171. Gill, Glenda Eloise. "Six Black Performers in Relation to the Federal Theatre." Ph.D. Thesis, Univ. of Iowa, 1981.

172. Gillen, E. and Y. Leonard, eds. *America: Traum und Depression 1920/40.* Berlin: Akademie der Kunste, 1980.

173. Goldman, Arnold. "Life and Death of the Living Newspaper Unit." *Theatre Quarterly*, 3(no.9 1973).

174. Goldman, Arnold. "Injunction Granted: An Introduction." *The Minnesota Review*, (no.1 1973).

175. Goldman, Harry Merton. "'Pins and Needles': An Oral History." Ph.D. Thesis, New York Univ., 1977.

176. Goldman, Shifra M. "Siqueiros and Three Early Murals in Los Angeles." *Art Journal*, 23(Summer 1974), 321-7.

177. Goldstein, Malcolm. *The Political Stage: American Drama and Theater of the Great Depression.* New York: Oxford Univ. Press, 1974.

178. Goodrich, Lloyd. *Reginald Marsh.* New York: Abrams, 1972.

179. Goodrich, Lloyd. *Raphael Soyer.* New York: Abrams, 1972.

180. Goodson, Martia Graham. "An Introductory Essay and Subject Index to Selected Interviews from the Slave Narrative Collection." Ph.D. Thesis, Union Graduate School, 1977.

181. Goossen, E. C. *Stuart Davis.* New York: George Braziller, 1959.

   On FAP artist.

182. Gorelik, Mordecai. "Legacy of the New Deal Drama." *Drama Survey,* 4(Spring 1965), 38-43.

183. *Graphic Works of the American Thirties.* New York: Da Capo Press, 1977.

   Reprint of *America Today: A Book of 100 Prints by the American Artists' Congress.*

184. Green, Archie. "A Resettlement Administration Song Sheet." *John Edwards Memorial Foundation Quarterly,* 11(1975), 80-7.

185. Green, Brenda Z. and Elizabeth D. Walsh. "The Research Center for the Federal Theatre Project." *Theatre Design & Technology,* (Fall 1978), 23-4.

186. Greenberg, Clement. "The Late Thirties in New York." *Art and Culture: Critical Essays.* Ed. Clement Greenberg. Boston: Beacon Press, 1961.

187. Guedon, Mary Scholz. *Regionalist Art: Thomas Hart Benton, John Steuart Curry, and Grant Wood: A Guide to the Literature.* Metuchen, NJ & London: Scarecrow Press, 1982.

188. Gurney, George. "Sculpture and the Federal Triangle." *National Sculpture Review,* 28(Fall 1979), 18-23+.

189. Gurney, George. *Sculpture and the Federal Triangle.* Washington, DC: Smithsonian Institution Press, 1985.

190. Hall, Daniel E. "Federal Patronage of Art in Arizona from 1933 to 1943." M.A. Thesis, Arizona State Univ., 1974.

191. Hamlin, Edith Dixon. "Maynard Dixon, Artist of the West." *California Historical Quarterly,* 53(Winter 1974), 361-76.

192. Harney, Andy Leon. "WPA Handicrafts Rediscovered." *Historic Preservation,* 25(July 1973), 10-5.

193. Harrison, Helen A. "American Art and the New Deal." *Journal of American Studies,* 6(Dec. 1972), 289-96.

194. Harrison, Helen A. *Dawn of a New Day: The New York World's Fair, 1939-1940.* New York: New York Univ. Press, 1980.

195. Harrison, Helen A. "Social Consciousness in New Deal Murals." M.A. Thesis, Case Western Reserve Univ., 1975.

196. Harrison, Helen A. "John Reed Club Artists and the New Deal: Radical Responses to Roosevelt's 'Peaceful Revolution'." *Prospects*, 5(1980), 241-68.

197. Harrison, Helen A. "Subway Art and the Public Use of Arts Committee." *Archives of American Art Journal*, 21(no.2 1981), 3-12.

198. Harrison, Lowell H. "The Folklore of Some Kentucky Slaves." *Kentucky Folklore Record* 17(no.2 1971), 25-30.
    Based on FWP interviews.

199. Harrison, Lowell H. "Recollections of Some Tennessee Slaves." *Tennessee Historical Quarterly* 33(Summer 1974), 175-90.
    On Slave Narratives.

200. Harrison, Lowell H. "Memories of Slavery Days in Kentucky." *Filson Club Historical Quarterly* 47(July 1973), 242-57.
    Based on slave narratives.

201. Hauptman, Laurence M. "The Iroquois School of Art: Arthur C. Parker and the Seneca Arts Project, 1935-1941." *New York History*, 60(July 1979), 283-312.

202. Haworth, Alfred. *Roosevelt's Image Brokers: Poets, Playwrights and the Use of the Lincoln Symbol.* Port Washington: Kennikat Press, 1974.

203. Heller, Nancy and Julia Williams. *The Regionalists.* New York: Watson-Guptill Publications, 1976.
    Includes material on FAP artists.

204. Hemenway, Robert. "Folklore Field Notes from Zora Neale Hurston." *Black Scholar* 7(no.7 1976), 39-46.
    Hurston's notes from the FWP.

205. Hendrickson, Gordon O. "Collections." *Annals of Wyoming* 49(no.2 1977), 175-92.
    On FWP in Wyoming.

206. Hendrickson, Gordon O., ed. *Wyoming Works Projects Administration Federal Writers' Project Collection Inventory.* Cheyenne: Wyoming State Archives and Historical Dept., 1977.

207. Hess, Thomas B. *William de Kooning.* New York: George Braziller, 1959.
    On FAP artist.

208. Heymann, Jeanne L. "Dance in the Depression: The WPA Project." *Dance Scope*, 9(Spring 1975), 28-40.

209. Hills, Patricia. *Social Concern and Urban Realism: American Painting of the 1930s.* Boston: Boston Univ. Art Gallery, 1983.
    Published in conjunction with the exhibit organized by Bread and Roses Cultural Project.

306

210. Hills, Patricia. "Philip Evergood's 'American Tragedy': The Poetics of Ugliness, the Politics of Anger." *Arts Magazine* 54(Feb. 1980), 138-43.
    On FAP artist.

211. Himelstein, Morgan Y. *Drama Was a Weapon: The Left-wing Theatre in New York, 1929-1941.* New Brunswick, NJ: Rutgers Univ. Press, 1963.

212. Himelstein, Morgan Y. "Theory and Performance in the Depression Theatre." *Modern Drama,* 14(Feb. 1971), 426-35.

213. Hirsch, Jerrold and Tom E. Terrill. "Conceptualization and Implementation: Some Thoughts on Reading the Federal Writers' Project Southern Life Histories." *Southern Studies,* 18(Fall 1979), 351-62.

214. Hirsch, Jerrold. "Reading and Counting." *Reviews in American History* 8(Sept. 1980), 312-7.
    Review essay on WPA Slave Narratives.

215. Hirsch, Jerrold. "Portrait of America: The Federal Writers' Project in an Intellectual and Cultural Context." Ph.D. Thesis, Univ. of North Carolina at Chapel Hill, 1984.

216. Hirsch, Jerrold. "From the FSA Files: The Rural Landscape of the Thirties." *Carolina Dwelling, Toward Preservation of Place,* 26(1978), 241-50.

217. Hobson, Archie, ed. *Remembering America: A Sampler of the WPA American Guide Series.* New York: Columbia Univ. Press, 1985.

218. Holcomb, Robert. "The Federal Theatre in Los Angeles." *California Historical Quarterly,* 41(June 1962), 131-47.

219. Hoover, Kathleen and John Cage. *Virgil Thomson, his Life and Music.* New York and London: Thomas Youseloff, 1957.

220. Houseman, John. "Working with Welles: Anecdotes from an Autobiography." *Audience,* 1(Nov. 1971), 61-77.

221. Houseman, John. *Run-through: A Memoir.* New York: Simon and Schuster, 1984.
    Recalls work on FTP.

222. Howard, Donald S. *The WPA and Federal Relief Policy.* New York: Russell Sage Foundation, 1943.

223. Hunter, John O. "Marc Blitzstein's *The Cradle Will Rock* as a Document of America 1937." *American Quarterly,* 18(Summer 1966), 227-33.

224. Hurlburt, Laurence P. "The Siqueiros Experimental Workshop: New York, 1936." *Art Journal,* 35(Spring 1976), 237-46.

225. Hurley, F. Jack. *Portrait of a Decade: Roy Stryker and the Development of Documentary Photography in the Thirties.* Baton Rouge: Louisiana State Univ. Press, 1972.

See also 1971 Tulane Univ. Ph.D. Thesis.

226."Interview:  Ben Shahn Talks with Forrest Selvig." *Archives of American Art Journal*, 17(no.3  1977), 14-21.

227. Jacob, Mary Jane and Linda  Downs. *The Rouge:  The Image of Industry in the Art of Charles Sheeler and Diego Rivera.* Detroit, MI: Detroit Institute of Arts, 1978.

228. Jewett, Masha Zakheim. *Coit Tower, San Francisco: Its History and Art.* San Francisco: Volcano Press, 1983.

229. Joe and Emily Lowe Art Gallery. *The Mural Art of Ben Shahn.* Syracuse: Joe and Emily Lowe Art Gallery, 1977.

230. Johnson, Evamarii A. "A Production History of the Seattle Federal Theatre Project Negro Repertory Company: 1935-1939." Ph.D. Thesis, Univ. of Washington, 1981.

231. Johnson, Jerah. "Marcus B. Christian and the WPA History of Black People in Louisiana." *Louisiana History*, 20(no.1  1979), 113-5.

232. Johnson, Nancy A. *Accomplishments: Minnesota Art Projects in the Depression Years.* Duluth: Tweed Museum of Art, Univ. of Minnesota, 1976.

233. Jones, Alfred H. "The Search for a Usable American Past in the New Deal Era." *American Quarterly*, 23(Dec. 1971), 710-24.

234. Jones, Len. "The Workers Theatre in the Thirties." *Marxism Today*, (Sept. 1974), 271-80.

235. Joslyn Art Museum. *The Thirties Decade: American Artists and Their European Contemporaries.* Omaha, NB: Joslyn Art Museum, 1971.
Introduction by William A. McGonagle.

236. Kelder, Diane, ed. *Stuart Davis.* New York: Praeger, 1971.

237. Kempton, Murray. *Part of Our Time: Some Ruins and Monuments of the Thirties.*  New York: Simon and Schuster, 1955.
Discusses the arts and the left in the 1930s.

238. Key, Donald. "Milwaukee's Art of the Depression Era." *Historical Messenger*, 31(Summer 1975), 38-49.

239. Kingsbury, Martha. *Art of the Thirties: The Pacific Northwest.* Seattle: Univ. of Washington Press, 1972.

240. Koch, John C. "The Federal Theatre Project:  Region IV - - A Structural and Historical Analysis of How It Functioned and What It Accomplished." Ph.D. Thesis, Univ. of Nebraska-Lincoln, 1981.

241. Korn, Majorie Susan. "It Can't Happen Here:  Federal Theatre's Bold Adventure." Ph.D. Thesis, Univ. of Missouri-Columbia, 1978.

242. Kornfeld, Paul Ira. "The Educational Program of the Federal Art Project." Ph.D. Thesis, Illinois State Univ., 1981.

243. Kostiainen, Auvo. "The Portrait of Finnish Americans: Materials on the Minnesota Finns Collected by the WPA Writers' Project." *Turun Hist. Arkisto (Finland)*, 31(1976), 414-31.

244. Kozloff, Max. "The Rivera Frescoes of Modern Industry at the Detroit Institute of Arts: Proletarian Art Under Capitalist Patronage." *Art and Architecture in the Service of Politics*. Ed. Linda Nochlin. Cambridge, MA: MIT Press, 1978.

245. Kreizenbeck, Alan Dennis. "'The Theatre Nobody Knows': Forgotten Productions of the Federal Theatre Project, 1935-1939." Ph.D. Thesis, New York Univ., 1979.

246. Kuh, Katharine. *The Artist's Voice: Talks with Seventeen Artists*. NY & Evanston: Harper & Row, 1962.

Includes artists Albers, Albright, Calder, Stuart Davis, Dickinson, Duchamp, and others.

247. Kunkel, Gladys M. "The Mural Paintings by Anton Refregier in the Rincon Annex of San Francisco Post Office, San Francisco, California." M.A. Thesis, Arizona State Univ., 1969.

248. Lally, Kathleen. "A History of the Federal Dance Theatre of the Works Progress Administration, 1935-39." Ph.D. Thesis, Texas Women's Univ., 1979.

249. Lancaster, Dorothy Mearle. "The Impact of the Works Progress Administration Upon Public Recreation in the United States." Ph.D. Thesis, Indiana Univ., 1967.

250. Laning, Edward. "Memoirs of a WPA Painter." *American Heritage*, 21(Oct. 1970), 38-44+.

251. Larsen, Susan Carol. "The American Abstract Artists: A Documentary History, 1936-1941." *Archives of American Art Journal*, 14(no. 1 1974), 2-7.

252. Larsen, Susan Carol. "The American Abstract Artists Group: A History and Evaluation of Its Impact Upon American Art." Ph.D. Thesis, Northwestern Univ., 1975.

253. Larson, Erling. "The 1930's, a Symposium." *Carleton Miscellany*, 6(Winter 1965), 6-113.

254. Lashbrook, Lawrence Gene. "Work Relief in Maine: The Administration and Programs of the WPA." Ph.D. Thesis, Univ. of Maine, 1977.

255. Lawrence, Ken. "Oral History of Slavery." *Southern Exposure* 1(Winter 1974), 84-6.

On Slave Narratives.

256. Leigh Yawkey Woodson Art Mus. *Wisconsin's New Deal Art*. Wausau: Leigh Yawkey Woodson Art Museum, 1980.

257. Levin, Howard M. and Katherine Northrup. *Dorothea Lange: Farm Security Administration Photographs, 1935-1939.*

Glencoe, IL: Text-Fiche Press, 1980.
2 volumes.
258. Lewis, Emory. *Stages: The Fifty Year Childhood of the American Theatre.* New Jersey: Prentice-Hall, 1969.
Interprets theatre in stages, including FTP.
259. Liasson, Mira. "The Federal Writers' Project and the Folklore of Cultural Pluralism." Senior Thesis, Brown Univ., 1977
260. Lippard, Lucy. *The Graphic Work of Philip Evergood.* New York: Crown Publishers, Inc., 1966.
On FAP artist.
261. Lloyd, Norman. "Norman Lloyd in Interview with Hilary Mackendrick." *Gambit,* (Oct. 1975).
262. Losey, Joseph. "Injunction Granted: Prefatory Notes." *The Minnesota Review,* (no.1 1973).
263. Lunde, Karl. *Isabel Bishop.* New York: Harry N. Abrams, Inc., 1975.
Bishop painted Post Office Mural in 1938 and was on FAP in New York.
264. Lyon, Edwin Austin. "New Deal Archeology in the Southeast: WPA, TVA, NPS, 1934-42." Ph.D. Thesis, Louisiana State Univ., 1982.
265. MacLeod, Bruce A. "Quills, Fifes, and Flutes Before the Civil War." *Southern Folklore Quarterly* 42(no.2-3 1978), 201-8.
Uses WPA Slave Narratives.
266. Madden, David. *Proletarian Writers of the Thirties.* Carbondale: Southern Illinois Univ. Press, 1967.
267. Mangione, Jerre. *The Dream and the Deal: The Federal Writers' Project, 1935-1943.* Boston: Little, Brown, 1972.
268. Mangione, Jerre. *An Ethnic at Large: A Memoir of America in the Thirties and Forties.* Philadelphia: Univ. of Pennsylvania Press, 1983.
269. Mankin, Lawrence David. "The National Government and the Arts: From the Great Depression to 1973." Ph.D. Thesis, Univ. of Illinois at Urbana-Champaign, 1976.
270. Marcello, Ronald Ely. "The North Carolina Works Progress Administration and the Politics of Relief." Ph.D. Thesis, Duke Univ., 1969.
271. Mardis, Robert Francis. "Federal Theatre in Florida." Ph.D. Thesis, Univ. of Florida, 1972.
272. Marling, Karal Ann. "A Note on New Deal Iconography: Futurology and the Historical Myth." *Prospects,* 4(Spring 1979), 420-40.
273. Marling, Karal Ann. *Wall-to-Wall America: A Cultural History of Post-Office Murals in the Great Depression.*

Minneapolis: Univ. of Minnesota Press, 1982.

274. Marling, Karal Ann. "Federal Patronage and the Woodstock Colony." Ph.D. Thesis, Bryn Mawr, 1971.

275. Marling, Karal Ann and Helen A. Harrison. *7 American Women: The Depression Decade.* New York: A.I.R. Gallery, 1976.

Catalog of exhibit at Vassar College Art Gallery sponsored by A.I.R. Gallery.

276. Marling, Karal Ann, et al. *Federal Art in Cleveland 1933-1943.* Cleveland: Cleveland Public Library, 1974.

Catalog of exhibit, September 16 to December 27, 1974.

277. Marter, Joan M., et al. *Vanguard American Sculpture, 1913-1939.* Rutgers, NJ: The State Univ., 1979.

278. Mathews, Jane DeHart. "Arts and the People: The New Deal Quest for a Cultural Democracy." *Journal of American History*, 62(Sept. 1975), 316-39.

279. Mathews, Jane DeHart. *The Federal Theater, 1935-1939: Plays, Relief, and Politics.* Princeton, NJ: Princeton Univ. Press, 1967.

See also 1966 Duke Univ. Ph.D. Thesis.

280. Maurer, Joyce C. "Federal Theatre in Cincinnati." *Cincinnati Historical Society Bulletin*, 32(Spring 1974), 28-45.

281. McCoy, Garnett. "Poverty, Politics and Artists, 1930-1945." *Art in America*, 53(Aug. 1965), 88-107.

282. McCreery, Kathleen. "Prolet: Yiddish Theatre in the 1930's." *Race and Class*, 20(Winter 1979), 293-305.

283. McDermott, Douglas. "The Living Newspaper as a Dramatic Form." *Modern Drama*, 8(May 1965), 82-94.

284. McDermott, Douglas. "The Theatre Nobody Knows: Workers Theatre in America 1926-42." *Theatre Survey*, 6(May 1965), 65-82.

285. McDermott, Douglas. "Propaganda and Art: Dramatic Theory and American Depression." *Modern Drama*, 2(May 1968), 73-81.

286. McDermott, Douglas. "Agit Prop: Production Practice in the Workers Theatre 1932-42." *Theatre Survey*, 7(July 1966), 115-24.

287. McDonald, William F. *Federal Relief Administration and the Arts: The Origins and Administrative History of the Arts Projects of the Works Progress Administration.* Columbus: Ohio State Univ. Press, 1969.

288. McKinzie, Kathleen O'Connor. "Writers on Relief: 1935-1942." Ph.D. Thesis, Indiana Univ., 1970.

289. McKinzie, Richard D. *The New Deal for Artists.* Princeton, NJ: Princeton Univ. Press, 1973.

See also 1969 Indiana Univ. Ph.D. Thesis.

290. Mead, Rita. *Henry Cowell's New Music, 1925-1936.*

Ann Arbor: UMI Research Press, 1981.

291. Mecklenburg, Virginia. *The Public as Patron: A History of the Treas. Dept. Mural Program Illustrated with Paintings from the Collection of the Univ. of Maryland Art Gallery.* College Park: Univ. of Maryland, 1979.

Catalog prepared to document a portion of the collection of New Deal art at the Univ. of Maryland.

292. Medovoy, George. "The Federal Theatre Project Yiddish Troups(1935-1939)." Ph.D. Thesis, Univ. of California, Davis, 1975.

293. Mehren, Peter. "San Diego's Opera Unit of the WPA Federal Music Project." *Journal of San Diego History,* 18(Summer 1972), 12-21.

294. Meltzer, Milton. *Violins and Shovels: The WPA Arts Projects.* New York: Delacorte Press, 1976.

295. Meltzer, Milton. *Dorothea Lange: A Photographer's Life.* New York: Farrar, Straus, & Giroux, 1978.

296. Mercer, P. M. "Tapping the Slave Narrative Collection for the Responses of Black South Carolinians to Emancipation and Reconstruction." *Australian Journal of Politics and History,* 25(no.3 1979), 358-74.

297. Miller, Dorothy C. and Alfred H. Barr, Jr. *American Realists and Magic Realists.* New York: Museum of Modern Art, 1943.

Also published by Arno, 1969.

298. Miller, Jeanne-Marie A. "Successful Federal Theatre Dramas by Black Playwrights." *Black Scholar,* 10(no. 10 1970), 79-85.

299. Miller, Lynn F. and Sally S. Swenson. *Lives and Works: Talks with Women Artists.* Metuchen, NJ: Scarecrow Press, 1981.

FAP artist Alice Neel is included.

300. Mitchell, Loften. *Black Drama: The Story of the Negro in the Theatre.* New York: Hawthorn, 1967.

Discusses Negro Unit of the Federal Theatre.

301. Mitchell Gallery. *WPA Revisited.* Carbondale: Southern Illinois Univ., 1972.

Catalog of exhibit, February 1 to 28, 1972.

302. Monroe, Gerald M. "The 1930's: Art, Ideology and the WPA." *Art in America,* 63(no.6 1975), 64-7.

303. Monroe, Gerald M. "The Artists Union of New York." Ph.D. Thesis, New York Univ., 1971.

304. Monroe, Gerald M. "Art Front." *Archives of American Art Journal,* 13(no.3 1973), 13-9.

305. Monroe, Gerald M. "Artists as Militant Trade Union Workers During the Great Depression." *Archives of American Art Journal,* 14(no.1 1974), 7-10.

306. Monroe, Gerald M. "The American Artists Congress and the Invasion of Finland." *Archives of American Art Journal*, 15(no.1 1975), 14-20.

307. Monroe, Gerald M. "Mural Burning by the New York City WPA." *Archives of American Art Journal*, 16(no.3 1976), 8-11.

308. Monroe, Gerald M. "The Militant Artists Union Treats with the New Deal." *Archives of American Art Journal*, 18(no.3 1978), 20-3.

309. Monroe, Gerald M. "Artists on the Barricades." *Archives of American Art Journal*, 18(no.3 1973).

310. Morris, George L.K. "The American Abstract Artists: A Chronicle 1935-56." *The World of Abstract Art*. Ed. American Abstract Artists. New York: Wittenborn, 1957.

311. Morse, John D., ed. *Ben Shahn*. New York: Praeger, 1972.

312. Museum of Modern Art. *U.S. Government Art Projects: Some Distinguished Alumni*. New York: Museum of Modern Art, 1963.
Mimeographed guide to exhibit, organized by Dorothy C. Miller.

313. Naison, Mark. "Communism and Harlem Intellectuals in the Popular Front: Anti-Fascism and the Politics of Black Culture." *Journal of Ethnic Studies*, 9(Spring 1981), 1-25.

314. Naison, Mark. *Communists in Harlem During the Depression*. New York: Grove Press, Inc., 1983.

315. Narber, Gregg R. and Lea Rosson De Long. "The New Deal Murals in Iowa." *Palimpsest*, 63(no.3 1982), 86-96.

316. National Museum American Art, Smithsonian Institution. *Perkins Harnly: From the Index of American Design*. Washington, DC: Smithsonian Institution, 1981.
Catalog of exhibit, October 16, 1981 to February 15, 1982.

317. Nelson Ruby, Christine. "Art for the Millions: Government Art During the Depression." *Michigan History*, 66(Jan. 1982), 17-20.

318. Nemser, Cindy. *Art Talk: Conversations with 12 Women Artists*. New York: Charles Scribner's Sons, 1975.

319. New Muse Community Museum, Brooklyn. *The Black Artists in the WPA, 1933-1943*. Brooklyn, NY: New Muse Community Museum of Brooklyn, 1976.
Exhibit catalog.

320. Noggle, Burl. *Working with History: The Historical Records Survey in Louisiana and the Nation, 1936-1942*. Baton Rouge: Louisiana State Univ. Press, 1981.

321. Noggle, Burl. *A Photographic Portrait, 1935-1941 Farm Security Administration Photographs*. Ohio: Akron Art Institute, 1980.

322. Norton, Sally O. "A Historical Study of Actor Will Geer, His Life and Work in the Context of Twentieth-Century American Social, Political, and Theatrical History." Ph.D. Thesis, Univ. of Southern California, 1981.
Geer worked on FTP.

323. Noverr, Douglas A. "Unlovely Subjects: Four Paintings from the Great Depression." *Landscape*, 27(no.2 1983), 37-42.

324. O'Connell, Barry. "In the Coal Mines Far Away: Russell Lee's Photographs of Mining Life." *Prospects*, 2(1976), 309-47.

325. O'Connor, Francis V. *Federal Support for the Visual Arts: The New Deal and Now*. Greenwich, CT: New York Graphic Society, 1969.

326. O'Connor, Francis V. "New Deal Murals in New York." *Artforum*, 7(Nov. 1968), 41-9.

327. O'Connor, Francis V. "A Sampler of New Deal Murals." *American Heritage*, 21(Oct. 1970), 45-57.

328. O'Connor, Francis V. *Federal Art Patronage: 1933 to 1943*. College Park: Univ. of Maryland Art Gallery, 1966.

329. O'Connor, Francis V. "The New Deal Art Projects in New York." *American Art Journal*, (Fall 1969), 58-79.

330. O'Connor, Francis V. *Jackson Pollock*. New York: Museum of Modern Art, 1967.
On FAP artist.

331. O'Connor, Francis V. "Philip Guston and Political Humanism." *Art and Architecture in the Service of Politics*. Ed. Linda Nochlin. Cambridge, MA: MIT Press, 1978.

332. O'Connor, Francis V., ed. *Art for the Millions: Essays from the 1930's by Artists and Administrators of the WPA Federal Art Project*. Greenwich, CT: New York Graphic Society, 1973.

333. O'Connor, Francis V., ed. *The New Deal Art Projects: An Anthology of Memoirs*. Washington: Smithsonian Institution Press, 1972.

334. O'Connor, Francis V. and Eugene V. Thaw, eds. *Jackson Pollock*. New Haven, CT: Yale Univ. Press, 1978.
On FAP artist.

335. O'Connor, John S. "'King Cotton': The Federal Theatre Project." *Southern Exposure*, 6(no.1 1978), 74-81.

336. O'Connor, John S. "But Was It Shakespeare? Welles's Macbeth and Julius Caesar." *Theatre Journal*, 32(Oct. 1980), 337-48.

337. O'Connor, John S. "Something to Be Whispered About Out Loud: Spirochete and the War on Syphilis." *Drama Review*, 73(March 1977), 91-8.

338. O'Connor, John S. "WPA Collection Available." *American Libraries*, (March 1975), 142.

339. O'Hara, Frank. *Jackson Pollock*. New York: George Braziller, 1959.
  On FAP artist.
340. O'Neal, Hank. *A Vision Shared, a Classic Portrait of America and Its People*. New York: St. Martin's Press, 1976.
341. O'Neill, Robert K. "The Federal Writers' Project Files for Indiana." *Indiana Magazine of History*, 76(June 1980), 85-96.
342. Ohrn, Karin Becker. *Dorothea Lange and the Documentary Tradition*. Baton Rouge: Louisiana State Univ. Press, 1980.
343. Orvell, Miles. "Letting the Facts Speak for Themselves: Thirties America." *American Scholar*, 43(no.4 1974), 671-8.
344. Osborn, David S. "Mural Projects of the United States Government in the Bay Area of Northern California." M.A. Thesis, Univ. of California, 1956.
345. Osnos, Nina F. "New Deal for New Deal Art: National Fine Arts Inventory." *Art in America*, 60(Jan. 1972), 19.
346. Papenfuse, Edward C. "'A Modicum of Commitment': The Present and Future Importance of the Historical Records Survey." *American Archivist*, 37(no.2 1974), 211-21.
347. Park, Esther A., ed. *Mural Painters in America*. Pittsburgh: Kansas State T.C., 1949.
348. Park, Marlene and Gerald E. Markowitz. *New Deal for Art: Government Art Projects of the 1930s*. Hamilton: Gallery Association of New York State, 1977.
349. Park, Marlene. "City and Country in the 1930's: A Study of New Deal Murals in New York." *Art Journal*, 39(Fall 1979), 37-47.
350. Park, Marlene and Gerald E. Markowitz. *Democratic Vistas: Post Offices and Public Art in the New Deal*. Philadelphia: Temple Univ. Press, 1984.
351. Parsons School of Design, New York. *New York WPA Artists: Then and Now*. New York: Parsons School of Design, 1977.
  Catalog of exhibit, November 8 to December 10, 1977.
352. Pearson, Ralph M. *Experiencing American Pictures*. New York: Harper & Bros., 1943.
  Discusses government art program and murals: focus on such artists as Gropper and Benton.
353. Peck, David. "Salvaging the Art and Literature of the 1930's: A Bibliographical Essay." *Centennial Review*, 20(Spring 1976), 128-41.
354. Pells, Richard H. *Radical Visions and American Dreams*. New York: Harper & Row, 1973.
  Cultural and intellectual history of 1930s, includes mention of arts projects.

315

355. Penkower, Monty Noam. *The Federal Writers' Project: A Study in Government Patronage of the Arts.* Urbana: Univ. of Illinois Press, 1977.

See also 1970 Columbia Univ. Ph.D. Thesis.

356. Perdue, Charles L., Jr., et al., ed. *Weevils in the Wheat: Interview with Virginia Ex-Slaves.* Charlottesville: Univ. Press of Virginia, 1976.

357. Perdue, Charles L., Jr., et al., ed. *An Annotated Listing of Folklore Collected by ...the Virginia Writers' Project: Held in the Manuscripts Department...University of Virginia.* Norwood, PA: Norwood Editions, 1979.

358. Pettis, Ashley. "The WPA and the American Composer." *Musical Quarterly*, 26(Jan. 1940), 101-12.

359. Pietan, Norman. "The Federal Government and the Arts." Ph.D. Thesis, Columbia Univ., 1949.

360. Poindexter Gallery. *The Thirties: Painting in New York.* New York: Poindexter Gallery, 1957.

Exhibit catalog.

361. Potter, Jeffrey. *To a Violent Grave: An Oral Biography of Jackson Pollack.* New York: G.P. Putnam's Sons, 1986.

362. Pratt, Davis, ed. *The Photographic Eye of Ben Shahn.* Cambridge, MA: Harvard Univ. Press, 1975.

363. Purcell, Ralph. *Government and Art, a Study of American Experience.* Washington: Public Affairs Press, 1956.

364. Rabkin, Gerald. *Drama and Commitment: Politics in the American Theatre of the Thirties.* Bloomington: Indiana Univ. Press, 1964.

365. Randle, Mallory B. "Murals and Sculpture of the Public Works of Art Project and the Treasury Section in the Southwest." M.A. Thesis, Univ. of Texas, 1967.

366. Randle, Mallory B. "Texas Muralists of the PWAP." *Southwestern Art*, 1(Spring 1966).

367. Rapport, Leonard. "How Valid Are the Federal Writers' Project Life Stories: An Iconoclast Among the True Believers." *Oral History Review*, (1979), 6-17.

368. Rawick, George P. *The American Slave: A Composite Autobiography.* Westport, CT: Greenwood Press, 1972.

Multi-volume compilation of Slave Narratives.

369. Reed, Alma. *Orozco.* New York: Oxford Univ. Press, 1956.

370. Refregier, Anton. *An Artist's Journey.* New York: International Publishers, 1965.

Autobiography of FAP artist.

371. Reuss, Richard A. "Folk Music and Social Conscience: The Musical Odyssey of Charles Seeger." *Western Folklore*, 38(no.4 1979), 221-38.

372. Reuss, Richard A. "American Folklore and Left-wing Politics: 1927-1957." Ph.D. Thesis, Indiana Univ., 1971.

373. Rhoads, William B. "The Artistic Patronage of Franklin D. Roosevelt: Art as Historical Record." *Prologue*, 15(Spring 1983), 5-21.

374. Rice, Elmer L. *The Living Theatre*. New York: Harper & Row, 1959.

Lectures on theatre, includes chapter on FTP which he helped organize and operate.

375. Ridge, Patricia Lin. "The Contributions of Hallie Flanagan to the American Theatre." Ph.D. Thesis, Univ. of Colorado, 1971.

376. Ring, Daniel F. "The Cleveland Public Library and the WPA: A Study in Creative Partnership." *Ohio History*, 84(Summer 1975), 158-64.

377. Robbins, Jhan and June Robbins. "The Man Behind the Man Behind the Lens: Roy Stryker." *Minicam Photography*, (Nov. 1947), 52+.

378. Roditi, Edouard. *Dialogues on Art*. Santa Barbara, CA: Ross-Erikson Pub., 1980.

379. Rodman, Selden. *Ben Shahn: Portrait of the Artist as an American*. New York: Harper & Brothers, 1951.

380. Rodman, Selden. *Conversations with Artists*. New York: Devin-Adair, 1957.

381. Rollins, Peter C. "Ideology and Film Rhetoric: Three Documentaries of the New Deal Era." *Journal of Popular Film*, 5(no.2 1976), 126,+.

382. Rosenberg, Harold. *Arshile Gorky*. New York: Horizon Press, 1962.

On FAP artist.

383. Rosenberg, Harold. "The Thirties." *The De-definition of Art*. Ed. Harold Rosenberg. New York: Horizon Press, 1972.

Also published by Univ. of Chicago Press, 1983.

384. Rosenstone, Robert A. "The Federal (Mostly Non-) Writers' Project." *Reviews in American History* 6(no.3 1978), 400-4.

Review essay.

385. Roskolenko, Harry. *When I Was Last on Cherry Street*. New York: Stein and Day, 1965.

Includes experiences on NYC FWP.

386. Ross, Ronald. "The Role of Blacks in the Federal Theatre." *Journal of Negro History*, 59(Jan. 1974), 38-50.

387. Ross, Ronald. "Black Drama in the Federal Theatre, 1935-1939." Ph.D. Thesis, Univ. of Southern California, 1972.

388. Ross, Theophil Walter, Jr. "Conflicting Concepts of the Federal Theatre Project: A Critical History." Ph.D. Thesis,

Univ. of Missouri, Columbia, 1981.

389. Rothstein, Arthur. "The Picture That Became a Campaign Issue." *Popular Photography*, (Sept. 1961), 42.

390. Rothstein, Arthur. *The Depression Years as Photographed by Arthur Rothstein.* New York: Dover, 1978.

391. Rubenstein, Erica Beckh. "Government Art in the Roosevelt Era: An Appraisal of Federal Art Patronage in the Light of Present Needs." *Art Journal*, 20(Fall 1960), 7-8.

392. Rubenstein, Erica Beckh. "The Tax Payer's Murals." Ph.D. Thesis, Harvard Univ., 1944.

393. Rubinstein, Charlotte Streifer. *American Women Artists from Early Times to the Present.* Boston, MA: G.K. Hall, 1982.
Includes chapter, "The Thirties: Daughters of the Depression".

394. Salzman, Jack. *Social Poetry of 1930s.* New York: B. Franklin, 1979.

395. Salzman, Jack, ed. *Years of Protest: A Collection of American Writing of the 1930's.* New York: Pegasus, 1967.

396. Schmeckebier, Laurence E. *John Steuart Curry's Pageant of America.* New York: American Artists Group, 1943.

397. Schrader, Robert Fay. "The Indian Arts and Crafts Board: An Aspect of New Deal Indian Policy." Ph.D. Thesis, Marquette Univ., 1981.

398. Schwartz, Lawrence H. *Marxism and Culture: The CPUSA and Aesthetics in the 1930s.* Port Washington: Kennikat, 1980.

399. Scott, Barbara Kerr and Sally Soelle. *New Deal Art: The Oklahoma Experience, 1933-1943.* Lawton, OK: Cameron Univ., 1983.
Survey of Oklahoma New Deal art.

400. Scott, David W. "Orozco's Prometheus." *Art Journal*, 17(Fall 1951).

401. Seeger, Charles and Margaret Valiant. "Journal of a Field Representative." *Journal of the Society for Ethnomusicology*, 24(May 1980), 169-210.

402. Severin, Werner J. "Cameras with a Purpose: The Photo-Journalists of F.S.A.." *Journalism Quarterly*, 41(no.2 1964), 191-200.

403. Severin, Werner J. "Photographic Documentation by the Farm Security Administration, 1935-1941." M.A. Thesis, Univ. of Missouri, 1959.

404. Shahn, Bernarda Bryson. *Ben Shahn.* New York: Abrams, 1972.

405. Shapiro, David and Cecile Shapiro. "Abstract Expressionism: The Politics of Apolitical Painting." *Prospects*, 3(1977), 175-214.

406. Shapiro, David, ed. *Social Realism: Art as a Weapon.* New York: Frederick Ungar, 1973.

407. Shapiro, David, ed. *Art for the People-New Deal Murals on Long Island.* Hempstead, NY: Emily Lowe Gallery, Hofstra Univ., 1978.

408. Sherwood, Leland Harley. "The Federal Sponsored Community Art Centers of Iowa as Part of the New Deal." Ph.D. Thesis, Indiana Univ., 1973.

409. Siskind, Aaron. *Harlem Document: Photographs 1932-1940.* Providence, RI: Matrix Publications, 1981.

410. Sittig, William J. "Luther Evans: Man for a New Age." *Quarterly Journal of the Library of Congress* 33(no.3 1976), 251-67.
On Historical Records Survey.

411. Slobodkina, Esphyr. *American Abstract Artists: Its Publications, Catalogs and Membership.* Great Neck, NY: Urquhart-Slobodkina, 1979.

412. Smiley, David L. "A Slice of Life in Depression America: The Records of the Historical Records Survey." *Prologue*, 3(Winter 1971), 153-9.

413. Smiley, Sam. "Rhetoric on Stage in Living Newspapers." *Quarterly Journal of Speech*, 54(Feb. 1968), 29-36.

414. Smithsonian Institution, Traveling Exhibition Service. *WPA/FAP Graphics: Catalogues.* Washington: Smithsonian Institution Press, 1976.
Catalog of traveling exhibit, May 1976 to April 1978.

415. Snyder, Robert L. *Pare Lorentz and the Documentary Film.* Norman: Univ. of Oklahoma Press, 1968.
See also 1965 Univ. of Iowa Ph.D. Thesis.

416. Soapes, Thomas F. "The Federal Writers' Project Slave Interviews: Useful Data or Misleading Source." *Oral History Review*, (1977), 33-8.

417. Soby, Jas. Thrall. *Ben Shahn: Paintings.* New York: Braziller, 1963.

418. Solomon, Izler. "A Decade to Defeat Decadence." *Musical Courier* 151(Feb. 1955), 46-8.
Overview of FWP.

419. Sprunger, Keith. "The Most Monumental Mennonite." *Mennonite Life* 34(no.3 1979), 10-6.
On WPA statue of Mennonite wheat farmer.

420. St. John, Bruce, ed. *John Sloan.* New York: Harper & Row, 1971.
On FAP artist.

421. Stanford, Edward Barrett. "Library Extension Under the WPA: An Appraisal of an Experiment in Federal Aid." Ph.D. Thesis, Univ. of Chicago, 1943.

422. Stange, Maren E. "American Documentary

Photography: The Mode and Its Style, 1900-1943." Ph.D. Thesis, Boston Univ., 1981.

423. Steichen, Edward, ed. *The Bitter Years, 1935-1941: Rural America as Seen by the Photographers of the Farm Security Administration.* New York, 1962.

424. Stevens, Errol Wayne. "The Federal Writers' Project Revisited: The Indiana Historical Society's New Guide to the State of Indiana." *Indiana Magazine of History,* 76(June 1980), 97-102.

425. Stewart, Ruth Ann. *New York/Chicago: WPA and the Black Artist.* New York: Studio Museum in Harlem, 1978.

426. Stokes, Ronald C. *Midwest - - The 30's.* Milwaukee, WI: Milwaukee Art Center, 1968.
Mimeographed exhibit guide.

427. Stott, William. *Documentary Expression and Thirties America.* New York: Oxford Univ. Press, 1973.

428. Stryker, Roy and Nancy Wood. "In This Proud Land." *American Heritage,* 24(no.5 1973), 40-55.
On FSA photographs.

429. Stryker, Roy E. "The Lean Thirties." *Harvester World,* (Feb. 1960), 6-15.

430. Stryker, Roy Emerson and Nancy Wood. *In This Proud Land: America 1935-1943 as Seen in the FSA Photographs.* Boston, MA: New York Graphic Society, 1973.

431. Studio Museum in Harlem. *New York/Chicago: WPA and the Black Artist.* New York: Studio Museum in Harlem, 1977.
Catalog of exhibit, November 13 to December 8, 1977.

432. Susman, Warren. *Culture as History: The Transformation of American Society in the Twentieth Century.* New York: Pantheon Books, 1984.
Includes three essays on the 1930s.

433. Susman, Warren, ed. *Culture and Commitment, 1929-1945.* New York: George Braziller, 1973.
Collection of documents on 1930s culture.

434. Swados, Harvey, ed. *The American Writer and the Great Depression.* Indianapolis: Bobbs-Merrill, 1966.

435. Swain, Martha H. "'The Forgotten Woman': Ellen J. Woodward and Women's Relief in the New Deal." *Prologue,* 15(Winter 1983), 201-13.

436. Swerdlove, Dorothy L. "Research Materials of the Federal Theatre Project in the Theatre Collection of the New York Library at Lincoln Center." *Performing Arts Resources.* Ed. Mary C. Henderson. New York: Theatre Library Association, 1980.

437. Swiss, Cheryl Dianne. "Hallie Flanagan and the Federal Theatre Project: An Experiment in Form." Ph.D. Thesis, Univ.

of Wisconsin-Madison, 1982.

438. Taber, Ronald W. "Writers on Relief: The Making of the Washington Guide, 1935-1941." *Pacific Northwest Quarterly*, 61(Oct. 1970), 185-92.

439. Taber, Ronald W. "Vardis Fisher and the 'Idaho Guide': Preserving Culture for the New Deal." *Pacific Northwest Quarterly*, 59(April 1968), 68-76.

440. Taber, Ronald W. "The Federal Writers' Project in the Pacific Northwest: A Case Study." Ph.D. Thesis, Washington State Univ., 1969.

441. Taubman, Howard. *The Making of the American Theatre*. New York: Coward-McCann, 1967.
Discusses Houseman and Wells on FTP.

442. Taylor, Joshua C. "A Poignant, Relevant Backward Look at Artists of the Great Depression." *Smithsonian*, (Oct. 1979), 44-53.

443. Teichroew, Allan. "As Far as the Eye Can See: Some Depression Photographs of Mennonite Farmers." *Mennonite Life*, 33(no.3 1978), 4-15.

444. Terrill, Tom and Jerrold Hirsch. "Such as Us." *Southern Exposure*, 6(no. 1 1978), 67-72.

445. Terrill, Tom E. and Jerrold Hirsch. "Replies to Leonard Rapport's 'How Valid Are the Federal Writers' Project Life Stories: An Iconoclast Among the True Believers'." *Oral History Review*, (1980), 81-92.

446. Thomson, Virgil. *A Virgil Thomson Reader*. Boston: Houghton Mifflin, 1981.
Autobiography: discusses FTP and FWP.

447. Tischler, Barbara Leonora. "Musical Modernism and American Cultural Identity." Ph.D. Thesis, Columbia Univ., 1983.

448. Tonelli, Edith Ann. "The Massachusetts Federal Art Project: A Case Study in Government Support for Art." Ph.D. Thesis, Boston Univ., 1981.

449. Tonelli, Edith Ann. "The Avant-Garde in Boston: The Experiment of the WPA Federal Art Project." *Archives of American Art Journal*, 20(Winter 1980), 18-24.

450. Troy, Nancy J. "The Williamsburgh Housing Project Murals and the Polemic of Abstraction in American Painting of the 1930s." M.A. Thesis, Yale Univ., 1976.

451. Tsujimoto, Karen. *Images of America: Precisionist Painting and Modern Photography*. Seattle: Univ. of Washington Press, 1982.
Includes "Photography in the Thirties" and "Changes in the Times".

452. Turchen, Lesta VanDerWert. "Dakota Resources: Mss.(Manuscripts)." *South Dakota History* 11(no.3 1981), 226-

35.
Discusses a publication of South Dakota FWP.

453. Tweed Museum of Art, Univ. of Minnesota, Duluth. *Accomplishments: Minnesota Art Projects in the Depression Years.* Duluth, MN: Tweed Museum of Art, 1976.
Catalog of exhibit, April 28 to May 30, 1976.

454. Twining, Mary. "Harvesting and Heritage: A Comparison of Afro-American and African Basketry." *Southern Folklore Quarterly* 42(no.2-3 1978), 159-74.
WPA project and revival of basketmaking.

455. University of Maryland. *The Spirit of the Thirties.* College Park: Univ. of Maryland Art Gallery, 1982.
Catalog of exhibit, February 24 to April 18, 1982.

456. University of Michigan, Museum of Art. *The Federal Art Project: American Prints from the 1930s in the Collection of the University of Michigan Museum of Art.* Ann Arbor: The Museum, 1985.

457. University of Minnesota, Univ. Gallery. *The American Scene: Urban and Rural Regionalists of the 30s and 40s.* Minneapolis: Univ. Gallery, Univ. of Minnesota, 1976.
Catalog including artists Benton, Wood, Marsh, R. Soyer, Grosz.

458. University of Minnesota, University Gallery. *Contact: American Art & Culture 1919-1939.* Minneapolis: Gallery of Univ. of Minn., 1981.
Exhibit catalog.

459. Vacha, J. E. "The Case of the Runaway Opera: The Federal Theatre and Marc Blitzstein's *The Cradle Will Rock.*" *New York History*, 62(April 1981), 133-57.

460. Valentine, Jerry W. "The WPA and Louisiana Education." *Louisiana History*, 13(no.4 1972), 391-5.

461. VanDeburg, William L. "Elite Slave Behavior During the Civil War: Black Drivers and Foremen in Historical Perspective." *Southern Studies* 16(no.3 1977), 253-69.
Uses WPA Slave Narratives.

462. VanDeburg, William L. "Slave Drivers and Slave Narratives: A New Look at the 'Dehumanized Elite'." *Historian* 39(no. 4 1977), 717-32.
Discusses WPA Slave Narratives.

463. VanDeburg, William L. "The Slave Drivers of Arkansas: A New View from the Narratives." *Arkansas History Quarterly*, 35(no.3 1976), 231-45.

464. Verdicchio, Joseph J. "New Deal Work Relief and New York City: 1933-1938." Ph.D. Thesis, New York Univ., 1980.

465. Vitz, Robert C. "Struggle and Response: American Artists and the Great Depression." *New York History*, 17(Jan. 1976), 80-98.

466. Vlatch, John. "Holger Cahill as Folklorist." *Journal of American Folklore*, 98(no.388 1985), 148-62.

467. "WPA Art: Rescue of a U.S. Treasure." *U.S. News and World Report*, 70(June 1971), 75-8.

468. "WPAccounting." *Time*, 41(no.7 1943), 95-6. Discusses final report on FWP.

469. Walker, Melissa C. "American Scene Art and Government Murals in Northern California." *The Development of Modern Art in Northern California*. Ed. Joseph Armstrong Baird, Jr. Sacramento: Crocker Art Museum, 1981.

470. Walker, Sam. "Documentary Photography in America: The Political Dimensions of an Art Form." *Radical America*, 11(no.1 1977), 53-66.

471. Wallis, John J. "Work Relief and Unemployment in the 1930's." Ph.D. Thesis, Univ. of Washington, 1981.

472. Walsh, Elizabeth D. "New Deal Theatre: The Best Art Is That Which Can Be Enjoyed by All the People." *Dramatics*, 8(March 1977), 15-9.

473. Walsh, Elizabeth D. and Diane Bowers. "WPA Federal Theatre Project." *Theatre News*, 8:7(April 1976).

474. Warren-Findley, Jannelle. "Musicians and Mountaineers: The Resettlement Administration's Music Program in Appalachia, 1935-37." *Appalachian Journal*, 7(Fall 1979), 105-23.

475. Warren-Findley, Jannelle. "Culture and the New Deal." *American Studies*, 17(Spring 1976), 81-2.

476. Warren-Findley, Jannelle. "Of Tears and Need: The Federal Music Project, 1935-1943." Ph.D. Thesis, George Washington Univ., 1973.

477. Watkins, Charles A. "The Blurred Image: Documentary Photography and the Depression South." Ph.D. Thesis, Univ. of Delaware, 1982.

478. Watrous, James S. "Mural Painting in the United States: A History of Its Style and Technique." Ph.D. Thesis, Univ. of Wisconsin, 1939.

479. Waugh, Thomas H. R. "John Ivens and the Evolution of the Radical Documentary, 1926-1946." Ph.D. Thesis, Columbia Univ., 1981.

480. Wechsler, Jeffrey. *Surrealism and American Art, 1931-1947*. New Brunswick, NJ: Rutgers Univ. Art Gallery, 1976.

481. Weigle, Marta. "From Alice Corbin's 'Lines Mumbled in Sleep' to Eufemia's 'Sopapillas': Women and the Federal Writers' Project in New Mexico." *New America*, 4(April 1982), 54-76.

482. Weir, Jean Burwell. "Timberline Lodge: A WPA Experiment in Architecture and Crafts (Volumes I and II)." Ph.D. Thesis, Univ. of Michigan, 1977.

483. Weisstuch, Mark Wolf. "The Theatre Union, 1933-1937: A History." Ph.D. Thesis, City Univ. of New York, 1982.

484. Welsch, Roger L. "Straight from the Horse Trader's Mouth." *Kansas Quarterly* 13(no.2 1981), 17-26.
Discusses horse trading stories collected by Nebraska FWP.

485. Werner, Alfred. "WPA and Social Realism." *Art and Artists*, 10(Oct. 1975), 24-31.

486. Werner, Alfred. *Moses Soyer*. South Brunswick: A.S. Barnes and Co., 1970.
On FAP artist.

487. Werthman, Joan B. "The New Deal Federal Art Programs, 1935-1939." Ph.D. Thesis, St. John's Univ., 1971.

488. Wheeler, Monroe, ed. *Painters and Sculptors of Modern America*. New York: Thos. Y. Crowell Co., 1942.
Collection of writings by painters and sculptors, originally published in Mag. of Art, 1939-1942.

489. Whisnant, David. "Finding the Way Between the Old and New: The Mountain Dance and Folk Festival and Bascom Lamar Lunsford's Work as a Citizen." *Appalachian Journal*, 7(Fall 1980), 135-54.

490. Whisnant, David. *Modernizing the Mountaineer*. New York: Burt Franklin & Company, 1980.

491. Whisnant, David. *All That is Native & Fine: The Politics of Culture in an American Region*. Chapel Hill: Univ. of North Carolina Press, 1983.

492. Whitney Museum of American Art. *American Art of the 1930s: Selections from the Collection of the Whitney Museum of American Art*. New York: Whitney Museum of American Art, 1981.
Catalog for traveling exhibit, 1981-1983.

493. Wickre, Karen. *An Informal History of Oregon's FTP*. Portland: Oregon Committee for the Humanities, 1982.

494. Willard, Charlotte. *Moses Soyer*. Cleveland: World Publishing Co., 1962.
On FAP artist.

495. Williams, Colleen Ingram. "Work Relief as a Social Service Delivery System: The Experience of the WPA." Ph.D. Thesis, Tulane Univ., 1976.

496. Williams, Jay. *Stage Left*. New York: Scribner's, 1974.

497. Wood, Darrell Gar. *Artist in Iowa*. New York: W.W. Norton & Company, Inc., 1944.
On Grant Wood.

498. Wooden, Howard E. *The Neglected Generation of American Realist Painters: 1930-1948*. Wichita, KS: Wichita Art Museum, 1981.
Catalog of exhibit, May 3 to June 14, 1981.

499. Woodward, C. Vann. "History from Slave Sources: A Review Essay." *American History Review* 79(no.2 1974), 470-81.

On WPA Slave Narratives.

500. Woodworth, William Harry. "The Federal Music Project of the Works Progress Administration in New Jersey." Ph.D. Thesis, Univ. of Michigan, 1970.

501. Wyman, Marilyn. "A New Deal for Art in Southern California: Murals and Sculpture Under Government Patronage." Ph.D. Thesis, Univ. of Southern California, 1982.

502. YM-YWHA of Essex County. *WPA Artists: Then and Now.* West Orange: YM-YWHA of Essex County, 1969.

Catalog of exhibit, October 29 to November 26, 1967.

503. Yasko, Karel. "Treasures from the Depression." *Historic Preservation*, 24(July 1972), 26-31.

504. Yeh, Jen. *W.P.A. - - The Writers Project: Selected from the Collection of Dr. Jen Yeh.* Hempstead, NY: Hofstra Library Associates, 1978.

Catalog from Hofstra Library Associates Exhibit, November 1978.

505. Yetman, Norman R. "Background of the Slave Narrative Collection." *American Quarterly*, 19(Fall 1967), 534-53.

506. Yezierska, Anzia. *Red Ribbon on a White Horse.* New York: Charles Scribner's Sons, 1950.

Includes experiences on NYC FWP.

507. York, Hildreth. "The New Deal Art Projects in New Jersey." *New Jersey History*, 98(Fall 1980), 132-74.

508. Young, James S. *Black Writers of the Thirties.* Baton Rouge: Louisiana State Univ. Press, 1973.

509. Young, Mahonri Sharp. "American Realists of the 1930s." *Apollo*, 113(March 1981), 146-89.

# 10. Films

The following films are of interest to those studying or teaching about the government-sponsored arts projects of the 1930s.

**Art for Main Street** is a twenty-minute, color film on the the thirty-six post office murals painted in Indiana towns and cities between 1936 and 1942. The film discusses the murals in five main categories: town founding and early days; local industry; festivals; farm life; and delivery and receipt of the mail. Contact: Interphase II Productions, PO Box 8032, Merrillville, IN 46410; 219-769-3995.

**Artists at Work** is a thirty-six minute, color film on the New Deal art projects by Mary Lance. It shows Alice Neel, Chaim Gross, Jacob Lawrence, Lee Krasner, James Brooks, Ilya Bolotowsky, Edward Laning, Joseph Delaney, Harry Gottlieb, and Joseph Solman discussing their experiences working under the New Deal. Contact: New Day Films, 22 Riverview Drive, Wayne, NJ 07470; 201-633-0212.

**Jack Levine: Feast of Pure Reason** is a sixty-minute, color film portrait of Jack Levine, the social realist painter who was one of the first participants in the Boston FAP. Levine, who got his professional start in the FAP, continues to paint bold realistic and satirical canvases long after the style has gone out of vogue. The artist is both the subject and the host of this documentary by filmmaker David Sutherland. Contact: David Sutherland Productions, PO Box 163, Waban, MA 02168; 617-244-5684.

The New Deal for Artists is a ninety-minute, color film which surveys the arts projects of the Roosevelt administration--the FTP, FWP, FAP, and the historical section of the FSA. Director Wieland Schulz-Keil interviewed many of the participants in those programs--including writer Meridel LeSeur, photographer Arthur Rothstein, actor Norman Lloyd, and painter James Brooks--to get their first-hand accounts of the Federal government's role in the arts of the 1930s. The interviews are interwoven with archival film footage, contemporary photographs, and other documents. Contact: Corinth Films, 410 E. 62nd St., New York, NY 10021; 212-421-4770.

One Third of a Nation is a videotape of the FTP's Living Newspaper produced by Multimedia Studies in American Drama at the Brooklyn College Humanities Institute. This 1930s play explores the history of slum housing in America. Also available from the Institute is a *Handbook of Source Materials on One Third of a Nation* and copies of the play. To order the videotape or the sourcebook and play, contact: Vera Jiji, Program Director, Multimedia Studies in American Drama, Humanities Institute, Brooklyn College, Brooklyn, NY 11210; 212-780-4158.

Paul Cadmus: Enfant Terrible at 80 is a sixty-five minute color film by David Sutherland, in which Cadmus tells his own story, including the controversies surrounding his public art works of the the Thirties. Contact: David Sutherland Productions, Box 163, Waban, MA 02168; 617-244-5684.

The People and the Land: The California Post Office Murals is a slide-tape on forty-three post office murals painted in California between 1934 and 1943. Contact: Interphase II Productions, PO Box 8032, Merrillville, IN 46410; 219-769-3995.

Roosevelt, New Jersey: Visions of Utopia is a fifty-five minute color film that documents how 120 families of Jewish garment workers from New York City created a government-sponsored, agro-industrial cooperative community in New Jersey during the middle of the Great Depression. Among the first residents of the community was artist Ben Shahn who painted a famous WPA mural of immigrant laborers on the wall of the local elementary school. Using archival footage and photographs and interviews with the original homesteaders and their children, director Richard Kroehling traces the origins and struggles of this experiment in cooperative living. Contact: The Cinema Guild, 1697 Broadway, New York, NY 10019; 212-246-5522.

**The World of Tomorrow** is a film by Tom Johnson and Lance Bird in which they use home movies, newsreels, cartoons, and promotional films from the 1930s to examine the social forces and ideals that shaped 1939 America. The film focuses on the World's Fair, what it meant and stated overtly, and what it deliberately did not say or masked. Shown in the film is GM's Futurama exhibit, the first TV broadcast, and a contest between Mrs. Modern and Mrs. Drudge. Contact: Liz Behken, Media Study, 305 West 21 St., New York, NY 10013.